ASPECTS OF SOCIAL CHANGE
IN MODERN JAPAN

This is the third in a series of six volumes to be published by Princeton University Press for the Conference on Modern Japan of the Association for Asian Studies, Inc. The others in the series are:

Changing Japanese Attitudes Toward Modernization, edited by Marius B. Jansen (1965)

The State and Economic Enterprise in Japan, edited by William W. Lockwood (1965)

Political Development in Modern Japan, edited by Robert E. Ward (1967)

Tradition and Modernization in Japanese Culture, edited by Donald Shively

Dilemmas of Growth in Prewar Japan, edited by James W. Morley

Aspects of
Social Change
in Modern Japan

Edited by
R. P. DORE

CONTRIBUTORS

REINHARD BENDIX   SOLOMON B. LEVINE

JOHN W. BENNETT   KEIICHI MIZUSHIMA

JOHN B. CORNELL   EDWARD NORBECK

GEORGE A. DE VOS   THOMAS C. SMITH

L. TAKEO DOI   GEORGE O. TOTTEN

R. P. DORE   EZRA F. VOGEL

ERWIN H. JOHNSON   HIROSHI WAGATSUMA

PRINCETON UNIVERSITY PRESS

PRINCETON, NEW JERSEY

HN
723
A8
cop. 3

Foreword

Scholarly studies of Japan have had a remarkable growth in the United States and other English-speaking countries since the end of World War II. To some extent this has been the natural result of the popular boom of interest in Japan stimulated by the war and its aftermath and by the increased opportunities Westerners had to associate with the Japanese people. But it is more directly the result of the spread of academic programs devoted to Japan and particularly the growing number of specialists trained to handle the Japanese language.

In the fall of 1958 a group of scholars gathered at the University of Michigan to seek some means of bringing together in more systematic fashion the results of the widely scattered studies of Japan which had appeared in the years since the end of the war. The Conference on Modern Japan which resulted was dedicated both to the pooling of recent scholarly findings and to the possibility of stimulating new ideas and approaches to the study of modern Japan. Subsequently the Conference received a generous grant from the Ford Foundation for the support of a series of five annual seminars devoted to as many aspects of the history of Japan's modern development. Recently the number of seminars planned by the Conference was expanded to six.

The Conference on Modern Japan exists as a special project of the Association for Asian Studies. The Conference is guided by an executive committee consisting of Ronald P. Dore, Marius B. Jansen, William W. Lockwood, Donald H. Shively, Robert E. Ward, and John W. Hall (chairman). James W. Morley joined the group as leader of the sixth seminar. Each member of the executive committee has been responsible for the organization of a separate seminar devoted to his particular field of specialization and for the publication of the proceedings of his seminar.

Although the subject of modernization *in the abstract* is not of primary concern to the Conference, conceptual problems are inevitably of interest to the entire series of seminars. Because of this, two less formal discussions on the theory of modernization have also been planned as part of the Conference's program. The first of these was held in Japan during the summer of 1960 and has been reported on as part of the first volume of published proceedings. The second will seek at the conclusion of our series to review whatever contributions to the realm of theory the six annual seminars may have made.

The present volume, edited by Ronald P. Dore, is the third in a series of six to be published by the Princeton University Press for the Conference on Modern Japan. The other volumes, of which the first two have already appeared, are: *Changing Japanese Attitudes Toward Modernization*, ed. Marius B. Jansen; *The State and Economic Enterprise in Japan*, ed. William W. Lockwood; *Political Development in Modern Japan*, ed. Robert E. Ward; *Tradition and Modernization in Japanese Culture*, ed. Donald H. Shively; *Dilemmas of Growth in Prewar Japan*, ed. James W. Morley.

As their titles suggest, the annual seminars have adopted broad themes so as to cast a wide net about a variety of scholars working within each major field. Within the broad fields, however, the seminar chairmen have focused on specific problems recommended either because they have received the greatest attention of Japanese specialists or because they seem most likely to contribute to a fuller understanding of the modernization of Japan. We trust, as a consequence, that the six volumes taken together will prove both representative of the current scholarship on Japan and comprehensive in their coverage of one of the most fascinating stories of national development in modern history.

Volume three of our series results from a seminar in Bermuda in January of 1963 under the chairmanship of

Professor Ronald P. Dore. In addition to the authors whose papers appear in this volume the following individuals took part in the seminar, serving as discussants or discussion leaders: Richard K. Beardsley, University of Michigan; George M. Beckmann, University of Kansas and the Ford Foundation; Dr. William Caudill, National Institute of Mental Health; John W. Hall, Yale University; Marius B. Jansen, Princeton University; Takeyoshi Kawashima, Tokyo University; Marion J. Levy, Princeton University; William W. Lockwood, Princeton University; W. H. Newell, International Christian University; Herbert Passin, Columbia University; Donald H. Shively, Harvard University; Robert E. Ward, University of Michigan; and Tōji Watanuki, Tokyo University. Thomas C. Smith, while presenting a paper, was unable to attend the seminar. Mr. Koya Azumi served as *rapporteur*.

The 1963 seminar was convened to study the theme of changing interpersonal relations in Japan since 1870. Papers were presented from the fields of sociology, anthropology, psychology, and social relations and were grouped to concentrate on a number of specific aspects of social change in modern Japan. Two papers deal with historical backgrounds, while others touch on changes in family and village life, group organization, labor relations, minority communities, and personal values. One paper offers comparison between Japan and Modern Germany. The Conference regrets that papers presented by Professor Kawashima and Dr. Caudill were not included in the present volume due to the manner in which the volume was finally organized. Both authors are thanked for their valuable contribution to the seminar sessions.

John Whitney Hall

Contents

ix

CONTENTS

ASPECTS OF SOCIAL CHANGE
IN MODERN JAPAN

Introduction

R. P. DORE

THIS IS an old-fashioned book. As one of the by-products of the present (entirely laudable) concern with the economic development of the poor countries of the world, the study of modern Japan is becoming, for social scientists, increasingly a "howdunnit" exercise. Japan, the one nation outside the European cultural sphere to industrialize successfully, is looked to for lessons as to how the trick might be repeated elsewhere. Some of the papers in this volume do indeed have some suggestive things to say on this question—Bendix on the preconditions for development in Japan and Germany, Smith on the Tokugawa bureaucracy, or Vogel on the family and migration, for instance. But most of the papers bear on a rather different set of problems, problems first posed by sociologists of the nineteenth century.

The latter were men who wrote with their eyes on Europe and who saw industrialization not as the chancy touch-and-go thing it seems in so many parts of the world today, but as an inexorable and inevitable process. Their problem was: what are the consequences for other parts of the social structure of the changes in economic organization which take place as society becomes more productive? Their varied answers are best known by the catchphrases under which their work is often subsumed. Maine saw the process as a movement from a society based on status to a society based on contract. Spencer spoke of the militaristic society giving way to the productive society, Marx of feudalism and capitalism, Weber of the "disenchanting" and all-pervasive process of rationalization, Toennies of *Gemeinschaft* and *Gesellschaft*, Durkheim of mechanical solidarity giving way with the division of labor to organic solidarity, Wirth of a shift from primary to secondary relationships. More recently Parsons, in

3

his pattern variables, has attempted to analyze the varying separable themes which many of these formulations have in common and to state in a set of polar categories the dimensions in which social action can vary.

It is from this tradition, and especially from Parson's analysis, that the following set of six hypotheses was derived. They are hardly formulated with the kind of precision which would make them testable in any definitive way. They were intended rather as a focus for discussion at the second seminar of the Conference on Modern Japan, for which the papers of this volume were originally written. They are suggestions, that is to say, concerning the type of change in interpersonal relations which, from one's knowledge of the society of Tokugawa Japan and in the light of theoretical formulations of the social change accompanying the growth of capitalist-type industrialization in Europe and America, one would have expected to occur in Japan as she became an increasingly industrial and urban nation in the last hundred years. The hypotheses were as follows. It will be seen that they may be roughly characterized as postulating a movement toward greater equality, greater individuation, and greater rationality.

1. The criteria determining status in social organizations tend to change, showing less emphasis on birth and seniority and more on merit.

2. Relations of authority become more circumscribed, more specific to the particular narrow functions of the organization and less "relations of the whole man."

3. In consequence, the "volume" of authority exercised by superiors vis-à-vis inferiors tends to diminish; there is less social distance between statuses; there are fewer formal marks of deference required in speech, gesture, etc.

4. A greater range of the individual's behavior is the result of choice between conscious alternatives rather than the following of tradition.

4

5. A greater range of an individual's choices is determined by reference to his own well-being or that of certain other specific individuals and less by reference to the well-being of some group to which he belongs.

6. A greater range of an individual's behavior is based on rational secular premises and with reference to situations and events beyond his personal experience.

Not all the papers bear directly on these themes. Some are more concerned with relationships between groups rather than between persons, and some with analysis of the peculiar differentiae of traditional Japanese culture. They do, however, contain a good deal that is directly relevant to these hypotheses and hence to the broader questions to which they are related: does industrialization—or at least capitalist industrialization—have the same social consequences everywhere? Are industrial societies destined to become more and more alike? Or what, alternatively, are the sources of variation in the forms they may assume?

Ascription and Achievement

As for the first of these hypothesized trends, any assumption that Japan's development over the last century represents a standard pattern starting from the base line of a standard "traditional society" needs the corrective of Smith's paper. He shows that over the last three centuries there has been a cyclical change in the criteria for allocating status within organizations, not a steady unidirectional trend. Merit was more important in making appointments in the rudimentary bureaucracies of the seventeenth century than in the more developed ones of the eighteenth. It was from the middle of the Tokugawa period that hereditary rigidity really set in. The paper by DeVos and Mizushima also shows how in one sector of premodern Japanese society, the world of the gambling gangs, leadership positions always were achieved. (The two things are doubtless related. The seventeenth century continued the patterns of the sixteenth, when the samurai lived, like the gangs later in the period, in a world of anarchic competition.) Perhaps the most striking point made by Smith's paper, however, is that the "merit ideology" held such dominant sway among the intellectuals of Tokugawa society that, despite the ascriptive principles which in fact operated, no counter-ideology was developed explicitly to justify the hereditary principle. If a shift from ascription to achievement is in fact a necessary prerequisite for industrialization or for the growth of efficient rationally organized bureaucracies, Japan was peculiarly well prepared. Social change in this respect required not the development of new social forms and a new supporting ideology, but simply the practice of what was formerly preached.

Smith notes that the concept of merit in the Tokugawa period was necessarily ill-defined. In the modern period the development of schools and universities provided, in graduation certificates and special-purpose examinations, at least one concrete means of defining it. It is one on which, perhaps, greater reliance has been placed for the allocation of occupational roles than in any other industrial society. My own paper describes some of the ways in which the ascriptive principles of patronage and family influence still operate to modify or to amplify the workings of merit criteria in the allocation of first jobs—of initial membership in industrial organizations. At this level the mixture of ascription and achievement seems not very different from that in most other industrial societies (though it is difficult to imagine what quantitative measures one might use to substantiate such an assertion). In the criteria for promotions and transfers *within* organizations, however, the mixture of seniority, patronage, and performance seems to be much more heavily weighted toward the first, and perhaps toward the second, than is the case in other industrial societies. Levine's paper describes how the labor unions, with their emphasis on se-

curity of employment and their defense of seniority incre-
ments, have in the postwar period given an extra rigidity to
organizational forms which were originally designed to retain
a skilled and loyal labor force. This feature of Japanese
industry would clearly seem to be related to the continuing
emphasis on group solidarity in Japanese society. If it is
true, as the analysts of "bureaucracy" have suggested, that
there is a basic incompatibility in the traditional Weberian
ideal type between fostering loyal commitment to the organization on the one hand and maintaining strict evaluation
procedures involving the invidious assessment of individual
performance as a basis for merit promotions on the other,
then the Japanese have quite clearly chosen to emphasize
the former at the expense of the latter.

In general terms, however, and in spite of the impossibility
of adducing conclusive evidence of a quantitative kind, it
seems undoubtedly true that, as compared with a century
ago, the allocation of prestige, power, and income in modern
Japan depends to a much greater degree on demonstrated
abilities and much less on ascribed characteristics.

This fact by itself, however, is no evidence of a secular trend
in this direction which will continue further to narrow the
role of ascription. The record of economic growth described
in Bennett's paper does not suggest that the present compromise between seniority and merit criteria seriously
hampers the efficiency of Japanese industry. Nevertheless,
Japanese management journals are full of exhortations to
rationalize evaluation and promotion procedures, and if
these exhortations have no effect, some would argue, as
Bennett argues by implication in his paper, that the changing
nature of the labor market will. Both the growing general
shortage of labor and the more frequent occurrence of particular shortages for particular high-grade skills are, it is suggested, likely to increase labor mobility. Once the "lifetime
employment pattern" is broken down the whole of the rest

of the structure will crumble. In another decade it will be possible to judge with some accuracy just how valid these arguments are.

There remains one more point to be made concerning the first hypothesis. Norbeck's paper records a method of allocating leadership roles common in Japanese villages—annual rotation on a more or less fixed roster. This is not easy to "place" in terms of the concepts in which the hypothesis is framed. In that it eliminates competition and the invidious assessment of merit, this method resembles use of the seniority criterion; it is certainly not an application of the merit principle. Yet, by carrying to an extreme the principle of equality of all members of the organization, it lacks the hierarchical emphasis usual in ascriptive systems. Once again, it is a device related to the emphasis on group integration.

Specificity of Authority

Discussion of the second hypothesis needs again to be prefaced by reference to Tokugawa society, which in one crucial respect differed from the feudal societies of Europe. In Europe the dissolution of feudalism was a prolonged process in which traditional relations of diffuse authority were gradually made more specific in overtly contractual forms. The same process was hardly apparent in Tokugawa Japan before the more abrupt political transition to a centralized state. The emphasis in the ideology on unconditional loyalty militated against any such evolution. One of the clearest indicators of the difference is the growth of a powerful class of lawyers in feudal Europe as guardians of the objective authority of contract, a phenomenon which had no counterpart in Japan. If, therefore, Japan entered her industrial phase as well prepared as European countries—or perhaps even better—for the acceptance of merit criteria for allocating roles, it was considerably less well prepared to accept the narrowing of authority relations to specific organizational contexts.

Nevertheless, the process has taken place. It is most clearly documented in the papers of Norbeck and Johnson. In the villages, at least, the proliferation of special-purpose associations, each with their own leadership positions, has destroyed the diffuse generalized authority of rural squireships though perhaps it was not until the land reform destroyed the economic basis of traditional hierarchies that the formal patterns of authority began very fully to coincide with the realities of the distribution of power.

In industry, too, it is quite clear that the authority attached to the employer's or manager's role has become more specific than in the master-servant pattern of Tokugawa employment relations. It seems clear, nevertheless, that the limits within which this process has taken place are narrower than in most industrial societies. For one thing, the separation of workplace from home, of occupational from private life, is inevitably less complete in a society where it is customary for employers to provide houses for their employees. The papers of Totten and Levine show the limits within which authority has been narrowed by contract in work relations. Totten describes the efforts which were made before the war to prevent the clear contractual specification of rights and duties—the government's provision of conciliation machinery for the ad hoc settlement of disputes, and the largely successful attempts to substitute factory councils (which left rights and duties undefined and provided only for consultation) for collectively bargained enforceable agreements. Levine shows how, since the war, although unions have gained legally sanctioned bargaining powers, they have generally chosen to confine the exercise of these powers to the two main matters of wages and the right of employment, leaving the authority of management in other respects—work arrangements, the settling of grievances, production processes, etc.—relatively unimpaired by contract and circumscribed only by loosely defined mechanisms for consultation. The picture which emerges is of groups internally organized on a basis of mutual trust and understanding between statuses recognized as diffusely subordinate and superordinate. The management is expected to consider the interests of the workers, and workers are expected to comply with the management's wishes, provided only that suitable arrangements are made for each party to make known its wishes and interests to the other. This contrasts with a system in which it is assumed that only the clear definition in contracts of the specific rights and duties of each party can prevent them from taking resented advantage of each other.

That the evolution of the present forms of Japanese industrialism is in part a product of deliberate social engineering is made clear in Totten's description of the activities of the government and semiofficial agencies such as the Kyōchōkai. At the conference at which these papers were presented Takeyoshi Kawashima described the application of similar policies in the prewar period in two other fields, within the family and in tenancy relations. In both cases pressure for a legal specification of rights—the rights of tenants vis-à-vis landlords or of wives vis-à-vis husbands—was resisted by prewar governments anxious to preserve the cellular community structure of Japanese society as a basis of social stability. Instead there were created new kinds of conciliation machinery which preserved the diffuseness of authority relationships but provided mechanisms to regulate what had become, by the new emerging standards of society, abuses of authority sufficiently flagrant to arouse protest and conflict.

Although none are contained in this book, studies of the internal organization of the civil bureaucracy, hospitals, universities, or political parties would also reveal the existence in Japan of authority relations of a degree of diffuseness unusual in other industrial societies. Still, the degree is considerably less than would have been considered normal in nineteenth century Japan.

Again, the question arises whether one can see this change as evidence of a trend which will continue, or whether in these respects Japanese society has reached a viable point of stability; or whether, indeed, the trend might in future be reversed, back again to greater diffuseness of authority—a not impossible alternative given the availability of the new organizational forms of the totalitarian party or state. Levine, who postulates at the beginning of his paper a universal trend toward an increasingly complex industrial "web of rule" and increasingly wide participation in rule-making as a necessary consequence of the growing complexity of industrial technology and organization, remains at the end uncertain whether Japan will proceed to prove the truth of the postulate or not. Only a very bold man would be more dogmatic.

The Volume of Authority

It is not difficult to distinguish conceptually between a change in the specificity of authority attached to a particular role and a change in what one might call its "volume." The authority of a superior who can only direct his subordinate's working activity for eight hours a day is more "specific" than that of a superior who can also require his subordinate to seek permission before marrying or moving house. On the other hand, one can talk of a difference in "volume" even if there is no difference in specificity, as, for instance, between a superior who gets an immediate and willing response to a peremptory order—"take the plate away"—and one who feels constrained to say politely "would you please take the plate away" and glances anxiously at his subordinate to make sure that the order was well received. Change in the two dimensions tends to be related, of course. It is in the small closed agrarian community, where the superior in one sphere of life is the superior in all, that the dominance of man over man tends to be most complete. Bouglé, writing at the end of the nineteenth century, was one of the first to make explicit the idea that in an economically developing society it is the increasing proliferation of special-purpose associations, each with their own disparate status systems, which, by ensuring that the superior in one context is the subordinate in another, produces a trend toward what de Tocqueville called a "general equality of condition." Armies may enforce discipline and insist on the completeness of the authority of superiors in the specific military context, but when officer and private frequent the same bars, when they are each worth only one vote in the polling booth, when the private's son is as likely to pass the university entrance examination as the officer's, the dominance of the one over the other even in the military context is likely to be attenuated.

One general indicator of such a change in Japan over the last century is well known, the slow withering away of forms of deferential behavior. The elaborately respectful forms of speech with special verb endings and honorific prefixes are much less frequently heard than they were. Forms of gift-giving to superiors which two or three decades ago would have been considered normal and proper expressions of respect are today condemned as degrading bootlicking. Subordinates bow less often and with a lesser degree of inclination. The taxi driver scolded by a policeman may still take off his hat and give a smart 20-degree bow, but he does not go down on his knees like a rickshawman of 1890.

Nevertheless, despite Bennett's assertion that the reticence and self-effacement of the "Japanese character" have now become rare phenomena, the taxi driver is still likely to bow. Those who exercise authority are likely to receive more overt deference and more real obedience than is common in most industrial countries. It is a significant indication of this that the factory representatives' congresses of the twenties described by Totten had as one of their main purposes the aim of destroying general attitudes of submissiveness. They provided a sense of mass anonymity which enabled workers to breathe defiance at their superiors. (The political demonstrations of modern times probably have something of the same appeal to their participants. Perhaps they would not be so well attended if the general level of submissiveness were not so high.)

Totten's paper, and Levine's by implication, also point up another important aspect of changes in this regard. A changing balance of power between groups may not be immediately reflected in a change in the "volume" of authority displayed in face-to-face relations between members of those groups. Labor unions may be able to hold the management to ransom, but the lathe operator called to the factory manager's office is still likely to be very respectful. On the other hand, the papers of Cornell and of Wagatsuma and DeVos show a contrasting situation. The *burakumin* organizations have been successful in removing overt forms of discrimination against the outcast groups, and even in extracting substantial subsidies from local governments. Concomitantly there has also, it appears, been an accompanying change in interpersonal relations. *Burakumin* are not usually treated with the rude scorn that they frequently encountered from other Japanese fifty years ago; discrimination today takes the form of avoidance and the polite refusal. Now it is the *burakumin* who is feared by other Japanese, rather than vice versa. One may think of several reasons for the difference in the two cases. Equal citizenship for all and the abolition of caste distinctions have been principles supported by all governments since the beginning of the Meiji period, whereas they were concerned to maintain, and not to weaken, management hierarchies. Second, there is an obvious difference between the continuing and functionally differentiated relationship of manager to worker and the less structured contacts between *burakumin* and other Japanese.

The assumption implicit in the preceding paragraph is that the complement of a strong "volume" of authority was an attitude of submissiveness and that this was a generalized personality trait. This is, of course, one of the assumptions underlying the psychologist's analysis of the "authoritarian personality." It is one that has yet to be conclusively proved, but Johnson's paper provides incidental support for the "general syndrome" thesis in his assertion that those villages which preserve a most authoritarian community structure tend also to be villages where the elder brother is given the greatest authority over his siblings within the family.

Specificity and volume are by no means the only measures which can be applied to authority relationships. An equal "volume" of authority may be admixed with (or achieved by) either terror or benevolence. Doi's analysis of the concept of *amaeru* points up the peculiar nature of Japanese authority relations in this respect. The subordinate, in his view, is constantly seeking the assurance that he is loved, an assurance which is essential for his security and sense of identity. This, too, Doi sees as a generalized need built into the personality, and although one might question his final conclusion that these personality traits will only be modified by "searching deeply into the foundations of Western culture," he is surely right in suggesting that changes in authority relations have been and will be brought about not only by the structural changes accompanying industrialization which were sketched in at the beginning of this section, but also by ideological influences. Ideas about what is proper respect and what degrading self-abasement, about what is legitimate leadership and what arbitrary dominance, have indeed been notably influenced by ideas originating outside Japan.

The Range of Choice

In the fluid and mobile society of present-day Japan, it is obvious enough that individuals more frequently have the opportunity and face the necessity of making deliberate individual choices. The mere following of tradition does not make one an electronics engineer. Nevertheless, several of these papers show ways in which individual freedom of choice is more limited than in many other comparably industrial societies. The relatively low level of mobility in that growing segment of the labor force employed in the big corporations, reinforced as Levine shows by the unions' stress on secure permanence of employment, means that the choice of occupation is often made once and for all, and is not seen by a good proportion of Japanese men as a constantly open choice. Equally, the smoothness of the patterns of migration described by Vogel—with the family structure determining who should migrate and joint family efforts helping in the process—meant that no rebellious individual initiative was involved. Equally, my own description of the job-seeking of university graduates in the mid-fifties suggests that the importance of patronage in getting jobs effectively reduced individual choice to a minimum.

Clearly, however, these phenomena are in part the consequence of the structure of the economy, of the fact that for most of Japan's industrializing period there have been more job-seekers than jobs. They may also be the result of an inability or unwillingness to make self-reliant choices which is built deeply into the personalities of a majority of the Japanese. But we shall only know how much to attribute to each of these factors after the objective economic situation has changed and a situation of labor shortage has existed long enough for all the consequent structural changes to be worked through. Bennett suggests that these changes are likely to be both radical and rapid, and the consequences for individual choice-making immediate.

If the new industrial economy does not offer as much freedom of individual choice as one would expect, it is not surprising that choice is even more limited in the villages where in their occupational lives a good many men are in effect "following tradition." Norbeck describes the great variety of common interest associations which have developed in Japanese villages, but he shows also how the "voluntariness" of voluntary associations is always very much open to doubt. In theory one may or may not belong to the agricultural cooperative. But such are the social pressures toward conformity—or, rather, so strong is the assumption that action is taken not by individuals but by groups—that the individual who perceives himself as actually having such a choice is rare, and the deviant who actually exercises it is rarer still.

The *burakumin* described by Wagatsuma and DeVos and also by Cornell do have a choice, as they make clear: the one big choice of whether to make what Cornell calls the "quantum leap" of "passing" into outside society, or whether to stay with his kind in a situation of very limited opportunity. And if he does opt out, the burden of his solitary "choosing" existence is very great, as is shown by the case studies which Wagatsuma and DeVos have collected.

Paradoxically—if one considers the expansion of choice as a function of modernity—it is the men in the traditional sector of small family businesses who in some respects have the greatest range of choice. The optical manufacturer mentioned in Bennett's paper, the small entrepreneurs mentioned at the end of Vogel's and my own papers, are not subject to the group constraints which confine the employee of a big corporation. Their scope for individual initiatives and their need for self-reliance are greater, their dependency relations more likely to be contingent, calculated and instrumental. But they are a declining group. If Riesman is right, and it is only in such entrepreneurial milieux that the "study individualism" of the Western tradition is born, they would seem to have a slim chance of radically affecting the norms and ideologies of Japanese society as a whole before they are engulfed by the big corporations.

The Criteria of Choice

One can at least conceptually separate a change in the opportunity or the need to make individual choices from a change in the criteria by which choices are made—whether they are guided by considerations of the welfare of oneself or of individual others, or whether the welfare of some group to which one belongs is a more dominant concern. Again, of course, changes in the two dimensions tend to be related, since the individual most subject to group pressures and hence most restricted in his freedom to make choices is also likely to have the emotional identification with the group which guides his choices toward a concern with group welfare.

Quite clearly there has been a change toward greater individuation in this latter dimension, too, most notably in the declining tendency to conceive of the family as a corporate group with a life and interests of its own. (This is related in part, perhaps, to the decline in family size as well as to the changing economic function of the family; a household with two children does constitute less of a "group" than one with six.) Sometimes the change can be concealed in the persistence of traditional behavioral forms. Marriages may continue to be arranged, but the arrangers are less concerned that "the house of Tanaka" should receive a worthy future mistress than that their Taro should get a girl who will look after him and make him happy.

But, if one focus of group identification has lost its importance, others have taken its place—notably "the firm" with its promise of permanent employment and its overwhelming claim on the individual's loyalty, characteristics which, as Levine describes, are reinforced by the enterprise union structure. Vogel suggests, indeed, that the member of a large organization is likely to have "the same all-embracing commitment to his firm, the willingness to undergo temporary sacrifice for the eventual good of the firm and himself, that the members of a family enterprise have toward their *ie*." The enterprise structure of unions is an important part of the picture, since it means that there is little to induce a sense of membership of class or craft or of any other unit which transcends the enterprise. The Mitsubishi man is a Mitsubishi man first, only secondarily a boilermaker or a member of the working class, and, in many cases, only secondarily a member of his nuclear family.

In the villages the farmer is still very much a member of his hamlet. Norbeck describes how this results in almost universal membership in hamlet associations, and Johnson shows, *inter alia*, how the hamlet organizes itself to ensure that all its votes should be used "for the good of the hamlet" in village council elections. He stresses, of course, that the degree of hamlet solidarity is considerably less than it was a century ago, but it is still greater than is found in the rural areas of other industrial countries.

For the *burakumin* there is the choice between a leap into individual isolation or a continued sense of identification with his group, which is likely to loom larger in his consciousness than ever before. As the papers of Cornell and of Wagatsuma and DeVos show, the erosion of the boundaries of the *buraku* and the increasing contacts of *burakumin* with outsiders have given them frequent opportunities for being reminded of their *buraku* origin, as a Japanese in Europe is constantly reminded that he is a Japanese. And the embattled *dōmei* organizations which seek to improve the *burakumin*'s lot serve to strengthen the solidarity of the *buraku* communities—*vide* Cornell's example of the *buraku* where the *dōmei* urged everyone to use the bathhouse even if they had a bath at home.

Again the question arises: how far is this continuing group solidarity, this low level of individuation, determined by transitional structural features—the nature of the labor market and the mode of industrialization determining the enterprise structure; the nucleated settlement pattern and the exigencies of irrigated rice culture determining the nature of the village community; the economic position of the *burakumin* enforcing their sense of group membership? Or how far, alternatively, is it a continuation of cultural patterns rooted in the structure of individual personalities, formed by the expressive culture and patterns of child training in such a way that individuals have a "need to belong"? Certainly the psychological need is no longer uncomplicated and uninhibited. The ideology of individualism has been imported into Japan. Self-reliance and individual initiative are accepted virtues. DeVos and Mizushima suggest that the legends of Tokugawa gangs, the theme of much popular fiction, serve to provide a dream world of unfettered masculinity and freedom of initiative which the real world does not permit, and they make the neat contrast between the identity crisis of the Japanese adolescent as a striving for freedom *from* something, and that of American youths as a striving for freedom *to* achieve something. Nevertheless, they suggest that a need to belong is one of the factors in the formation of juvenile gangs.

In their view, however, the need is not just for identity with a group, but for membership in a group which also provides a strong relation of dependence on a dominant leader figure. Throughout the discussion of individuation it is difficult, but necessary, to separate that derogation from an individual's independence which results from merging his identity in a group, and that which results from his surrender to dependency on a particular person. In the case of a job-seeking youth who allows himself to be guided in his choice—to be "taken care of"—by a patron, it is clearly the latter; in the case of the member of an egalitarian hamlet, voting for his hamlet's chosen candidate, it is equally clearly the former; but when the group is under authoritarian leadership, as in a criminal gang, the two mechanisms coincide.

The distinction becomes important in considering how far "the nation" began in the modern period to loom in the individual's consciousness as a new group in which his membership was for him psychologically important, a focus of loyalty strong enough to satisfy the "need to belong" for those individuals who had no secure membership in firm, community, or family. Culturally, membership in the nation was, until 1945, typically expressed as personal loyalty to the emperor. Doi, in his analysis, perhaps because he is chiefly concerned with personal relationships, stresses this emperor-centered aspect of the national bond. On the other hand, the continuing strong degree of national consciousness since the war, despite the virtual elimination of the emperor as an effective national symbol (especially when "the honor of Japan" is at stake in, for instance, Olympic games) suggests that the sense of group membership may be more important. Whichever is the case, it makes no difference to Doi's point that the development of national loyalties had ambiguous effects for individuation. On the one hand the national loyalty had a prior claim over family or community solidarity, and so helped to loosen primary affiliations. On the other hand, for those who were shaken loose from such affiliations by circumstances, it provided the refuge of an alternative form of group identification which prevented individuals from coming to terms with their aloneness in more individually self-reliant ways.

Whatever the force of transitional economic features, no one can doubt that one of the reasons why most modern Japanese are more firmly bound in group affiliations than most members of other industrial societies is that the Tokugawa society of a century ago had a more tightly organized structure of corporate groups than was found in Europe, even perhaps at the height of European feudalism. (One may leave aside the question of whether this continuity depends on the direct persistence of structural forms or on the characteristics of the modal personality seeking expression in new forms.) In feudal England a serf who escaped to a city and lived there for a year thereby acquired a right to his freedom. The preindustrial societies of Europe were more individualistic than that of Japan. Again, this raises interesting questions of the interrelation of structure and culture. Is the difference between Japan and Europe in this regard a function of power relationships, of the fact that there *were* free cities in the feudal societies of Europe and none in Japan? Or is it a function of the ideological difference between the individualistic emphasis of Christianity and the collective emphasis on the residential community in the Shinto tradition and on the family and its analogues in that of Buddhism and Confucianism? And if the ideological difference is important, how far does it in turn depend on structural differences, on the fact that the church in European societies had its own centralized organization which disposed of secular power capable of balancing that of the state, a dualism absent in Japan?

Rationality and Secularism

An increasing tendency toward the instrumental adaptation of behavior to consciously conceived goals and toward the elimination of supernatural considerations from the determinants of behavior is something implicitly assumed in most of these papers, rather than something which emerges as a demonstrated conclusion. Some of its less obvious manifestations and mechanisms are touched on, however. DeVos and Mizushima see a shift within criminal gangs toward a greater emphasis on the rational instrumental value and a lesser emphasis on the expressive value of personal relationships, but remain doubtful whether this is a real shift or an illusory result of romanticization of the gang loyalties of the past. Totten's discussion of union activities mentions the effect of their educational efforts to make their members think rationally of their situation and the means of improving it. Undoubtedly, however, the major causal factor in this regard has been the development of sophisticated forms of secular education and the broadening of horizons—the "expansion of empathy"—brought by the development of the popular press. One side effect of educational developments, touched on in the paper by DeVos and Mizushima, is the delaying of adulthood, the creation of the special limbo of adolescence with its own special problems. They are problems which Japanese society has not learned to handle much better than the societies of the West.

General Considerations: Universal Trends?

If one were to give a one-sentence epitomization of the above discussion it would be that there is more evidence of change in the directions suggested by the first three hypotheses than in the directions suggested by the fourth and fifth; that is to say, more evidence of a move toward greater equality than of a move toward greater individuation.

The question naturally arises, however, and is explicitly posed in Bendix's paper, whether one has any right to expect a move in either direction. Do these hypotheses about trends have even enough plausibility to make them worth considering as perspectives for the analysis of social change in Japan? In their defense it can be said that they rest on a little more than the simplistic correlational argument: "European societies seem to have moved in these directions in the course of capitalist industrialization; a Japan going through the same economic process should show the same trends." It is possible to indicate the mechanisms by which one expects economic development and social change to be linked. The arguments used earlier about mobility, cross-cutting group membership, the noncoincidence of statuses, and changes in the volume of authority are an example. So is the discussion which introduces Levine's paper, suggesting that a trend toward an increasingly elaborate objective web of rule and wider participation in rule-making is a necessary consequence of technological development.

But these, Bendix would suggest, are not enough. The functional requirements for operating a modern industrial system are such that they can be met by a wide variety of structural and cultural forms. In the first place, there is a fundamental difference between the first endogenous industrializers and the late developer. One aspect of this difference, the role of imported ideology, was already mentioned above, a propos both of egalitarianism and individualism. A second aspect is that in the late-developing society the role of political agents in determining the pattern of change tends to be greater. There is evidence enough of this in these papers—in the deliberate efforts of prewar governments to preserve diffuse patterns of authority described by Totten, in the postwar creation of labor unions mentioned by Levine. And in the particular cases of Japan and Germany discussed by Bendix an important part has also been played by external political agents, the armies of foreign powers. He would go so far as to say that if these two societies today resemble others in the West, this is chiefly because of the activity of those external political agents: the "significant" changes in both countries "have come about as a result of conquest and externally induced change."

The role of political leadership in late-developing societies may be accepted. It might still be argued that the functional necessities of an industrial society are such that there is only one direction in which change can go, and within broad limits the role of political leaders can only be to accelerate or hinder changes likely to take place eventually anyway. To this Bendix would reply that the effects of political action depend as much on (a) the cultural orientations and economic interests of those who hold power, (b) the structure of group relations, and (c) the nature of the tensions within it (all determined by the unique structure of the traditional society) as on the strains and needs set up in the process of economic development itself. In particular he points out that the contrast between the preexisting class antagonism of Germany, already ideologically canalized, and the acceptance of interpersonal status distinctions in Japan, or the contrast between the ingrained militarism of the Junkers and the demilitarized orientation of the samurai, were significant factors in making for different patterns of personal relationships in Japan and Germany.

Granted the existence of such differences rooted in the past, it could still be argued, as Veblen argued fifty years ago, that these differences are bound to disappear. This, indeed, is Bennett's assumption. Only now, he would argue, in the very rapid economic growth of the last few years based on a rapid expansion of domestic consumption, has the breakthrough occurred. Hitherto traditional forms have remained dominant; now the landslide into Westernization has begun. It is a sad thought that even if he does turn out to be right, this might still prove nothing much about the functional necessities of industrial societies—only about the processes of cultural diffusion. It might, that is to say, simply be that when the Japanese have been sufficiently persuaded on all eight of their television channels that they too like Lucy and that they need the same deodorants as Americans and the same electric toothbrushes, they will come increasingly to behave like Americans in other respects too.

PART ONE

A Comparative Perspective

CHAPTER I

Preconditions of Development:
A Comparison of Japan and Germany[1]

REINHARD BENDIX

THE GREAT CLASSICS of comparative analysis have in common that they focus on one issue with reference to which they analyze materials from different countries and civilizations. Max Weber studied the secular repercussions of different religious doctrines, de Tocqueville contrasted equality in American and in French society, Fustel de Coulanges examined the religious foundation of civic unity in ancient Greece and Rome, Henry Maine used the familial versus individual basis of contract as the criterion for analyzing ancient legal history, and so on. Unfortunately, we do not possess models of similar simplicity for the comparative study of social and political change in the modern world.

While the renewed interest in this field is only some twenty years old, the difficulty is less one of inexperience than of conceptualization. The whole vocabulary of modern sociology originated in a few countries of northwestern Europe, where it was natural to consider change as indigenous to the societies changing, and where change had been sufficiently gradual and pervasive to affect all aspects of the social structure and the cultural life of the people. Yet this setting and the theoretical assumptions appropriate to it are irrelevant outside the area in which modern technology and the modern processes of social and political change originated. It is as true of Germany as it is of Japan that many of these changes were either taken over from abroad or developed in

[1] Research for this essay was begun during a three-month stay in Japan made possible by a "reflective year" grant of the Carnegie Corporation. I am indebted to Henry Rosovsky for his encouragement and critical comment.

conscious reference to changes that had taken place abroad, often in the effort to increase the economic and military viability of these countries. Other, major changes have resulted from conquest. As modern technology and various aspects of modern Western societies have been "transplanted" by one means or another, Germany and Japan along with many other countries have had to cope with the problems arising from the symbiosis of tradition and modernity.

To avoid ambiguity, I state here my use of three terms. By "industrialization" I propose to refer to the changes brought about in the economy by the use of a technology based on inanimate sources of power as well as on the continuous development of applied scientific research. "Modernization" is sometimes used as a synonym for all those social and political changes which accompanied industrialization in many countries of Western civilization, such as urbanization, changes in occupational structure, social mobility, development of education, as well as the development of political institutions from absolutist to responsible to representative government and from a laissez-faire to a modern welfare state. More simply, the two terms refer to the technical-economic and the sociopolitical changes familiar to us from the recent history of western Europe, and the term "development" will be used where reference is made to correlated changes in both of these spheres. The appropriateness of these proximate definitions will be questioned in the course of the following discussion, especially with regard to the correlation between industrialization and modernization. There is, however, nothing inherently wrong about using the development of Western societies as the basis of what we propose to mean by development—as long, that is, as the purely nominal character of this definition is understood. The past development of industrialized societies must certainly be one basis for our definitions in this field. Trouble arises only when it is assumed that these are "real" definitions, that "development" can mean only what it has come to mean in the West.

Germany and Japan are today highly industrialized countries. Consequently, the two countries share a large number of characteristics which follow from industrialization itself and are either the direct product of technological and economic change or variable by-products of that change. An incomplete list of the first would include the change from a traditional technology toward one based on the application of scientific knowledge, a change in agriculture from subsistence farming toward commercial production of agricultural goods, a change in industry from the use of human and animal power toward the use of power-driven machines, and a change in workplace and residence from the farm and village toward urban centers. An incomplete list of the second would include the effects of a growing market economy upon dependency relations and the division of labor, namely the substitution of contractual and monetary ties for the earlier familial or quasi-familial relation between employer and worker, the diversification of the occupational structure, increased social mobility, the development of universal elementary education, and others. These and related changes have occurred in all countries that have industrialized successfully, including Germany and Japan, though this is not to deny the quantitative and qualitative distinctions which remain even with regard to these comparable products and by-products of industrialization.

The two countries are comparable in a number of other respects. Both began their most rapid development at roughly the same time, Japan after the Restoration of 1868 and Germany after her political unification following the Franco-Prussian war of 1870–1871. This accident of timing meant that the two countries began the rapid industrialization of their economies on a broadly comparable technological and scientific basis, though at that time Germany could look back to a more sustained indigenous development of science and technology than Japan. As industrial latecomers both countries were dependent for a time upon borrowing technical and scientific know-how from abroad, though here again Germany preceded Japan by several decades. In the political field the two countries shared a preference for monarchical institutions and a tradition of bureaucratic government controlled by a ruling oligarchy—a similarity which accounts for the degree to which the Meiji oligarchs took the government of Imperial Germany as their model. This common tradition of bureaucratic government also imparted a certain similarity to the aristocracies of the two countries, at any rate to the extent that aristocratic title depended upon or was directly associated with high office. Finally, both countries were broadly similar in the relatively weak development of the middle class, in the uneasy development of democratic institutions and the readiness with which they resorted to authoritarian and dictatorial forms of government.

Considered as a whole, the similarities mentioned above provide a promising basis for a comparative study of the two social structures. With reference to each of these similarities it is possible to point to striking differences as well; a number of these differences will be noted in due course. It is well to bear in mind, however, that the analysis of dissimilarities is illuminating because the common ground between Japan and Germany improves our ability to pinpoint the significance of the elements in which they differ.

"Partial Development"

The conventional approach to the study of development has been to consider tradition and modernity mutually exclusive; the more you have of one, the less you have of the other. Examples of this dichotomy can be cited, beginning, say, with Adam Ferguson's contrast between aristocratic and commercial nations and ending, for the time being, with the pattern variables of Talcott Parsons. Robert Redfield's *Folk Culture of Yucatan* is an outstanding empirical study of this type. Certainly there has been considerable advance from the earlier contrasts between tradition and

modernity, which barely disguised a largely ideological reaction to a rising commercial civilization. But while comparisons between the inequities of that civilization and the
"golden age" of tradition may receive little credence among
scholars, it is still difficult to avoid the developmental generalization implicit in this intellectual legacy. We are so at-
tuned to the idea of a close association among the different
elements of "tradition" or "modernity" that wherever we find
evidence of industrialization we look for, or tend to expect,
those social and political changes which we are accustomed
to find associated with industrialization in some countries of
Western civilization.

Many years ago Veblen questioned this assumption in his
essays on Germany and Japan.[2] Borrowed industrialization
in those countries had *not* had the same solvent effect on
"archaic" social institutions as original industrialization
in England, and he was concerned to show the special problems and special opportunites of the "unstable cultural com-
pound" which resulted. Nevertheless, Veblen assumed, as
is implicitly assumed by the hypotheses listed in the introduction to this book, that this was a transitional phase. In the
end social institutions would adapt to conform with the new
technology.

Schumpeter went further than Veblen: the partial nature
of development was likely to be not a temporary but a lasting phenomenon.[3] "Social structure, types and attitudes are
coins that do not readily melt," and a variety of forms of
them are compatible with industrialism. Every industrial

[2] Thorstein Veblen, *Imperial Germany and the Industrial Revolution* (New York: Viking Press, 1954, and "The Opportunity of
Japan," in *Essays in Our Changing Order* (New York: Viking Press,
1934). For additional remarks on Veblen's discussion of Germany
and Japan and on similar analyses by Talcott Parsons, see my *Nation-
Building and Citizenship* (New York: John Wiley and Sons, 1964),
pp. 6–7, 210–11.

[3] Joseph Schumpeter, *Capitalism, Socialism, and Democracy* (New
York: Harper and Brothers, 1947), esp. pp. 12–13.

country retains features of its preindustrial society, and the forms of industrial societies are likely to differ widely depending on their earlier traditions.

Schumpeter was obviously right. One might add further that "iron rules" of development are subject to variation not only because of different traditions but also because of events that impinge upon a society from outside. In both Japan and Germany the symbiosis between tradition and modernity was destroyed, and the most drastic social and political change was induced not by the slow adaptation to the matter-of-fact outlook of modern technology which Veblen extrapolates from the English experience, but by conquest, military occupation, and partition.[4]

Two Aristocracies

If all developing countries exemplify a more or less viable symbiosis of their traditional social structures with the direct and indirect products of industrialization, the task is, therefore, to distinguish between different types of "partial development." In the case of Germany and Japan this may be attempted by comparisons between the samurai and the Junkers, two traditional ruling groups which exemplify how past formations of a socal structure can facilitate or hinder the process of development.

Perhaps a word is needed to explain this emphasis on ruling groups, since in Germany and Japan the process of industrialization came to pervade the whole society. Most obviously, ruling groups are best documented in the history of any country. Since political initiative is important in countries that were "industrial latecomers," it is appropriate to give special attention to the social groups that were politically prominent in the traditional social structure. Whether or not such groups take a leading role in the industrialization of the country, it is clear that their social and cultural influence is

[4] I have elaborated on this point in *Nation-Building and Citizenship,* pp. 210–13.

pervasive. If we are to understand types of "partial development," and in particular changes in interpersonal relations that accompany industrialization, then we must give special attention to the "baseline" of tradition with reference to which these changes are to be gauged. To do this, a knowledge of traditional ruling groups is indispensable, and a comparative analysis can help us to define their distinguishing characteristics. My emphasis is also determined by Professor Thomas Smith's recent interpretation of the "aristocratic revolution" in Japan, which represents and specifically calls for a comparative analysis.[5]

Smith points out that ordinarily one expects aristocracies to defend their established positions, not to take the lead in transforming their society and in the process abolish their own privileges. Why was Japan different? In his answer to this question, Smith examines the changes in the position of the samurai prior to the Restoration, how these changes were related to Japan's "aristocratic revolution," and what distinctive traits emerged in Japan because her revolution was aristocratic. On all three points Smith's treatment is a brilliant summation of research on the social history of Japan. Rather than repeat what he has stated, I shall single out specific points which invite comparison with the divergent history of the ruling strata in Prussia and Germany since the seventeenth century.

A. IDEOLOGICAL ARTICULATION?

Referring first to conditions under the Tokugawa shogunate, Smith makes the hypothetical point that the Japanese aristocracy might not have initiated a wholesale transfor-

---

[5] See Thomas Smith, "Japan's Aristocratic Revolution," *Yale Review*, L (1960–61), 370–83. Two other contributions of the same author, "The Discontented," *Journal of Asian Studies*, XXI (1962), 215–19, and "Merit as Ideology in Tokugawa Japan," in this volume, in addition to his earlier works, fit into the framework of this interpretation and will be noted in due course.

mation of their own position in society if their privileges had ever been challenged by a rising "democratic" movement. They could be revolutionary only because there was no democratic revolution in Japan. Why did the Japanese townsmen fail to launch such a challenge? Neither numerical weakness, poverty, illiteracy, political innocence, nor a lack of resentment can well serve as an explanation. "There was resentment aplenty and there were many instances of private revenge; but for some reason resentment never reached the pitch of ideology, never raised private hurts to a great principle of struggle between right and wrong."[6]

With this suggestion let us look at Prussia and Germany at the end of the eighteenth century. As in Japan, the aristocracy was *not* challenged in its privileged position. The quiescence and pietism of the German burgher are proverbial, coming to consummate expression in Goethe's epic poem *Hermann und Dorothea*, in which the upheavals of the French Revolution are recorded as from afar, while by contrast the modest well-being and contentment of the average citizen is praised in a quietly glowing panegyric.[7] It is true, however, that liberal tendencies were present. But police control was sufficient to force such tendencies "underground" in the sense that the Freemasons with their secret assemblies became the forum for mildly liberal, frequently mystical expressions of opinion.[8] But if liberal views were

---

[6] Smith, "Japan's Aristocratic Revolution," p. 372.

[7] For a documentation of these quietistic tendencies in the middle-class society of the eighteenth century, see W. H. Bruford, *Germany in the Eighteenth Century* (Cambridge: Cambridge University Press, 1939), pp. 206-34. See also Koppel Pinson, *Pietism as a Factor in the Rise of German Nationalism* (New York: Columbia University Press, 1934).

[8] Two studies enable us to follow both trends in detail. For an analysis of the first very mild expressions of opinion and the relation of these expressions to public affairs, see Fritz Valjavec, *Die Entstehung der politischen Strömungen in Deutschland, 1770-1815* (Munich: R. Oldenbourg, 1951). The Freemasons as a forum for the formation of

hardly public enough to account for the aristocratic reaction, it was otherwise with their literary expression. It has often been observed that the German classical drama of Lessing, Schiller, Goethe, and many lesser writers broadcast the message of the French Enlightenment, of liberty and the inviolable claims of the individual personality, in a manner that reached the widest possible audience with the greatest possible effect in a society in which public life, publicity, and the expression of political views were virtually nonexistent.[9] Thus, in Germany, "private hurts [were raised] to a great principle of struggle between right and wrong," because the country's opinion leaders were influenced directly by liberal ideas from abroad, even though there was very little internal stimulus in this direction. Conversely, the absence in Japan of a comparable ideological polarization may be attributed, at least proximately, to the effective seclusion of the country.[10] It is difficult to give a convincing explanation for the

---

"public" or politically relevant opinion are examined in Ernst Man-heim, *Die Entstehung der öffentlichen Meinung* (Brünn: R. M. Rohrer, 1933).

[9] From the standpoint of the present one can only look back with nostalgia to a time when it was sufficient for a writer to place his action in the Middle Ages, in Spain, or in the far-off Near East in order to disguise the contemporary political relevance of his theme. It should be mentioned, however, that most of the classical German literature originated outside Prussia and, although subject to some police controls, was probably more at liberty to reflect current ideas than would have been the case in Prussia. There are, of course, hundreds of studies of this matter, but one of the most comprehensive and judicious is probably Ernst Cassirer, *Freiheit und Form, Studien zur deutschen Geistesgeschichte* (Berlin: Bruno Cassirer, 1916).

[10] I am tempted by the intriguing byways that this contrast suggests. To understand the social-psychological correlates of modernization we require some basis for comparison between past and present. In the absence of interviews or questionnaires, we must rely on the indirect evidence of literature, the theater, diaries, and so forth. In this respect a comparison between Japan and Germany would seem to be especially rewarding. Perhaps the most striking contrast in the literature of the two countries is related also to the restrictionism of

absence of a phenomenon such as the ideological articulation of middle-class resentments, even where a directly contrasting development can be found as in this instance. But these negative considerations do not stand alone.

B. RELATION TO LAND AND ITS IMPLICATIONS

Smith points out that following the Restoration the Japanese samurai were in no position to resist the transformation of their position in society, because some three centuries earlier they had been removed from the land. Until the late sixteenth century warriors had been scattered over the land, where they were overlords of villages, levying taxes, administering justice, and keeping the peace. In the course of the protracted civil wars preceding the Tokugawa shogunate the great lords restricted the power of these vassals over their fiefs, i.e. forbade them to administer justice, eventually took

---

the Tokugawa regime. In Japan sumptuary laws and police controls sought to regulate the entertainment appropriate for each class and to exclude from the theater any politically suspect themes. As a result, Kabuki seems to have been channeled in the direction of situation comedy, taking its themes from the foibles of stock characters derived from the social scene of the time. The fact that police controls proved very difficult to enforce and that political themes kept reappearing despite efforts to suppress them only accentuates the political significance of cultural seclusion. Germany in the eighteenth century also witnessed considerable censorship, but she was the recipient of influences from abroad and her classical literature reflects this in the sense that here themes derived from the suppressed social and political controversies of the time were given a universal meaning. This classic literature then was joined to a romantic idealization of personality; this blend became the dominant "high culture" of Germany during the nineteenth century; and under the influence of a dominant militarism some unsavory synthesis resulted between this humanistic tradition and the power orientation of *Realpolitik*. Unfortunately, I know too little to follow through with a proper comparison of literary traditions in the two countries. A glimpse of the contrast may be had, however, by comparing Donald H. Shively, "Bakufu versus Kabuki," *Harvard Journal of Asiatic Studies*, xviii (1955), 326-56, with Bruford, *Germany*, pp. 291 ff.

the power of taxation into their own hands, and compensated their warriors directly by stipends in money or in kind. Thus by 1560 fiefs had been consolidated into large tracts of land and seignorial rights concentrated in the hands of some two hundred daimyōs, each governing on the average a population of some one hundred thousand people. These large realms were administered from the newly erected castle-towns in which the expropriated samurai came to reside as rentiers and officials of their lords.

The chronology of these and related events is instructive. Hall states that most of the first-ranking castle-towns were founded between 1580 and 1610 after a large number of lesser castles had been destroyed, a process which culminated in the Shogunal edict of 1615 ordering the destruction of all but one castle in each province.[11] This wholesale removal of warriors from the land was the action most likely to provoke their intense resistance, and there is evidence that it was accomplished by superior force.[12] It is significant in this respect that the first decree promulgating the expulsion of Christian missionaries was issued in 1587, right in the midst of the struggles eventuating in the consolidation of daimyō power and culminating in the Battle of Sekigahara of 1600, which established the national supremacy of the Tokugawa family. The ferocity with which the Christian missions were suppressed in the 1620's and the policy of seclusion which followed was prompted not just by general fears of what might befall the country if contact with the West was permitted to continue, but probably by the specific fear that this

[11] See John W. Hall, "The Castle Town and Japan's Modern Urbanization," *Far Eastern Quarterly*, xv (1955), 42–44. He cites the case of Bizen, which had some twenty to thirty castles during the fifteenth century. This number was reduced to four by 1615, at which time the edict led to the destruction of three more, leaving the castle-town of Okayama.

[12] Cf. the brief description of the principal methods used by Hideyoshi in C. R. Boxer, *The Christian Century in Japan, 1549–1650* (Berkeley: University of California Press, 1951), pp. 173–74.

contact, if continued, would provoke the warriors to organize a more concerted resistance against the consolidation of daimyō and Tokugawa power.[13] Seclusion insulated the struggles of the Japanese warrior-aristocracy sufficiently to enable them to fight it out among themselves, and continued insulation was used by the victors to stabilize the resulting power relationships.

The contrast with Prussia enables us to strengthen this interpretation, though in such complex matters one cannot expect confirmation. Here also the struggles among the ruling strata of the country culminated in the supremacy of one ruling family, the Hohenzollern dynasty, but political unification was achieved to the accompaniment of a rapid decline of towns, the political and economic ascendance of the rural nobility, and an eventual victory of the ruler over the Estates on the basis of military mobilization and foreign involvements. Toward the end of the sixteenth century the later state of Prussia consisted of a number of scattered territories in northeastern Germany and elsewhere, only nominally held together by the Hohenzollern rulers whose center of power lay in the province of Brandenburg.[14] In these territories the

[13] This is the interpretation of C. R. Boxer. Cf. *ibid.*, especially pp. 338–39. Professor Boxer emphasizes that among Japanese Christian converts who remained true to their faith unto death during the persecution, *heimin* (peasants, artisans, and merchants) constituted a much higher proportion than samurai. Out of two to five thousand martyrs who died for their faith in 1614–1643, less than seventy were Europeans (pp. 358, 448). Accordingly, it is probable that the persecution was motivated by the fear that conversion to Christianity would undermine obedience to temporal lords among the population at large as well as by the more specific fear of the disgruntled *rōnin* and the possibility of an alliance between these elements and Catholic Spain (pp. 317, 373, and *passim*).

[14] The diversity of these territories is suggested by their divergent legal status. "The Prussian 'kingdom' was confined to the province of East Prussia only. The 'King of Prussia' (since 1701) was at the same time 'Elector' of Brandenburg, 'Duke' of Pomerania, Magdeburg,

towns had been relatively prosperous and the peasants free under the stimulus of the Hanseatic towns on the Baltic Sea and the political stability provided by the Teutonic Order. By the sixteenth century, however, the Hanse was declining and the Order was dissolved in 1525. All resistance to the landed nobility crumbled. The result was a steady encroachment by the nobility on the commercial and political prerogatives of the towns and on the customary rights of the peasants, leading to an almost precipitous decline of the former and the establishment of serfdom for the latter by the middle of the seventeenth century. Still, the sixteenth century was a period of peace and prosperity. Feudal knights turned themselves into merchants and entrepreneurs who, having broken the urban monopoly on trade and industry, proceeded to make the most of the ample opportunities in foreign and domestic trade, which their prominent social and political position made available to them.[15]

At first the Hohenzollern rulers were entirely powerless against this landed but commercialized nobility. Though their territories were scattered, they succeeded during the sixteenth century in adding to them through a series of marriages; the consequent involvement with the power-struggles of Europe proved later on to be an important vantage point in their struggle against the Estates. But at the beginning of the seventeenth century the Hohenzollern were at the lowest point in their fortunes. The Thirty Years

---

Cleves, and Silesia (since 1740), 'Prince' of Halberstadt and Minden, 'Count' of Mark and Ravensberg, etc." See Hans Rosenberg, *Bureaucracy, Autocracy, and Aristocracy* (Cambridge: Harvard University Press, 1958), p. 28. The territory of "East Prussia" was a Polish fief until 1657 when Poland recognized the sovereignty of Prussia.

[15] For documentation cf. F. L. Carsten, *The Origins of Prussia* (Oxford: Clarendon Press, 1954), Chapter XII. Note that the towns continued to pay two thirds of all taxes, even in this period of their decline, while the landed nobility was tax-exempt.

War (1618–1648) engulfed all of their possessions, the Hohenzollern did not take part in the struggle, and while the Elector chose to reside in far away Prussia, his home province of Brandenburg was occupied by Imperial or Swedish troops from 1627 onward. Yet this occupation helped to change the internal balance of power. Since the foreign army leaders made short shrift of all existing privileges, the prolonged occupation weakened the political power and economic strength of the landed aristocracy. This weakness played into the hands of the Hohenzollern, who strengthened their military preparations, especially in connection with the war between Sweden and Poland from 1655 to 1660, in which they took an active part. Frederick William, the Great Elector (1640–1688), "considered it the obvious duty of the Estates not only of Prussia which was directly involved in the war, but equally of Brandenburg and of Cleves, to grant him the money for the conduct of the war. When they failed to do so, he raised it without their consent. At the end of the war he had gained great strength and a standing army, capable of breaking any resistance against the collection of taxes required for its maintenance."[16] Frederick William and his successors compensated the aristocracy for their submission not only by a continuation of their privileges in all fiscal and local administrative affairs, but also by the transformation of an army of mercenaries into one in which especially the poorer nobility made up the overwhelming majority of the officer corps that was loyal to the Hohenzol-

---

[16] *Ibid.*, p. 189. When the Great Elector came to power in 1640, the total revenue of his realm amounted to one million taler; at the time of his death in 1688 the total came to over three million. During the same period the strength of the standing army increased from approximately forty-five hundred men to some thirty thousand, although these numbers fluctuated greatly. The financial burden of this effort fell on a population of one million people, who had to pay nearly twice as much per head as their much more prosperous contemporaries in France. See *ibid.*, pp. 266–71.

lern dynasty and indeed opposed to some extent the more parochial interests of the landed nobility.[17]

Japanese and Prussian social history in the sixteenth and seventeenth centuries thus provides a series of striking contrasts. In Japan, centralization of power occurred in the course of protracted civil wars under conditions of increasing isolation; in Prussia it occurred as a result of (or in relation to) events outside the country which altered the internal balance of power, e.g. decline of the Hanse, dissolution of the Teutonic Order, Hohenzollern marriage alliances, the Thirty Years' War. The Hohenzollern used foreign involvements and the divisions within the aristocracy to subdue the recalcitrant nobility and weaken their opposition to specific policies. From the standpoint of the internal social structure the importance of external events for this build-up of the Prussian state may be considered "fortuitous." Yet in the present context these fortuitous events have significance because their absence or deliberate exclusion from the course of the Japanese development helps to account for the successful removal of warriors from the land and hence for their greater receptivity to change in comparison with the Junkers.

Japan experienced a rapid rise of urbanization, Prussia a rapid decline. In Japan the warrior-aristocracy was separated from the land, which was tantamount to its urban concentration, its anti-rural bias, its relative demilitarization, or, conversely, its increasing bureaucratization, about which more presently. In Prussia the aristocracy strengthened its ties to the land by virtue of the widening of economic opportunities that resulted from the destruction of urban monopolies. This development led to a strong anti-urban bias and a concerted resistance to the demands of the ruler and his officials; even

[17] See Rosenberg, *Bureaucracy*, p. 70. Rosenberg's study contains an excellent comparative analysis of the "Prussian case" in its relation to the general European development (pp. 1–45).

when this resistance was finally overcome in matters of taxation, military affairs, and foreign policy, it continued still in all local affairs where the nobility remained paramount.[18]

This difference between an urbanized and a rural aristocracy is related in various ways to the different significance of military affairs for the political unification of the two countries. German unity was achieved through military victory over France. Prussia, the leading German state prior to unification, was itself largely the product of military preparedness and army organization. This accounts for the special position of the Hohenzollern kings and for the special virulence of the constitutional conflict of 1862–1866, for the Prussian king was above all the personal leader of the army. The constitution of 1850 specifically noted this position and excluded military affairs from the purview of legislative oversight, so that the Reichstag's refusal to endorse the proposed increase in military preparedness struck at the root of the king's prerogative. The subsequent military victory appeared to give a retrospective endorsement to the king and Bismarck's position and brought about—for the time at least—a genuine acceptance of "dynastic militarism" in the ranks of the liberal opposition. I note this development of ascendant militarism in the German case in order to emphasize the contrast with Japan.

[18] At the same time, one can speak of a "remilitarization" in so far as these Prussian aristocrats who now became army officers were descendants of feudal knights who had cultivated the military arts as a way of life at one time, but had become peaceful landowners and landed merchants during the peace and prosperity of the sixteenth century. However, one should remember that this was East European frontier territory, which had been settled not only by knights, but by "professional promoters of frontier settlements, and numerous noble *condottieri* immigrants." In addition, some of these noble families were descendants of "horse and cattle thieves, dealers in stolen goods, smugglers, usurers, forgers of legal documents, oppressors of the poor and helpless, and appropriators of gifts made over to the Church." See Rosenberg, *Bureaucracy*, p. 30.

Seen in the large, one may characterize the Tokugawa sho-gunate as a period of descendant or quiescent militarism. Hideyoshi's sword hunt of 1588, the consolidation of local daimyō rule through the establishment of castle-towns (from 1580 to 1610), the consequent removal of samurai from the land, and the formalization of the *sankin-kōtai* system for *tozama* daimyō in 1635 (and for *fudai* daimyō in 1642) were major steps in the thorough subjugation and control of the Japanese warrior-aristocracy, and this control remained intact until the Meiji Restoration. In terms of their education, bearing, and ideas, the samurai certainly remained attached to their tradition of physical prowess and chivalric honor, as Veb-len might say, but this was a militarism without war and above all it was an individualized military stance. Thus Japan entered the modern world in 1868 under the leadership of a demilitarized aristocracy that was turning its attention to the promotion of education and economic enterprise as a neces-sary precondition of the country's eventual political and military renaissance, whereas Germany did so under the leadership of the Prussian king, the Prussian army, and the Prussian bureaucracy whose *raison d'être* was a military posture and whose success in achieving national unity pro-vided a framework of militancy for the resolution of most internal conflicts.

The foregoing comparative analysis has examined two points. In the absence of a "democratic challenge" the Japa-nese aristocracy possessed a greater tolerance for change, even in its own privileged position, than would have been the case otherwise. Second, the Restoration movement under the leadership of the Meiji oligarchs could accomplish a wholesale transformation in the position of the samurai, be-cause the latter had been removed from the land three centu-ries earlier and were in no position to resist. Both the lack of ideological articulation and the failure of the warriors to resist their removal from the land may be related to the policy of seclusion, an interpretation which is strengthened by the contrasting development of Prussia during the same period. But it is one thing to show why the Japanese aristocracy did not resist the development of their country; it is another to show why they took the lead in accomplishing this result and in so doing greatly altered the preconditions of their own privileged status. In his answer to this last question, Professor Smith points to a series of conditions which induced the samurai to take an active interest in development under the aegis of the Meiji government, even at the risk of actual or eventual deprivation. Conflicts of interest between the ranks of the aristocracy, the bureaucratization of *han* government, the development of new aspirations, and changing interpersonal relations between lord and vassal are among these conditions.

C. RULING-CLASS TRADITIONS AND DEVELOPMENT

The Tokugawa settlement had resulted in a genuine class division within the aristocracy. A few thousand families of superior lineage monopolized the important offices of government, while several hundred thousand families of samurai were cut off from all opportunities of appointment, high or low. Though some samurai became officials in their respective daimyō domains, most of them were modest retainers. Many samurai families lived in real poverty, resorted to by-employments they considered degrading, and greatly resented the impropriety of merchant wealth. Yet such differences in rank or condition did not affect samurai ideology. The tradition of loyalty to the lord, the cultivation of a militant stance of daring and prowess were not only retained by the samurai but encouraged by the shogunate and the daimyō. One can suppose that the samurai sensed this discrepancy between their lives and their pretensions. Military men who live as rentiers and have little chance to see action may strut about in language and gesture, but the more sensitive among them must have resented the falsity of this position and many more developed strong hostilities against the higher ranks of the aristocracy, especially at the shogunal court.

Other considerations support this speculation. The consolidation of daimyō power led to the bureaucratization of *han* government and hence to increased career opportunities for some of the samurai who had been removed from the land and could now exercise a larger, albeit delegated authority. By the late eighteenth century writers on government were in strong and general agreement on merit as the criterion which should govern selection for office. It is uncertain at what levels and how widely this new principle was applied. But impressive public works were undertaken in some well-administered daimyō domains, which suggests that merit was recognized occasionally.[19] Where such practices prevailed, upward mobility based on achievement became possible. "Men of lower rank were sometime promoted to high office; merchants and occasionally even peasants with specialized qualifications were ennobled that they might hold office; and promotion in the bureaucracy became for warriors an im-

[19] Both the emphasis on merit and the uncertainty of applying this principle under the Tokugawa shogunate are discussed in Smith's contribution to this volume. It would be instructive to know the social position of these writers and in particular whether they have reference primarily to the Tokugawa or the daimyō bureaucracy. The transformation of samurai from vassals into officials and the increasing use of impersonal administrative considerations is described by John W. Hall, "Foundations of the Modern Japanese Daimyo," *Journal of Asian Studies*, xx (1961), 327–28. The same author discusses the construction of waterworks undertaken during and since the seventeenth century in Richard Beardsley, John W. Hall, and Robert E. Ward, *Village Japan* (Chicago: University of Chicago Press, 1959), Chapter 3, especially pp. 51–55. However, the two studies cite evidence from the same area (Bizen and environs), and conditions varied among the *han*. One such variation is analyzed in Robert K. Sakai, "Feudal Society and Modern Leadership in Satsuma-han," *Journal of Asian Studies*, xvi (1957), 365–76. Note especially the decentralized administration of Satsuma and the quite high proportion of samurai in the population (26 percent in 1874 against 5.6 percent of the total population).

portant means of improving status."[20] But however sporadic such instances may have been, the impoverished samurai families provided a ready audience for writers who made "merit" their watchword. Since the highest offices usually went to well-placed families, it was easy to exacerbate the invidious contrast between the incompetence of high officials and the lowly samurai whose sterling virtues went unrewarded. Accordingly an ideology of merit was fashioned which satisfied the pride and aspirations of the samurai while it also increased their provincialism and the tensions existing between the daimyō domains and the shogunate in Edo.

Smith argues that the ideal of the warrior was gradually superseded by ideals of personal conduct more appropriate for a bureaucrat. Relations between lord and vassal became more impersonal, after the samurai were removed from the land and the country had become pacified, as the administration of the consolidated daimyō domains became more bureaucratic and a new ideology of aspiration developed among the lower samurai. For two centuries prior to the Restoration, the samurai had been schooled in envy and emulation by the example of *han* officials of samurai rank, whose successful careers presumably goaded on the pretensions and self-confidence of men who had to live on a modest rent or in penury.[21] Accordingly, the very rapid ex-

---

[20] Smith, "Japan's Aristocratic Revolution," p. 375.

[21] In this context, Smith refers in a review article to "able and rising men destined to form a new ruling class who felt unjustly cut off from positions of power and respect." See his "The Discontented," *Journal of Asian Studies*, xxi (1962), 218. While this characterization applied to men from all social ranks, it applied with special force to the lower samurai, as Jansen's case study of *Sakomoto Ryōma and the Meiji Restoration* (Princeton: Princeton University Press, 1961) makes clear. The curious combination of radicalism and conservatism among these petty and frustrated aristocrats may be explained by the fact that some of their number were successful; there was hope in principle, a condition highly conducive to revolution as de Tocqueville already suggested; but no one in high office questioned that men of

pansion of opportunities after 1868 was tailor-made for men who suffered from the acute discrepancy between their high social rank and their lowly economic position, who were free of bias against change since they had long since been severed from the land, whose educational preferment under the Tokugawa regime provided them with an immediate advantage over all competitors, and whose traditional cult of action, habits of frugality, aristocratic aversion to money-making, and new ideology of aspiration had prepared them psychologically for a bureaucratic career.[22] In a society which heavily underscored status distinctions, the samurai could now rise to the highest positions. This hope, combined as it was with the collectivist ideal of national advance, outweighed the real deprivations to which they were at first exposed, and this occurred the more easily because the Restoration leaders left no doubt that the new government's obligations toward the ex-samurai were taken seriously.[23]

---

samurai rank had first claim, certainly a reassuring note even in a dismal economic situation.

[22] Smith, "Japan's Aristocratic Revolution," pp. 378–79. R. P. Dore has stated in an unpublished paper that the samurai class made up 6 percent of all families, and that two samples of samurai participation in the Meiji elite yield the proportions of 45 and 53 percent respectively. That the response of the samurai was instantaneous and disproportionately high is suggested by the fact that in the years 1863–1871 Fukuzawa's Western-oriented Keio school was attended by 40 commoners and 1,289 samurai. See Johannes Hirschmeier, S.V.D., *Entrepreneurship in Meiji Japan* (Ph.D. Dissertation, Harvard University), p. 69.

[23] In 1867 payments in rice to the samurai amounted to 34.6 million yen, while in 1876 the value of yearly interest paid on a commutation basis had fallen to 11.5 million. But this decline should be compared with the fact that in 1871 the government spent 15.3 million yen or some 36 percent of its total budget on stipends for *han* samurai who had become prefectural samurai. Cf. Hirschmeier, *op.cit.*, p. 62. Note also Itō Hirobumi's telling comments that "most of the men of spirit and argument have come from among the former samurai," that these men have been deprived of their former high position in society and

Once again, comparisons and contrasts with Prussia and Germany may be made. The consolidation of Tokugawa and Hohenzollern power was similar in one respect: the daimyō and the Junkers were left with considerable local powers in contrast to several European countries like France and Bohemia, where dynastic absolutism greatly disorganized or actually destroyed the old aristocracy. Yet daimyō and Junkers or the samurai and the lower landed nobility of Prussia were not aristocrats of the same type, either in their relation to local government, in their military role, or in their manners and general culture.

In Prussia, the Hohenzollern rulers subjected a once-free peasantry to serfdom and thus vastly increased the local power of the landed aristocracy (even of its lesser ranks) in return for political submission. The Junkers remained on the land and lorded it over a servile peasantry as landowners, administrators, judges, prosecutors, and police officers, thus combining personal dominance with governmental authority. In Japan the samurai were removed from the land in the sixteenth century, while the social structure of the village community remained intact. The daimyō along with their samurai retainers became town residents and as such did not intervene in village affairs as long as they received their stipends and contributions from the villagers. This setting greatly encouraged local autonomy, albeit one combined with a strongly collectivist orientation. Under the Tokugawa shogunate governmental controls were highly centralized and responsibilities were imposed on the community as a whole. As a result the exercise of local authority by government officials tended to be relatively impersonal in contrast to the Junker estates in Prussia with their highly personal exercise of authority. It is probable, therefore, that these two countries possess strikingly different traditions of interpersonal

are, consequently, the source of unrest. Quoted in George Beckmann, *The Making of the Meiji Constitution* (Lawrence: University of Kansas Press, 1957), p. 131.

relations, despite their common and long-standing emphasis on status distinctions and hierarchy. For *in the sphere of local government* high social rank and governmental authority went hand in hand in Prussia, whereas in Japan high rank did not confer authority under the Tokugawa regime.

In the military sphere the two groups also contrasted sharply. The Tokugawa shoguns pacified the country as a whole and ensured the loyalty of their aristocratic vassals by elaborate police controls. The daimyō and samurai, nevertheless, retained the exclusive right to carry a sword; hence this right was an index of high social rank. Meiji military reforms abolished this right and established a system of national conscription with the result that a significant measure of equality was introduced in Japanese society through the army. In Prussia, on the other hand, all independent military action on the part of the Junkers was suppressed and the absolute ascendance of the central government was assured by making the army directly subordinate to the monarch. At the same time the Junkers were given the privilege of exclusive access to the officer corps so that high military rank and high social rank were closely related. In the army the very harsh relations between officers and men tended to replicate and reenforce the harsh civilian relations between landlords and peasants, since the composition of the two groups largely overlapped. Accordingly, interpersonal relations between military ranks were a major buttress of inequality and invidious status distinctions in Germany until well into the twentieth century.

There are parallel distinctions between the two aristocracies in the field of culture and manners. The Tokugawa shoguns required that all daimyō maintain a residence in Edo in which the daimyō or his relations vouchsafed for the loyalty of those absent by their presence at court (*sankin-kōtai* system). The system imposed very heavy expenditures, since it greatly increased the conspicuous consumption of the daimyō and his relations who sought to hold their own in the competition for preferment at the shogunal court.[24] It would be of interest to compare the resulting refinement in etiquette with the development of polite manners at the French court in Versailles, since both may be considered a by-product of absolutism following the decline of feudalism.[25] The Junkers, by contrast, were not subjected to comparable controls. They were complete masters in their own domains. As such they combined the arbitrary benevolence or puni-tiveness of the personal master with the authoritarianism of the government official and military commander. They be-came "experts in local tyranny" (Rosenberg) for several reasons. As colonizing territory East Germany attracted its complement of adventurers and outlaws. The serfdom of the peasantry brutalized masters and servants alike. And the masters, who stayed on the land and entertained themselves with the crude pleasures of provincial squires, lacked the polished manners and cultural refinements which in the seventeenth and eighteenth centuries were typical by-products of court life.[26] In the Prussian "garrison state" there was little room for the cultivation of manners, which helps to account for the "militarization of civilian life" that exacer-bated the class and status distinctions of German society until the twentieth century.

As a consequence of these and related differences the two aristocracies played quite different roles in the industriali-

[24] Incidentally, this put a premium on a more efficient organization of the *han*, which in many instances passed into the hands of samurai officials. May this not be an instance in which "wasteful expenditures" proved to be on occasion at least a positive incentive for a more efficient administration of the *han* domains, Veblen to the contrary notwithstanding?

[25] Such an interpretation of the evidence from France is contained in Norbert Elias, *Über den Prozess der Zivilisation* (Basel: Haus zum Falken, 1939), 2 vols.

[26] Until well into the eighteenth century many of these Junkers definitely preferred a military as against a bureaucratic career, be-cause they lacked the educational background for the latter. See Rosenberg, *Bureaucracy*, p. 59.

zation of their countries. In Japan the lower nobility of samurai and ex-samurai took the initiative and at the beginning furnished the majority of the key figures. In Prussia, members of the aristocracy remained landowners or became military officers; a certain number became government officials and rather few became businessmen.[27] Among the samurai there was a strong antirural bias, much indignant envy of wealthy merchants, and a prejudice against materialism and moneymaking, but this last disappeared quickly as soon as "economic development" became a national cause. Among the Junkers an antiurban bias prevailed,[28] which was combined with a strong prejudice, not against moneymaking (in many ways the Junkers were rural capitalists), but against merchants and commercialism, an attitude that was buttressed both by the real conflicts of interest between the agrarian East and the industrial West of Germany and by the anticommercial attitudes typical of military officers. In Germany, therefore, it was not the landed aristocracy but government officials of an absolutist government and much later middle-class entrepreneurs who took the initiative in the economic development of the country.

These government officials had been at one time a major weapon in the hands of the Hohenzollern in subduing the Estates and in building Prussia into a major European power. By the device of appointing commoners rather than native aristocrats and of ennobling these officials if they performed well, or by enlisting the services of aristocrats from other parts of Germany and by subjecting these personal servants of the monarch to a detailed system of legal rules, prescribed procedures, and disciplinary codes, the Prussian

---

[27] This statement is confined to the Prussian aristocracy, and it is admittedly impressionistic, since no survey of the entire group is available. Among the non-Prussian German aristocracy, the proportion of government officials and businessmen would be significantly higher.

[28] Is there anything in Japanese literature like the *romantic* idealization of the German peasant?

rulers created one of the earliest models of a modern bureaucracy.[29] In this way government officials were inculcated with loyalty to the monarch, habits of frugality, the ideal of hard work, and a patriotic ideology of aspiration for their country which became serviceable eventually to the economic development of Germany. Thus in Japan and in Germany development originated with that sector of society which first moved away from considerations of inherited privilege to principles of action based on more impersonal criteria.[30]

D. SUMMARY

In commenting on the changes brought about in Japanese society as a result of an "aristocratic revolution" which on his own showing was neither quite aristocratic nor quite revolutionary in the conventional meaning of these words, Professor Smith points to two distinct features. Acknowledging that there was tension in Japan between tradition and

---

[29] See Rosenberg, *op.cit.*, p. 48 and *passim*. A full-scale study of Tokugawa bureaucracy does not seem to be available in English. But a comparison between Rosenberg's *Bureaucracy, Aristocracy, and Autocracy* with John W. Hall's *Tanuma Okitsugu (1719–1788)* (Monograph Series XIV, Harvard-Yenching Institute; Cambridge: Harvard University Press, 1955) suggests that nothing quite like the Prussian bureaucracy developed in Japan until 1868.

[30] Hence a comparison of Germany and Japan provides a long overdue corrective to the large, critical literature focusing on Max Weber's *The Protestant Ethic and the Spirit of Capitalism*. In its single-minded preoccupation with that essay this literature has largely overlooked the problem with which Weber was concerned. If it be true that an important measure of economic rationalism first developed in western Europe (and no writer criticizing Weber's thesis of the *Protestant Ethic* has denied this, nor have many come up with alternative explanations of this phenomenon!), then Germany and Japan provide examples of economic rationalism arising from other sources. Perhaps Lutheranism affected the orientation of Prussian bureaucrats as much as, according to Bellah, Tokugawa Religion affected the samurai, but in both cases religion probably played a secondary role.

modernity, Smith asserts that nevertheless in the absence of an aristocratic defense of the old regime there was "no radical cleavage of the two by ideology. All parties were more or less reformist, more or less traditional, and more or less modern; excepting perhaps the Communists whose numbers were insignificant, no pre-war party thought of the past as such as a barrier to progress. It was a barrier in some respects, in others a positive aid. Modernization appeared to most Japanese who thought about it at all, not as a process in which a life-or-death confrontation of traditional or modern took place, but as a dynamic blending of the two. I wonder if this does not account in large part for what has seemed to many people the uncommon strength of tradition in the midst of change in modern Japan." Following this he continues with the observation that "status-consciousness is relatively strong in Japan in part because there was no revolutionary struggle against inequality, but for that reason class-consciousness is relatively weak. These attitudes are by no means contradictory. The nervous concern of Japanese for status is quite consonant with their relatively weak feeling about classes—higher-ups to some extent being looked on as superior extensions of the self."[31]

Comparison with Germany suggests the pertinence of these observations. There, the ideological cleavage between tradition and modernity was a by-product of the French Revolution, which in Prussia brought the ideals of equality and freedom into direct confrontation with a society in which "stiffly martial concepts of authority and of military virtues were established as the models for peacetime civil government and for civil life in general."[32] The idea that masters and servants view each other as inferior or superior extensions of themselves is a typical feature of societies which take the existence of inequality for granted.[33] In Germany this

[31] Smith, "Japan's Aristocratic Revolution," p. 382.
[32] Rosenberg, op.cit., p. 41.
[33] See the chapter on "Masters and Servants" in Alexis de Tocque-

acceptance of inequality was destroyed, and hence inferiors and superiors who had always been status conscious also became class conscious. Accordingly, interpersonal relations tend to be hierarchic, master-and-servant relations in Germany, whereas in Japan hierarchy is softened by kinship simulations, and status equals have an elaborate ritual of collaboration which—as far as I am aware—is altogether missing in Germany.

Development as a Political Problem

The discussion so far has questioned the mutual exclusiveness of tradition and modernity. It has compared the traditional ruling classes of Germany and Japan in order to illustrate two symbiotic patterns, one which facilitated and one which hindered development. Taken by itself, this comparison would be misleading, since German industrialization preceded that of Japan and was rapid despite Junker obstruction, whereas Japanese industrialization did not become significant under the Tokugawa despite the propensities of the samurai that were repressed until the Restoration provided them with opportunities for constructive action. Indeed, this difference is only one of many dissimilarities between the two countries.

Japan is an island empire that was successfully conquered only once (at the end of World War II) in her entire recorded history. Thus the tremendous internal divisions which mark Japanese medieval history had no adverse effect upon the cultural coherence of the country. Because of her insular position, Japan's political divisions and instability never exposed her to the cumulative effect of wars and alliances from the outside. On the other hand, Germany has experienced changes in her territorial composition throughout her history. Her exposure to outside forces at all times greatly intensified her cultural and political heterogeneity. This

ville, *Democracy in America* (New York: Vintage Books, 1954), ii, 187–95.

difference is associated with the dynastic and religious traditions of the two countries. In one case there is an unbroken tradition of the emperor as the single source of legitimacy (despite the political impotence of the emperor for long periods of Japanese history). In the other there is a succession of reigning houses during the medieval period and a history of conflicts over the principle of legitimacy as well as over questions of succession. Again, Japanese religious history is marked by a high degree of doctrinal syncretism, making for a considerable degree of toleration, whereas Germany reflects the doctrinal orthodoxies of Christianity generally and reveals to this day the legacies of past conflicts based on religious belief.[34]

Moreover, the basis from which the two countries began their most rapid industrialization in the 1870's was not the same despite the important similarities noted earlier. By the time of the Meiji Restoration, Japan had had 250 years of seclusion, which had been accompanied on the positive side by administrative consolidation, significant developments in agriculture, a population increasingly disciplined both by police supervision and education, and a pent-up preparedness for change on the part of the lower nobility, which was analyzed earlier. On the negative side we must put the high cost of isolation: the exclusion of ideas from abroad, the consequent lack of technical advance, the cultural provincialism which perhaps jeopardized even the native arts with stagnation, and above all the hidden danger (which became visible only

---

[34] These religious and dynastic differences between Japan and western Europe have important ramifications for the comparison of feudalism and the preconditions of representative institutions in the two settings. On feudalism, cf. F. Joüon des Longrais, *L'est et l'ouest* (Tokyo: Maison Franco-Japonais, 1958) and now John W. Hall's excellent essay, "Feudalism in Japan: A Reassessment," *Comparative Studies in Society and History*, v (1962), pp. 15–51. A comparative study of preconditions of representative institutions is contained in Otto Hintze, "Weltgeschichtliche Bedingungen der Repräsentativverfassung," *op.cit.*, pp. 140–85.

in retrospect) that the precipitous industrialization which followed the opening of the country would subject its social structure to strains of a magnitude that was difficult to manage politically.

On the other hand by the time Germany became unified in 1870 she had undergone a very different experience. Instead of isolation she had been exposed to the impact of the French Revolution and its Napoleonic aftermath, thus setting the stage for her political bifurcation between revolution and reaction. During the eighteenth and nineteenth centuries, every idea propounded in England or France found an echo as well as a creative response in Germany. Her cultural cosmopolitanism was not matched for many decades in the technical and industrial fields, but from the late eighteenth century onward there was a steady advance here also, often based on borrowings from England.[35] Her economy was stimulated also (and at an increasing rate) by indigenous developments, at first by bureaucratic initiative and scientific developments at academic institutions and supplemented eventually (roughly from the 1830's on) by entrepreneurial efforts as well. Germany's liabilities were largely in the political field. Instead of administrative consolidation of more or less equal component territories under the central government as in Japan, Germany was fragmented into very un-

[35] As a result of these early developments, Germany was at a markedly different economic level in the 1870's when developments in both countries began their most rapid spurt forward. The Japanese population of 33 million in 1872 compares with the German population of 42.5 million in 1875, but in 1871, 36 percent of the German population was classified as urban whereas as late as 1890 only 10 percent of the Japanese population was so classified. Germany's railroads measured 37,650 kilometers in 1885, whereas Japanese railroads measured 1,024 kilometers in 1887. Japan's distribution of her labor force in 1920 corresponds roughly to the German distribution of the 1880's. Perhaps most striking of all, Prussia had 86 percent of her children (7–14 years of age) attending school as early as 1820, as contrasted with Japan, whose elementary school attendance developed from 28 percent in 1873 to 94 percent in 1903!

equal units and she lacked central authority. Moreover, one of the units (Prussia) was clearly ascendant over all others by virtue of its military strength and efficient administrative organization. Political unity, when it came in consequence of the Franco-Prussian War, came under the aegis of Prussia, the Prussian army, and the Hohenzollern legacy of monarchical and bureaucratic rule. Economic development after 1870 was not nearly as precipitous in Germany as in Japan, but on the other hand Germany's oligarchic rule was not nearly as undisputed as that of the Meiji bureaucrats, who derived considerable strength from the cumulative legacies of Tokugawa rule, even though these did not include much economic advance. In this concluding section I wish, therefore, to discuss development as a political problem.

It is pertinent to do so because both Germany and Japan were latecomers to the industrialization of their economies compared with countries like England, France, and the United States.[36] Today we are concerned with the spread of "modernization" from the West to societies all over the world in contrast to an earlier focus of attention on the Western development. English and French industrialization occurred in the late eighteenth and early nineteenth centuries with considerable emphasis upon private initiative and a curtailment of political controls over the economy, whereas the industrialization of countries that have come later typically involves a relatively high degree of political initiative.[37] Ger-

---

[36] Veblen was perhaps the first to emphasize this distinction. Since the renewal of interest in this problem after World War II, a number of scholars like Alexander Gerschenkron, Bert F. Hoselitz, Marion Levy, Henry Rosovsky, and others have developed the distinction in several directions.

[37] Cf. Talcott Parsons, "Some Reflections on the Institutional Framework of Economic Development," in *Structure and Process in Modern Societies* (Glencoe: Free Press, 1960), pp. 99, 102, and *passim* for an elaboration of these points. The importance of political initiative in industrialization is, of course, a matter of degree. It was never absent even in England at the height of laissez-faire policies, and it varies

many and Japan are, therefore, early examples of this spread of "modernization" not only because they borrowed a ready-made technology from the industrially more advanced countries, but also because both countries witnessed the importance of political initiative in attempts to promote economic change and to cope with the intensified divisions of the population.[38] In Japan as well as in Germany government and political ideas were considered major factors in the development of these countries. This emphasis together with the political considerations animating it are another basis on which the two countries may be compared and contrasted.

To do this, it will be useful to cite a forceful statement, of 1880, by Itō Hirobumi, one of the architects of the Meiji Restoration. After referring to the major transformations brought about in Japanese society by the destruction of the *han*, the system of conscription, and the decline of the samurai, Itō continues as follows:

It is easy to control the popular sentiments of a single village, but it is difficult to control the public opinion of an entire nation. Moreover, it is easy to change the conditions of a country, but it is difficult to alter world-wide trends. Today, conditions in Japan are closely related to the world situation. They are not merely the affairs of a nation or

---

greatly among countries like Germany, Japan, and Russia which are notable for their emphasis upon political measures.

[38] I note in passing that in the absence of abundant resources and a widespread "achievement motivation," many countries borrow selected aspects of modernity, and some of these such as education or medicine are more easily borrowed than modern technology. Under these conditions politics and administration can become a panacea for all the ills besetting an economically backward country. For an interesting discussion of this perspective in the context of the contemporary African experience, cf. the analysis by David Apter, "Political Religion in the New Nations," in Clifford Geertz, ed., *Old Societies and New States* (Glencoe: The Free Press, 1963), pp. 57-104. However, we are dealing here with Germany and Japan, both of which possessed the requisite resources and motivation.

province. The European concepts of revolution, which were carried out for the first time in France about one hundred years ago, have gradually spread to the various nations. By combining and complementing each other, they have become a general trend. Sooner or later, every nation will undergo changes as a result.

In this period of changes from old to new, revolution often broke out. In fact, revolution continues at present. It has not yet stopped. Elsewhere enlightened rulers, with the help of wise ministers, led and controlled these changes, thus solidifying their nations. In brief, all have had to discard absolutist ways and share political power with the people.

Now, European ideas and things are coming into our country like a tidal flow; moreover, new opinions concerning the form of government have become popular among the ex-samurai. Within a few years' time, these ideas have spread into the towns and countryside, and this trend cannot be halted immediately. Thus, there are persons who surprise the public by voicing misleading views. Their thoughtless, disorderly acts pay no attention to the considerations of the Emperor. They groan although they are not sick, and their violent acts have evil effects upon others. However, if we take a general view of causes, it appears that this experience is common to the whole world. Like the rain falling and the grass growing, it is no wonder that we, too, have been affected. . . .

At present it is the responsibility of the government to follow a conciliatory policy and accommodate itself to these tendencies so that we may control but not intensify the situation, and relax our hold over government but not yield it.[39]

There is a whole literature dealing with the comparable orientation of ruling strata in Imperial Germany. Among the

[39] Quoted in George M. Beckmann, *The Making of the Meiji Constitution*, pp. 131–32.

many sources that could be cited, I would call attention to an analysis by the German historian Otto Hintze, who pointed out in 1911 that, owing to the rifts characterizing German society, English parliamentary methods were inapplicable. Then, turning to the factors which made a monarchical constitution mandatory for Germany, Hintze states that first Prussia and then Germany were specifically military states by virtue of their location in Central Europe.

In his relations to the army the monarch is not bound by any constitutional considerations [*Rücksichten*]. The constitution is in fact only related to the people in its capacity as a bourgeois society. But the military structure is after all the backbone of the organization of the state, so that the representation of bourgeois society, i.e. the Landtag, can never acquire a dominant influence in the state. Moreover, this representative body thoroughly lacks the necessary inner unity which would be the indispensable precondition of a dominant political role [*politische Machtrolle*]. Unity and cooperation are prevented by the great social and economic cleavage which has always divided East from West in Prussia, a division which has its origin in the diversity of the agricultural economy in the two regions and the different distribution of agrarian and industrial interests between them. Likewise, unity is prevented by the conflict of religious faiths, whose virulence and repercussions in Prussia and the German Reich are greater than in any other state in the world. There is further the radical opposition to the state [*radikale Staatsfeindlichkeit*] on the part of the Social Democratic Party.

In England, the development of a parliamentary regime was conditioned by the unity of the polity [*Einheit und Geschlossenheit der politischen Gesellschaft*], which was reflected in the party system of the Old Whigs and Tories. Both of these were aristocratic parties of the same political, social, and religious basis, and the distinctions between them involved relatively subordinate nuances. A system of party government can be constructed only on such a homogeneous basis. . . . [However] among us parties are not so much political as economic and social or religious group formations. This is related to the fact that our representative bodies only reflect the life of bourgeois society in contrast to the specifically political structure. From the standpoint of monarchical government Bismarck wishes to have the parties appear as clearly articulated, socioeconomic interest groups, with which one can bargain and do politics on the *do ut des* principle.[40]

These statements present some interesting similarities and differences. Foremost in both is the conviction that the monarchical or Imperial government is the guarantor of order, and to this end the inviolable authority of the emperor (or Kaiser) must be assured. In both cases the government is conceived as the indispensable "balance wheel" among the antagonistic forces which threaten the stability of the country.[41]

[40] Otto Hintze, "Das monarchische Prinzip und die Konstitutionelle Verfassung," in *Staat und Verfassung*, pp. 377–78.

[41] No doubt these two considerations prompted the statesmen of the Meiji Restoration to look to Imperial Germany as the constitutional model most appropriate to their own needs. George M. Beckmann has described the visit of the leading Meiji oligarchs to Europe and especially their attendance at lectures delivered by Rudolf Gneist and Lorenz von Stein. While the general affinity between the German and the Japanese outlook is clear enough, the actual differences between the two countries were considerable. I have the impression, which I cannot document, that men like Gneist, Stein, and others made a system out of the uneasy truce between Wilhelm II and the Reichstag, or that they extrapolated the claims of the Kaiser in the light of what they thought their Japanese visitors wanted to hear. In the process they may have greatly enlarged the prerogatives of the Kaiser, large as these were, while underemphasizing their limitations and the considerable development of quasi-parliamentary methods, political parties, freedom of the press, etc. Or, perhaps, this extrapolation was the work of the Japanese, since in Germany at the time knowledge of Japan was rudimentary. Cf. Beckmann, *The Making*

Yet beyond these well-known similarities, many contrasts stand out.

First, there is the difference between Japan coming into contact with Western ideas after 250 years of seclusion, and Germany being a seedbed as well as a recipient of these ideas throughout her history. Hence it is quite appropriate for Itō to refer to the intrusion of ideas which have disturbed Japan's domestic tranquility, while Hintze speaks of the religious and political divisions of the German population as an established fact. Itō's implication is that the upheavals and divisions resulting from the Western intrusion are controllable in principle, Hintze's that the divisions are so pervasive as to make national unity precarious. Both, of course, consider the emperor or Kaiser as the mainstay of the nation.

Second, Itō's principal concern is the internal unity and development of the country. Japan's military weakness at the time of the Restoration was so manifest that any attempt at an immediate and rapid military buildup was foreclosed as unrealistic. Certainly a gradual buildup was undertaken, but in the years immediately following the Restoration, Japan benefited from the fact that her situation made the promotion of industry the precondition of a later military preparedness.[42] The German situation was quite the reverse. Some of the earliest governmental efforts to promote industrial production (in the eighteenth century) were directly related to military considerations.[43] Moreover, the predomi-

---

of the Meiji Constitution, Chapter VI. No other monographic study of this "borrowing" process has come to my attention.

[42] Cf. Thomas Smith, Political Change and Industrial Development in Japan: Government Enterprise 1868–1880 (Stanford: Stanford University Press, 1955), p. 35.

[43] The contrast is perhaps lopsided, since in the interval between the reign of Frederick the Great and the years following the Meiji Restoration military technology underwent a complete transformation. In the eighteenth century production of simple arms and the promotion of industrial enterprises could go hand in hand, while in the later

nance of the army and of the monarch as its personal leader was dictated by the fact that only through these means were many scattered territories first united into the state of Prussia. It was on the same foundation that Prussia eventually became the predominant political and military power within Germany and the fountainhead of her political unity. Accordingly, "militarism" was a building block of the German social structure which cannot be explained as a response to the strains arising from the precipitous confrontation between tradition and modernity, whereas in Japan that explanation appears to be more nearly correct.[44]

---

nineteenth century it was necessary to create an industrial base before the production of military equipment could be undertaken. Cf. Henry Rosovsky, *Capital Formation in Japan 1868–1940* (Glencoe: Free Press, 1961), p. 27, for related comments. These considerations do not, however, nullify the major contrast made in the text.

[44] Otto Hintze's major work, *Die Hohenzollern und Ihr Werk* (Berlin: Paul Parey, 1915), especially pp. 202–21, 280–306, and *passim*, is the classic analysis of the early development of Prussian militarism. Note also Hintze's comparative treatment of this problem in his essay "Staatsverfassung und Heeresverfassung," *Staat und Verfassung*, pp. 53–83. In the latter essay, Hintze shows that the militarism of the German Reich was a continuation on a larger scale of the militarism that was the foundation of the Prussian state. It is impossible to ignore this background of militarism when an attempt is made to interpret the rise of National Socialism. However much this movement may have been a "fundamentalist reaction" against "the rationalization in the Western world," the fact remains that this reaction took a paramilitary form and thus followed as well as bastardized models derived from the Prussian military tradition. The great social and political strain between the Reichswehr and the Nazi Party and its paramilitary formations reveal, among other things, the great social distinction between the failures and outlaws who rose to leadership in the party and the aristocratic officers who commanded the army. Hence the "fundamentalist reaction" was also a protest against the German aristocracy, hardly a part of the "rationalization in the Western world" which both Veblen and Parsons emphasize. In this respect it is indeed striking, as Masao Maruyama has observed, that the Nazi elite consisted of "rejects" from bourgeois society, while the

Third, there is the matter-of-fact manner in which Itō refers to the vast changes which the Restoration government has brought about: the abolition of the *han* system, the establishment of universal conscription that was tantamount to the final "demilitarization" of the samurai, and the fact that several hundred thousand samurai were deprived of their property and their stipends. Manifestly, the Meiji government possessed a great reservoir of power and unity to have accomplished such results, a fact which stands out in bold relief against the confusion and disunity and powerlessness of the immediately preceding period.[45] In a comparison with the contemporaneous German experience this unity of the Restoration government is impressive. The Meiji oligarchs constituted a relatively cohesive group of political leaders, largely from the Satsuma and Chōshū *han*, who had acquired considerable political experience in achieving a compromise prior to the Restoration.[46]

---

top leaders of the Japanese military establishment certainly belonged to the highest strata of Japanese society. See Masao Maruyama, "Japan's Wartime Leaders," *Orient/West*, VII (1962), 37–45.

[45] Cf. the characterization of successive constellations of leadership and compromise from the 1830's on in Yoshio Sakata and John W. Hall, "The Motivation of Political Leadership in the Meiji Restoration," *Journal of Asian Studies*, XVI (1956), 31–50. The authors conclude with the observation that the leaders of the Restoration movement had no aim other than the elimination of Tokugawa despotism, and in particular that social and economic reorganization was not part of their objective.

[46] More than opposition to the Tokugawa united these men, as Beasley has shown in his analysis of the latent unity underneath the conflict between the *joi* and the *kaikoku* advocates. See W. G. Beasley's introduction to *Select Documents in Japanese Foreign Policy, 1853–1868* (London: Oxford University Press, 1955), pp. 8–10 and *passim*. This unity could emerge once the bakufu had turned to the imperial court for an endorsement of the treaty with Townsend Harris. The steps by which this opening wedge was eventually used to effect a compromise between the Satsuma and Chōshū leaders which took the form of "returning" the *han* lands to the emperor are traced from a

There is nothing really to equal this record in the German case. Hintze maintains, correctly enough, that the ascendance of Prussian military might was the foundation of the German Reich and hence of her monarchical constitution. Here, political unity was achieved by the ascendance of one territory and its leading strata over all other territories and strata. One could say that this ascendance of Prussia was not unlike the rise of the Tokugawa shogunate, but this comparison is vitiated by the fact that the ascendance of Prussia was *not* accompanied by any significant transformation of her ruling groups. These ruling groups simply expanded the range of their social and political predominance, culminating in the unification of the German reich in 1871 as a result of the successful war against France. In the process the social and economic divisions of the population were intensified, which only accentuated the militarism of the Prussian ruling strata and the drive for unification. These facts are reflected in a striking speech by Max Weber, given in 1893: "Tremendous illusions were necessary to create the German empire, but now that the honeymoon of unification is over these illusions are gone and we cannot recreate them artificially. . . . No doubt, the nation would rally to the colors to defend the frontiers of the country. But when we undertake the peaceful defense of German nationality on the eastern border, we encounter several mutually conflicting interest groups."[47] Accordingly, the German slogan of the *Primat*

---

worm's-eye perspective in Jansen, *Sakamoto Ryōma and the Meiji Restoration.* These superb studies appear to give evidence both for the difficulty of interpersonal contacts leading to eventual compromise and for the tenacity with which a compromise once achieved is maintained. The balanced discussion of the positive aspects of this cultural characteristic, such as that contained in E. O. Reischauer, *The United States and Japan* (Cambridge: Harvard University Press, 1950), pp. 133–40, may have to be put alongside an analysis of the same traits in their negative potentialities as revealed by Masao Maruyama, "Japan's Wartime Leaders," pp. 37–53.

[47] Quoted in Reinhard Bendix, *Max Weber, An Intellectual Portrait*

der Aussenpolitik (primacy of foreign policy) over all internal political issues reflected the military and political vulnerability of Germany. The country's internal divisions reenforced the need for diplomatic and military successes as a means to unity—certainly a major theme in the political role of Bismarck. It is not surprising that in this use of foreign policy issues for the purpose of maintaining an internal balance less could be done about the internal transformation of the country than in Japan—quite aside from the question whether or not there was any intention of pointing in this direction. Moreover, comparison with Japan during this critical period makes one thing quite clear: the unity of leadership in Japan was collective while in Germany it depended on one man, Bismarck.

Both government and political ideas played a major role in the development of Germany and Japan, and more particularly in the attempts to cope with the divisions of the population. It is not clear, however, that these divisions were primarily a result of that confrontation between modern technology and "archaic institutions," which Veblen emphasized in his earlier analysis. For even where this confrontation gave rise to "strains" or "malintegration," it is highly probable that these only compounded tensions which existed prior to the introduction of modern technology and other aspects of Western rationalism. When Hintze cites the religious divi-

---

(Garden City: Anchor Books, 1962), pp. 30–31. Hintze appears to confirm this view when he stresses the endemic disunity of Germany, and this confirmation has additional weight in view of his profound political disagreement with Weber. To my knowledge, the works of the two men have not been analyzed in relation to each other. Since I have quoted from Hintze's essay "Das monarchische Prinzip . . . ," it is worth adding a reference to Max Weber's "Parlament und Regierung im neugeordneten Deutschland," in *Gesammelte Politische Schriften* (Tuebingen: J. C. B. Mohr, 1958), pp. 294–431, which is the liberal counterargument to Hintze's conservative position.

sions of the German population as one major reason for the need of a strong monarchical constitution, it is apparent that these divisions greatly antedate the impact of modern technology, even if it be true that they were also compounded by that impact. This consideration certainly supports Schumpeter's view that once they are formed social structures and attitudes persist, sometimes for centuries, and many tensions we observe today may, therefore, be legacies from the past which have little to do with the development process. Nor is it clear, on the other hand, that even the more or less precipitous introduction of a modern technology and its sudden confrontation with established institutions and habits of thought always results in "strain" or "malintegration." When the Meiji oligarchs "engineered" major changes of the Japanese social structure in their effort to meet the Western threat more effectively in the future, they apparently could rely upon certain aspects of Japanese tradition in order to facilitate these efforts. A comparison of German and Japanese development certainly underscores the consideration that traditions can facilitate as well as hamper rapid development. But to what extent "tradition" will do the one or the other depends not only on these legacies themselves but also on the manner in which these enter into the "political management" of a country.

We must remember that the social sciences originated in England where the impetus to change arose in the economic sector and appeared to many unilinear and progressive, so that politics and political ideas were all too readily considered a dependent variable. To this day sociologists (like the Marxists before them) tend to consider political ideas and solutions matters of negligible interest compared with the imperatives of the social structure which circumscribe such ideas and solutions. Yet comparative studies such as the preceding one suggest that "partial development" is the rule rather than the exception and that the further "development" of a country depends in some measure upon the political management of group relations in the context of each country's changing blend of tradition and modernity.[48]

[48] For a "companion piece" of the preceding discussion cf. Reinhard Bendix, "A Case Study in Cultural and Educational Mobility: Japan and the Protestant Ethic," in Neil J. Smelser and S. M. Lipset, eds., *Social Structure and Mobility in Economic Development* (Chicago: Aldine Publishing Company, 1966), pp. 262–279.

PART TWO

Mobility and Migration

CHAPTER II

"Merit" as Ideology in the Tokugawa Period

THOMAS C. SMITH

OFFICIAL APPOINTMENTS in the Tokugawa period were based mainly on social rank, though it was widely held that, as a matter of principle, they ought to be based on ability alone. This conflict between theory and practice lay near the center of both political thought and practical politics. To a considerable extent the issue was between upper and lower samurai, between those with more and those with less rank. As time passed it became more intense, creating frustration and despair, and finally raising questions about the legitimacy of existing government.

The argument for merit[1] appointment and promotion was, of course, Confucian. Given the ruler, it was self-evident that the quality of government depended on the ability of officials, who therefore ought to be chosen on the basis of merit. Because merit was rare, moreover, the recruitment net ought to be thrown wide—though perhaps not so wide as to cover the entire population.

"Merit," it was held, was a product of natural gifts, education, and environment: all three were equally essential. Natural superiority of intellect, temperament, and physique —the potential for merit—was a rare and mysterious gift which appeared at all social levels. In fact, the largest supply was probably among commoners because of their number. But among commoners it rarely grew into merit. They had little time for education owing to the demands of work; and

[1] An anachronistic term which I use here to summarize all the various qualities Tokugawa writers thought fitted men for office— intelligence, wisdom, understanding, humanity, generosity, courage. They had no term with quite the omnibus meaning of "merit."

71

as their work was organized around incessant efforts for self-advancement, it engendered a crabbed selfishness quite inimical to the qualities merit implied. Those qualities occurred only when, in addition to natural gifts, there was time for education, proper instruction, and a certain freedom from want making for generosity and boldness of spirit.

Thus, for all practical purposes, merit was confined to samurai. But among samurai, who were minutely graded with great differences between top and bottom, it was as often found in one rank as another, taking into account the different numbers in the various ranks. Since men fit for high office were rare, while the lower ranks of samurai were most populous, it followed that considerations of rank ought never to interfere, among samurai, with the discovery and employment of talent. Curiously, considering that practice largely followed other precepts, this proposition was generally treated as unexceptionable. No one seriously challenged it; no one developed the formidable counterargument that rank itself was possibly an aspect of merit. What, it might have been asked, was so likely as rank to give the absolute inner assurance that made other men obey instinctively, or to give the lofty freedom from personal interests so desirable in public life. The argument, though known, was scarcely used. Tokugawa Yoshimune (1684–1751) stated it in essence when he opined that men of high rank were less likely than others to use office for personal advantage or to endanger the ruler's power—though in the next breath, reverting to the conventional view, he spoke as if rank and merit were quite unrelated.[2]

THE MERIT PRINCIPLE was as much a part of political polemics as of abstract speculation. Politics in both *bakufu* and *han* turned largely on factional struggles between groups that were socially similar. Nonetheless, the "outs" were forever

[2] Tokugawa Yoshimune, *Kishū seiji gusa*, in Horiuchi Makoto, ed., *Nanki Tokugawa shi*, 1 (Wakayama, 1930), 592–98.

charging the "ins"—and being charged in turn, when themselves in—with making official appointments based on party, rank, and other inadmissible criteria, rather than merit. Merit being a subjective attribution, this charge was impossible to refute and therefore much used. For all that, it would have been less used had it not been capable, on the right occasions, of inflaming samurai feeling.

But why was the merit principle warmly regarded if so little honored in practice? Partly this was because few samurai held office and all wanted it. Office gave power and prestige and was nearly the only means of advancement in income and rank. In peacetime it was also the only way of serving the lord, and the urge to serve was exceedingly strong. Besides, given the taboo on business and the special temperament required for the arts and scholarship, it was nearly the only escape from inactivity and boredom. For a large number of samurai, therefore, the merit principle held out the only hope of office and office the only hope of self-fulfillment.[3]

Educational opportunity was also substantially equal within the samurai class; many contemporaries claimed the lower-middle ranks were better educated than the upper.[4] In any case, the *han* schools did in fact regularly register instances of lower-rank excellence and upper-rank dullness by seating students according to achievement. As a consequence the distribution of offices according to rank was not supported by an educational system that made the people who received office appear abler than those who did not; indeed, it often

[3] Yamaga Sokō (1622–1685), an influential expounder of *bushidō*, held that a warrior who did not perform his role (*shokubun*) properly, including of course serving his lord, was no better than a robber because he took a living he had no right to, and that such a person would do well to become a merchant or a peasant and so make himself an honest man. *Shidō* in Katō Setsudō, ed., *Kokumin shisō sōsho*, IX [1929], 5.

[4] Anon., *Shōhei Yawa* in Takimoto Seiichi, ed., *Nihon keizai taiten*, pp. 14, 416, 425, and Sakurada Komon, *Kakenroku*, in Honjō Eijirō, ed., *Kinsei shakai keizai sōsho*, V (1926), 106-107.

seems to have had nearly the opposite effect. Although those who long for blessings often feel themselves unworthy, this was not always, perhaps not usually, the case with aspirant samurai; they might yearn for office with the firm conviction that many office-holders were less worthy than themselves.

Still another reason for the strong appeal of the merit principle was that, after all, things were going badly in the country. After the late seventeenth century, the *bakufu* and the *han* were in serious financial difficulties, which was perhaps the least of their troubles. Peasants were abandoning farming for trade, merchants growing so powerful they could bring all but the greatest lord to heel by withholding credit, samurai losing their martial qualities, and the lower ranks being ground down by frightful poverty. To all these classic symptoms of dynastic decay was added, toward the end of the eighteenth century, the threat of barbarian domination and debauchment. If things were to be put right and the country saved, clearly the bunglers (proved so by the troubled times) must be got rid of and abler men given power.

To WHAT EXTENT was merit in fact taken into account or disregarded in appointments? It is difficult to know precisely, since there is no certain way of distinguishing between merit appointments and other appointments; some men of high rank were appointed for ability, some of low rank despite lack of it. To the extent that appointments *generally* corresponded to rank, however, we may say that merit, though not necessarily ignored, was at least subordinated to other considerations.

The voluminous samurai genealogies of Matsue *han*[5]

---

[5] *Resshiroku,* MS 24-H: 17-1 (Shiryōkan, Tokyo). These genealogies, totalling 59 volumes, provide invaluable material for the study of mobility within the warrior class. Compiled in the last years of the Tokugawa period, they give an immense amount of data—on inherit-

throw some light on the question; they would throw a good deal more if carefully studied. But even on casual examination they show clearly enough that mobility, as measured by changes in stipend, was common in the seventeenth and early eighteenth centuries. Nearly all families of direct Matsue vassals in this period moved up or down the income scale, or both up and down—often drastically and within a single generation. During the last two thirds of the eighteenth and the first decades of the nineteenth centuries, however, there was astonishingly little mobility up or down. The majority of families went through the whole period with no change in incomes whatever, or with very slight changes only. The last decades of the Tokugawa period brought more movement again, though nothing like the mobility of the first period.

Changes in income were usually occasioned by changes in office. Sometimes a man was promoted or demoted beyond the normal range for his rank, which made an increase or decrease in stipend necessary, or he was deprived of office and income as punishment for an offense. On the other hand, a man was rarely given a considerable cut or increase in stipend without a roughly corresponding change in his office, if he had one. Thus income mobility reflects to a considerable extent the degree of constraint by rank on official appointment, promotion, and demotion; and it is evident that the constraint was far greater after 1700 than before. In short, although rank was always a factor in appointment and promotion, it only became the dominant factor in Matsue in the early eighteenth century. If the experience of other parts of the country was similar, merit appointment may have be-

---

ance, marriages, adoptions, income, offices, ranks, honors, and other outstanding events, generation by generation, from the Kan'ei era (1624–1642) down to the time of compilation in the last years of the Tokugawa period, for each samurai family in existence in Matsue at the latter date.

come a sore issue in the second half of the Tokugawa period partly because rank was a *more* severe bar to advancement than previously.

It is at least certain that over the country as a whole large numbers of samurai were barred by considerations of rank from any office of consequence, and nearly all were barred by rank from further advancement at some point up the official ladder. For one thing, fief income, an aspect of rank, was usually a formal criterion of eligibility for important offices. Thus, in the *bakufu*, ten thousand *koku* income was required for *rōjū, wakadoshiyori*, and *jisha bugyō*; five thousand *koku* for *onkoshōgumigashira* and *onsobago-yōnin*; and so on.[6] After 1723 fief income was theoretically irrelevant to *bakufu* office holding, because provision was made in that year for supplementary grants of income (*tashi-daka*) during the term of office for vassals with less than the required minimum for the various offices. But the value of this system was mainly symbolic. For financial reasons, if no other, the *bakufu* chose to fill offices with men who required little or no additions to fief income; and few *han* had even this slight offset to formal income requirements.

For another thing, in both *bakufu* and *han* income requirements for office were fortified by the tendency of offices to become hereditary. In Daishōji *han*, a branch of Kaga, the highest group of officials, called *karō*, were chosen from a number of families of the highest rank. None of the Daishōji *karō* of the late Tokugawa period represented the first generation of his family in this office; several represented the eighth, ninth, or tenth.[7] In the lists of holders of high *bakufu* offices, the same surnames, with nearly identical

[6] Yokoi Shōnan, *Yokoi Shōnan ikō*, Yamazaki Masataka, ed. (Tokyo, 1938), p. 805.

[7] A total of ten *karō* served under the last daimyō between 1854 and 1870. Of the ten, one represented the third generation in this office, two the fourth, one the fifth, one the sixth, one the eighth, two the ninth, and one the tenth. (Daishōji han shi Hensakai, ed., *Daishōji han shi* [Kanazawa, 1938], 495–96).

personal names, often recur in the same offices, suggesting dynasties of fathers, sons, and grandsons.[8]

Nor was hereditary succession confined to high offices (to which relatives of the shogun or the daimyō in the *han* may have had special claim). In Kaga, offices pertaining to finance, trade, and monetary policy were typically held by merchant families in which they were handed down from generation to generation like property. Even if a father died when his son was a child, the son succeeded to the office upon reaching a suitable age. The son even succeeded when the father was removed from the office for misconduct.[9]

Another link between rank and office was the system by which many subordinate offices, in the *bakufu* at least, were filled. Numerous bureaus, and not always the least important, had no permanent staff. Each head, therefore, was obliged to staff the bureau with his own vassals and, if he had too few, with additional persons hired at his own expense.[10] Thus in governing the city of Edo, for example, the *machi-bugyō* used their own retainers as assistants, judges, clerks, police, runners, and so on.[11] This system restricted the free use of talent in three ways. (1) It tended to limit the headship of such bureaus to *bakufu* vassals who had numerous vassals of their own; that is, to men of wealth and high rank, usually daimyō. (2) It limited the subordinate positions to the vassals of such men; hence direct *bakufu* vassals of middle rank were barred from staff positions as well as from the headships. (3) Moreover, since the staff

[8] Tōkyō Teikoku Daigaku, Shiryō-hensanjo, ed., *Dokushi biyō* (1935), pp. 495–526.

[9] Anon., *Chōnin yuishochō*, MS in Kanazawa City Library.

[10] Thus, when a certain Toda Izumo no kami stationed at Nagasaki died in 1785, his 72 retainers who had assisted him in office there left the city and were replaced by the retainers of Matsuura Izumi no kami, his successor. (Takayanagi Shinzō and Ishii Ryōsuke, eds., *Ofuregaki Temmei* shūsei [1936], p. 804.)

[11] Ogyū Sorai, *Seidan*, in Takimoto Seiichi, ed., *Nihon keizai taiten*, pp. 9, 97.

changed when its head changed, the most merit-minded ruler might hesitate to replace an incompetent head for fear of losing the experience of his staff.

Primogeniture was still another link.[12] Except for very large fiefs, which were sometimes divided among heirs, younger sons rarely inherited property, rank, or eligibility for office.[13] The younger son of a middle- or low-ranking family was thus virtually excluded from office, high or low. He might hope for a small pension from the lord, especially if he excelled as a scholar or swordsman, or for adoption as an heir by another samurai family—though, if this entailed marrying a daughter of the family, it could be the least happy of all solutions. If both of these hopes failed, he could either drop into the class of commoners and go to work or live off his elder brother as an unwanted dependent. This array of life chances was not likely to make younger sons, as a group, the stoutest supporters of appointment by rank, or of any other tenet of the establishment. If, as contemporaries thought, younger sons were especially given to rowdy and delinquent behavior[14] or, later, were overrepresented in the Restoration movement, this was probably the reason.

IT WOULD BE WRONG to suppose, though, that because rank outweighed talent in bureaucratic practice, government, as opposed to its critics, cared nothing for the merit principle. The *bakufu* persistently tried to check nepotism, bribery, and favoritism in appointments. An administrative regu-

[12] If, as happened frequently, a younger son inherited owing to the incapacity of the eldest son, the latter was then in the position of a younger son with respect to inheritance, the lord, and future prospects.

[13] That is, after about 1700; before that the partitioning of fiefs was far commoner.

[14] Buyō-inshi, *Seji kemmonroku*, in Honjō Eijirō, ed., *Kinsei shakai keizai sōsho*, pp. 1, 19–20; Sakurada Komon, *Keiseidan*, in Takimoto, *Nihon keizai taiten*, pp. 16, 351; Yokoi Shōnan, *Ikō*, pp. 2, 35; Takayanagi Shinzō and Ishii Ryōsuke, eds., *Ofuregaki Tempō shūsei* (1937), p. 359.

lation of 1787 illustrates this effort: it stated that the cardinal duty of group commanders (*kumigashira*) was to recommend from their groups for appointment to office men of outstanding ability (*kiryō*), character (*jimbutsu*), and skill (*tagei*); shortly after, another regulation reminded the same commanders of their oath to recommend persons on the basis of ability only, threatening punishment for contrary recommendations.[15] Since these regulations[16] did not define ability, they can hardly have had any deep influence on practice; nevertheless, they held up an ideal of impersonality that was, perhaps, as widely accepted among officials as others.

The sensitiveness of group commanders to any imputation of impropriety in their recommendations—revealed by an incident in 1787 reported in the *Tokugawa jikki*—illustrates the importance of the ideal of impersonality among officials. According to the story, one of the commanders hinted to his colleagues that their recommendations, unlike his own, were not above suspicion of influence by gifts. Incensed, they planned revenge for the insult and got their chance at festivities one evening at his home. One of them picked a quarrel with him, and the quarrel soon grew into a brawl during which the guests upset food and drink, broke down sliding doors, ripped up the mats, and urinated on the floor. But perhaps they objected more to his holier-than-thou attitude than to the specific charge.[17]

As noted earlier, in 1723 the *bakufu* instituted the system

[15] Takayanagi and Ishii, *Tempō shūsei*, pp. 367, 520.

[16] Other similar orders may be cited. A directive of 1793 says that sons serving as understudies to their fathers in the office of *kanjō* in the Bureau of Finance were to be examined, before appointment, on their technical qualifications. Another of 1794 provided that the sons of *hatamoto* could not be enrolled in command groups (*ōban-iri*) and hence could not succeed to their fathers' fiefs, without examination as to character and skill. (Takayanagi and Ishii, *Tempō shūsei*, pp. 314–15, 348.)

[17] Narushima Motonao, ed., *Zoku Tokugawa jikki* (1), 1905, 37–38.

of supplementary income grants making it possible, in theory, for low-ranking warriors to hold all but the highest offices of *wakadoshiyori* and above, which were excluded from the system. This was going a long way toward merit egalitarianism, even in theory. A similar reform, about the same time, concerned the assignment of residences (*yashiki*) to *bakufu* vassals. Residences, which varied greatly in size and desirability of location, were assigned according to rank. One effect of this system, which was necessary to maintain the proper social distance between ranks, was to restrict eligibility for each office to those *bakufu* vassals with residences of an appropriate dignity. A noble fool living in a great residence, enclosed with walls and garden, could not be assigned to a minor clerkship nor a sage in a hovel be made a minister without exposing rank to public ridicule. The reform did nothing about the first case; but it provided for the second by stipulating that, irrespective of rank, officials upon appointment be assigned appropriate residences if they did not already have them.[18] Like the supplementary-grants system, however, this removed an obstacle to the use of ability in government without in the least assuring the use of ability.[19]

Critics continued to claim that rank, not ability, determined appointments. Before these reforms, Ogyū Sorai had charged that, because of their relatively low rank, *hatamoto* were virtually barred from high office in the *bakufu*; and long after, on the eve of the Restoration, Yokoi Shōnan was making the identical charge. *Han* practice seems to have been no

[18] Takayanagi and Ishii, *Tempō shūsei*, p. 465.

[19] Not all *han* were willing to concede so much to talent, even in theory. The regulations concerning warrior residences in Sendai, for example, stipulate that size should correspond precisely to fief income, and they lay down a detailed schedule of income categories with their corresponding residential sizes. The intent was clearly to prevent any blurring by accidents of officeholding of the distinctions of rank based on birth. (Sendai-shi Shi Hensan-iinkai, ed., *Sendai-shi shi* [VIII], 1950–1956, pp. 404–05.)

more liberal than the *bakufu's*, and may have been less so. Hayashi Shihei (1738–1798) held that, in Sendai, high office was restricted to upper-income families (*tairoku no mono*), with deplorable results for government.[20] An anonymous writer who may have been Murata Seifū said that, in Chōshū, the size of a warrior's fief determined the offices he was eligible for; consequently men were frequently appointed to high office who were young, inexperienced, and physically and morally unfit, while on the other hand men of talent with smallish stipends had no hope of important office.[21] In his memoirs, Ōkuma Shigenobu (1839–1922) stated that, in Saga, official appointments were determined by rank; intelligence and character counted for little.[22]

WHILE BUREAUCRATIC PRACTICE was coming to take more account of ability very slowly, if at all, the inability of government to cope with domestic and external problems was rapidly being revealed. This encouraged stronger statements on the conflict between rank and merit, and an increasing number of writers overstepped the conventional position that the two did not always go together, to suggest that they hardly ever went together. For some writers it was almost as if they were inversely correlated: the more of the one, the less of the other.

Although not the first to take this position, Ogyū Sorai was perhaps the first to support it with a plausible argument. When a country is at peace for a sufficiently long time, he argued, it nearly always happens that the men at the top of the social and political system have less ability than men below them.[23] War no longer weeds out the unfit; families at the top consequently maintain themselves there through

[20] Hayashi Shihei, *Jōsho sampen*, in Takimoto, *Nihon keizai taiten*, pp. 20, 48.

[21] Anon. (Murata Seifū?), *Bōshi ikensho*, pp. 48–53.

[22] Ōkuma Shigenobu, *Ōkuma-haku sekijitsudan* (1895), pp. 12-13.

[23] Ogyū Sorai, *Seidan*, p. 114.

political influence, enjoying by birth the positions their ancestors had to win by deeds; and, possessing everything one could wish without effort, they develop no talent—such native ability as they have is ruined. How could it be otherwise? Raised in ease and indolence, never rebuked, constantly praised by retainers who do everything for them, they grow up soft, ignorant, proud, self-indulgent. Above all, they have no feeling for or understanding of the common people, a defect utterly unsuiting them for high office. In such circumstances, the wise ruler will recruit his ministers from men of low rank whose character and talents and sympathies have been formed in harsher circumstances.[24]

All human ability rises from the difficulties of life. The part of one's body a person habitually uses becomes strong. If he uses his hands, they become powerful; if he walks much, his legs become sturdy. If he practices with a bow or gun, his eyes become sharp; if he uses his mind, it grows penetrating. Every difficulty and hardship refines and strengthens. This is the rule of nature, and is why Mencius said that when Heaven would entrust men with great responsibilities, it first sends them troubles. Talent therefore develops below, and hence it is essential for government to be informed of affairs below. It is the way of the sage in recruiting talent to raise it up from below: the wise and talented men of history rose from low rank: it is exceedingly rare for wisdom and talent to carry over from one generation to another in families of high rank.[25]

If, Sorai said with obvious reference to Japan, recruiting from below has been neglected for a long time, one cannot quickly set matters right, throwing down the high and raising up the low. Those who thought so were clearly mistaken; such violent change would only result in chaos, and there-

[24] *Ibid.*, pp. 112–13.
[25] *Ibid.*, p. 114.

fore new talent from below should be introduced gradually. If even a few men of low rank were promoted to high positions, it would break the monopoly of birth; others, seeing what could happen, would suddenly come alive with hope. A rush of talent would result; the age would be reborn.

But not if able men from below were merely made advisors to high officials, as some urged. That would leave them in reality powerless, for "talent standing below" cannot speak up. The man of low rank is so overwhelmed by the rank and power of the high official he cannot look him directly in the eye but "looks involuntarily at his collar," saying not what he thinks but what the official wants to hear. Therefore the only way to use able men of low rank is to give them the power and prestige of high office.[26]

By recruiting talented officials from below, Ogyū continued, the governing elite would be continuously renewed. As new men rise to positions of honor and power, they replace others who have become a drag on government and whose biological lines naturally tend to die out—"according to Heaven's rule," Sorai said hopefully. Thus the able rule the less able; meritocracy prevails and can last forever. However, if talent is not continuously recruited from below, if government tries to keep the high high and the low low, as it unfortunately tends to, its quality will deteriorate; it will lose touch with the people, and finally men of talent will rise up from below, where they are bred, to replace it.[27] "It is the unvarying rule of nature," Sorai wrote, "that old things disappear and new things take their place. Everything in creation is subject to this rule. However one may wish to preserve something forever, it is beyond anyone's power to do so. . . . To wish for this reason for the quick demise of the old would be harsh; but to hope it may last for forever is folly. In all human affairs, the way of the sage is to keep

[26] *Ibid.*, pp. 115–16, 121.
[27] *Ibid.*, p. 113.

human feelings in mind and not outrage them, at the same time seeing clearly what must be done and not being blinded by human emotion."[28]

All this, tasteless and innocuous in China, perhaps, was far from that in Japan. Sorai was proposing nothing less than the transformation of an aristocracy of birth into an aristocracy of talent, claiming that nature itself made the transformation inevitable. His writings must have thrilled men of low rank who believed that merit would solve the ills of the age and that merit and low rank went hand in hand.

Kaiho Seiryō spelled out the kind of economic changes that in his view would have to accompany merit appointment. If one presently put the ablest men in office regardless of rank, Seiryō said, samurai income would have to be thoroughly redistributed, or it would often occur that officials would have little income, while men with no office at all had a great deal. To avoid such injustice and waste it was necessary to establish a new system of stipends. First, all samurai should receive a basic rank-stipend (*iden*); then, in addition, officials should receive a salary (*yakumai*), the amount varying with the office and rising to a very large sum for the highest offices. Fief income would disappear. Therefore, since rank-stipends would be small, significant income differences henceforth would depend exclusively on officeholding; families would move up or down the income scale, irrespective of rank, as they moved up or down the administrative ladder according to the merit of family heads. Thus, for Seiryō at least, meritocracy was quite specifically an economic as well as a political order.[29]

This meritorious economic order, according to Seiryō, was

---

[28] *Ibid.*, pp. 112–13.

[29] Kaiho Seiryō (1755–1820), *Keiseidan*, in Takimoto, *Nihon keizai taiten*, pp. 27, 75–76. The son of a *karō* of Miyazu *han*, Seiryō became a *rōnin* and lectured on political economy to townsmen audiences in Osaka, Kyoto, and Kanazawa, facts which show that merit ideology was not confined to the lower and middle warrior ranks.

essential if "intelligent and wise men of low rank are to serve in high office and foolish and lazy men not."[30] The necessary adjustments to bring this order about, he recognized, would be painful to people presently at the top whose income would be drastically cut: a three thousand *koku* income would shrink to about thirty *koku,* according to one of his illustrations. There would be fierce resistance to such economic leveling unless care were taken to see that it did not entail a simultaneous social leveling. To preserve the social significance of rank, of which fief income (*chigyō-daka*) was the main indicator, he suggested that present fief income rankings, as rankings, be retained; thus the family with three thousand *koku* would remain for ceremonial purposes a three thousand *koku* family, though its actual income was reduced to thirty *koku.* If this was done, Seiryō claimed, there would be relatively little opposition to the actual loss;[31] and one cannot be sure that his optimism was wild, so often have Japanese eased the loss of power by preserving its forms.

Nevertheless, Seiryō was aware of the harshness of his proposals, which he took pains to justify. Heaven, he said, going against the common view that men were born unequal, endowed every man with the same capacity for understanding. If, nonetheless, some men were incapable of effort, unable to use their minds, unfit for work, it was their own fault. Having squandered Heaven's gift by idle living, it was Heaven's will and simple justice that they be punished for their folly.[32]

How DID THE REFORMERS suppose that merit appointment, with all its disturbing social implications, was to be brought about? Not of course by force; not by persuading high-ranking samurai to give up their offices to the lower ranks; but by the easiest, quickest, and oldest agency of reform under monarchy, the benevolence and wisdom of the ruler.

[30] *Ibid.,* p. 597.   [31] *Ibid.,* pp. 75–76.   [32] *Ibid.,* p. 77.

Nevertheless, just here was the supreme difficulty. For, according to the merit reformers, rank corrupted very nearly in proportion to its eminence; hence of all men the lord must be the least able to conceive, understand, and carry through so far-reaching and difficult a program as merit appointment. How was he who lived among courtiers to see through social appearances to men's real worth? And if he could not, how were simple, direct, unpolished men of low rank, however able, to come to power?

The merit reformers were under no illusions about the difficulties they faced. The daimyō, said Sakurada Komon scornfully, were brought up by women in the interior of the palace where no sound of the outside world penetrated and not even officials or retainers dared enter; therefore they knew nothing of men and affairs. Whatever nonsense they spoke was praised as wisdom, every action treated as a miracle of grace and dexterity. If they played chess or any other game, their companions contrived that they won, then threw up their hands, exclaiming "My, how clever the lord is!" Hence the phrase "a daimyō's skill" (*daimyō-gei*), which meant just the opposite. No wonder the daimyō for generations had been pictured in comic drama as fools. By the time a young daimyō left the palace interior, his character was ruined—he was willful, weak, pompous, foolish. And the situation was not improving: "As time passes one lord is succeeded by another like himself."[33]

Sakurada's daimyō were no worse—though certainly no better—than those of many other writers. Daimyō, in the view of men like Sakurada, were scarcely fit to referee an archery contest, let alone stand as judges of other men's qualifications. Yet this was their unique function, the essence of monarchy—the only way a single man could make his influence felt over an entire country. A ruler cannot and should not try to rule directly with his own intelligence (*chi*), Oka Hakku wrote, but by the intelligence of others

[33] *Keiseidan*, pp. 282–83.

magnify his own a thousand times. Take away this power and nothing was left to lordship but its name.[34]

Meanwhile, daimyō were donkey dull and peacock proud, and Sorai and others proposed various amelioratives for this sadly normal condition. One was to improve the education of daimyō;[35] another to secure the appointment as chief minister of men of outstanding wisdom and character.[36] But none of these suggestions was very promising. All required the daimyō to rise above himself; to make appointments of a kind that were critically needed precisely because of his inability to make them in the past.

Sorai suggested four ways that a ruler could compensate to some degree for his own social biases, which Sorai took for granted: (1) deliberately favor men of low rank in appointments; (2) be careful to appoint men representing different personalities and viewpoints, to avoid a single yes-man type; (3) start all officials at the bottom and promote no one except on the basis of performance; (4) take care that high officials never gave detailed instructions to a subordinate—otherwise subordinates would slavishly follow their superiors' orders, nothing would be revealed of their abilities, and conformity would become the standard for promotion.[37]

Further than this Sorai could hardly go in hedging against the defects of rulers. He could hope they would follow his advice, he could exhort them to be wiser than they were, but he would not deny them the power to appoint if he

[34] Oka Hakku, *Chikoku shūshin roku*, in Takimoto, *Nihon keizai taiten*, pp. 13, 289.

[35] Sakurada, *Kakenroku*, 141; Anon. (Murata Seifū?), *Bōshi ikensho*, pp. 127–28.

[36] According to Shingū Ryōtei, there were even those who suggested that it was a good thing if a daimyō were plain stupid since it would be easy in that case to keep him from interfering with his ministers. (*Yabureire no tsuzukuribanashi*, in Takimoto, *Nihon keizai taiten*, pp. 33, 116–17.)

[37] Ogyū Sorai, *Seidan*, pp. 120–24.

could. Yet, if he was right about the debilitating effects of the social system on their character, nothing short of curtailment of their power was likely to bring any lasting improvement to government.

GIVEN THE IMPOSSIBILITY of curtailing the daimyō's power and the difficulty of living with it, it is no wonder "present-day rulers"—the usual discreet generality—came in for much abuse. Daimyō were commonly called weak, ignorant, stupid, self-indulgent, ostentatious, and a great deal else. Honda Toshiaki, Kaiho Seiryō, Yokoi Shōnan, Murata Seifū, Shingū Ryōtei, and Sakurada Komon were some of the more intemperate name-callers.[38] Diatribe against daimyō was common, defense of them rare—though many writers praised individual daimyō, often to set off the others' lack of virtue.

Enmity to the daimyō was not confined to the abstraction of "present-day rulers," nor was it devoid of subversive sentiment. Writers frequently spoke of the hatred of vassals for their lords.[39] One anonymous writer predicted that in a crisis of civil strife vassals would desert their present lords, and he thought it proper they should: "Can it be virtue to help such princes rule?" he asked.[40] Sakurada thought that when the competence of government had declined sufficiently, the country would be plunged into a new civil war, and that the daimyō would be destroyed by tougher and abler men because "those who go soft cannot last long."[41] The idea of Heaven's mandate was frequently cited with a special sense of aptness to the condition of present rulers. Matsudaira Sadanobu, himself a daimyō, wrote that "Heaven

[38] Honda Toshiaki, *Keisei hisaku*, in Takimoto, *Nihon keizai taiten*, pp. 20, 120–21; Kaiho Seiryō, *Keiseidan*, pp. 77, 274; Yokoi Shōnan, *Ikō*, pp. 2, 39, 813; Anon. (Murata Seifū?), *Bōshi ikensho*, pp. 61, 90, 93, 121–23, 127; Sakurada, *Kakenroku*, 78–79, 82, 85–86, 138–39; Sakurada, *Keiseidan*, p. 309.

[39] Anon. (Murata?), *Bōshi ikensho*, pp. 90–91.

[40] Anon., *Shōhei yawa*, pp. 396, 398, 402, 413–14.

[41] Sakurada, *Kakenroku*, pp. 85–86.

orders what the people wish. . . . The preferences of a man, a family, or a village are a private matter, but what the masses (*okuchō no hito*) wish *is* the will of Heaven." If a ruler disregarded Heaven's will, he would eventually be destroyed and his state perish. Now "present-day rulers," said Sadanobu, becoming quite specific in his reference to Japan and repeating the customary charges against the daimyō, were brought up by women; they were used to people approaching on their knees saying "yes, yes"; if a minister dared tell them of the people's sufferings, they put their hands over their ears and the minister was condemned for his thoughtlessness. Such men, said Sadanobu grimly, do not know Heaven's will or rule in Heaven's name.[42]

Honda Toshiaki was as explicit about his readiness for a change in Heaven's mandate as he dared be. In a long passage in one of his major works, *Keisei hisaku*, he showed how throughout Japanese history Heaven had destroyed bad rulers. Then coming to his own time, he described the evils of the day, tracing them to the influence of the rulers. All of these evils would vanish, he said, if an enlightened ruler were to appear; but no such thing was likely, and he placed his hope on Heaven's intervention. "Whose fault is it that the people starve and good fields turn to waste? These evils cannot be blamed on laziness or disloyalty [in the people] but are owing to the crimes of the rulers [*kokkun no zaika*]. When I think of this I forget myself and breathe 'Heaven's punishment comes too slowly!'[43]

AFTER HONDA'S TIME in the late eighteenth century, merit ideology was increasingly obscured by two more dramatic issues—Japan's relations with the West and the relation of the emperor to the government. Since these issues led more or less directly to the Restoration, they have usually been

[42] Matsudaira Sadanobu, *Kokuhon ron*, in Takimoto, *Nihon keizai taiten*, pp. 13, 330–32.
[43] Honda, *Keisei hisaku*, pp. 120–21.

seen as the chief intellectual causes or antecedents of that event. But one wonders whether, on a longer view, either was more important than the merit issue in undermining the legitimacy of the *bakufu* and *han* and arousing feeling against them. On no broad political principle, not even perhaps on the emperor, were the anti-*bakufu* agitators so nearly united. And for the majority of the samurai, one must remember that the opening of careers to talent was no abstract issue but a matter of the greatest personal urgency —offering hope of escape from poverty, boredom, and helplessness. One is reminded of Sir George Sansom's judgment: "There can be no doubt that, of all the causes of the anti-Tokugawa, loyalist movement which ended in the fall of the *bakufu*, the ambition of young samurai was the most powerful."[44]

[44] G. B. Sansom, *The Western World and Japan* (New York, 1950), p. 254.

CHAPTER III

Kinship Structure, Migration to the City, and Modernization

EZRA F. VOGEL

CONSIDERING the scope, depth, and sophistication of kinship studies, it is surprising how little attention has been devoted to the relation of various kinship structures to the processes of urbanization and industrialization. In cases where this problem has been studied, the general conclusion has been that kinship systems inhibit and are disrupted by modernization.[1] The central argument of the present paper is that the Japanese kinship system adapted relatively easily to modernization and that its continued strength helped make the transition a relatively smooth process. The author cannot hope to examine kinship organizations in all parts of Japan at all times. Rather, the present paper will focus on one crucial change which can be traced with somewhat greater clarity and certainty: the relatively recent migration from country to city. An attempt will be made to present the overall pattern even at the risk of ignoring some of the subtleties and complexities of this migration. The data for this paper are based in part on interviews in the Tokyo area in 1958–1960 with middle-class migrants and children and grandchildren of migrants, and on the implications of already well-known features of the Japanese kinship system.

The Traditional Kinship System

As students of Japan know, the crucial kinship unit in

---

[1] One exception is Manning Nash, *Machine Age Maya* (Glencoe: Free Press, 1958). But even Nash is less concerned with the type of kinship system than with the type of economic organization which can take advantage of certain kinship systems.

rural Japan has been the *ie*. The *ie* is a patrilineal organization with rapid segmentation in each generation. One son, usually the first, inherits all the family property, including land, home, and ancestral treasures. Daughters enter their husband's *ie* upon marriage, and sons who do not succeed to their parents' *ie* can either be adopted as heirs in families with no sons or start relatively independent "branch" lineages of their own. *Ie* organization has been firmly institutionalized, being supported by religious practices associated with the lineage, by the ethical teachings and laws and regulations emanating from the government, by local community organization in which an *ie* was considered a single unit, and by the small size of land plots which made it impractical to divide land between all sons in a family. While in some cases the clan organization (*dōzoku*) comprising several *ie* was a viable and powerful organization, the information from urban informants indicates that in recent times the power of the *dōzoku* over the *ie* has been limited. Unless several related *ie* were living in the same village, each *ie* had virtual autonomy from the *dōzoku* in most spheres of activity.[2] But the head of the *ie* had considerable power over the members, and the national government and local community lent support to this power, enabling him effectively to control and supervise the activities of its members.

[2] For an excellent brief summary of the Japanese kinship system, see Kizaemon Ariga, "The Family in Japan," *Marriage and Family Living*, XVI (1954), 362–68. For a case of an extremely strong *dōzoku* group (based on the work of Ariga), see Michio Nagai and John W. Bennett, *Dōzoku: A Preliminary Study of the Japanese Extended Family Group*, Ohio State University, 1953 (mimeo.). Recent field studies like those of Edward Norbeck indicate that the *dōzoku* is no longer such a powerful group in many areas. Unfortunately, in this brief overview it is not possible to treat variations, but one particularly crucial variation has been in villages dominated by *dōzoku* and those dominated by collateral ties. See Tadashi Fukutake, *Studies on the Rural Community in Japan* (Tokyo: Tokyo University Press, 1959).

Kinship as the Regulator of Migrations

In contrast to many of the large migrations in Europe and especially the migrations to the United States, the Japanese migration to the city was not a result of sudden spurts of economic growth that demanded large masses of labor supply. Nor did sudden and disruptive famines or political upheavals force starved or dissident elements to migrate elsewhere. The continued economic expansion of Japan in the post-Meiji period and the political stability, once the Satsuma rebellion had been subdued in 1877, meant that migration within Japan could be a continuous and orderly process.[3]

The social, economic, and political orderliness of Japanese society made it possible for the migration to be controlled by and subordinated to the existing kinship organization. Because there were no sudden massive migrations, the selection of those who would and would not go to the city was determined by a primogeniture kinship system which provided a steady exodus to the city, and an orderly basis of rural organization during the period of migration. Because one son remained in the rural area and inherited the family property, the *ie* was maintained and remained the basic unit of rural organization. Sometimes it was the first son who migrated to the city,[4] but in any case the head of the *ie* has remained remarkably powerful in deciding who would and

[3] Irene Taeuber notes that the migration to cities in Japan was very steady over many decades. "Family, Migration and Industrialization in Japan," *American Sociological Review*, XVI (1957), 149–57. Taeuber's data are presented much more fully in her excellent book *The Population of Japan* (Princeton: Princeton University Press, 1958).

[4] In one study of 7,000 families in twelve villages, of the men who had left the village in the 1930's for work elsewhere and not returned, 20 percent were eldest sons. (Nojiri Shigeo, *Nōmin rison no jisshōteki kenkyū*, 1949, p. 502. Cited in R. P. Dore, "Japan: Country of Accelerated Transition," *Population Studies*, XIII (1959), 103–11.) See also Harumi Befu, "Corporate Emphasis and Patterns of Descent in the Japanese Family," in Robert J. Smith and Richard K. Beardsley, eds., *Japanese Culture* (New York: Werner Gren Foundation, 1962).

would not go to the city. Work opportunities in the city were relatively limited, and most economic organizations in the city preferred to use personal connections to insure getting a devoted and reliable labor supply.[5] Even if the head of the household did not directly make the arrangements for his son's employment, he controlled access to prominent people, who through personal connections would be of assistance in making these arrangements.

The existence of a primogeniture system only partly explains the orderliness of the migration. Japan not only had primogeniture but required children to leave home in their adolescence or by their early twenties at the latest. But the Irish, despite a primogeniture system with single inheritance, allowed excess sons and daughters to remain in the family until their thirties or even forties, when the father retired and an heir was selected.[6] It is not completely clear why the *ie* had begun to require excess children to leave home at such an early age.[7] But in any case, even though the pattern of early migration was not strictly a result of the primogen-

[5] For large companies this applied to only a small proportion of the personnel, the most trusted members of the company. Many companies had a much lesser commitment to the masses of laborers. Cf. unpublished manuscript by Kazuo Noda. Most families studied by the author, however, were middle-class families, and they reported close connections with the company.

[6] Conrad Arensberg and Solon Kimball, *Family and Community in Ireland* (Cambridge: Harvard University Press, 1940).

[7] Perhaps farm plots had been too small to divide for centuries, and the pattern of leaving home had become fully institutionalized before large-scale migration began in the Meiji period. Feudal lords or, later, landlords might not have permitted excess sons to remain and use up the limited supply of consumers' goods. (By contrast the Irish family had considerable autonomy.) Perhaps opportunities for economic success were for those who migrated at a younger age because loyalty and long apprenticeships were regarded as so critical, or possibly at the time of population expansion, more economic opportunities were available in Japan than in Ireland.

iture system alone, the pattern of primogeniture was the basis for the requirement that excess sons be sent elsewhere.

In Japan placing a child in the city meant finding him a job in a good organization.[8] The success of the placement depended in large part on the status and the contacts which the rural family was able to command. In some cases the family had only a single channel to use to make the placement. Tenant farmers, for example, were frequently dependent on their landlords for assistance. But some economic organizations had direct ties to certain villages, and arrangements could be made through them, and if a family had relatives or close friends of power and importance, they would provide the necessary channels. By and large, the son going to the city could not make these contacts by himself but depended on other members of the *ie*, particularly the head, to make the necessary arrangements. An employer expected to give a young man on-the-job training and so did not look for specific ability, but rather sought a young man who had good general intelligence, reliable character, and most important, a special personal connection with his friends or relatives so that he could be assured of the employee's loyalty and willingness to work long hours without high wages.[9]

There is no reason to suspect that the urban employer, even a few generations ago, was not interested in obtaining com-

[8] Again, why the tie with the economic organization was the crucial group for integrating the newcomer into the city rather than organizations based on the country of origin, religion, region, craft guild, or the like is beyond the scope of the present paper. It is important to note, however, that this became the basic membership group in the city. For example, ritual kinship relations generally grew up between people in the same company rather than on some other basis.

[9] It should be reiterated that while this applied to middle-class workers who were closely identified with the company, the mutual commitment between employer and employee was much less in the case of the laboring classes.

petent employees. The problem was that he had a limited range of acquaintances within which he could select a competent person. In addition he had to rely on judgments of friends and relatives about competence, and there were occasions when he felt obliged, because of personal relationships, to accept a young man he did not regard as very competent. Furthermore, often boys were hired at such a young age that they had no chance to prove themselves before coming to work, and it was highly unlikely that any would already have acquired the specific skills necessary for performing the work.

Because the employer and employee both relied on personal connections for arranging employment, and the number of such connections was limited, it was difficult for an employee who left one organization to find a job elsewhere and for an employer who lost employees to find other men who would be equally devoted and hard-working. Employees were rewarded for competence, and there was usually some opportunity for talented and hard-working employees to rise within the organization, but only very rarely could a man change firms and rise more rapidly than before. A man who left his job usually had to rely on the *ie* from which he had come for a new placement. In a sense the early system of placement and promotion might be called "universalism with a limited particularistic framework," a phenomenon essentially like what Marion Levy called "family civil service."[10] There were opportunities for placement and promotion based on competence, but these opportunities were restricted to a narrow range of people.

It is still true that particularistic contacts are used in arranging employment, and those who have important connections can sometimes rise more rapidly than those without them. But on the whole, within the last generation the importance of universalistic criteria for hiring and promot-

[10] Marion J. Levy, *The Family Revolution in Modern China* (Cambridge: Harvard University Press, 1949).

ing has increased drastically as a result of the increased size of business organizations. In the first place, large organizations hire so many people that for efficiency in selecting new members, they must rely on such universalistic criteria as educational achievement, school or university attended, entrance examinations, and specific skills. The higher educational level of the population and the later age of hiring gives a young man more opportunity to demonstrate his competence and to acquire skills before being selected by the firm. Hence specific skills and competence have become relatively more important than general ability and personal connections in the labor market. A second result of growth of firms is a greater range of possible positions within the firm, which permits a more refined matching process of person and work. As opposed to a small organization, which may have no important managerial positions available, a large organization will have many levels of positions open, and the more talented as well as the less able man can find a post commensurate with ability.

Despite these fundamental changes in the direction of increased universalism in the labor market, most Japanese rural *ie* have continued to be able to control the entrance of their children into the labor market. It is easy to understand why the family maintained control over migration in previous time. The eldest son inherited the family property, and his prospects were generally much brighter than those who migrated. Second and third sons who had no hope of sharing in the family inheritance could not find a desirable position in the city without their family's assistance. The family started making suitable contacts and introductions years before the young man had to go to the city and in general did everything it could to secure the young man a good position in the city. The young man knew he had to remain in the city all his life and that with personal introductions the chances of an employer taking an interest in his long-run livelihood were much greater. He had everything

to gain by going through the usual channels of family introduction.

The family's ability to maintain control appears related in
part to its control of access to education. As in other countries, the family is probably the most important source of
motivation for educational ambitions, and family funds are
often needed later for school fees. In addition, entrance paths
are highly competitive, and examinations ordinarily stress
the acquisition of factual information more than innate ability.
Generally, it is not felt that a young person can acquire
this large fund of information without considerable family
help. The family must support the child who is preparing
for examinations, pay entrance and tuition fees, and because
homework assignments during the year and even in summer vacation are often difficult, either the parents or tutors
hired by the parents often provide assistance in studying.
Furthermore, while universalism is increasing, it is often accompanied by particularistic connections. Introductions by
friends of the family to schools and prospective employers
are often routine procedures. It is assumed that everyone can
get such introductions, and while differences in introductions are not very useful for differentiating between
most applicants, the fact that they are required has served
to help maintain the family's control.

Quite possibly there were other factors that accounted for
the rural *ie*'s ability to control the migration. The close
parent-child relationship, for example, encouraged by traditional values and modern child-rearing practices as well,
has undoubtedly contributed to the *ie*'s ability to control the
decisions of the children. What is crucial for the present
argument, however, is not which factor led to the *ie*'s ability
to maintain control but that it did in fact control the migration process. It is now necessary to consider some of the
effects of this control for the migration.

Some Effects of Kinship Structure on the Migration Process

THE INDEPENDENCE OF THE FIRST GENERATION URBAN FAMILY
FROM THE RURAL *ie*

The family which established itself in the city was typically a nuclear family of husband and wife with considerable independence from the rural *ie*. This is again in striking contrast, for example, to many areas in China and to the Batak of Indonesia where the migrants to the city maintained ownership or some hope of eventual ownership of property in the rural areas.[11] In those cases the urban family felt much more tied to the rural society. It is also in contrast to migrations such as the European migration to America where large numbers of elderly parents migrated with young couples and exerted a considerable restraining force in the adoption of new patterns of life.[12] In Japan the *ie* system meant that the migrant to the city had no hope of settling in the rural area and that the elderly parents were cared for by the son who remained in the country. The rapid segmentation of the lineage in each generation meant that there was no large kinship group for a person to join when he came to the city.[13] Kinship ties did not interfere and, if anything, worked to reinforce the ties between the employer and the employee. The common ritual kinship relationship between employer and employee became the basic tie in the city, and

[11] Cf. Edward Bruner, "Urbanization and Ethnic Identity in North Sumatra," *American Anthropologist*, LXIII (1961), 508–21, 1961; and Marion Levy on the Chinese family in *op.cit.*

[12] See for example Carolyn Ware, *Greenwich Village, 1920–1930* (Boston: Houghton Mifflin, 1935).

[13] This is in striking contrast to the Chinese, and the difference between the Chinese and Japanese is vividly presented by Stanford Lyman in his analysis of Chinese and Japanese settlement in the United States. Stanford Lyman, *The Structure of Chinese Society in Nineteenth Century America* (Ph.D. Thesis, University of California, 1961).

the migrant's original *ie* stood ready to see that that tie was maintained.

The young man typically migrated to the city alone, and once he had economic security in the city he would have his original *ie* in the rural areas select a bride. Unlike the European immigration to the United States, it was rarely necessary for a nuclear family to be split during the process of migration. Because the decision about inheritance was made early and because migration was controlled by the kinship system, the migration consisted essentially of single young people. Thus from the time of marriage the young couple was united but independent of control by kin, and they had a measure of financial stability through the husband's firm.

Even the employer, once he approved the selection of the bride, usually did not exert close supervision over family relationships. It is true that before his marriage, a young man often lived in housing provided by his employer, and after marriage an employer closely supervised many aspects of an employee's life, but ordinarily this supervision did not interfere with the details of family life. In some ways this freedom was comparable to the freedom which had been granted in rural Japan in the previous era to the semi-independent farmers (*nago*).[14]

Even if the young couple officially established themselves as an urban branch family, they had great autonomy in running their own affairs. Only rarely did they return to the rural village. At most the husband would return at New Year or for the O-bon Festival, and in many cases his visits to even a nearby rural home were less than once a year. When they did return it was usually for a ritual occasion and a personal visit which did not encroach on their autonomy in the city; typically their parents virtually never came to see them in the city.

This autonomy permitted the urban family to adapt to the

[14] Cf. Thomas C. Smith, *The Agrarian Origins of Modern Japan* (Stanford: Stanford University Press, 1959).

Even after the children had grown, there seemed to be little meaning for man and wife in continuing the *ie* form of organization. They were a branch family with no responsibility for the rural *ie*, and their sense of involvement diminished as they became established in the city; and there was little drive to establish a new *ie* in the city. The *ie* was well adapted to rural land organization but had little economic meaning in the city. An employee in the city generally could not pass his job on to his son. The crucial factor in one's livelihood had changed from property to position, and the position could not be passed on by inheritance. There were exceptions. Certain craftsmen and skilled workers did pass down skills and shops from one generation to the next, and some independent professionals such as doctors and dentists selected heirs for their practice. In these families and in certain business families the concept of *ie* remained strong even in the city. But, by and large, for those who entered the large organizations (and today this is by far the largest group in contemporary urban areas), the consciousness of *ie* became weaker and weaker. This means that, unlike the rural families, there was less necessity to distinguish first and second sons, with the kind of training given the children depending more on their individual interests and abilities than on their birth order in the family. In previous times a family had at least one position, that of family heir, which had to be filled. Now the occupation of the sons of the organization man is not determined by the father's occupation, and distinctions between heir and nonheir have greatly decreased in importance.

Though the rural *ie* gave initial assistance in getting the branch established in the city, the urban family did not have to engage in any emotional revolt to achieve independence. In China, with a much larger kinship unit, for one son to establish his independence often meant serious quarrels with a father or a brother or quarrels between wives of brothers. In Japan, because of the *ie* system, the second and third sons broke off and moved to the city without this kind of family disruption.[17] The move to the city was not a break in the kinship structure, but rather a natural development which proceeded within the structure of the kinship organization.⟩

MIGRATION WITH MINIMAL SOCIAL DISRUPTION

When one considers the massive disorganization in European cities resulting from the migrations described by Le Play[18] or the massive disorganization in American cities, it appears that urbanization in Japan proceeded quite smoothly. It is true that the migrants in Japan often suffered from economic deprivation, and in some cases they hesitated to let their rural relatives know how difficult conditions actually were. It is true that some employers took advantage of paternalism and exploited the workers, requiring very long hours with very low wages. But these were not part of a massive disorganization of the basic social structure. Indeed, the young migrant was generally integrated into society through his place of work, and since the *ie* in the rural areas had been instrumental in making this placement and had used important intermediaries to make the arrangements, they and the intermediaries stood behind the young man in case of difficulty with the employer. The employer, with this personal connection to the intermediary and the rural family, could not easily dismiss an employee. Many an employer who went out of business exerted considerable effort in trying to find new places of work for his workers. Because the migration had been relatively steady, the rural *ie* had ample time to locate the most secure employment situation possible, and since they had made the original arrangements, if a young man did lose his job, they would permit

[17] This does not mean there were no difficulties between rural families that tried to keep more control or provided less help to the urban branch than the urban branch desired, but only that the kinship structure served to minimize this difficulty.

[18] Frederic Le Play, *Les ouvriers Européens* (Tours, 1877).

him to return to the rural areas temporarily while they made new arrangements for him.

Those who left the rural area departed only with the encouragement, or at a minimum the tacit approval, of the *ie*, and so the exodus did not constitute a threat to the local rural authority structure. The *ie* was the basic unit of rural social structure, and because one son remained to take over the *ie* a continuity in local village structure was provided. It is true that some *ie* rose or declined in relative status within the rural community, and these shifts created strains and required painful adjustments. But rarely did an established *ie* leave the community entirely and rarely did a new *ie* come into a community from the outside. This continuity of the *ie* which resulted from the kinship system provided a large measure of stability during the peak of the migration to the city. Even today, when a very large proportion of farmers are entering the industrial labor force, it is common to continue the *ie* on the same plot of land; the husband commutes to work, doing the farm work in spare time or turning it over entirely to his wife and children.

The urban family in Japan has shown remarkable stability. Evidence presented by Kawashima and Steiner show that in contrast to many modern countries the divorce rate actually went down with urbanization.[19] It may be suggested that the ability of the rural *ie* to place the young couple in a relatively stable economic situation and the fact that the young couple was not separated during the migration process were important elements in this stability.

Some Implications of the Migration Process for Contemporary Society

THE COMMITMENT OF THE LABOR SUPPLY

For people who remained attached to their *ie* in the coun-

[19] See Takeyoshi Kawashima and Kurt Steiner, "Modernization and Divorce Rate Trends in Japan," *Economic Development and Cultural Change*, IX: i, pt. 2 (1960), 213–39.

try, there was a pattern, known as *dekasegi*, whereby people worked for a brief period of time away from home. This pattern was particularly common for young girls prior to their marriage and for others in the household who were for some reason free for part-time work. But this *dekasegi* pattern has not generally applied to the excess sons who separated from the *ie* and moved to the city. Many migrants in other countries (for example, Chinese migrants to cities or Italian migrants to American cities) hoped to acquire money and then to return to their original home. The Japanese migrants' main desire was to obtain a secure place in the city, and they were willing to undergo long periods of apprenticeship at low wages. Unlike Japanese migrants, Italian migrants to American cities only wanted short term jobs with high pay, and they were unwilling to acquire skills that would pay off only much later. In Japan many parents in the rural areas actually told their migrating children that they should make good in the city so they would not have to come back. One of the crucial requirements for industrialization in any country is the development of a skilled labor force. Because the Japanese *ie* removed the migrant from its membership and did not expect him to return once he had gone to the city, the *ie* played an important role in motivating the migrant to acquire these skills that would give him sufficient security to remain.[20]

CAPITAL ACCUMULATION

Although much of the initial capital investment in Japan in the early Meiji period was provided through the government, many small businesses throughout Japan were essentially family enterprises, and these family enterprises managed to accumulate a sizeable amount of capital. The *ie*

[20] The importance of the stem family system in providing a committed labor supply in urban areas in Europe has already been noted by economic historians. See for example H. J. Habakkuk, "Family Structure and Economic Change in Nineteenth Century Europe," *Journal of Economic History*, xv (1955), 1–12.

system had two important contributions to the accumulation of capital. First, it had an extended time perspective, which sanctioned the postponement of gratification. The *ie* provided a link with one's ancestors, and to the extent that immortality was thought to exist it was dependent on the continued prosperity of the family line. Most *ie* had treasures and heirlooms which had been passed down for many generations, and it was extremely important to preserve the vitality of the *ie* for the future generations. Hence it was considered very important to make short-term sacrifices for the benefit of the *ie* in the future. One such sacrifice was the willingness to curtail spending and make investments which would offer profit and stability for the *ie* in the future.

A second contribution was that the capital remained in the hands of a relatively small group, the members of the *ie*. The average poor farmer in rural Japan could not save much, but richer farmers or small industrial enterprises in rural areas could accumulate capital, and the system of having only a single heir did not force the dissipation of this wealth. In China, by contrast, any family's wealth was always rapidly dissipated within two or three generations because it was divided between all the children. The family firm in Japan could acquire and maintain capital investment not possible in countries where the family would be expected to provide for a much broader range of friends and relatives.[21] Wealth could be retained in the enterprise, and in contrast to other countries which had large numbers of absentee landlords, the head of the local *ie* remained in the rural areas to apply his energy and skills to the wise utilization of this capital.

CHANGE WITHOUT DIVIDED LOYALTIES

Compared to other industrialized societies, Japanese society is still composed of tight-knit groups with relatively

[21] A good example of some of the problems of rationalizing family firms can be seen in the case of France. See Jesse Pitts, *The French Bourgeois Family and Economic Retardation*, Ph.D. Thesis, Harvard University, 1959.

few channels for contact and movement between groups. The commitment of an individual to his own group is much stronger than any commitment to a transcendent value system or to a professional, occupational, or union organization tying him to others occupying the same position in other groups. The basic cleavages in Japanese society have not been between different social classes but between one corporate group (composed of people at different social positions) and other corporate groups. The strong commitment of an individual to his group and the lack of cross-cutting membership to other groups has not been conducive to the smooth integration of groups in the wider society, but it has been conducive to a very high degree of solidarity and conformity within any single group.

Relations between members of a given group have generally been sufficiently close and humane, and opportunities for members to find equally good opportunities in other groups so limited, that people have been very willing to make sacrifices for the group to which they belong. Because of this very deep commitment to their group, they have been willing and even eager to take on new techniques and develop new organizational procedures to improve their organization relative to other organizations, even if it requires a considerable measure of personal sacrifice. Many of the pressures for modernization and rationalization come from members of a given *ie* or a given firm trying to improve their competitive position. This pressure for achievement and sacrifice within the context of primary commitment to the group is fully consistent with the traditional value system which subordinated patterns of achievement to loyalty to the group.[22] It is also fully consistent with the child-rearing practices which tend to make the individual dependent on his group.[23]

[22] Cf. Robert N. Bellah, *Tokugawa Religion* (Glencoe: Free Press, 1957).

[23] Cf. Ezra F. Vogel, *Japan's New Middle Class* (Berkeley: University of California Press, 1963).

In the *ie*, as in other groups in Japanese society, the individual is subordinated to the group, and achievement is rewarded within the context of the group. In order to preserve the *ie*, members have been willing to undergo personal sacrifice and to introduce changes for the benefit of the *ie*. If a first son was not sufficiently capable of taking over the family enterprise or unwilling to place the interests of the group above outside or personal interests, the *ie* would pass the position of family head on to another son or would adopt the most suitable young man available. This does not, of course, mean that every *ie* throughout the society was composed only of able people, but only that as much as possible the head of the *ie* tried to choose the successor who was most likely to preserve the *ie* as a flourishing corporate group.

As long as the same unit, the *ie*, was both the familial and the economic unit, the individual's allegiance could be united in a single group. In the most industrialized sector of society, the *ie* has declined in importance, but there is still no reason for an individual to have divided loyalties. The *ie* is replaced by the large economic firm on the one hand and the small nuclear family on the other. Since most of the workers in these large organizations are recruited from branch rather than main family, they do not have an *ie* to support which might conceivably conflict with the firm's activities. The individual thus comes to have dual membership which might conceivably lead to cross-cutting ties interfering with a complete commitment to the other group. This dual commitment, however, generally has not led to problems because the two organizations, the business firm and the family, have been kept perfectly distinct. The wife has virtually no contact with anyone in the husband's firm, and the husband's work associates are kept quite apart from any family affairs. The modern nuclear family is so small and its sphere so limited that it in no way interferes with the husband's commitment to the firm, which is the important group to which he belongs. The large corporation, like the *ie*, is a clearly distinct corporate group, and an individual ordinarily expects to work in the same place throughout his lifetime.

Not all people in Japan enjoy membership in a secure corporate group. Very small individual enterprises sometimes lack capital and equipment that would make the inheritance of property through the *ie* at all meaningful. Among these families there is no large stable group to which they can belong. The same is true of some families where the husband has a job in a small enterprise which lacks the capital and adaptability to meet changing economic and technical developments and offer secure long-term employment to the individual. In some new enterprises where there is a critical shortage of skilled labor other organizations are sometimes willing to offer very high rewards to people willing to change organizations, and many people have shown a willingness to make such moves.

For the large mass of workers in the larger organization, there is no such willingness to change organizations. Here the critical problem is getting admitted to the organization when one enters the labor force. Once admitted a person is firmly attached to the organization. He can thus have the same all-embracing commitment to his firm, the willingness to undergo temporary sacrifice for the eventual good of his firm and himself, that the members of a family enterprise have toward their *ie*.

In those sectors of society where the *ie* continues as an important economic unit (among farmers, independent professionals, and small businessmen), it continues to serve as the basic solidarity group. The *ie* is generally committed to preserving these enterprises and is willing and even anxious to undergo changes that would help ensure the future of the enterprise.

It is because the loyalty to a given group has been so strong and the future association of an individual with the group so certain that people have been willing to undertake painful changes in their group which would help them better meet the future. The structure and practices of the *ie* have helped to preserve this relatively undivided loyalty. Overlapping membership in groups of primary significance and conflicting loyalties have been virtually absent. The distinction between member and nonmember has been drawn very sharply. Unlike the Chinese clan, in which one might have some loyalties to more than one clan and in which it was not always clear whether or not distant relatives were members of a given clan, in the Japanese *ie* it was always very clear who was or was not a member. The name of the bride or young man who married into another family was crossed off from the family register. This rapid and sharp segmentation from the *ie* permitted a very high degree of solidarity within the *ie*, and it also helped minimize the conflicts of loyalty of the member who left the *ie*. It was very clear that the second son or daughter who left an *ie* owed primary loyalty to the group he was entering. The fact that it was so clear which group should be the object of one's primary loyalty served to strengthen this commitment and to weaken ties with other groups. The members who remained in a given *ie* considered nothing so important as the continued success of that *ie*. Even disruptive changes necessary for modernization were accepted but adapted so as to strengthen the *ie* or, when one was detached from his *ie*, his new firm.

CHAPTER IV

Mobility, Equality, and Individuation in Modern Japan

R. P. DORE

A<small>N INDUSTRIALIZING SOCIETY</small> is bound to be a mobile society. The towns must take population from the countryside, some men must do new jobs, some sons must enter different occupations from their fathers. *How many* can vary from society to society depending on the extent to which there is further mobility between existing occupational groups. Societies may also differ in the extent to which the occupational mobility which does take place involves changes in individuals' relative position in the hierarchies of prestige and power attaching to these shifting occupational structures (i.e. how far the new groups at the top of the new hierarchies are recruited from old groups at the top of the old hierarchies, groups at the bottom of the new from groups at the bottom of the old, and so on). They may differ, too, in the extent to which these differentials of power, income, and prestige are considered important, the extent to which they are considered legitimate, the extent to which changing one's relative position in these hierarchies is a dominant preoccupation of the individuals in the society, the extent to which raising that position is considered possible, and the extent to which the possibilities of changing that position depend on personal enterprise, intellectual ability, character, educational qualifications, or patronage.

This paper will be concerned chiefly with the latter questions concerning aspirations and the mechanisms of mobility and what they reveal about trends to greater equality and individuation in Japanese society. First, however, it will be useful to summarize the evidence concerning the *amount* of mobility in the last century. Beliefs and hopes are not always based on a realistic appreciation of possibilities, but in the long run the actual amount of mobility is bound to have some influence on what people think or hope are their prospects.

Mobility Data

There is little basis for quantitative assessments of the pattern of mobility during the initial transition from the feudal to the new occupational hierarchy. What seems fairly well established is: first, that a high proportion of the governmental, professional, and even business elites were drawn from that 6 percent of the population which was of samurai ancestry; second, that, nevertheless, within this group there was considerable mobility—a good many of those in positions of the greatest power, prestige, and wealth came from the humbler ranks of the samurai class; third, that this proportion of ex-samurai in the elite was steadily declining; and fourth, that insofar as it did not decline more quickly this was less and less because of advantages attaching to samurai ancestry as such. (The privileges attaching to the legal status of *shizoku* [given to former samurai families] had disappeared before the end of the century, and the social prestige value of that status was rapidly attenuated thereafter.)

By the first decades of this century an individual's life chances were determined not so much by his family's feudal status in itself as by the income and amenities attaching to his father's occupational position. The pattern of occupational mobility became not so very different from that of Western societies. How mobility rates have changed over time it is impossible to say, but for the most recent period certain rough statistical comparisons can be made between Japan and other countries, based on studies of the family history of their adult male populations carried out since the last war. The main features are summarized in Table 1.

TABLE 1

Comparative Mobility Data

e figures for the United States, Great Britain, and France indicate a degree of mobility
ich is: slightly lower (*l*), definitely lower (*L*), slightly higher (*h*), or definitely higher
*) than comparable figures for Japan. Lower-case letters indicate a difference on which
le reliance should be placed, given the sampling problems and difficulties of definition.

	Japan	*United States*	*Great Britain*	*France*
bility with respect to:				
Chance of a farmer's son becoming a top business leader		*l*		
Chance of a nonagricultural manual worker's son becoming a top business leader		*h*	*h*	
Percent of farmers' and agricultural laborers' sons entering nonmanual occupations	22%	*h* (24%)		*L* (16%)
Percent of other manual workers' sons entering nonmanual occupations	25%	*h* (31%)		*H* (36%)
Percent of all manual workers' sons entering nonmanual occupations	23%	*H* (29%)	*H* (27%)	*l* (22%)
Percent of nonmanual workers' sons entering manual occupations	27%	*L* (23%)	*H* (42%)	*h* (28%)
Chance of a manual worker's son being in nonmanual occupation as percentage of chance of a nonmanual worker's son staying nonmanual[1]	31%	*H* (38%)	*H* (47%)	– (31%)
Among mobile farm sons, the ratio of those entering nonmanual to those entering nonagricultural manual occupations	1.4:1	*L* (0.5:1)		*L* (0.3:1)
Percent of farmers' and agricultural laborers' sons entering professional and managerial occupations[2]	7%	*h* (8%)	*L* (2%)	*L* (3%)

Notes to Table 1

I.e., the percentage of manual workers' sons who have moved into nonmanual occupa-
s divided by the percentage of nonmanual workers' sons who have stayed in non-
ual occupations, a version of Miller's "index of inequality" (*Comparative Social
bility*, p. 36) which to some extent discounts different rates of change in the occupa-
al structure.

The category "professional and managerial" seems to be slightly wider in the Japanese
1 in the British and French surveys; more restricted than in the U.S. survey. The
entages in these categories are: Japan, 10.9%; U.S., 16.0%; Britain, 7.5%; France, 8.0%.

SOURCES: For rows 1 and 2: J. C. Abegglen and H. Mannari, "Leaders of Modern Jap Social Origins and Mobility," *Economic Development and Cultural Change*, IX, i, pt (1960), and G. H. Copeman, *Leaders of British Industry* (London, 1955).

For the rest: S. M. Miller, *Comparative Social Mobility* (*Current Sociology*, IX, i, 196 S. M. Lipset and R. Bendix, *Social Mobility in Industrial Society* (Berkeley: University California Press, 1959), and Nihon Shakai Gakkai Chōsa Iinkai, ed., *Nihon shakai kaisoteki kōzō* (1958). Miller's figures for Japan were recalculated from the tables gi in the last work, since those he used excluded sons whose occupations were unclassifia The French figures were recalculated from tables given by Miller to include farmers manual workers and so improve comparability with Japanese data. The dates of th surveys were, respectively, Japan, 1955; France, 1948. The figures from the British sur (1950) were taken from Miller. For the U.S., the figures for rows 5, 6, and 7 were ta from Miller's report of the 1956 Michigan Survey data, 3, 4, and 8 from Lipset Bendix's reports of the 1952 Michigan Survey. (These figures have been challenged Miller [p. 28], but no alternatives are available.) The figure for row 9 derives Miller) from Centers' 1945 survey.

It is clear enough that there is no "normal" pattern of social mobility with which modern Japan can be compared, but one can single out one or two features in which Japan seems to be somewhat exceptional. For a society as generally mobile the proportion of nonagricultural laborers' sons who move up the prestige scale seems to be low. Conversely, the proportion of farmers' sons who move into nonmanual occupations seems to be unusually high. Japan is not *quite* an exception to the generalization supported by every other national study that it is more difficult to enter white-collar work from a rural background than from urban origins.[1] But it *is* an exception to the corollary that *a fortiori* it is more difficult to enter professional and managerial occupations from a rural background. (The difference is actually small: 6.7 percent of farm sons entered these occupations as opposed to 6.6 percent from the urban manual group.) That Japan, in the last generation at least, does not fit the usual picture of the "rural exodus" (which derives ultimately from the experience of nineteenth century England) is clear enough from the fact that the number who left farm families for *non*manual occupations exceeded the number who left for

[1] Miller, *Comparative Social Mobility*, p. 31.

urban manual occupations by 40 percent.[2] Others have noted the very high rate of recruitment of landlords' sons into the business elite,[3] and it seems likely that in the early Meiji period they had an equally disproportionate share in staffing many other elite occupations. The 1955 figures indicate that at more modest nonmanual levels, the inflow of farm sons has also been heavy.

Mechanisms of Mobility: Enterprise and Education

As in other countries, in modern Japan industrial or commercial enterprise and patronage (possibly formalized by marriage or adoption) have been joined and overshadowed by another major mechanism of intergenerational occupational mobility—educational selection. The professions, as elsewhere, were the first to be rationalized. In the early Meiji period one became a doctor or a lawyer, a journalist or a politician, by finding a patron—a friend of the family, a native of one's own district, or just a stranger whom one could manage to beard in an unguarded moment and impress with the sincerity of one's intentions and the earnestness of one's ambitions. Once taken into his household as a *shosei*, a secretary and runner of errands, one was assured of food and shelter, the chance to learn his profession and earn his continued patronage and perhaps one of his daughters.

[2] This result may be in part influenced by the slight overweighting of the Japanese sample with higher-status occupations. (See Nihon Shakai Gakkai Chōsakai, ed., *Nihon shakai no kaisoteki kōzō*, pp. 86–87.) Any adjustment on this score is unlikely to affect the striking contrast between Japan and France or the U.S., however, though according to one survey Switzerland is one European country which is similar to Japan in this respect. (See Lipset and Bendix, *Social Mobility*, p. 20.)

[3] See, in addition to the Abegglen and Mannari articles quoted above, T. C. Smith, "Landlords' Sons in the Business Elite," *Economic Development and Cultural Change*, ix, i, pt. 2 (1960).

The development of schools and universities changed all this. Competitive examinations for the civil service and state regulation of professional standards made it impossible by the turn of the century to enter government, medicine, teaching, or the law without a university degree.

The same trend can be traced in industry. Japan still has its self-made captains of industry, but in the upper and even in the middle reaches of the business hierarchy they are easily outnumbered by men who have made their careers in established corporations and prepared themselves for it with a university training. Smith has suggested that this process of bureaucratization in industry and emphasis on educational qualifications has proceeded more rapidly and at an earlier stage of industrial development in Japan than elsewhere, in part because in a late-developing country industry represents a sharper break with tradition and depends to a greater extent on learning than on inventiveness.[4] Another factor may well be the predominance from an early stage as pace-setters in the economy of the big *zaibatsu* enterprises which were closest to the bureaucratic traditions of the samurai with their emphasis on learning as a moral qualification for executive position.[5] At any rate the existence of the trend is not hard to document. Of a sample of business leaders in a directory of 1915, only 15 percent had been to a university. The figure was 83 percent for a similar sample from the 1955 edition. In the latter year 48 percent of the sample had spent all their working lives in salaried employment, compared with only 5 percent in the earlier sample.[6]

[4] Smith, "Landlords' Sons," p. 100.

[5] A random sample of men born between 1850 and 1869 who achieved enough "eminence" to appear in biographical dictionaries contained 13 directors of the big four *zaibatsu* companies and 63 directors of other companies whose backgrounds could be ascertained. Twelve of the 13 were of samurai or aristocratic origin, compared with 37 out of the 63.

[6] Asō Makoto, "Kindai Nihon ni okeru eriito-kōsei no hensen," *Kyōiku shakaigaku kenkyū,* xv (1960), pp. 158–59.

A wider survey, covering most of the directors of companies employing more than 1,000 workers, found in 1957 that of the 96 percent whose educational background was known, 70 percent had university degrees and another 20 percent some form of higher technical education.[7]

At more modest levels the picture is somewhat different. Another survey conducted by the Ministry of Education in 1955 found that the number of directors who had only an elementary school education—only 5 percent in the firms with more than 1,000 employees—increased to 15 percent for firms with 50–200 employees, and 30 percent for firms with 5–50.[8] It should not be forgotten that Japan is still a country in which a large section of the population are workers on their own account; craftsmen, shopkeepers, service workers, small workshop proprietors—men whose ambitions are directed not toward promotion but toward expansion. Since 1930, in a period when the number of wage-and-salary employees has risen from about ten to about twenty million, the number of self-employed has fluctuated around the four million mark (agriculture excluded), and they seem to have more than maintained a proportionate share in the national income; 19.9 percent in 1930 and 15.4 percent in 1959.[9]

Even so, this does not mean that there are four million "eels in the basket," to use the Japanese metaphor, all struggling and hoping to get to the top. In both 1950 and 1955, two thirds of these self-employed workers were in tertiary occupations, nearly a half in the wholesale and retail trade.[10] Many of these run inherited businesses and are, perhaps, no

[7] Shimizu Yoshihiro, *Shiken* (1957), p. 107. The survey covered 3,552 directors in 316 companies.

[8] Japan, Mombushō, Chōsakyoku, Chōsaka, *Shokushu to gakureki* (1955), p. 23.

[9] Japan, Keizai Kikakuchō, *Kokumin shotoku hakusho 34-nendo* (1961), p. 166.

[10] Japan, Prime Minister's Office, Statistics Bureau, *1955 Population Census of Japan,* II, 2 (1957), p. 56.

less conservatively oriented to maintaining their present position than that other large sector of independent enterprisers, the nation's five million farmers. Of those who started a business in their own lifetime, a good proportion have probably done so by the *noren-wake* process of commercial parthenogenesis, and the employee who is set up on his own is likely to depend on the patronage of the "main house" in a way which inhibits expansionist ambitions. (It would be bad form, at the very least, to excel the *honke,* at any rate during the first master's lifetime.) Of the million or so independent workers and unincorporated enterprisers in the manufacturing sector, too, a good many are dependent on subcontracting from the major firms, with only limited chances of breaking free. In established industries, in any case, the small man has little chance of wresting a corner of the market from the bureaucratized corporations. New fields offer better chances, and it is significant that some of today's best-known self-made men, such as Matsushita or Ibuka the creator of Sony, are in the electrical industries. These, however, are increasingly fields in which the entrepreneur must have, or be able to hire, highly educated technological skill.

Even Without an Education is the title of one of the "success books" published in 1957,[11] but its biographies of ten company presidents, politicians, artists, and trade unionists dwell on how they *overcame the handicap* of not having a university education. For those who hope to get to the top a degree is not simply a short cut, it is the only route which does not lead through bogs and thickets.

And so it has been for the last half-century. If the typical aspirant of the early Meiji period was the *shosei,* his early twentieth century equivalent was the *kugakusei,* the lad from the country inspired by articles in the magazines on "How To Live in Tokyo on 6.50 Yen a Month," making his way through the university on a diet of rice, dried fish, and

[11] Ogiya Seizō, *Gakkō wa denakute mo* (1957).

bean curd, supplementing a meager parental allowance with his
own occasional earnings but sustained through it all by
hopes of glittering rewards to follow, of honor in his
native village,[12] of the gratifying glow of virtue fulfilled in
which he would kneel at the *butsudan*—the ancestors' shrine
—and tell them that he had made—or restored—the family's
fortune.

Just as higher education became necessary to enter the
professional and managerial classes, so secondary schools
played an increasingly important part in selecting and
training the lower grades of nonmanual workers: the technicians and supervisors, bookkeepers and draftsmen of the
larger firms—and also many of those who inherited small
businesses or succeeded in developing their own. The following figures give an indication of the development of secondary education and of the way in which, as the pace of industrialization quickened in the twenties and thirties, the academic middle schools, with curricula primarily designed for
that fifth of their pupils who went on to high school and
university, began to be overtaken by the development of
technical and commercial secondary schools.

TABLE 2

Boy Pupils per 10,000 Population
in Secondary Schools[13]

	Academic	Technical and Vocational
1895	6.2	1.5
1920	31.9	26.3*
1930	54.1	48.0*
1940	60.5	65.5
1959 (High Schools)	101.4	143.3

* Figures include some girls, though not more than 20 percent.

[12] For illustrations of the importance of the village community as
a reference group, see Iwai Hiroaki, *Kyōsō, seikō, shusse* (1956), p. 36.
[13] Figures from Japan, Mombushō, Kyōikushi-hensankai, *Meiji ikō
kyōikuseido hattatsushi* (1938) and (last two rows) Japan, Prime
Minister's Office, Bureau of Statistics, *Statistical Yearbook of Japan*.

Because the expansion of education kept up with the changing demands of industry so well that in depression years and slow-growth years the secondary schools and universities have "overproduced" graduates, it has been possible for employers gradually to raise their recruiting standards. The position has long since been reached where it is next to impossible to enter a firm at managerial level without a university degree or to obtain a clerical position without high school graduation. Today many of the most go-ahead firms in leading sectors such as the electrical, optical, and chemical industries, whose high wages enable them to take their pick on the labor market, accept none but high school graduates even for manual occupations.

This gradual raising of educational barriers has presumably been even more decisive for intergeneration mobility because of the declining rate of intrageneration mobility. Larger firms are the ones which adopt "the typically Japanese" employment practices of the Abegglen pattern (the life-long commitment, and the status systems inhibiting promotion from manual to nonmanual and from clerical to managerial positions). As they come to occupy a growing sector of the economy, an individual's first job is increasingly likely to determine the rest of his career.

The importance of educational selection very probably explains the peculiar features of the Japanese mobility pattern that were noted in the last section. Except for the lower normal schools that trained elementary school teachers and the military schools, both of which were open to families that could just manage to forego a child's earnings beyond the age of thirteen even if they could not contribute to his support, secondary education has been beyond the reach of the poorest families.[14] But if the urban working class could

---

[14] Some other forms of secondary education were state subsidized, but, as a writer giving advice to students pointed out in the magazine *Seikō* (Sept. 1915), although students at the Higher Normal School got a subsidy of 7 yen a month and those at the Communica-

not afford the education which would make their children candidates for nonmanual jobs, small landlords and owner-farmers with largish holdings probably could—if not out of income at least out of capital. It was always possible to sell a small piece of land or fell a few trees and so give a younger son his customary inheritance portion in cash. In 1939 farmers' sons accounted for 16.2 percent of Tokyo University students. Manual laborers' children were included in the 1.4 percent of "others" in the classification of parental occupations.[15]

The same cost factor still operates to reduce the possibility of upward mobility from the working class. With considerably higher present-day incomes nearly half of the nation's parents can now manage the expense of keeping their children at high school for three years beyond the compulsory education period,[16] and another 10 percent of each age group work their way through part-time high schools. But the $2,000 or more which it can cost to put a son through a private university is beyond the means of manual workers. State universities with much cheaper fees require about half that amount and a bright child can cover most of the cost with scholarships and side earnings, but the son of a manual worker, living in a crowded home, unable to buy the

---

tions Technicians Center 10 yen a month, candidates had to be middle school graduates (5 years of fee paying) and the courses took 4 years. The best bargain he could recommend was the Waseda technical school, which offered a 2½-year education for upper elementary graduates (i.e., those already 2 years beyond the compulsory level) at an average expenditure of 3 yen a month (plus 7–11 yen a month living expenses if one's home was not in Tokyo). This would guarantee a starting wage of 15 to 18 yen a month.

[15] Shimizu Yoshihiro, *Shiken*, p. 110.

[16] For an analysis of the relation between I.Q., parental income, and high school entrance in a Hikone middle school, which shows that ability and economic circumstances are about equally determinant factors, see Moriguchi Kenji, "Nyūgaku-shiken no genkyō to sono shakaigakuteki bunseki," *Kyōiku shakaigaku kenkyū*, x (1956), p. 19.

books or the private tuition of his middle-class competitors (70 percent of Tokyo University entrants have spent one or two years after high school in special cram schools preparing for the entrance examination) has a poor chance in the stiff competition for places at the best state universities.[17] Prefectural universities are easier to enter, but they offer less chance of scholarship assistance, fewer opportunities for side earnings, and much inferior chances on the labor market after graduation.

Mechanisms of Mobility: Patronage

The patronage on which the *shosei* relied did not totally lose its importance with the development of the school system. The schools provided a preliminary filter which screened candidates for jobs. The practice of further rationalizing the process of selection by competitive entrance examinations was started by the bigger firms early in this century and now has become almost universal in all but the smallest firms. But these are only eliminating contests. There is still scope for patronage to operate in the final de-

[17] Two analyses of the occupations of fathers of Tokyo University students produce the following figures:

	All Entering Students, 1957[a]	4th-Year Students, Faculty of Arts, 1955[b]
Business proprietors	18.7%	15.9%
Independent merchants, craftsmen	—	18.4%
Government officials	22.8%	11.2%
Teachers	—	12.9%
(Other) professionals	11.8%	8.2%
Other salaried workers	29.8%	18.9%
Farmers	5.4%	6.9%
Laborers	—	4.3%
Others	1.9%	4.3%
Not employed	9.6%	

[a] Shimizu, *Shiken*, p. 110.
[b] Ozaki Morimitsu, "Kyōiku, toku ni kōtō-kyōiku to shakai-kaiso no kankei," *Kyōiku shakaigaku kenkyū*, xi (1957), p. 95.

cision taken at the second—the interview—stage of selection. The personal connections along which it flows, however, are not simply of the old type based on kinship and local community ties. Of nearly equal importance are connections formed within the school or university—themselves, therefore, a product of the educational selection process.

At the university level the appointments bureau—a large organization employing, in the big universities, twenty or thirty people under the direction of a professorial committee —exists to forge these links. How they work is described in an unusually frank contribution to a book entitled *How I Got My Job*,[18] by a journalist who graduated from Hōsei University in the slump year of 1955, when the universities were producing more graduates than the market would bear. He describes how he began planning his "job-getting strategy" in a mood of despair. This was a difficult year, many of his classmates already had assured niches thanks to some family connection, and his one single hopeful *kone* (connection), an uncle, was likely (as he did) to prove a broken reed. He decided to let no considerations of pride block his chances. His first move was to ingratiate himself with key officials in the appointments bureau by helping to stick on stamps and address envelopes. The normal procedure is for firms to use the appointments bureau to secure recommended candidates for their initial entrance examinations, usually by a quota system, inviting a fixed number of candidates from favored universities. In his year there were enough invitations for each graduating student to make only three applications, but his softening-up of the appointments bureau enabled him to make six. With applications sent in, the business of establishing *kone* began. A professor of the appointments committee gave him an introduction to one of the school's trustees, who passed him on to a Hōsei graduate now managing a branch of one of the banks he had applied to enter.

[18] Koyama Shoten, ed., *Watashi wa kōshite shūshoku shita* (1956), pp. 10–39.

Presents were presumably taken to each, and he describes how each piece of "inside news" about his chances which the manager vouchsafed him—including the final tip that he had failed in the interview—was faithfully reported back with grateful expressions of thanks to the two intermediaries in his chain of introductions. Eventually these tactics succeed at the *Yomiuri* newspaper, where again he was introduced to an influential Hōsei graduate. In this case the introduction took the form not of a note scribbled on the back of a visiting card but of a full-scale delegation—he went accompanied by a professor and a member of the appointments bureau in one of the university cars, which at this season of the year scurry all over Tokyo on such errands. Thanks to the intervention of his *sempai* (senior fellow alumnus) his good showing in the written examination got him the job, despite a miserable performance in the interview.

Schools perform a similar function lower down the scale. Some elementary school teachers spend weeks of each school year touring factories—preferably those whose owner or manager is a native of their district—to arrange employment for the children about to leave school, or at least to arrange that they be allowed to take the manual aptitude and intelligence tests by which the firm selects its employees. When the textile workers' union tries to enforce wage agreements it is to school teachers (through the teachers' union) that it sends circulars warning against sending children to firms which underpay.

But here too the *kone* (or rather the indigenous Japanese word *enko* is the one used at this level of society) created by the school is only an alternative—and a weaker alternative—to the use of kinship connections. These count for a good deal in the still-large sector of the small and medium enterprises, and it is probable that they always have been of major importance, especially for rural migrants. The boy who goes to the city and tramps the streets looking for work seems to have been a rarity in the history of Japanese industrialization. In a society where personal connections are sedulously cultivated (and in which the populace was literate and capable of writing letters before industrialization started) most people could find some lever to use on behalf of their spare sons, and employers who were willing to take all comers, unintroduced and unguaranteed, were rare.

The guarantee aspect of the personal connection is an important one from the employer's point of view. Most personnel managers in the larger firms acknowledge that they always take *kone* into account in the marginal case for the perfectly rational reason that the string-puller within the firm can act as guarantor for the inductee's good behavior.[19] Some firms, particularly old established ones,[20] carry this principle to the point of limiting applications for their entrance examinations to those who have a personal connection with an established employee. The function of the "personal guarantor," a relic of the preindividuated days of the five-man group system, is taken much more seriously in Japan than in the Anglo-Saxon world, where he survives solely as a writer of references and a witness to signatures on legal documents. Employers usually require a personal guarantor (*mimoto hoshōnin*), and he may be sued successfully if the guaranteed employee absconds with the firm's funds, provided that the employer plays his part by sending the guarantor regular annual reports on his protégé's conduct.[21]

There *are* firms, however, which eschew the use of personal connections as a matter of rigid policy on the grounds that favoritism creates bad feeling and prevents objective personnel management. Thus a father or an uncle in one of the Mitsubishi enterprises can help one to get a job in another

[19] See the discussion between personnel managers in Koyama Shoten, *Watashi wa kōshite*, p. 75.

[20] Such as the department stores Mitsukoshi and Isetan, the Tokyo Gas Company, Ajinomoto and Nippon Cement. (*Ibid.*, p. 175.)

[21] *Ibid.*, p. 164.

Mitsubishi firm, but not in his own. Even such firms, however, may be influenced by personal connections for different profit-maximizing reasons—as, for instance, when they give special consideration to relatives of major creditors or customers of the firm.

Thus, in these marginal forms the older particularistic patterns of behavior survive around the edges of the new objective selection procedures. So well have they survived, in fact, that Kawashima has described the careful nurturing of personal connections and the formation of patron-client relations as the major ingredient of the typical Japanese recipe for success.[22] It is true that the use of patronage has reverberating consequences. The young man whose Hōsei connection got him into the *Yomiuri* is in duty bound to count himself a member of the Hōsei *batsu*—his university's faction—within the firm, with its hierarchical structure of relations between *sempai* and *kōhai*—seniors and juniors. He must loyally support his *sempai* (in particular the one who got him his job) in any internecine struggle; he must help *kōhai* to get into the firm and so increase the *batsu*'s strength: his own chances of advancement may depend on it. How far the resultant cliquishness really impedes the efficiency of Japanese bureaucratic organizations is doubtful; the same personality characteristics which breed loyalty to the clique also develop loyalty to the firm or to the ministry (more especially to the firm than to the ministry, though the "family feeling" of ministries like Agriculture and Forestry is well known). Hence sectional interests are less likely to take absolute precedence when they conflict with the goals of the whole organization. It is clear, too, that the initial screening procedures reduce the damage of patronage in personnel selection. The effects of nepotism are considerably modified if all the nephews are of uniform ability.

It seems, in any case, that reliance on personal connections

---

[22] See his article on "Risshin shusse" reprinted in Kawashima Takeyoshi, *Nihon no shakai to seikatsu ishiki* (1955).

is not an immutable Japanese cultural pattern unrelated to the market situation. The last few years have seen a growing shortage of middle-school graduates (fifteen-year-olds who leave school at the end of the compulsory education period). One result has been a marked increase in the use of state labor exchanges for factory labor recruitment. Employers apply to the exchanges because they can no longer be sure of getting all the workers they want by personal recommendations. Hence the school-leaver finds that the labor exchange offers a more attractive choice of jobs than he could get through the good offices of his teachers or his uncles. He can get his job, moreover, without the *cost* of patronage, the cost in thank-you presents, in anxiety over whether the present is of the right value, in a continuing sense of obligation to his patron. Similarly, at the university level, as graduates have recently been in little danger of not finding a job, fewer are reduced to licking stamps in the appointments bureau office.

Ideals and Aspirations: Meiji Japan

The Meiji Restoration, and the drive to "civilization and enlightenment" which followed it, probably left the majority of Japanese little affected, hoping for and expecting out of life not much more than their fathers had had. But for the young ex-samurai, and for those among the wealthier commoners who had absorbed enough of the culture of their betters to feel at home in the samurai world, the new regime ushered in an age of opportunity. As Fukuzawa Yukichi wrote in 1882, it was (or it was believed to be) an *udemae no shakai*[23]—a society in which only ability counted and a self-made younger brother could laugh at the petty authority of his poverty-stricken elder brother. The prevalence of this belief that courage, energy, and initiative could carry a man anywhere, however humble his origins, is clear enough in

[23] Quoted from *Tokuiku ikan* in Kamishima Jirō, *Kindai Nihon no seishin kōzō* (1960), p. 327.

the biographies of those who were young at the time. It accounts for the enthusiastic reception of Nishimura's translation of Smiles' *Self-Help*, for the fact that an American
missionary teacher who stayed in Japan for only a few
months could earn a permanent place in Japanese folklore by
uttering the slogan "Boys, be ambitious!" and for the frequency with which popular writings and books of moral
exhortation reechoed the phrase *risshin-shusse*—"raise yourself
and make your way in the world."

This was not a sudden and aberrant eruption of an ideology totally at variance with the ethos of the preceding
regime. Bellah has shown how, according to the ideal ethic
of the Tokugawa period at least, mere ascription was not
sufficient validation of claims to status without adequate
performance of the roles prescribed for that status.[24] What
is more, by the nineteenth century it was more than ever
possible for status to be achieved. The bureaucracies of the
fiefs and of the *bakufu* provided opportunities, occasional
and precarious though they might be, for ambitious men
to rise to positions of power and prestige. The development of formal education in Chinese ethical and political
philosophy and in Chinese and Japanese history gave many
young men the hubris and the theories to set about trying
to remake their world after their own ideas—and a good
many of them found satisfaction in dying heroically in the
attempt. The schools also gave them, as did their training in
the individualistic military skills of fencing and the use of
the lance, the experience of competitive striving. A prize
pupil at the Akita fief school describes how he and three
of his dormitory friends engaged in a prolonged reading
competition, and describes it in a success magazine in 1904
as experience relevant to twentieth century youth:[25] "We
really went all out that month. If one of us got a page ahead
the others would turn pale. We hardly took time off to chew

[24] R. N. Bellah, *Tokugawa Religion* (1957).
[25] Nemoto Tsūmei in *Seikō*, 1, 1 (1902), p. 8.

our food properly, and we drank as little water as possible in order that the others should not get ahead in the time wasted going to the lavatory—so keen were we to get a line or two ahead of the others."

The Meiji period greatly widened the prospects of those who had this kind of drive to succeed, and it set the seal of official approval on their ambitious efforts, for it was now official doctrine that the *nation* had to progress and that it could only do so by mobilizing all the talents of individuals devoted to strenuous self-improvement.

The new ethic was gradually diffused beyond the circle of the ex-samurai elite, by example, by the gradual removal of all legal status distinctions, and more particularly by the schools. The virtues of independent initiative, of dogged determination and healthy ambition, the possibility of rising from humble origins to positions of eminence, were illustrated in the ethics text books used in elementary schools by stories of Abraham Lincoln and Benjamin Franklin, of Florence Nightingale and the persevering bridge-builder George Edwards, of Ninomiya Sontoku, the Tokugawa peasant exemplar of the virtues of studious diligence, thrift, enterprise, and public service, and of Toyotomi Hideyoshi, the poor peasant who conquered Japan.

By the time these attitudes and beliefs spread to the mass of the Japanese people the change in the mechanisms of mobility noted earlier was already well under way. Educational qualifications had become all-important, and the rising level of aspirations was reflected, therefore, in a growing pressure on the schools. At the lowest level this can be seen in the sudden rise in the number of elementary school pupils after 1890. (Fees were not abolished until 1898.) By the turn of the century the compulsory provisions of the educational ordinances had ceased to be declarations of pious intention. Whereas for the first quarter-century statutory provision had been ahead of public demand, thereafter it lagged behind. When the period of compulsory education was extended to six years in 1907 the vast majority of children were already taking the voluntary two extra years of the upper elementary school beyond the compulsory four. The situation was similar at the next extension of the compulsory period in 1940.

The same expansion in demand took place at the secondary levels. In 1896, 25,000 pupils competed for the 18,000 places in middle schools, and 2,159 applied for 1,210 places in the upper secondary schools which led directly and almost automatically to Tokyo University. By 1909 the numbers of places in both kinds of school had nearly doubled, but the numbers of applicants were respectively three and four times the earlier figure. Only 56 percent of applicants were successful for middle schools and only 23 percent for high schools, compared with 71 percent and 56 percent in the earlier year.[26] These figures make no allowance for multiple applications, so that it is impossible to estimate how many were in fact thwarted in their ambitions, but they are a sufficient indication of the stiffening competition which set in train that process, lamented by Japanese educators since the twenties, whereby school education has become increasingly geared to securing successes in the entrance examinations of schools at the next highest level.

But if the expansion of educational facilities could not keep up with the demand, it did run ahead of the expansion of industry and the bureaucracies. A contributor to a *Taiyō* symposium on the state of the nation wrote, in 1911, that whereas in the early Meiji period a student could get through a university at a cost of 15 to 20 yen a month and walk into a 100-yen-a-month job when he graduated, the modern student expected to spend 40 to 50 yen a month and could hardly hope to earn more than 20 yen at the end of it; indeed, if he were at one of the lesser private universities, he would be lucky not to find himself unemployed.[27]

[26] Figures from the various volumes of Japan, Mombushō, *Meiji ikō*.
[27] Nakamura Fusetsu in *Taiyō*, xvii, 3 (1911), p. 17.

Thus the shining ideal of success was already somewhat tarnished by the early years of the twentieth century. The formalization of the criteria for entry and promotion in the civil service, the armed forces, the professions, and the bureaucracies of the favored *zaibatsu* firms made the possibility of meteoric advancement more and more remote. The struggle to get one's foot on the right educational ladder was harder, and the pay-off less certain. As the new ruling class settled comfortably to the enjoyment of its perquisites, it became less concerned to use patronage for the purpose of advancing the able in the national interest (which certainly was *one* important consideration of the early Meiji oligarchs) and more concerned to advance the prospects of family dependents—and the older those philoprogenitive "young men of Meiji" got, the more dependents they had to promote. There is not much confident optimism about the hero of a *Mita bungaku* short story written in 1910. As he wavers between the defeatist impulse to give up the fight and leave Tokyo for his country home and the still surviving hope that *luck* will come his way, his dream of success is provided by a former classmate who marries the daughter of a rich banker.[28]

The ideology was not immediately modified, however, although it was subject to greater doubts. In its early twentieth century version it is reflected in a magazine called *Seikō—Success*—which was founded in 1902 and published monthly until 1915. The foreign sources of its inspiration are clear. It was avowedly modeled on an American magazine of the same title and frequently reprinted some of its articles. Its first issue featured a picture of Lincoln's log cabin, and later issues carried large advertisements for American success books such as Roosevelt's *Strenuous Life* and Marden's *Pushing to the Front*, translated by members of the *Seikō* staff. The editor claimed Samuel Smiles as his great forerunner and used "Self-Help" as his own main pen name. Smiles was, indeed, very much a living force. When *Seikō*,

[28] Kuroda Kōzan, "Tateta hashi," *Mita bungaku*, I, 1 (1910).

for one of its New Year issues, asked thirty eminent contemporaries to recommend for modern youth a work of spiritual sustenance "equivalent to the Bible for Christians," half of them suggested Smiles' *Self-Help*.[29]

The purpose of the magazine, as the editor described it in his initial statement of principles,[30] was indeed to keep alive the Smiles tradition. He was concerned at the growing predominance of the organization man, the "clever young modern who has no fixed principles and knows only to ingratiate himself with people by smooth words and a smiling face." He would not advocate a return to the ideal of the late Tokugawa *rōnin*, the "Oriental-style hero with wildly unkempt hair and no manners, given to loud, large, and boastful talk but lacking in practical ability." His was rather the ideal of the "man of character who helps himself and respects himself, lives by his own enterprise and his own toil, and creates his own fate by the exercise of his own abilities." It was the object of the magazine to encourage the development of such character, to counter undesirable trends among contemporary youth, to give spiritual encouragement to the *kugakusei*—the student struggling under difficult conditions—and at the same time to give practical advice on the choice of occupation and methods of study.

And as in Smiles, the keynote of the magazine's moral message is perseverance, determination, and self-denial. Even the great inventors, we are told in the first issue (p. 48) were not just the happy recipients of a sudden flash of inspiration. Many men are called to have ideas, but only the few choose to show the determination which enables them to persevere and develop these ideas into something of value. Likewise, the man who seeks wealth without work by speculation is condemned out of hand on the authority of Andrew Carnegie (p. 50).

But compared with its foreign counterparts the magazine offers a distinctly studious and bookish version of success.

[29] III, 4 (Jan. 1904).   [30] I, 1 (Nov. 1902).

Its readers were mainly middle-class students. The samurai traditions which elevated government and warfare above the baser pursuits of industry and trade could be carried over into the Meiji period because the political revolution preceded the industrial revolution and businessmen remained the clients of the statesmen rather than vice versa. The result was that the prime object of the young aspirant's ambition remained an official or a military career. The list of supporters in the first issue contains many famous names from the universities and journalism, doctors of philosophy and science, generals and admirals, but hardly any businessmen. The famous Japanese held up as models to contemporary youth are mostly scholars, writers, or military men. The translated articles featuring Carnegie and Vanderbilt and American agricultural millionaires are almost the only ones which laud the businessman, and when the magazine does print an article on Shibusawa Eiichi, the Meiji entrepreneur par excellence, the emphasis is all on the perseverance with which he pursued his studies in youth.[31]

In effect, *Seikō* was a journal of the official and semiofficial establishment written for aspirants to establishment positions. As such there was a contradiction between its concealed assumptions and the overt ideal of self-help. The original Smilesian doctrine was planted firmly in the context of laissez-faire liberalism. Success, by individual self-cultivation, was possible for *every* man.[32] The competition of the market was only the mechanism by which each individual could be guided into the field where his talents gave him comparative advantage and where he could best contribute to the welfare of his fellow men, not a battleground where one man's success could be bought only at the price of another man's failure. It was this generous, optimistic side of the Smiles message which commended him to

[31] VIII, 2 (1906).
[32] See Asa Briggs' introduction to the centenary edition of *Self-Help* (London, 1958).

Robert Blatchford in England and which explains, perhaps, why the early issues of *Seikō* contained contributions from Nishikawa Kōjirō, advertisements for the socialist journal *Rō-dō no Sekai*, and answers to questionnaires by socialist leaders such as Abe Isō, Sakai Toshihiko, and Kōtoku Shūsui. But the success aimed at by the *kugakusei* reader of *Seikō* was success in competitive examinations which *was* success only because others failed. Inoue Tetsujirō strikes a strident and somewhat discordant note in the first number of the magazine (p. 30). "Today, competition is the keynote of the field of learning, a place where examinations sort out the superior from the inferior. It is the battleground of intellect. The inferior are pushed to the rear and only the victorious advance from victory to victory."

The competition was to grow keener in the succeeding years, the chances of failure more apparent, the confident self-helper less and less common than the anxious climber "who has no fixed principles and knows only to ingratiate himself with people by smooth words and a smiling face." A decade later the tenor of the magazine changed. More space is devoted to readers' bread and butter queries, the careful requests for practical information from humble aspirants to middle-income security—which schools are cheapest, will this or that career offer better chances of promotion, what of pension prospects, and the chances of exemption from conscription? The brusqueness with which the answers are given and the high-handed tone of the instructions to readers which head the section suggest a certain irritation, as if this were a grudging concession to the weakness of the flesh, an unwilling perversion of the editors' original intention to keep the whole affair on a plane of moral uplift.

Eventually, in 1915, the editor finds a way out of the tension between the grandeur of his ideals and the reality of the selfish competitive ambitions to which he is ministering. The solution is one in keeping with the growing nationalism of the times and with the growing emphasis in education on "loyalty and filial piety" which pushed some of the earlier success stories out of the primary school text books and replaced them with anecdotes of loyal retainers devoted to the service of the Imperial throne. The September 1915 issue of the magazine proclaims a new editorial policy based on "the doctrine of strength." Whatever the outcome of the struggle in Europe, runs the editorial declaration, it is certain that the world which emerges will be one of intensified struggle for survival. Weak countries will go to the wall. *Seikō* will henceforth preach the "doctrine of strength" to ensure that Japan secures "absolute victory" in the struggle. It will foster the development of strong men, "of iron will and iron physique," men with "a positive aggressive energy, a spirit of independence, men of a healthy outlook, abreast of their times." This is no time for "empty theories and empty argument." The nation needs wealth as well as intelligence and ability; it must produce the men who will advance to seize this wealth in the competitive markets of the world. Science must be developed for the national advantage. A new original culture blending East and West must be created; the superior qualities of the Japanese race must be fostered by ever greater emphasis on the essence of the "national morality," the nurturing of the *Yamato-damashii*, the spirit of Old Japan. Japan must learn the lesson of the strong nations, that only those peoples come out on top who direct their energies to expansion abroad.

Competition in the struggle for survival is thus brought to the forefront, but in terms of national, not of individual, goals. Attention is to be focussed on the international competition in which the failures are Japan's defeated competitors, not on the internecine competition in which it is one's less successful classmates who have to go to the wall. And it is not without relevance that success in the international competition was to provide more jobs and reduce the number of disappointed failures at home. The same issue of the magazine contains articles on opportunities in the colonies and on how to become a farmer-colonist in Manchuria. The cover illustration showing the predatory hands of the Western powers clawing at a map of China shows the immediate direction of the contemporary nationalist's ambitions.

It would be too simple to suggest that it was the internal pressure caused by the excess of awakened aspirations over opportunities which accounted for the development of nationalism in twentieth century Japan and its direction into channels of military expansion, though this may well have been one factor. It may at least be true that fervent nationalism took an easier grip on the nation in that it provided vicarious alternative satisfactions to those who had been disappointed in the struggle for success. A writer who suggests this quotes as a telling illustration Tayama Katai's novel *The Country Schoolmaster*.[33] The hero, a young man of burning ambition, is thwarted in his plans for self-advancement partly by circumstances, partly by his own lack of persistence. He drowns his disappointment and self-contempt in drink and dissipation, recovers his pride and discipline only when it is too late; he finds himself hopelessly consumptive. But he dies happily, for the Russo-Japanese war is being fought. He follows Japan's successes with enthusiasm and is killed by his joyous excitement at the news of the fall of Port Arthur.

Ideals and Aspirations: Postwar

Postwar Japan is no longer engaged in the same kind of competitive struggle against the rest of the world. Except in the periods of national hysteria set off by each Olympic Games, or in the odd moment when he reads in his newspaper of Japanese exporters' efforts to capture the transistor market, the success the average Japanese looks forward to is

[33] Ogawa Tarō, *Risshin-shusse-shugi no kyōiku* (1957), p. 116. The novel is *Inaka kyōshi*.

not Japan's success. It may sometimes be his firm's success, or the success of his favorite baseball team or *sumō* wrestler, but most commonly and universally it is his own success or that of his children.

Of the very wide diffusion of the ambition to "get on," the postwar development of schools and universities is sufficient evidence. In no other country outside the United States are 60 percent of the nation's parents willing to buy for their children three years' extra education beyond the compulsory nine. The vast expansion in university education (in 1940 there were twelve, and in 1959 fifty-five, university students per 10,000 population) has not been induced by public provision and state scholarship aid but as a private enterprise response to an effective economic demand. Sixty-four percent of these students are (1959) at unsubsidized private universities, and the majority of the remainder at public universities get no scholarship help toward paying the more modest fees required.

The tendency for overproduction of graduates to cheapen the value of a degree has made it increasingly important not just to get to a university but to get to the *best* university. There are enough students who would prefer to spend one, two, or even three years preparing for renewed attempts at the entrance examination of a high-prestige university, rather than accept a place at a second-rate institution, for hundreds of preparatory cram schools to flourish in all the major cities. In 1957, 46 percent of the successful applicants to Tokyo University were taking the examination for the second, 18 percent for the third, and 8 percent for the fourth or more time.[34] In all state universities in that year students coming straight from high school made up only 52 percent of successful entrants. At Hitotsubashi, the former State University of Commerce, and at Keio, the businessman's university par excellence, the proportion has been as low as 21

[34] Shimizu Yoshihiro, *Shiken*, p. 32.

percent and 19 percent respectively.[35] The social cost of this competitive pressure can be seen in the drawn faces and cat-napping exhaustion of fifteen-year-olds commuting for hours across Tokyo to a "good" high school, in the women's magazine articles on nourishing diets for examinees, in the sales of Benzedrine to teenagers, most ominously in the sui-cide statistics. The ages fifteen to twenty-five, which in most countries have one of the lowest suicide rates, in Japan have one of the highest.

Much of the success literature of modern Japan is aimed at the university student, and the career for which it as-sumes him to be headed is that of the *sarari-man*, the organiza-tion businessman not, as in the earlier literature, for govern-ment, scholarship, or the professions. A correlative difference is that these books have a much less confident tone than their earlier counterparts; their authors are more openly aware of the dilemmas which afflicted the editors of *Seikō* half a cen-tury before. In a society where old Japanese ideals of service to the nation are now reinforced by—or reinterpreted into—a left-wing condemnation of capitalist self-seeking, moneymak-ing is an ambition which has to be defended. One writer acknowledges a tendency (which he dates from the twenties) to associate the word "success" solely with unworthy ambi-tions to enter the ruling capitalist class. Now, he urges, trade union leadership offers a new, and from this point of view unexceptionable, route to success.[36] Another rejects the view he finds implicit in school children's answer to a question-naire—that worldly success is incompatible with the desire to lead the just life. The world is, in fact, designed to produce a perfect harmony between the two.[37] His is not the classical liberal doctrine whereby individual self-seeking is translated into the common good by the mechanism of the market, how-

[35] Ogawa, *Risshin-shusse*, p. 182.

[36] Ishimori Kenkichi, *Seikō suru hito no tame ni* (1957), preface.

[37] Yarita Ken'ichi, *Seikō e no nijū no michi* (1957), p. 18. For a similar defense of "success" see Fujiwara Ginjirō, *Shose no gijutsu 50-kajō* (1957), p. 8.

ever. Divine providence works the other way round—the Calvinist way—to ensure that only those who lead the moral life and have the common good in mind *do* succeed. "The first thing to consider is not how you can make money, but how you can benefit other people. In other words, altruism should be your starting point. If it is, then you are bound to succeed and the money will pile up."[38]

These authors are also disturbed that so many Japanese youths have learned to tailor their ambitions to their realistic prospects. They deplore (and this, again, they have in common with left-wing writers) the privatized pettiness of the young men who have lowered their sights to a cosy little home in the suburbs, a pretty wife, a couple of kids, and the occasional game of golf. They object not only to the meanness of these aims, but also to the consumption orientation revealed in the openness with which so many young men nowadays acknowledge them. Real success does not come to those who concentrate on the emoluments. These books do not dwell on the glamor and glitter of the rewards; the emphasis is all on the virtuous traveling rather than the arrival. Hard work and perseverance have a value far beyond their instrumental efficacy.

This is, indeed, an element of tradition still very much alive, and it is one which has institutional support in the schools, where there is a considerable reluctance to acknowledge the importance of innate ability in determining academic or any other kind of success. Determined application, it is thought, can compensate for most natural deficiencies. It is significant that intelligence tests have never been popular in Japan. They were introduced for university and high school selection after the last war, but by 1955 they were almost everywhere abandoned in favor of tests of academic achievement which the persistent can take year after year until they succeed.

But if hard work and persistence are important in getting

[38] *Ibid.*, p. 291.

into a good firm, are they enough to guarantee one's rise within it? Here again the more sententious authors have a hard time trying to impose their moral order on a recalcitrant world. They are aware of a persistent and widespread view that the road to success involves a departure from the norms of personal integrity, truthfulness, and independence which are acknowledged by the modern Japanese middle class. *Twenty Roads to Success* quotes Genji Keita, a bestselling novelist who has catered for the salary-man's taste for tolerant self-contempt by a fairly realistic portrayal of life in the offices and in the restaurants and brothels where business is done. Genji's recipe for success as a salary man is first of all ability, then luck and graduation from the right school. You must get on well with people. Finally, you must be able to flatter your superiors and keep cleverly abreast of the currents of clique politics within the firm (p. 44). These remarks, says the author, "raise very important issues" which unfortunately he has no space to go into. Instead he offers his own prescriptions—honest devotion and application to whatever task is set you, speedy and accurate work, and nice manners.

Faithful and loyal service is the message of another writer. The salary man is selling his labor. He should make sure that it is of good quality. Get enough sleep at night to make sure you are alert. To avoid tiredness never push back when you are pushed in the rush-hour crush. "Remember that even in the sixteen hours of the day when you are not working your body is, as it were, only partly put in your safe keeping."[39] Give that little bit extra. If you are told to fetch the boss's shoes, fetch them *and* give them a little polish (p. 67). Show your respect for your superior's expertise—but without too ostentatious flattery. Don't try to buy favors with gifts. If you do see something which exactly suits your superior's tastes, you may bring it along to him and say "I

[39] Fujiwara, *Shose no gijutsu*, p. 44.

142

thought you would be sure to like this." But to buy the banal box of cakes and offer it with the traditional formula, "It is an unworthy thing, but . . ." is simply self-abasing.

These middle-class modifications of the morality typical of traditional Japanese relations of patronage disappear as soon as one moves down the scale to the success literature written for those who do not begin their career as university graduates. The heroes of the monthly magazine *Life: In Full* are not the big corporation presidents but the smaller men who have carved out their own tiny territory in the shadow world of commerce and the smaller industrial enterprises, the owner of a chain of Osaka restaurants, the farmer who eventually succeeds in a life-long search for a new hot-spring well and becomes proprietor of a large tourist hotel, the drapery shop assistant who sets up on his own account, the men who have made their pile playing—but not manipulating—the stock exchange. There is not much moralizing here about service to society, though in the "this is my life" department, a barber speaks feelingly of the opportunity his profession gives him to live a life of sincerity, and deplores the world's general lack of recognition of the high standards of scientific knowledge required for good barbering and of its importance as a means of realizing the potentialities of human beauty (p. 72). Perhaps more typical, however, is the man who describes as the drive which has carried him to success his youthful ambition "to ride to Tokyo second-class, smoking Shikishima [the best] cigarettes" (p. 27).[40] The December 1961 issue has a special collection of articles on "How To Charm Your Way through the World" containing practical advice which might have been drawn straight from the pages of Ruth Benedict or Professor Kawashima. The way to impose *on* others: give gifts regularly to those whom you might need to call on for favors; look on it just

[40] *Ooru seikatsu.* The examples here are all drawn from the Dec. 1961 issue.

as building up credit in the bank by regular saving. If you neglect to mend your fences in this way, you can always repair the damage. Take a good big box of cakes on the pretext that you "just happened to be passing." When you go along with your request a week later "he won't be able to give you a scowl and he won't say no. Afterward he might even chuckle at the thought that he had been had." How to win an argument without actually appearing to do so: never speak up first, let the others talk themselves to an impasse until you see the lie of the land, then appear to agree with everyone with slight modifications which let you have your own way. How to say no delicately: always put off a creditor by telling him that you have a big deal in hand and expect the money next week; it reassures him and such white lies are harmless provided that you do have a sincere intention to repay (pp. 62–65).

The patterns are traditional enough, but they are drained of moral content. The principles of reciprocity, of modest self-effacement, of consideration for others, of sincerity, are reduced to rules of the game which must be observed to pursue one's own personal ends. There always was such an element of manipulation in the morality of Japanese personal relations, of course, just as the Anglo-Saxon world has never been sure whether honesty was just the best policy or an absolute value in itself. But here there is no ambivalence and no hypocrisy.

In one respect this picture of the go-getter differs from that presented by Kawashima (see above, p. 128); the techniques are illustrated not in the context of hierarchichal relations, but in the context of relations between equals. This is advice for the man who is on his own in a competitive world, not for the climber who depends on patronage and recognition by superiors. The soliciting and extracting of favors is only between the temporarily advantaged and the temporarily disadvantaged, not between different statuses. The wholesaler can no longer count on the "loyalty" of his dependent shops and craft workers; the branch shop is no longer simply the retainer of the main shop.[41]

One element this poor man's version of the route to success contains in common with that which is urged on the salary man—the emphasis on diligence and industry. One article (p. 120) features a *sake* retailer's son who has made a small fortune by his bold and shrewd dealings on the stock market. He is praised for his courage in taking risks, his single-minded devotion to moneymaking, and his readiness to learn from experience, but the really clinching final sentence points out that "a good many people with the gambling instinct are lazy. But Kajiwara is different. He never neglects his work in the shop and applies himself to it with all his might. And this, I think, is the reason for his success."

Mobility and Social Change

Some of the foregoing discussion has a clear relation to the hypotheses about trends set out in the introduction to this book. First, as to the criteria which determine the status of individuals within organized groups, obviously in one sense the importance of hereditary factors has now greatly declined. The prestige attaching to samurai ancestry gets a man nowhere today. The prestige value of birth in what were until recently titled families still counts for something— especially in the marriage market—but its importance *per se* is probably less than in a society such as England which still has a titled aristocracy. Family background has, how-

[41] It seems, indeed, that the pattern of establishing branch shops has changed. A young *tofu*-maker who had recently set up his own (taking his shop's name from his former employer in the traditional *noren-wake* manner) describes in *Ooru seikatsu* how he created his capital largely by his own efforts—by saving, learning economics in night school and investing on the stock exchange. For the rest his money was borrowed only partly from his former employer, partly from the Satomi-kai, a group of *equals* who have all branched out independently from the parent Satomi shop.

ever, a very important bearing on the status which can be *achieved*.

To start with, it affects the kind of merit an individual is likely to acquire by (a) influencing his aspirations and (b) his access to education. The effect on aspirations is rapidly declining with the increasing homogenization of Japanese culture, though still a large section of the urban working class (larger than in the U.S. though not, probably, than in England) looks on higher education as "not for the likes of us" and limits its aspirations to the ranges indicated by magazines such as *Life: In Full*. (A 1953 opinion survey found the proportion of laborers desiring a university education for their son as 52 percent, compared with 86 percent of executive managers.)[42] The effect on access is also great, given the cost of higher education, though this too is diminishing with the increase in incomes, which both makes it easier for working class families to forego a son's earnings and contribute to his expenses, and also makes it easier for students to support themselves by tutoring the younger children of middle-class families.

Second, family background directly affects occupational destination and status within organizations by the operation —acknowledged and overt operation—of patronage in selecting between equally qualified candidates. The inheritance of family businesses, the clearest case of this, probably affects fewer individuals than the activation of family connections in getting positions in larger corporations. Here too, however, the importance of patronage is likely to decline as a seller's market for labor develops, and the importance of *family* connections has declined as university appointments bureaus offer alternative—though less effective—means of establishing connections. Patronage itself may be achieved.

[42] Quoted in W. D. Baker, *A Study of Selected Aspects of Japanese Social Stratification: Class Differences in Values and Levels of Aspiration* (Ph.D. Thesis, Columbia, 1956), p. 57.

The second hypothesized trend concerns the absolute narrowing of status differences and reduction of the "volume" of authority attaching to superior status within organizations. In this respect it seems that it is the lower-middle-class world of the small businessman which has come closest to breaking loose from the framework of traditional patron-client relations. The salary man's world is still the hierarchical world though styles of deference have changed. The subordinate should show respect and obedience, but what might once have been unquestioningly accepted as proper respect may now be branded boot-licking flattery and a derogation of individual dignity. But this, one suspects, is an anomic field where the variance between ideal and actual norms has been great and where there is much confusion of cues and uncertainty of expectations.

The third hypothesized trend concerning the specificity of authority relations recalls the instruction to the salary man that his body is only "put in his safe keeping" for the sixteen hours a day when he is not working. But this is ostensibly presented as a matter for his own self-respect that he should make the provision of good-quality labor the dominant objective of his daily life, and as such it is placed in the context of a limited specific contract for the sale and purchase of labor. It is the relationships of patronage which still preserve the diffuse authority relations unrelated to the overt functions of the organization. If it be granted that the importance of patronage for securing a foothold in a firm will diminish with changes in the labor market, it still remains an open question whether the strength of patron-client cliques within the firm will automatically diminish. One's prophecy in this regard depends on whether one believes that patron-client cliques are primarily the direct consequence of the acceptance of patronage for gaining employment (this acceptance being now usually unwilling and determined solely by the client's weak bargaining position) or whether one believes that it is due to the fact that the personality typically produced by Japanese families and schools is one which has a *need* for the security afforded by a powerful patron, in which case although patronage may be dispensed with for job-getting if other alternatives become available, once in the organization the individual would still be likely to cover his naked vulnerability by—to use the proverbial phrase—"wrapping up in something long."

In this context one may note the development of a new kind of diffuseness in the relations between superior and inferior which in contacts outside the firm does not overtly involve the asymmetry of the authority relations which apply within it. The old pattern was of unilateral visits and formal presentation of gifts and greetings by the subordinate—at New Year, at mid-summer, to celebrate a daughter's wedding or a son's examination success. The new "organization man" pattern is contact on the golf course, at the *go* table, in a tea house (ceremonial, not August Moon), or at a *nō* recitation club, the chirpy conversation of the subordinate's wife enlivening the boss's party at the firm's sports day.[43] The boss does not necessarily have to be allowed to win. The wife (in part taking over *geisha* "privilege") does not have to use respect language.

Finally, it is suggested that individuals make more choices, with regard to more rational secular premises, and in doing so are influenced by personal rather than by group goals.

It is obvious enough that mobility accelerates individuation in a number of important ways. The city-dweller now chooses how to spend his income, where to live, what films to see, how many children to have, with a latitude impossible a century ago, and even the village is far less ruled by tradition and the need to conform. But in respect of one of the most fundamental decisions—the choice of occupation—the possibilities of free and independent choice have been more

[43] See, for lively illustrations, Iwai, *Kyōsō*, pp. 79–86.

limited than in most industrializing societies. Because of the surplus of labor at almost every level of educational training at almost any time in the last sixty years except for the war periods, and because of the preference of employers for "personally guaranteed" labor, individuals' choices have had largely to be determined by the availability of useful personal connections, and this has applied equally to the farm lad who goes to work in an uncle's shop in Tokyo and to the journalist quoted earlier who in his first interview with a member of his university's appointments bureau was told, "Yes, I think we'll put you in for a bank," and accepted the suggestion meekly because he had no other ideas. First jobs have not by any means always been final jobs and the small-business world of *Life: In Full* still offers chances for individual initiatives, but this is a world which, although it once embraced the majority of Japan's urban population, is gradually being squeezed out by the salary man's big corporations.

As far as the nature of the goals is concerned, mobility quite clearly weakens family solidarity and so weakens the importance of raising the *family's* prestige and increasing the *family's* wealth as a motive for the choosing and striving individual. The modern salary man or the modern restaurant proprietor is concerned for the welfare of his children or his parents as individuals. He cares very little about the "House of Tanaka" or its prestige, for only in the village are there still local communities of a kind in which a "house" *can* have prestige.

A further intriguing aspect of the individuation problem is that of nationalism. For how many people did identification with the nation and an earnest devotion to its goals provide a new self-submerging "sense of belonging" for the man emerging to individuation from the womb of the primary group— as it did, for instance, for the hero of Tayama Katai's novel quoted earlier? Of this one can never be sure, particularly since, in a culture which set such store on patriotism, patriotic words and deeds provided a guaranteed way to *personal* prestige and power.

Once again—to sum up the implications for the hypothesized trends—it seems that there is better evidence of a trend toward greater equality resulting from the social changes of the last century than of an increase in self-sufficient individuation.

PART THREE

The Villages

CHAPTER V

Status Changes in Hamlet Structure Accompanying Modernization[1]

ERWIN H. JOHNSON

Types of Hamlet Structure

THE HAMLET in Japan ("hamlet" is used as a translation of *buraku*) is a social unit having a number of households as constituent units. Quite a few hamlets of the present time can be traced back many hundreds of years, since each unit almost always had, and has, a unique identifying name.

Actually, since the term *buraku* was coined in the Meiji period, there is no reference to such units in the earlier Japanese literature. There are, however, in the earliest of the historical writings still extant, references to social units which were probably in form like the present hamlets; and archaeological data from the earliest agricultural communities indicate that residence units, not unlike present-day hamlets in shape, were already in evidence.[2] Thus, taken

[1] The author carried out primary field work in Japan supported by a two-year grant from the Social Science Research Council, from 1956 to 1958. He also received a Small Grant from the National Institute of Mental Health, and a Faculty Grant-in-Aid from the University of Rhode Island, with the help of which some of the following material was collected. These sources are gratefully acknowledged without committing them in any way to the ideas expressed here. I wish to thank Miss Estellie Smith for help in revising the earlier draft. Thanks for helpful comments are due to several members of the Conference on Modern Japan, but specially Messrs. Cornell and Hall.

[2] References to *uji, ujiko, ujigami, ujinokami, muraji*, etc., in the *Kojiki* and *Nihongi*, as well as other early histories, are tantalizing adumbrations of later units. Three terms, *mura, agata*, and *sato*, all refer to *buraku*-like groups. See Kuroita Katsumi, ed., *Kokushi taikei*,

in toto, the evidence for the antiquity of some sort of hamlet is great.[3]

While the specific shape of the settlement patterns of hamlets varies, generally in accordance with the topography,[4] al-

1 (1929), pp. 92, 108-09, 161-62 for examples. For the archaeological information, Toro is described well in J. Edward Kidder, *Japan before Buddhism* (London and New York, 1959), pp. 95–103. For a second well-described site, see Hiraide Iseki Chōsakai, ed., *Hiraide* (Tokyo, 1955).

[3] The literature in English on the *buraku* is extensive. The interested reader is referred to the following works: John B. Cornell and Robert J. Smith, *Two Japanese Villages* (Ann Arbor, 1956); Ronald P. Dore, *Land Reform in Japan* (London, 1959); Paul S. Dull, "The *Senkyoya* System in Rural Japanese Communities," (*Occasional Papers*, No. 4, Center for Japanese Studies: Ann Arbor, 1953), pp. 29–39; Paul Dull, "The Political Structure of a Japanese Village," *Far Eastern Quarterly*, XIII (1954), 175–90; Iwao Ishino and John Bennett, *Types of Japanese Rural Community* (Interim Technical Report No. 6, Ohio State University Research Foundation, Columbus, 1953); Iwao Ishino and John D. Donoghue, "The Loss of Peasant Heritage in Japan," in Edgar A. Schuler *et al.*, eds., *Readings in Sociology* (New York, 1960); Edward Norbeck, *Takashima* (Salt Lake City, 1954), and "Postwar Cultural Change and Continuity in Northern Japan," *American Anthropologist*, LXIII (1961), 297–321; Robert J. Smith, "Cooperative Forms in a Japanese Agricultural Community" (*Occasional Papers*, No. 3, Center for Japanese Studies, Ann Arbor, 1952), pp. 59–70; R. J. Smith and Eduardo P. Reyes, "Community Interrelations with the Outside World: The Case of a Japanese Agricultural Community," *American Anthropologist*, LIX (1957), 463–72; Thomas C. Smith, "The Japanese Village in the Seventeenth Century," *Journal of Economic History*, XII (1952), 1–20; Kurt Steiner, "The Japanese Village and Its Government," *Far Eastern Quarterly*, XV (1956), 185–99; Mischa Titiev, "Changing Patterns of Kumiai Structure in Rural Okayama" (*Occasional Papers*, No. 4, Center for Japanese Studies, Ann Arbor, 1953), pp. 1–28; Robert E. Ward, "The Socio-political Role of the *Buraku* (Hamlet) in Japan," *American Political Science Review*, XLV (1951), 1025-40, and "Some Observations on Local Autonomy at the Village Level in Present-day Japan," *Far Eastern Quarterly*, XII (1953), 192.

[4] R. B. Hall, "Some Rural Settlement Forms in Japan," *Geographical Review*, XXI (1931).

most all of them are clusters of households showing a discernible physical break from one to the next. While many were once independent political units,[5] they are now almost always part of larger political units.

As noted above, the hamlet is made up of households, not of individuals. Characteristically, the constituent households remain basically the same—in the same general location, and in the same hamlet—for many generations, with personnel changes occurring only as people are born, die, or marry into and out of the household. Some gradual change may be noted however. For example, some households may fission, and the two newly created units remain in the hamlet, thus expanding it in size. On the other hand, some households may, in desperation, fold up and leave for the city, or become dependent households in another agricultural area, thus reducing the hamlet in size. Rarely does an outside family with no connections move in, but if one does it may have to buy a share in the communally held property and be formally accepted by the households already present before it can become a functioning part of the larger unit.

If the word *buraku* is sometimes used for a territorial unit, it is also more commonly and more importantly a social unit.[6] Here, therefore, we may ignore the variety of settlement patterns subsumed under the category of hamlet and concentrate our attention solely on a description of the various types of social structures to be found.

Recently, Izumi Seiichi and Gamō Masao suggested two major models for hamlet structure which are relevant here.[7] The first is based on a vertical orientation in which power,

---

[5] See Ward, "Socio-political Role of the *Buraku*," and Erwin H. Johnson, *Nagura Mura: An Historical Analysis of Stability and Change in Community Structure* (Ann Arbor, 1961, microfilm).

[6] Johnson, *Nagura Mura*, pp. 45ff.

[7] Izumi Seiichi and Gamō Masao, "Nihon shakai ni okeru chiikisei," in *Nihon chiri shintaikei*, II (Tokyo, 1952), 37–73. Translated at the Center for Japanese Studies, University of Michigan.

prestige, and wealth are concentrated within relatively few households, and in which concomitant patterns of social deference are important. This hierarchical model is contrasted to one based on a coordinate or egalitarian orientation. The above two classificatory systems conform closely to what Levi-Strauss calls "mechanical models."[8]

If there are, indeed, divergent patterns of social relations, they must be noted, for such a divergence would affect the hypothesis that the influences making for social change, whatever they may be, affect all village units in the same way. If the starting points are quite different, the result would be parallel but *non*convergent patterns of change. In other words, similar influence on dissimilar units may result in equal, but not in identical, change.

Izumi and Gamō break each of the above types down further into kin and nonkin forms of social control. The first subtype of the hierarchical unit (IA in the diagram) depends upon genealogical ties between or among households in the hamlet. The households so tied comprise a corporate kin group[9] in which there exists a hierarchy of prestige and influence. There may also be a hierarchy of wealth and differential ceremonial access to the ancestral spirits. All of these differences are based on birth order of the founders of the "branch" households and are fixed or ascribed for as long as the household continues. The kin unit so formed is referred to in modern scholarly literature as the *dōzoku* and while based on kin ties is also frequently a territorial unit. Within the *dōzoku* there are classes of membership based on the genealogical relationships between the main line—that of the founder of the *dōzoku*— and the founders of the various households. Thus in an

---

[8] Claude Levi-Strauss, "Social Structure," in Sol Tax, ed., *Anthropology Today: Selections* (Chicago, 1952), pp. 321–50.

[9] For the corporate nature of the group, see Seiichi Kitano, " '*Dōzoku*' and '*Ie*' in Japan: The Meaning of Family Genealogical Relationships," in Smith and Beardsley, eds., *Japanese Culture*, pp. 42–46.

ideal-typical *dōzoku* the main house, or *honke*, is occupied by the *ōya*, the direct descendant of the founder of the *dōzoku* as traced through a line of first sons. At a level just below that of the *honke* are the *bunke*, or branch households formed by younger sons born in the *honke*. Second degree *bunke*, formed by younger sons of already established *bunke*, rank lower and are designated as *mago bunke*, i.e. grand-child *bunke*.

One final word is necessary for the *dōzoku* subtype. It is quite unusual to find a hamlet nowadays consisting of a single *dōzoku*. Sometimes there are nonmembers in an otherwise single-*dōzoku* hamlet; sometimes more than one *dōzoku* is present; or there might be a combination of both, that is, several *dōzoku* and some non-*dōzoku* members. In any event, where the kin hierarchy type is found, the apex or apices of the *dōzoku* will dominate hamlet life and especially hamlet decision-making. The discussion of *dōzoku* as kin units is probably as extensive in the Western language studies as is the discussion of the hamlet itself,[10] and it occupies a large

[10] See, among other works, Kitano, " '*Dōzoku*' and '*Ie*' "; Ariga Kizaemon, "The Contemporary Japanese Family in Transition," in International Sociological Association, *Transactions of the Third World Congress of Sociology*, I (1954), 83–89; Richard K. Beardsley, "The Household in the Status System of Japanese Villages," (*Occasional Papers*, No. 1, Center for Japanese Studies, Ann Arbor, 1951), pp. 62–74; Richard Beardsley, J. W. Hall, and Robert Ward, *Village Japan* (Chicago, 1959), especially ch. 10; Harumi Befu, "Corporate Emphasis and Patterns of Descent in the Japanese Family," in Beardsley and Smith, eds., *Japanese Culture*, pp. 34–41; Cornell, *Two Japanese Villages*; Takashi Koyama, "The Changing Family Structure in Japan," in Smith and Beardsley, eds., *Japanese Culture*, pp. 47–54, and *The Changing Social Position of Women in Japan* (Paris, 1961); Michio Nagai and J. W. Bennett, *Dōzoku: A Preliminary Study of the Japanese Extended Family Group and Its Social and Economic Functions* (Interim Technical Report No. 4, Columbus, Ohio State University, Research Foundations, Research in Japanese Social Relations, 1953); Norbeck, *Takashima*; Yuzuru Okada, "Kinship Organization in Japan," *Journal of Educational Psychology*, XXVI (1952), 27–31; and

proportion of the literature in Japanese on rural social structure.[11]

The non-kin vertically oriented hamlet appears in the diagram as Ib. Ideally, it relies on ritual kin relationships, which need not be hereditary in household lines, although they are frequently so. A man desiring to associate himself with a stronger man will establish an *oya-ko* relationship. The *oyakata* (boss) protects his *kokata* (followers) and they in turn are loyal to him, support him, and generally enhance his prestige and power. Such *oya-ko* relationships are not restricted to the rural hamlet. Far from it; they constitute a prevalent form of social relationship throughout Japanese history. They have gained most recent notoriety in reference to urban gangs, both adult and teenage, and to internal relationship within work teams in the cities.

There are certain important features which distinguish the *oyakata-kokata* system from that of the *dōzoku*. One difference is the fact already mentioned that the relationship need not be hereditary. Perhaps the most important, however, is that for a rural hamlet the various *kokata* of a single *oyakata* do not consider themselves to be a group. They all have direct ties with the *oyakata* but need not have them with each other. Thus while the corporateness of the *dōzoku* may serve a divisive function within the hamlet, the *oya-ko* dyadic relationship does not necessarily lead to the development of factions within the hamlet.

The vertically oriented hamlet models may be contrasted with egalitarian ones. As an ideal type, an egalitarian orientation suggests the absence of ascribed differentials based on anything other than relative age, and perhaps on sex. In other words, households will be coequal unless an individual

---

Thomas C. Smith, *The Agrarian Origins of Modern Japan* (Stanford, 1959).

[11] A long bibliography would be possible here, but much of the recent work is well summarized in Fukutake Tadashi, ed., *Kazoku: Sonraku: Toshi* (*Kōza shakaigaku,* iv) (Tokyo, 1958).

household head happens to be more influential than an-other, but such a head would not establish *permanent* ties of a superordinate-subordinate sort with other households. No great inequality in land holdings would be expected in such a unit. However, exact or absolute equality in holdings would probably only be possible if the hamlet owned all the land as a corporate group. While it has been suggested that such a condition may have existed in early Japan, it has never been discovered in contemporary Japan.

Izumi and Gamō suggest that this egalitarian form may be divided into two subtypes diagrammed here as IIa and IIb. In each case group consensus rather than majority rule characterizes decision-making. This and its contrast to type III, Australian ballot "democracy," is discussed later. In type IIa the constituent units are the households, the *ie*, which comprise the hamlet. The principal decision-making rests with the various household heads. In type IIb age grading appears to be quite important, with each generation tending to decide for itself and control its own affairs except when its interests conflict with those of another generation.[12] Despite the implicit generational conflict in this subtype, which incidentally is itself a quite rare form, both types IIa and IIb have several important egalitarian features. For example, the household head in the older generation retires much earlier in the egalitarian hamlet than in the hierarchical one. Differential treatment of the eldest son is weaker in the egalitarian hamlet than in the hierarchical one, although it is certainly not absent. Consistent with this general equating of status levels, the position of the bride is more secure in the egalitarian unit and the status of women in general is higher.[13]

---

[12] Age grading seems to survive in fishing villages especially. See Izumi and Gamō, "Chiikisei." Norbeck discusses it in *Takashima*, p. 51; and Professor Kawashima has discussed it in a number of works.

[13] Izumi and Gamō, "Chiikisei," p. 45.

MODELS FOR COMMUNITY CONTROL

I. HIERARCHY

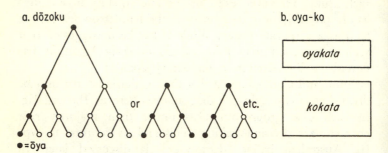

a. dōzoku

• = ōya

or

etc.

b. oya-ko

oyakata

kokata

II. EGALITARIAN

a. Emphasizing household

b. Emphasizing age grades

III. SECRET BALLOT "DEMOCRACY"

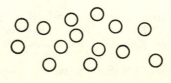

There is much discussion in the literature as to which of these two models is the older.[14] Many feel that the earliest form of community structure in Japan rested on a hierarchical lineage structure which, it would seem, could be a perfectly reasonable prototype for the contemporary *dōzoku*. There is evidence enough that villages of such a hierarchical type existed.[15] But equally, there is evidence enough to suggest that egalitarian communities were also present in Japan by Nara times. There may have been different pre-Nara populations arriving with different social structures from different parts of the world.[16] However that may be, it seems unnecessary to derive the contemporary egalitarian community from an early hierarchical one rather than accepting it as itself an ancient form. There seems to be no basis for assuming that all agricultural communities in Japan were homogeneously of a hierarchically structured type during the Yamato period.

The problem of the nature of the pre-Tokugawa hamlet structure lies outside the scope of this paper, but it does seem reasonable to postulate two patterns, both of which appeared to function and maintain themselves throughout the Middle Ages, and both of which have survived in some contemporary Japanese villages.[17]

[14] See especially Ariga Kizaemon, *Nihon shakai no kenkyū* (Tokyo, 1940), and *Sonraku seikatsu* (Tokyo, 1948). In English see Okada, "Kinship Organization," for a fairly clear statement, and almost any of the works cited above for the *dōzoku*.

[15] Cf. the *ujinokami*, clearly a lineage head.

[16] Four recent articles, all in Smith and Beardsley, eds., *Japanese Culture*, provide a fine foundation for such speculation: Ishida Eiichiro, "Nature of the Problem of Japanese Cultural Origins," pp. 3–6; Yawata Ichiro, "Prehistoric Origins for Japanese Cultural Origins," pp. 6–10; Egami Namio, "Light on Japanese Cultural Origins from Historical Archeology and Legend," pp. 11–16; and Ono Susumu, "The Japanese Language: Its Origin and Its Sources," pp. 17–21. Richard Beardsley postulated biethnic communities to account for two pottery styles where there should not be such (personal communication).

[17] Johnson, *Nagura Mura*, pp. 45ff.

Hamlet Functions in Tokugawa Times

No characterization of a time past and of a complex society can avoid making general statements for which there are many exceptions. Any attempt at a general description of hamlet structure in Tokugawa times must presuppose variants, differing according to region, specific economic activity, and historical accident.

It would seem safe, however, to suggest that generally the Tokugawa hamlet was a self-sufficient unit of social cooperation. Individual families carried out most activities needed for survival, and what they did not do was largely handled by the hamlet. It was the community, the *gemeinde*, consisting of contiguous households which considered itself a social whole. Virtually all activities critical to the people of the time were carried out within this hamlet unit. While aware of, and even related through consanguineal and conjugal ties with, members of other hamlets, their own hamlet would have been a distinct community in their minds. Except for extreme cases of isolated mountain hamlets, of course, it is doubtful that complete isolation has characterized the Japanese community for many, many centuries. Indeed, as Redfield notes, except for one doubtful Eskimo case, no such community is known.[18]

What we are saying, therefore, is that there was a much greater intensity of interaction within rather than between hamlet units. It is not clear whether endogamous or exogamous practices were characteristic of the Tokugawa hamlet. Our search of the firsthand evidence from Nagura Mura for three generations in Tokugawa times found only one case of hamlet endogamy (and that a son-in-law adoption, not an ordinary marriage). It might well be that for some hierarchical hamlets, endogamy characterized the lower status positions within the hamlet, and that exogamy characterized the upper status positions. For such families marriage within the

[18] Robert Redfield, *The Little Community* (Upsala, 1956).

162

same social class required looking far afield for an acceptable spouse.

What is today the modern hamlet was usually a separate unit (a *mura*) for the purposes of *han* administration, paying its taxes to the *han* representatives. *Han* government encouraged the hamlets to settle internal difficulties themselves, thus relieving the *han* of burdensome litigation. Generally, the hamlet members farmed land adjacent to their homes. Because of this the land units were contiguous to one another and hence the hamlet tended also to function as an irrigation association. Since the amount of water available determined the extent to which new fields could be opened, the hamlet served as the group which decided whether paddy lands should be extended. When, in times of drought, the availability of water was crucial to the entire community utilizing water, the hamlet, or some agency within it, had to decide on the allocation of this scarce resource. Where several hamlets were integrated into a single waterway system, the indications are that each hamlet acted as a unit within this supra-hamlet organization. Disputes over water rights tended, then, to be between hamlets, not between individuals from different hamlets, and what disputes there were between fellow hamlet members were generally settled informally within the hamlet.

The hamlet maintained control over other important aspects of production. One of the most important factors other than water was grasslands. The heavy application of fertilizers was necessary for double or triple cropping and generally to maintain high yields on arable fields. Before the development of commercial fertilizers, the main fertilizer source was either grass directly (as green fertilizer), or animal manure from animals, which were generally stall-fed—again chiefly on grass—rather than put out to graze. A portion of this grass was grown on the mud retaining walls separating the individual paddies, but most was the product of upland areas, which tended to be hamlet-owned.

Until recently, the importance of grass was neglected in much of the Western-language material on rural Japan.[19] Where estimates are available, they indicate that the volume of grass utilized by farming households required, in large holdings, several hundred trips annually by a draft animal and a man from the uplands to the fields.

The roofs of farmhouses were thatched with a special and quite tough grass called *kaya*. With minor repairs a roof lasted about twenty-five years. There was often an informal, though sometimes formal, system of rotation for roof thatching, so that a hamlet of about twenty-five houses would reserve a tract of land which grew enough *kaya* to rethatch the roof of one house each year. This stand, like the uplands, was also communal property.

Communally held uplands could supply firewood and timber for buildings. Of course, villages varied greatly in the availability of such land. Even in a single region different hamlets had quite different amounts of upland holdings. The type of holdings in mountain land also varied widely. There are cases where hamlets had different rights to the same land; one hamlet might have the right to glean firewood, and one the right to timber resources; one the right to raise mushrooms and another the right to burn charcoal; and so on. In some cases a clear title rested in the hamlet, in others the land was shogunal or daimyō land to which the hamlets had certain customary rights.

The importance of these hamlet holdings lies in more than just their economic value. Through the collective control of important factors of production the hamlet group (comprising, in the case of the egalitarian hamlets, the heads of the constituent households, and in the case of the hierarchical hamlets, the power centers of the constituent kin groups) possessed a potentially strong hold on recalcitrant

[19] Thomas Smith, *Agrarian Origins, passim*; Johnson, *Nagura Mura*, pp. 120ff.

households. The ultimate sanction of cutting off the water supply, grass, or firewood was always present.[20]

In addition to the above economic features there were a number of ceremonies and social mechanisms which bound the hamlets into tight social units. Through these, each hamlet family was regularly aware of the importance of the community, both to its economic and its social well-being. For example, the hamlet assisted as a cooperative unit in the construction of new houses or the rebuilding of old houses. There is some evidence that professional carpenters were employed for their technical knowledge (at least by late Tokugawa times), but the greater part of the labor was supplied by hamlet members and by kin of the family. Ultimate reciprocity in a delayed form is implied here since eventually, if not in one's own lifetime then in that of one's son, any labor an individual contributed would be returned. Community irrigation systems required cooperative work to open new ditches for the community fields and to keep the already present ditches in constant repair. Roads (through the fields or connecting the hamlet with others) and bridges (spanning the irrigation ditches and the rivers which were the sources of water for the ditches) also had to be built and repaired.

Communal worship also emphasized the spiritual well-being of the family as a member of the community. Through these ceremonies, and through intensive primary relations, the members of the hamlet were welded together into a single entity. Virtually every hamlet possessed a cemetery and a shrine. Both served as physical symbols uniting the living members with their ancestors and their ancestral deities. Festivals, whether of Buddhist or Shinto origins, took on a community character which was typical of what

[20] Erwin Johnson, "Perseverance through Orderly Change: The 'Traditional' *Buraku* in a Modern Community," *Human Organization*, XXII (1963–1964), 218–23.

Redfield called the "little tradition";[21] that is, they were oriented toward village deities, ancestral to leading families or to all families of the village. Both the shrine and the cemetery were symbols of continuity from the ancient past to the present. It is true that the village was not the only ritual unit; each household had its own set of ancestors commemorated by name within the confines of the house, and where larger units of kin existed, each of these might well have its own separate cemetery or shrine. The hamlet shrine, however, was the focal point for the important annual ceremonies symbolizing the continuity of the entire village. Festivals were frequently designed in such a way that each of the significant age groups within the village, and each sex, had its representatives participate, and this, naturally, reinforced the integration of these various segments into the hamlet community.

Rites of passage were also community rites. Funerals and weddings were perhaps the most important of these. Neighbors and kin served both as guests and as assistants to the hosts on these occasions. Modest as these ceremonies were for some villagers, they (and the many ceremonies accompanying the numerous cooperative tasks performed by the community) were important in integrating this *gemeinde* unit.

At each point in the life cycle of a hamlet member he was allied in one way or another with peer groups comprised of fellow hamlet members. There seems little doubt that the children of the hamlet—in the days before regular school was instituted—comprised the play group.[22] Young adults had their own organization, the *wakamono gumi* or the *wakashū nakama*. This group, comprised of young men who would soon be household heads, possessed a small house in

[21] Robert Redfield, *Peasant Society and Culture* (Chicago, 1956).

[22] Erwin Johnson, "Children's Play Groups and Village Social Organization," in *Proceedings* of the Joint Meeting of the Anthropological Society of Nippon and the Japanese Society of Ethnology, Twelfth Session (Tokyo, 1958).

the hamlet in which the young men spent much of their leisure time; in this way the group controlled, to some extent, the behavior of its members and had much to say about marriage arrangements as well.[23]

The hamlet was, then, a relatively closed and self-contained unit comprising many households. The major social activities of all of the members focused inward on the hamlet. Economic and political spokes went out to the regional *daikan* who taxed them, but the spokes were from the hamlet, not from the individual households within them and certainly not from the individuals within the households. The individual was, perhaps, first a member of his own family; next, clearly, a member of his hamlet. Beyond this there was, no doubt, a regional loyalty; a vague feeling of oneness with other peasants within the vicinity—those who shared certain customs and traditions with him.

Hamlet Structure in Tokugawa Times

A detailed description of hamlet structure in Tokugawa times is difficult because the evidence is inadequate. The sophisticated observational techniques developed in the twentieth century cannot be applied in retrospect, though it is possible to attempt historical reconstruction using modern conceptual categories. For instance, the specifically named formal positions of leadership in Tokugawa hamlets are known to us, and these can be used as a basis for sorting social relationships during this period. Information about the personnel who occupied the various status positions (by which I mean positions in the social structure and their accompanying rights and duties[24]) can frequently be reconstructed.

On the hamlet level in the Tokugawa period there were usually several positions of authority. These are referred to

[23] See Kawashima Takeyoshi, *Kekkon* (Tokyo, 1962), and *Ideorogii to shite no kazoku seido* (Tokyo, 1959).

[24] Ralph Linton, *The Study of Man* (New York, 1936), pp. 113-31.

167

collectively as the *murakata sanyaku*. The most important of these was generally called *nanushi*, a word characteristically translated as headman. In large villages he would be assisted by elders and neighborhood group leaders, given a variety of local names. Even in the egalitarian communities there was a tendency for a successful functionary to retain his position throughout his active life. In the hierarchical communities posts appear to have passed from lineage head to lineage head in important *dōzoku*.[25]

The formalization of these posts, of course, is a result of the imposition of a pattern of government on the village during the Tokugawa period, and to understand their significance one must take national, economic, social, and political developments into account. There may well have originally been folk counterparts for these posts. Certainly the variations in the patterns of assuming these positions must be accounted for not as the result of governmental forces but rather as corresponding to internal structural variations between hamlet and hamlet.[26]

There is a great range of social-status terminology in the Japanese literature indicating the general position of a household vis-à-vis other households within the hamlet. The main household and its master in a *dōzoku* were often called *ōya*. Frequently, the *ōya* comprised the hamlet council with other household heads eliminated from the decision-making apparatus. Within the *dōzoku* groups, *bunke* or branches from the older stem families, while free from legal subservience, were nevertheless one rung down on the hamlet ladder and distinguished from the *ōya* groups. Below these were hereditary groups of *nago*, the fictive kin, and of servants. There were also bond servants, whose positions were not hereditary but instead were contractually fixed for a restricted length of time.

[25] Tsuneo Yamane, *Social Change in Japan* (Ann Arbor, 1958), mimeographed; and Thomas Smith, *Agrarian Origins*, chs. 1–3.

[26] The case for this is put forth in Johnson, *Nagura Mura*, pp. 67ff.

Much the same titles for official positions were found in the egalitarian hamlets as well as in the hierarchical ones, but officers tended to circulate more freely, at least among the class of fully established farmers. In such communities, a branch household head could assume office shortly after he had established himself.[27] (Though there was, of course, no guarantee that he would do so, and new households—those admitted from outside the hamlet—seemed generally to have been denied access to these positions during their first generation of residence within the hamlet.) Great variation occurs in the rules regarding who could occupy official positions, but it is still possible to distinguish an egalitarian pattern from a hierarchical one. It was a pattern not of complete absence of social inequality, but rather of status equality among *full farmers*—i.e. the *hombyakushō*, as they were legally described. While branch families were denied full status in hierarchical hamlets, they were admitted to it in egalitarian ones, though even in egalitarian villages there might be a group of second-class citizens—outsiders who were not *hombyakushō* and only attached as laborers or tenants. (Even today, in hamlets which are clearly dominated by an egalitarian ethic, outsiders may be denied entry. They are egalitarian *for those who are members*.) At any rate, the difference between the egalitarian and the hierarchical models is clear. In the latter, powers of decision-making were restricted to a small group of households with a particular ascribed status. Branch families and new families might even be denied rights to participation in ceremonies even though they had been established in the village for hundreds of years.[28]

Izumi and Gamō noted specific variations between the two models. To what extent these can be projected back into the Tokugawa period is not clear. They note that while the first son is given deferential treatment in all rural Japan,

[27] *Ibid.*, p. 86.
[28] Thomas Smith, *Agrarian Origins*, pp. 50ff.

169

he is accorded less deference in the egalitarian hamlet than in the hierarchical one. This would seem primarily due to the fact that in the case of the hierarchically oriented *dōzoku*, the *ōya*'s first son will succeed to a position of great importance. They note further that the position of the bride is higher in the egalitarian hamlets than in the hierarchical one. It is possible that the aristocratic values of inferiority for women never penetrated the egalitarian villages.[29] The presence of highly elaborated patterns of superordination and subordination in some hamlets clearly hearken back to a *bushi* origin for the household head.[30] Perhaps a strong case can be made for seeing the egalitarian hamlet as remaining less contaminated by hierarchical developments in the social structure of the nonpeasant classes.

Izumi and Gamō note also that retirement of the older household head is earlier in the egalitarian hamlets and furthermore that when he does retire he does so more completely. There is often a retirement house to which the former head, his wife, and their still minor children move. This, too, seems consistent with the earlier mentioned egalitarian sentiment of this hamlet type which not only puts the main and branch families on a par and allows each household head a full and free position in the hamlet, but which also would appear to place less emphasis on sexual differences in prestige rankings.

Changes in Hamlet Function from the Tokugawa Period to the Present

This paper will only offer a contrast between late Tokugawa and present day Japan. The data readily available do not enable me to fill the gap very easily by a clear indication of the sequence of change.

Recent studies of Japanese communities indicate many changes in hamlet structure and function. These changes are

[29] Takashi Koyama, *The Changing Social Position*, p. 17.
[30] Beardsley, "Household in the Status System."

far from uniform from village to village, although basically they all appear to be in the same direction. Their variation cannot be detailed here, but an attempt will be made to indicate general trends. For example, there are several cases where hamlets have maintained their internal hierarchical organization with remarkable tenacity,[31] and many where earlier hierarchies have disintegrated.[32] There are no cases noted, however, in which hamlet-level hierarchies have emerged where none were present before. Where hamlets have maintained their hierarchy, though, some economic resource other than land generally provides the means whereby the main family has been able to maintain its position of power. Indeed, many of the largest and most complex hierarchies which survive are themselves products of late Tokugawa and early Meiji entrepreneurship, where a merchant or manufacturer invested capital in a land reclamation program or an extensive irrigation program and then constructed, almost out of whole cloth, a fictive kin *dōzoku.*[33]

Both hierarchical and egalitarian hamlets have frequently retained their exclusive, or closed, nature. That is, while people may freely pass through their villages and while their people may freely enter the outside world, still no one can enter hamlet organizations without the consent of the hamlet itself. A village is considered closed when it is very difficult to get this permission, where one is not welcome unless he is related (at least matrilineally) to someone in the hamlet who will vouch for him.

There are perfectly clear and logical reasons why the *buraku*'s function is different now from what it was in the past. For one thing, after 1865 there was a complete reorganization of all village political units which took from the hamlet its relative political autonomy and made it a sub-

---

[31] Kondō Yasuo, *Mura no kōzō* (1955), pp. 224ff.
[32] *Ibid.*, pp. 338ff.
[33] John D. Eyre, "The Changing Role of the Former Japanese Landlord," *Land Economics,* xxxi (1955), 34–46.

division of a larger unit, the *mura* or the *machi* of today. With this reorganization there was created a new superior administrative structure consisting of a mayor, town council, etc., and, along with these, of course, a social system, an agricultural cooperative, and the inevitable roster of local committees, all on a *mura* rather than a hamlet basis.

It is important to note that not all *mura* activities were simply old hamlet activities upgraded one step. Indeed, most of the *mura* activities were new to rural Japan and fitted in with the rapidly increasing complexity of village life. This flourishing of activities on the *mura* level did not destroy the hamlet. It did, however, make the hamlet *relatively* less important to the villager than it was before.[34] The sequence of changes can be illustrated by an actual example. Although the details and specific activities within any one community will vary from village to village, the general pattern of change which it illustrates applies to a fairly wide range of Japanese villages.

In the village in question,[35] the hamlet had, as one of its major tasks, the control of timberland and grassland. A land tax in early Meiji times put the hamlet at an economic disadvantage, since no money was raised by the use of these lands. Encouraged by the government, the villagers divided the lands and sold the tracts to individuals among themselves who cared to buy them and assume the tax obligations. Some grasslands were retained, but the increasing use of chemical fertilizers reduced the need for grass greatly.[36] The need for fodder also declined. At one time the villagers raised many small horses. These animals ate large amounts of grass, serving as veritable fertilizer machines. As vehicles replaced horses in Japan the market for horses gradually declined. Cattle continued to be used locally for draft purposes, but they ate much less than the ponies. The necessary

[34] Johnson, *Nagura Mura*, pp. 117ff.
[35] *Ibid.*, p. 123.
[36] *Ibid.*, pp. 128ff.

grass could now be raised on small, individually owned tracts.

Commercial fertilizer is now purchased through the *mura* cooperative, of which the hamlet has a sub-unit, called the *jikkō kumiai* or action group in this context. Elsewhere, where hamlets are large, smaller divisions of the hamlet comprise the *jikkō kumiai*. Here is one example in which hamlet tasks have atrophied and new tasks have been taken up by *mura* agencies, in this case the *kumiai* and the *yakuba*, the village office.

Tile and board roofs have almost completely replaced the thatch of the past. The hamlet still cooperates in thatching the few grass roofs which remain. As a matter of fact, when someone converts to tile, the hamlet men dutifully assist in laying the tile, forming a chain as long as need be, to give each individual something to do in passing the tile up to the man who actually puts it on. Although nearby towns have dropped this, and the villagers realize that such cooperative effort is not necessary, tradition can be quite strong. When new houses are built, the whole hamlet still helps in the roof raising, the principal result being a fine celebration after the day's work is through. Professional carpenter teams do most of the work, but the convention of mutual aid remains and the resulting work and festivities certainly assist in the integration of the social group.

It is not clear whether the hamlet households cooperated in the home manufacture of staples such as *miso* and *shōyū* in the Tokugawa period. They definitely did during the Taishō and Shōwa austerity drives. During these lean years the village office, in cooperation with the national government, encouraged a variety of economies and found it convenient to use the hamlet as the unit for implementation. They pitted hamlet against hamlet in an effort to see which one would be the first to get all its households to balance their budget. (Few ever did.) During this period, cooperative manufacture of important staples was also encouraged. Today, a number of hamlets have formed cooperative purchasing groups for relatively nonperishable staples. In this case they send a single large order to a less expensive city store and have the supplies delivered by a local truck driver. The cooperative production of these staples by the hamlet, however, has ceased.

High voltage electrical lines were put up for agricultural purposes just after the war. The hamlets now purchase electric motors cooperatively and charge each family for the amount of time they use these machines. Each hamlet maintains a large inventory of agricultural tools and equipment which any member may use.

The hamlet no longer maintains detailed tax records. This task has been assumed by the village office. In general, no one regrets losing this somewhat odious task at the hamlet level. A single hamlet headman has replaced the Tokugawa *mura-kata sanyaku*.

Ten hamlets, all small and comprising about half of the village, belong to a major Shinto shrine congregation. Each hamlet is a unit of membership, and individual families have not become separated in this membership. So much is the hamlet a unit that the Buddhist priest in one of the hamlets who is a household head must serve his term as hamlet representative to the Shinto shrine. Each hamlet takes a turn at shrine maintenance and each elects a representative to the shrine council. Two important festivals, one in the fall and one at New Year's, draw almost all of the congregation to the shrine. In addition to this, the council meets there for several other events. Each hamlet still maintains its own smaller shrine as well, and on two or three occasions during the year, depending on the hamlet, rather attenuated festivals are held. Ceremonial unity has decreased somewhat at the hamlet level, but it still has an importance.

Rites of passage remain hamlet functions, with hamlet neighbors assisting, as before, at weddings and funerals. Many of the hamlet members will attend the weddings as guests if they can trace some sort of remote kinship to the host household. Those that either cannot or do not wish to trace such kinship merely assist in preparation. Births, once handled by skilled women in the hamlet, are now handled by professional midwives, but neighbors assist.

In an amazingly large number of *mura*-wide associations, the hamlet serves as a subunit. The shrine was one example and the agricultural *jikkō kumiai* another. In addition, every parent of a school-age child belongs to the Parent-Teachers' Association. Dues for this are collected by hamlets. One woman in each household is a member of the *mura fujinkai* (women's association). Each hamlet serves as a subunit of this group also, and for villagewide meetings one representative from each subunit usually attends. The young people's group, the *seinendan*, is now a voluntary group although in the past it was a compulsory membership group. Since the hamlets tend to be too small to maintain independent units, larger geographical subdivisions have been established for these organizations consisting of a number of nearby hamlets, but at no point is a hamlet boundary violated.

In the elections for the *mura* council each adult casts a single vote on a single *mura*-wide list of candidates. The hamlet recognizes that it still has a collective vested interest in the *mura* government, and the larger hamlets elect one member by mutual agreement. The smaller hamlets form groups, each large enough to guarantee one member's election. They take turns in presenting candidates and members of all the associated hamlets vote for him. There are a few more seats than those assured by this informal subdivision so that at each election two or three members are elected at large.

The hamlet is still the only unit of importance for preschool and early-school-age children. Even where hamlets geographically merge into one another, children in adjacent houses but in different hamlets tend not to play with each other. School children assemble by hamlet and go to school each morning, but they return home by themselves. As the children get older their range of friends spreads out around the hamlet. Hamlet and kin provide the major social channels for the women but not especially for the men, who, through business activities, are drawn into *mura*-wide social relationships.[37]

Greater dynamics of change are apparent in one hamlet in the *mura* which, in the course of the last one hundred years, has increased in size from about eighteen houses to close to one hundred. That which is *mura* and not hamlet (i.e. new, not old) tends to be located in this hamlet. Here are found the buildings of many *mura* organizations, the lower and middle schools, the village office, the agricultural and forestry cooperatives, the police station with the village's only policeman, the agricultural cooperative's mill and the forestry cooperative's saw mill. There are many stores in this hamlet and several inns and restaurants. The only theater in town is located here. The newly built town meeting hall is also here. In this hamlet we find many non-agricultural households, specialists such as truck drivers, dyers, *tōfu* makers, and at least ten carpenters. This hamlet, unlike the others, freely admits new households, and families refused admission to purely agricultural hamlets have entered this hamlet and prospered. Many houses of shop-keepers, often younger sons of farming families from other hamlets, practice agriculture as a sideline.[38] This hamlet differs in character from the others, but to detail this difference would be to go beyond the scope of this paper. Perhaps, however, it can be suggested that this hamlet exaggerates,

[37] Erwin Johnson, *Nagura Report*, manuscript submitted to Interdisciplinary Project in Personality and Culture, Nagoya National University, 1958, and summarized in Muramatsu Tsuneo, ed., *Nihonjin* (Tokyo, 1962).

[38] Erwin Johnson, "The Emergence of a Self-conscious Entrepreneurial Class in Rural Japan," in Smith and Beardsley, eds., *Japanese Culture*, pp. 91–99.

but does not violate, general statements about change from the traditional mechanically integrated community to the modern organically integrated one.

Changes in Hamlet Status Structure from Tokugawa to the Present

While some of the hierarchically structured hamlets clearly remain today, their number is quite small and they are, to a great extent, museum-like communities. The evidence is strong that, in general, these communities are losing their extreme hierarchical, or vertical, orientation.[39] Where they have lost it they resemble the egalitarian stem-family type of hamlet (model IIa in the diagram on page 160).

Birth and seniority, the most important determinants of ascribed status, still operate on the hamlet level in all types of organization, but there have been some changes. For example, although in most rural communities (despite the legal provisions against unitary inheritance) the eldest son characteristically inherits the entire family property, and though he therefore has a position clearly different from that of his brothers,[40] unless specific household business is involved, the eldest son no longer appears to possess greater authority, and younger sons, while distinguished as younger sons in many aspects of life, are by no means subservient.[41] This situation may be new in certain regions but quite old in others. One can speculate, in the case of the hierarchical community structure, that the superiority of the first son and his authority was less specific to family affairs in the past, and that the growing availability of alternative employment, knowledge of the outside world, etc., undercut this general authority and restricted it to more and more specific areas.

In the hamlet structure itself the shift to specific rather

[39] Ishino and Donoghue, "Loss of Peasant Heritage," and Edward Norbeck, "Postwar Cultural Change and Continuity in Northeastern Japan," *American Anthropologist*, LXIII (1961), 297–321.
[40] Johnson, "The Emergence."   [41] *Ibid.*

than general authority is quite clear. Since the hierarchical hamlet structure parallels that of its family structures, what was said above about the family would also apply to the hamlet. The land-reform program, the general process of economic diversification, outside job opportunities, increased communication of new ideas, and other changes have combined to undercut rural squireships.[42]

The development of a sociological community[43] much larger than the hamlet has led to a diversification of activities which almost assures that authority will become much more restricted and specific—even though aspects of control over the "whole person" may remain. In contrast to the former situation of a single social group, comprised of multifunctioning individuals (e.g. the hamlet functioning simultaneously as a water control group, a land-holding group, and a labor exchange group), there are now a variety of forces operating which all have worked to counter the tight control possible when the same social group directed virtually every aspect of local life. These new forces include the proliferation of social activities for both youth and adults; the possibility of individuals going outside the village, acquiring prestige within the national, rather than the local system, and returning with this prestige to the village; and the opportunities for nonagricultural employment within the villages themselves. To be sure, the hamlet still serves as the membership unit for many of these special groups, but there have developed many other groups in recent times which draw their membership from many hamlets, and which do not include all the villagers. The lumber cooperative is one such group, the agriculture association another. Political parties have made modest starts in the villages; various study clubs, the 4-H clubs, dance ensembles, and other community groupings based on common interests are becoming stronger all

[42] Norbeck "Postwar Cultural Change."
[43] Conrad Arensberg, "The Community Study Method," *American Journal of Sociology*, LX (1954), 109–24.

the time. Merchant associations have even spread beyond the
mura lines and on to the regional level.

There are signs of rational choice based on secular premises in rural behavior, and, indeed, there have been for
many decades, though within a basic framework which is
traditional. Economic diversification in the rural village has
a history extending well back in Meiji times for remote
villages, and into Tokugawa times for villages near good
markets. There has been an extensive discussion of peasant
attitudes toward "progress" in a series of issues of *Human
Organization*.[44] The controversy there dealt with whether
or not peasants resented the success of their neighbors because,
as one of the discussants suggested, the village was looked
upon as a limited pie, where one larger cut means smaller
cuts for everyone else. Clearly, when the hamlet controlled
the important means of production in the era before the
introduction of commercial fertilizers, there was a finite
limitation to the resources for growing the principal field
crops. However, economic diversification does not appear
to have been resisted in most Japanese communities—
where it was feasible. Whether it seemed feasible or not
depended on knowledge of markets and on transportation.
The roads in rural Japan are not noted for their efficiency.
Since product transportation in Tokugawa times was
handled by either human or animal pack carriers, not draft
animals, the roads were narrow and not readily adapted to
vehicles of any sort. Furthermore, in the mountainous and
hilly areas, the roads tended to be quite straight with steep
inclines, rather than following gradual contours which could
readily be adapted to motor use. Thus when motor vehicles
and cart transport were introduced, entirely new routes had
to be planned and built. This meant, in effect, that no suitable roads were available for quite some time in the hinter-

[44] George M. Foster, "Interpersonal Relations in Peasant Society,"
with comments by Oscar Lewis and Julian Pitt-Rivers, *Human Organization*, xix (1960-1961), pp. 174–84.

land. This has now changed, and almost all villages have good access to the urban markets. Where train transport is not readily accessible, truck and bus transport is available.

Along with this improvement in transportation have come new commercial factors of production. Store-bought staple goods and chemical fertilizers, replacing the heavy use of grass, have freed the rural farmer from much of the close control of production which previously was imposed through the communal ownership of production factors. In one *mura*, new land uses not involving irrigation have been instituted by individual entrepreneurs, and have never been placed under hamlet cooperative control.[45] The mutual distrust which was exemplified in the latifundia system (heavily relied on in the *Human Organization* discussion) just simply did not appear.

While the young people tend to think in terms of their own well-being to some degree, there is little doubt that the well-being of the entire family is also an important consideration. The children still believe to a great extent that their parents can better decide their future than they themselves can. The parents also take the personal feelings of their children into account. The parents are conscious, on the whole, of the changes occurring in the cities and thus their decision as to the future of their children (other than the first son) will vary as conditions vary.

The parents still look to their holdings as an investment not only for themselves but for future generations. This feeling can be so extreme that sometimes market conditions are ignored, and aging trees will lose value because a farmer is reluctant to sell a stand of timber which represents a family investment. One of the major functions of local lumber brokers is to talk the farmers into selling their timber, though some of the better-informed and more self-confident owners will readily sell when prices are good and then invest the money in industry.

[45] Johnson, *Nagura Mura*.

Kin remains the strongest group of individuals a person may call on in times of emergency. This group is a bilateral extension, the size of which is moderated by such considerations as spatial and genealogical closeness, and personal friendship. Tradition calls for such rites of passage as weddings and funerals to be attended only by relatives. But hamlet neighbors who are present assist the host household.

Many changes have affected the Japanese countryside, but traditional ways of organizing life are still utilized where applicable. The development of *mura*-level organization did not impose a simple change in attitude or a conscious shift in levels.[46] Rather, the functions originally served by the hamlet have continued to be served by it, but new functions have been added at the *mura* level, and new organizational forms devised to fulfil them.

It would follow from this that the peculiarly Japanese hamlet will remain so long as agriculture—as presently practiced—remains. Were the Japanese to shift from intensive to extensive agriculture as has been recently suggested,[47] some changes in hamlet structure would be necessary. The increasing frequency of part-time farming, with the younger men working in factories or offices while women and old men run the farm, will clearly weaken hamlet structure, since the hamlet serves traditional work groups well but is ill suited to serve the commuter. It may be that improved agriculture and favorable economic conditions throughout the country will turn most hamlets into commuter dormitories. Until this happens, however, the hamlet will survive as part of the Japanese way of life.

Some Implications for the Problem of Democracy in Japan

Many Japanese social scientists and social critics have viewed the hamlet as clearly detrimental to the establishment

[46] *Ibid.*

[47] Iwao Ishino, "Social and Technological Change in Rural Japan," in Smith and Beardsley, eds., *Japanese Culture*, pp. 100ff.

of democracy. Some, for example, have seen roadblocks to independent agricultural entrepreneurship in the communal ownership of factors of production. Others see the close social control exercised by the hamlet as stifling individual initiative. The Japanese remember quite well the case of the young lady who, by complaining to the press of "undemocratic" practices in her community, brought upon her family the disgrace of being declared village outcasts. In general, it seems almost a foregone conclusion that, among other things, the postwar economic changes in Japan and the shift from traditionalism will result in a more democratic system.

Dore, however, has pointed out a rather interesting potential contradiction. He suggests that the land reform has given former tenants a new feeling of hamlet solidarity which now makes them more interested in the local level decisions. They are now cooperatively committed to the group that previously only dominated them. This new type of hamlet solidarity may be leading toward the third major hamlet pattern included in the diagram on page 160. It is termed the "secret ballot democracy," a situation where majority rule replaces either of the consensus patterns. If this pattern exists in reality, it has not been well publicized. It does seem to be the pattern which some social commentators consider desirable, though there are reasons for thinking that the land reform and other modernizing factors have worked against it.

Dore and Smith and Reyes have independently noted that some hamlet patterns are being strengthened.[48] As Dore notes: "It is difficult to forget the quiet pride with which a formerly very poor tenant in the Yamanashi village spoke of his election as hamlet chief designate for the following year. He had, he said, long been saving up to buy a power thresher. He would now have to postpone his plans because

[48] Smith and Reyes, "Community Interrelations," and Dore, *Land Reform*.

182

being hamlet chief is 'bound to be a bit expensive.' He 'belonged' to the hamlet in a way that he had never done in the days when it would have been unthinkable that he could ever become hamlet chief."[49]

There certainly remains room for considerable doubt of the superiority of a majority rule over consensus in moral terms. It is also somewhat debatable whether as a practical matter it is any more probable that consensus will lead to undue influence than that voting will lead to ballot tampering.

What is clear is that the land reform and other antihierarchy measures and influences have broadened the basis for decision-making. Where all, or almost all, household heads participate, whether the method is through ballot or through a consensus device, the process must be regarded as a step in the direction of democracy, no matter how the latter is defined. Where the hamlet is small, consensus can be reached; where it is large and the number of participants great, the vote will probably be more readily resorted to.

Whatever the future of the hamlet might be, its continued existence will depend upon its utility to those who live in it. Moral judgments will probably not affect the hamlet's continuing existence one iota. If they did, however, anyone raised in the impersonal neighborhoods of Western cities but exposed to the warmth and closeness of hamlet ties would have to suggest that all the morality is not on one side.

[49] Dore, *Land Reform*, p. 386.

CHAPTER VI

Associations and Democracy in Japan

EDWARD NORBECK

I HAVE RECENTLY attempted to describe the general characteristics of common interest associations in Japan and
have offered suggestions concerning their relationships to
other social groups and to economic conditions.[1] I wish now
to explore the question of the role of these associations in
promoting democracy in Japan. The present paper must, like
its forerunner, be regarded as a preliminary formulation
based upon incomplete information. We lack essential information on many aspects of rural and, particularly, urban
associations, including their internal structure, their procedures of operation, and their roles in local and national
politics. The discussion that follows concerns chiefly the
associations of rural Japan, which I shall first briefly describe
and compare with similar social groups elsewhere.

As a preliminary step, it is desirable to have some understanding of the meaning of the word "democracy." Scholars
writing on the subject of associations and democracy have
seldom given explicit definitions. De Tocqueville writes in
this context of "general equality of condition,"[2] and others
appear to imply egalitarian circumstances that allow relative
independence of action for the citizenry. I shall here use the
term to mean an ethic of social equality, and freedom from
any excessive restraint of action imposed by political or other
authority.

Many of the common interest associations of modern
Japan find their roots in antiquity, but the greatest develop-

[1] Edward Norbeck, "Common Interest Associations in Rural Japan,"
in Smith and Beardsley, eds., *Japanese Culture*.

[2] Alexis de Tocqueville, *Democracy in America*, 1 (New York: Century Co., 1898), 1–2.

ment of these social groups came after the beginning of the industrialization of Japan, about a century ago. Today, common interest associations are common and important, and they are particularly prominent in rural areas. Membership in twenty to thirty associations is ordinarily to be found among the residents of the hamlet (the *buraku*, the small, fact-to-face community of rural Japan, a number of which compose a village or town).[3] Following a recently formulated typology of associations based upon circumstances in the United States,[4] we may classify Japanese rural associations into those organized principally to reach goals of social and economic welfare and change (instrumental); those centering primarily upon recreation or other pleasurable activities (expressive); and those combining both sorts of objectives (instrumental-expressive). All of these types are well represented in rural Japan, and the associations may be described as entering most aspects of social life.

The greatest growth of rural associations occurred after World War II and is linked with a number of other social and economic changes. These I have discusssed elsewhere[5] and shall here note only in passing. Important among the changes is a decline in the importance of kinship. The rural household remains a vitally important social unit, but larger kin groups have lost much of their functional importance. Interpersonal relations in the small community are increasingly channeled through common interest associations, many of which have ties to neighboring communities and the nation as a whole. Much of the economic and social life of the hamlet is conducted through these associations, and social interaction outside the hamlet comes chiefly through involvement in the associations.

[3] See Norbeck, "Common Interest Associations in Rural Japan."

[4] C. W. Gordon and N. Babchuk, "A Typology of Voluntary Associations," *American Sociological Review*, xxiv (1959), 22–29.

[5] Norbeck, "Common Interest Associations in Rural Japan," and "Postwar Cultural Change and Continuity in Northeastern Japan," *American Anthropologist*, lxiii (1961), 297–31.

Most important in these respects today are the associations connected with occupations, particularly the Farmers' Co-operative Association, a national organization that exists in every agricultural community. Under the provisions of the postwar Agricultural Cooperative Law, activities in which these associations may engage embrace a broad range, in-cluding credit, marketing, purchasing, guidance in farming, mutual relief, medical services, and management and finance.[6] Activities unrelated or not directly related to farm-ing are also permitted. Agricultural cooperatives are primary sources of recreation and entertainment, provide adult edu-cation in a large variety of subjects, and are one of the most important media of intra- and interhamlet communication. Approximately three fourths of the agricultural cooperatives had several years ago developed women's divisions or aux-iliaries, which are concerned with agricultural matters but also with recreation, civic affairs, and general education, and about 40 percent had similar youths' divisions.[7]

Membership in instrumental associations is customarily limited to one person for each separate household. Expres-sive associations may include more than one member of any given household. Theoretically, each member of an associ-ation has an equal voice in elections and decisions on policy. Agricultural cooperatives and all other rural associations holding communal funds or property customarily have a panel of officers whose tenure of office ordinarily extends from one to three years. Secret ballot seems presently to be the most common means of selecting officers in large and important associations. Until after World War II, officers were often appointed by local people in positions of au-thority, but the extent of this practice today is uncertain. A survey conducted between 1947 and 1949 of election prac-

[6] Yoshio Hoynden, *Agricultural and Fishery Cooperative in Japan* (*Cooperative Movement in Japan*, Vol. II) (Tokyo: Azuma Shobō Co., 1960). The normal romanization of the name of the author, a pro-fessor of economics at Tokyo University, would be Hon'iden.

[7] *Ibid.*, pp. 95, 102.

tices in PTA's, women's associations, and youths' associations of Shikoku reports selection of officers by ballot or hand voting in 82 percent of a sample of 140 associations.[8] Office in associations that limit their concerns to the affairs of the local hamlet and have no great power seems often to be accepted unenthusiastically as a civic responsibility. Officership in the powerful agricultural cooperative, however, may be eagerly sought. Informants in one Miyagi community I visited in 1959 stated that in their region candidates for the highest office in the farmers' cooperative sometimes attempted to purchase votes.

Before considering directly the question of the democratic potentials of the Japanese associations, it is useful to review information and hypotheses concerning the nature of their counterparts in other areas of the world. Common interest associations are absent from the smallest and culturally simplest of primitive societies. They appear, but do not stand out prominently, in primitive societies of larger size and greater cultural development, those Lowie describes as being of a "medium level" of development.[9] They are present but not strongly developed in folk societies,[10] and their most elaborate development occurs among certain of the modern industrial nations. Where kinship serves as the organizing scheme in social and economic organization, common interest associations find no place. The fundamental issue does not seem, however, to be the strength or weakness of kinship. Any small, homogeneous group without intensive specialization in labor that can act as an all-inclusive corporate

[8] Fred N. Kerlinger, "Local Associations of Shikoku" (University of Michigan, Center for Japanese Studies, *Occasional Papers*, No. 2, 1952), p. 65.

[9] Robert H. Lowie, *Social Organization* (New York: Rinehart and Co., 1948). See also Heinrich Schurtz, *Altersklassen und Männerbünde* (Berlin: G. Reimer, 1903).

[10] Robert Redfield, "The Folk Society," *American Journal of Sociology*, LII (1947), 293-308.

body has no place for associations composed of segments of its members. When kinship and personalized ties with unrelated people of the small community fail for any reason to meet instrumental or expressive needs, however, the common interest association has very often arisen. Urbanization has often been accompanied by a blossoming of associations. The growth of associations is nevertheless poor in industrial nations with totalitarian governments and those wherein familial ties have managed to remain strong.

In rural Japan, a network of postwar economic and social innovations has profoundly affected kin and community organization, resulting in a social world in which many of the roles formerly performed by kin or through personalized ties with unrelated community members have been taken over by governmental institutions providing for social welfare and by common interest associations.[11] The relatively democratic atmosphere of postwar years has encouraged the growth of associations, but many questions arise as to whether or to what degree they are themselves democratic or democratizing.

Social theorists have long entertained the idea that voluntary associations are important for promoting democracy. Alexis de Tocqueville's *Democracy in America*, first published in 1835, presents an elaborate statement of this view. During his visit to the United States in 1831, de Tocqueville was struck by the proliferation of voluntary associations, which he saw as effective devices for democratic action and the spread of democratic ideas. He states: "Wherever, at the head of some new undertaking, you see the government in France, or a man of rank in England, in the United States you will be sure to find an association."[12] Later observers, foreign and American, have repeatedly commented upon the prevalence of associations in America. From these writings has emerged a conception of the United States as the "land

[11] See Norbeck, "Postwar Cultural Change."
[12] De Tocqueville, *Democracy in America*, ii, 129–30.

of joiners," a stereotype that has only recently been discredited.[13]

Theories concerning the democratic value of associations for society in general have also found frequent restatement. John Stuart Mill, writing in 1859,[14] advanced ideas much the same as those of de Tocqueville. Among modern writers, Arnold Rose[15] has suggested that association membership is important in a democratic society as a mechanism for creating an informed citizenry, providing both factual knowledge and the understanding of the issues necessary for rational decisions and effective action.

The writings of de Tocqueville and later theorists on the democratic nature and effects of associations have been concerned with groups that are voluntary in two senses: creation of the associations represents independent action by members and does not come about at the instigation of political authority; and membership at any time is a matter of choice. When we examine the rural Japanese associations from these viewpoints, little freedom of action seems evident, at least with reference to the important associations promoted by the national government and those with primarily nonexpressive goals. All of the modern rural Japanese associations are nominally voluntary in the sense that no laws

[13] Bernard Barber, "Participation and Mass Apathy in Associations," in Alvin Gouldner, ed., *Studies in Leadership* (New York: Harper, 1950); Floyd Dotson, "Patterns of Voluntary Association among Urban Working Class Families," *American Sociological Review*, xvi (1951), 687–93; Howard Freeman, Edwin Novak, and Leo G. Reeder, "Correlates of Membership in Voluntary Associations," *American Sociological Review*, xxii (1957), 528–33; Murray Hausknecht, *The Joiners* (New York: Bedminster Press, 1962); C. R. Wright and H. H. Hyman, "Voluntary Association Membership of American Adults: Evidence from National Sample Surveys," *American Sociological Review*, xxiii (1958), 284–94.

[14] John Stuart Mill, *Prefaces to Liberty*, Bernard Wishy, ed. (Boston: Beacon Press, 1959).

[15] Arnold M. Rose, *Theory and Method in the Social Sciences* (Minneapolis: University of Minnesota Press, 1954), p. 69.

compel membership in them. In several agricultural communities of Miyagi Prefecture investigated by the author in 1959,[16] only a very few farmers were not members of the farmers' cooperative. We are informed that in an area of Okayama Prefecture the new freedom not to join was "rather widely popular" during the early postwar period, but by 1954 over 90 percent of the farm households had memberships in the farmers' cooperative.[17] The numerous advantages offered by the farmers' cooperatives—advantages otherwise generally unavailable to the farmer—have made membership general throughout the nation. The number of member households of the agricultural cooperatives in fact exceeds the total number of agricultural households in the nation.[18] Although not quite all farming households are members, the total is swelled by auxiliary members—merchants, teachers, civil servants, and other people following nonagricultural occupations who live in rural areas. Laws governing the cooperatives allow these people auxiliary membership, with no voice in management, so that they may benefit from the educational, recreational, and economic advantages the associations provide. Governmental promotion of any association appears still to be accepted by most of the rural population as a moral obligation to participate in it.

Membership in certain expressive intrahamlet associations, such as wives' groups for the worship of Kannon or holiday travel savings groups, may be a matter of choice; since these are expressive organizations, they have essentially no political or economic import. Even for these associations, however, it seems probable that social pressures might induce membership, but information available does not allow assured statements on this point. It seems clear that social pressures en-

---

[16] Norbeck, "Postwar Cultural Change."

[17] R. K. Beardsley, J. W. Hall, and R. E. Ward, *Village Japan* (Chicago: University of Chicago Press, 1959), pp. 280–81.

[18] Hoynden, *Cooperative*, p. 26.

force membership in instrumental associations of the hamlet. Failure to participate in such organizations as the local funeral association would constitute a moral failing and is probably seldom even contemplated. In former times, when the hamlet was a much more autonomous unit separated politically and socially from its neighbors, local cooperative associations were often important, but today their roles are small as compared with those of associations organized on a national level.

Independent action in establishing associations seems limited to small expressive organizations, including study groups (*kenkyūkai*), which may come and go. Instrumental intra-hamlet associations are generally old and continue to be regarded as economically essential. It is noteworthy that the associations with membership confined to the individual hamlet seem never to be ad hoc organizations seeking to bring about social reform. The same may be said of the large rural associations organized into national networks. The programs of governmentally sponsored associations such as the PTA and the farmers' cooperatives do indeed include goals of civic and social improvement, but these stem from national officialdom. Neither personal experience[19] nor the written accounts of others provides any example in modern times of a rural association arising independently in an attempt to make social changes.

The Japanese population as a whole has not been averse to independent action in forming associations. When circumstances have permitted, they have often arisen among urban Japanese. After the end of the Tokugawa regime, the Japanese took readily to creating associations, and among the educated citizenry of the cities, associations seeking social reforms arose repeatedly. Control by the Japanese government over associations, however, was always maintained, and

[19] Honjō-chō, in Okayama Prefecture, during 1950–1951, and five communities of Miyagi Prefecture, in 1959 (see Norbeck, "Postwar Cultural Change and Continuity in Northeastern Japan").

it grew increasingly strict in the twentieth century. By the 1920's all organizations were subjected to the closest scrutiny. Douglas Haring, in a personal communication, described the difficulties shortly before 1920 of Americans who attempted to form a club of Phi Beta Kappa members in the Tokyo-Yokohama area with an idea of establishing the society in Japanese colleges. Hounded by the police, they finally abandoned the venture.

Agricultural and other cooperatives of an economic nature had received much encouragement from the government from the turn of the century. Although always guided by the government, they were first given a fair degree of autonomy. In regions where tenant farming prevailed, however, prewar farmers' cooperatives were hardly democratic bodies. Hoynden describes the circumstances briefly, referring to "class antagonisms" between landowners and tenant farmers, and stating: "Sometimes the cooperatives were looked upon critically as organs protecting landowners' interests, and the management was in reality somewhat paternal."[20] By the late 1930's the government had taken rigid control over the cooperatives, requiring all villagers to become members and appointing their executives through the prefectural governments. Youths' and women's associations were similarly nationalized, and membership was obligatory. These organizations, existing as they did in every rural community of the nation, provided a very effective channel of communication and control.

Postwar legislation has given much legal freedom to organize associations. Laws and policies established by the government regarding agricultural and fishing cooperatives seem consciously democratic. Yet there is much guidance from the top, and the postwar growth of important rural associations has come with the urging and strong encouragement of the national government. "Guidance" takes many forms

[20] Hoynden, *Cooperative*, pp. 15–16.

that enter strongly into the lives of rural residents. Legal provisions require that farmers' cooperatives belong to a central union of cooperatives, which appears to be intimately connected with the national government. Much of the credit, finance, and insurance available through cooperatives stems from national funds and goes through governmental agencies. Governmental programs of many kinds continue to flow to the people through the rural associations. Included in these programs have been such diverse items as instruction in techniques of birth control, education concerning health, nutrition, and sanitation, and adjurations to shorten traditional festival periods.

Hoynden writes of the democratic character of the postwar farming and fishing cooperatives, but at the same time his discussion often suggests that the associations are bureaucratic and that the government continues to exercise considerable control over them. The following citations will serve as examples: "After the war, a better-living campaign has been carried on in the villages. In order to accelerate this campaign, some 1,500 better-living promoters are dispatched to each prefecture."[21] "According to the 'Three-Year Program for the Reorganization and Expansion of Agricultural Cooperatives' recently laid down, the planning of farm economy is taken as next in importance to the dissemination of agricultural cooperative ideology."[22]

Writing shortly after the end of World War II, Braibanti[23] has described the manner in which neighborhood associations and their subdivisions, and, in rural areas, neighborhood associations, hamlet associations, agricultural cooperatives, and women's associations, were consolidated by the government during the war to form a tight network providing rigid control over the population. He suggests

---

[21] *Ibid.*, p. 95. [22] *Ibid.*, p. 43.

[23] Ralph J. O. Braibanti, "Neighborhood Associations in Japan and Their Democratic Potentialities," *Far Eastern Quarterly*, vii (1948), 136–64. See also John W. Masland, "Neighborhood Associations in Japan," *Far Eastern Survey*, xv (1946), 355–58.

that this same network be used to promote democracy. This may indeed be possible, although instruction in democracy backed by the force of authority seems curiously contradictory.

It seems clear that nothing democratic inheres in the structure of these Japanese organizations. As structural forms for organizing people into groups, they can be used for either democratic or totalitarian ends. Given organization on a national level, the associations may easily be used for imposing upon the people policies formulated by the national government. They are at the same time economical devices since it is possible through them to make the people themselves responsible for local administration of the policies.

These remarks lead to the question of the extent to which the modern associations are operated in a democratic fashion. The modern rural resident unquestionably has a greater voice in at least local affairs than he did during or before World War II. We have already pointed out that the important associations are hardly voluntary, and we have expressed doubt that selection of officers is everywhere conducted on a democratic basis. Fukutake[24] expresses the opinion that the democratization of rural Japan "is not yet complete," and discusses many obstacles that stand in its way. Among these are poverty, lack of education and understanding of social and political issues of importance to the people themselves, and, curiously, cooperation itself: ". . . the peasants still depend on cooperation to a certain extent. In spite of their selfishness, they are forced to maintain friendly relations with all members of the community because otherwise they would lose the advantages of cooperation. This is an important barrier to the independence of individual families." In the same context, however, Fukutake recommends cooperation, suggesting joint use of expensive farm machinery and, through the agency of the farmers'

[24] Tadashi Fukutake, "Post-war Democratization of Rural Society in Japan," *International Social Science Journal*, XIII (1961), 65–77.

cooperatives, collective management of farming. He emphasizes the democratizing value of both general and technical
education: "Japanese peasants and their social life will become more democratic if general education and the diffusion
of advanced farm technology through extension work help
to establish their economic and social independence." There
seems little doubt that the farmers' and other similar cooperatives have been very important economically to rural
residents, giving them through joint activities a considerable
measure of financial security.

The value in promoting democracy of the educative role
played by the Japanese associations is open to many questions. Social theorists have long laid stress on the role of
voluntary associations in teaching members how to use social
and political mechanisms to achieve their goals. Arnold
Rose[25] has stated that membership offers the individual the
opportunity to learn "how things are done" in a democratic
society. Reviewing available data on voluntary associations
in the United States, Hausknecht[26] doubts the importance
of their educative function, however, arguing that knowledge of social and political mechanisms can be enhanced
only if association membership actually results in introducing the individual into the mainstream of social and
political life. He points out that in the United States those
who would benefit most from membership (the working
class) are least commonly members and that the spread of
formal education among those who are most commonly members (the middle class) renders the educative role of the
associations superfluous. The middle class is already educated
in the necessary matters. The rural residents of Japan may be
equated with the American working class, and levels of formal education among them are not high. They stand indeed
to benefit from the educational functions of voluntary associations, and these have undoubtedly served importantly to

[25] Rose, *Theory and Method in the Social Sciences*, p. 69.
[26] Hausknecht, *The Joiners*, pp. 111–12.

create an informed citizenry, providing both factual knowledge and some understanding of local and national problems. Decision as to the areas in which the rural citizenry should be informed, however, continues to be made by representatives of the central government.

Hausknecht[27] calls attention to features inherent in the structure of associations which encourage bureaucracy and oligarchy rather than democracy:

> The slow erosion of democratic processes which is found in many voluntary associations is due in part to the interrelated factors of size and bureaucratization, and the latter, when seen from another perspective, may also have functional consequences. In a society which has passed through the "organizational revolution" adequate leadership supposes certain administrative and social skills appropriate to bureaucratic contexts. That is, the contemporary leader needs knowledge of and insight into bureaucratic processes as well as more general and diffuse processes. To the extent that voluntary associations are bureaucratic structures, it is possible to hypothesize that they serve as valuable training grounds for potential leaders in wider spheres of action. This may be true in some cases, but the other side of the coin carries greater weight. Leadership in voluntary associations may be denied to those who have not already acquired the necessary bureaucratic skills and knowledge elsewhere; instead of being the training grounds for leaders, associations become the contexts for the further exercise of skills learned in other spheres.

Writing in the same context, Barber discusses "structural necessities in democratic associations which impede the full realization of democratic values."[28] Barber's ideas may be briefly summarized as follows. Any association requires for

[27] *Ibid.*, p. 113.
[28] Barber, "Participation and Mass Apathy in Associations," p. 489.

its operation specialized executive functions and legitimate authority. Those in executive positions have generally acquired their skills in leadership elsewhere, and the association offers little opportunity for the development of qualities of leadership to rank and file members. Because of the inactivity of the majority of the members, the leaders must assume much authority. Given national organization, professional leadership and bureaucracy are fostered.

These circumstances apply much more strongly in rural Japan than in the United States. Active minorities and passive or inactive majorities seem to be characteristic.[29] For the majority of the population, established traditions of subservience to authority and submersion of the individual in the group stand in the way of independent and democratic action. "Approvers," those who meekly follow the minority capable of leading, appear to be abundant in Japan.[30]

Summary and Conclusions

Since the end of World War II, common interest associations have assumed increased importance in rural Japan. They, together with governmental institutions of social welfare, have taken over many of the functions formerly performed by kin or through personalized relations with others. Interrelated sociopolitical and economic changes have resulted in a comparatively democratic atmosphere in rural Japan. These changes in turn have encouraged the growth of associations, and much of the economic and social life of the rural resident revolves about them.

The democratic nature of these associations, however, is open to doubt, in part because of circumstances peculiar to Japan and in part because of characteristics that inhere in this kind of social group. The associations bring the villager in closer contact with outside communities and the nation

[29] See, for example, Kerlinger, "Local Associations of Shikoku."
[30] *Ibid.*, p. 68; see also Edward Norbeck, *Takashima* (Salt Lake City: University of Utah Press, 1954), p. 97.

as a whole, and they serve effectively as media of communication on matters of local, national, and even international concern. The cooperatives connected with rural occupations have unquestionably aided the rural resident economically, bringing him near to the financial independence necessary for democratic action. Through participation in these and other associations, the average villager has a larger voice in local affairs than in former times. The functions performed by the most important associations, however, are precisely those which the government urges on them and implements by nationalization and other encouragement. Although membership is theoretically voluntary, in fact it cannot be so described. Truly independent associations with aims of social reform seem at best rare.

The extent to which individual associations are democratic in their operations is unclear and needs investigating. The lone account in English dealing directly with this subject[31] describes conditions in Shikoku some years ago and reports that progress has been slow. Requirements of leadership necessary for any associations are undemocratic in placing much of the control in the hands of a few. In rural Japan, where few persons have had training in leadership, this circumstance seems especially to inhibit democratic action. Nationalization and the associated bureaucratization of the most important associations serve as additional obstacles. Discussing the decline of the importance of voluntary associations in the United States during the past century, Hausknecht states: "In the past voluntary associations have performed those functions that government was unwilling or unable to perform; as more and more of those functions have been assumed by government—ironically enough, often as a result of the activities of voluntary associations acting as pressure groups—a powerful force sustaining associations and motivating membership has been sapped of

[31] Kerlinger, "Local Associations of Shikoku."

strength."[32] In Japan the circumstances appear to be the reverse; the government has been the pressure group, making the nationalized associations assume many of the functions performed by the national government in the United States.

It seems evident from their history in Japan that common interest associations may be used for either totalitarian or democratic ends, but, unless they are in fact voluntary, their effectiveness in promoting democracy seems doubtful. The utility of voluntary associations in a changing society seems potentially great. They can be created quickly to meet needs and disbanded when their goals have been reached without affecting other social groups or seriously disturbing affective relationships. They are both instruments of change and themselves objects of change.[33] Whether or not they are democratic in nature appears to depend largely upon the social atmosphere in general. The associations of rural Japan seem to be principally reflectors rather than creators of postwar democratic trends. So long as they remain centrally organized on a national scale and under governmental guidance, democracy in them will continue to battle bureaucracy and authoritarianism.

John Stuart Mill's observation on the problems of democratic government is applicable to the dilemma Japan faces with regard to democratic action: ". . . to secure as much of the advantages of centralized power and intelligence as can be had without turning into government channels too great a proportion of the general activity—is one of the most difficult and complicated questions in the art of government."[34]

[32] Hausknecht, *The Joiners*, p. 115.

[33] See David L. Sills, "Voluntary Associations: Instruments and Objects of Change," *Human Organization*, xviii (1959), 17–21.

[34] Mill, *Prefaces to Liberty*, pp. 364–65.

PART FOUR

Managers and Workers

CHAPTER VII

Collective Bargaining and Works Councils as Innovations in Industrial Relations in Japan during the 1920's*

GEORGE O. TOTTEN

EVEN the diffusion of the wheel brought similar changes in a variety of widely different societies, posing for each of them similar problems of social readjustment. So, on a far larger scale, has the diffusion of the great complex of technological change which is industrialization.

For the late-developing nations the channels of communication which bring the technology of industrialism also offer solutions to the social problems which an industrializing society must solve—solutions rooted in the culture of the West which may or may not be optimum solutions for other societies. In this paper I propose to examine one such instance of borrowing and adaptation in Japan, the introduction during the decade after World War I of the concept of collective bargaining—one type of solution for the universal industrial problem of regulating the relations and resolving the tensions between those who direct and those who are directed in the large-scale enterprises of industrial societies.

The Westernizing 1920's

Rapid social, economic, and political change characterized the decade known in Japan as the "Taishō democracy" and the "early Shōwa" periods. It was marked by flamboyant Westernization and cosmopolitanism that caused political and cultural reactions in the 1930's, especially following the

* I am indebted to Mr. Rei Itō for assistance in preparing this paper.

Manchurian and China incidents, when ultranationalism provided the political impulse for sometimes ludicrous attempts to rid Japanese culture of Western elements and reinstate social patterns of a more traditional mold.

Considering the reaction of the 1930's, the 1920's were perhaps misleadingly Western and modern. In politics the "party governments" never really achieved power. "Universal suffrage" left out both youth and women and was accompanied by vague and restrictive police powers. Socially, the permanent waves, the "modern boy–modern girl" types, and the flood of Western literature, though permeating certain classes, were luxuries the masses could ill afford because of lack of money, time, and education. And even in economic development the sprawling *zaibatsu* battened, while the overwhelmingly large number of so-called middle and small enterprises starved for want of capital, markets, and raw materials and remained stunted in the shadow and on the sufferance of the giants.

The experience of this decade nevertheless constituted the most relevantly applicable aspects of Japan's legacy, when she entered a new era under the impact of defeat and the Allied Occupation. Whatever existed in the way of parliamentary and political party expertise, of familiarity with mass voting behavior, utilization of free media of communication, assertion of women's rights, knowledge of what constitutes a labor movement, all derive largely from the fecund post-World War I decade.[1]

Out of the wartime boom a new labor force emerged. While in general carrying forward attitudes from before the war, it found itself having to react to the postwar and later minor slumps, the world depression after 1929, and Japanese aggression abroad. Prewar labor, aside from the small number of skilled workers, was characterized, Professor Ōkōchi

---

[1] For the author's ideas on this subject see the Introduction and selections in George O. Totten, ed., *Democracy in Prewar Japan: Groundwork or Façade?* (Boston: D. C. Heath and Company, 1965).

Kazuo suggests, by the "poor man's" attitude; labor disputes resembled intrinsically the peasant uprisings of the Tokugawa period. They often erupted as spontaneous strikes, ignited by some small action but fed on the desiccated discontent of unbearable conditions. Workers reacted simply from a feeling that something had to be done if they were to survive, not from any calculation of what the results of their action were likely to be.[2] This type of attitude lay back of the great rice riots of 1918. There were no labor or socialist parties prepared to mobilize this released energy into political action.

But after this, glimmerings of "class consciousness" did appear. "Proletarian" concepts were imported from abroad to give form and direction to these stirrings of self-consciousness on the part of social strata that were undoubtedly new in the Japanese social structure. The postwar labor movement was led by an "elite" (it can be called so because it was so different from the rank and file) composed of two main elements: intelligentsia (products of the Westernized universities) and former craft or skilled workers (a kind of labor aristocracy with the experience and wherewithal for self-education). Examples of the former were Suzuki Bunji, Kagawa Toyohiko, Katō Kanjū, Nozaka Sanzō, and Asō Hisashi; examples of the latter Noda Ritsuta, Watanabe Masanosuke, Taniguchi Zentarō, Matsuoka Komakichi, and Nishio Suehiro.[3] Gradually, following the development of the Communist movement, this leadership split, throwing elements of both types of elite into both the Communist and non-Communist camps. But during the first few years after the war, before the sharp ideological division set in, they were all engaged in eclectic borrowing from the trade union movements of the West. It was in this period that we find great emphasis placed on claiming, on the workers' behalf, the right to bargain collectively.

[2] Ōkōchi Kazuo, *Reimeiki no Nihon rōdō undō* (Tokyo, 1952), p. 214.

[3] For the backgrounds of these men and their political roles see George Oakley Totten, III, *The Social Democratic Movement in Prewar Japan* (New Haven: Yale University Press, 1966), pp. 111–30, 324.

Collective Bargaining as a Crucial Demand

Theoretically, collective bargaining presumes that there are two sides, the employer and the employees. Beyond a minimal size, both sides have to resort to representation. Representation implies some kind of organization. Management, hierarchically organized, stands on one side and the workers, organized in some way to represent a collective will, typically in a trade union, stand on the other. Both sides possess power. One aspect of the company's power lies in its ability to hire and fire; the organized workers can, among other things, slow down or stop production. Except in certain special cases, the employer wants to keep production going, since that is what gives him a profit, and that in turn is why he is in business (as far as economic theory is concerned). The workers want a livelihood and prefer to have better conditions of work and better remuneration and also better compensation, in whatever terms, for their work. They dislike and fear the opposites, though they are willing to undergo temporary hardships for future rewards.

The interests of the employer and the employees are, in theory, always antithetical in that an increase in the rewards for either side reduces those of the other. But when the existence of the firm is at stake and the demand for labor low, the differences may be submerged. Here the workers are at an especial disadvantage. Conversely, in conditions of an extensive, open, and organized labor market with a larger demand than supply of labor, the clash of interests becomes clearer and labor more powerful.

The employer desires freedom to do what he wants with the workers in order to increase productivity, that is, to retain as many or as few of the workers as necessary and order them to do different tasks as needed. The workers, in contrast, want to be able to influence the employer and thus cut down his freedom with regard to wages and working conditions and tenure of employment and, lacking that, want to be able to leave if better jobs can be found. Collective bargaining and union organization are means to these ends.

Among the workers, however, certain fundamental differences in approach exist between the craftsman and the unskilled worker. To increase the remuneration for his time the skilled worker must see to it that his skill is scarce, and so he wants to form a union to limit and safeguard the procedure whereby his skill is acquired. That is why craft unions strive to be exclusive and tightly organized. But for the unskilled worker, strength lies in numbers. Because he is so easily replaceable, his goal is the closed shop. In the long run he realizes that increased productivity will enable the employer to raise wages generally. Therefore, unlike the skilled worker, he is not fundamentally opposed to mechanization, or even automation, if he can be assured of job security during the transition.

These general trends in the structure of the labor market and in the consequent development of trade union patterns were thwarted in Japan due to a number of special conditions, but they did operate among certain segments of Japanese labor into the late 1920's to a degree that is surprising in the light of subsequent enterprise-oriented labor control and/or trade unionism. If we exclude the large number of "transient female workers" (*dekasegi jokō*) engaged in textiles, it can be said that a labor market characterized by horizontal mobility (to a degree decisively higher than in postwar Japan) existed.[4] This was especially true of skilled work-

[4] Ōkōchi Kazuo, "Nihonteki rōshi kankei to sono dentō," *Keizaigaku ronshū*, XXIX (April 1963), 3. Taira has also shown that horizontal labor mobility was high in Japan before World War I. After that it became more stable, due, among other things, to the stagnant state of employment which reached a trough in 1932. Thereafter, as war requirements grew, labor mobility increased again in the late 1930's and during the war. After the surrender, it plummeted again and has remained low. Kōji Taira, "The Characteristics of Japanese Labor Markets," *Economic Development and Cultural Change*, X, ii, pt. 1 (Jan. 1962), 158–60.

ers who had learned a craft or technique, such as lathe operators or typesetters.

Up until the few years following World War I, this labor market did level off differences among wages and certain other labor conditions among enterprises, and the mobility between enterprises as a rule served to raise wages. The skilled workers played a large part in recruitment, since they brought their own apprentices with them. They thus responded to conditions outside the firm and were more independent in attitude toward management than became the case later on. Nevertheless, they were unable to organize craft unions mainly because of governmental suppression of such attempts after the promulgation of the Peace Police Law of 1900. (The unions that had grown up prior to this were almost all craft unions, such as the printers and ironworkers.)

In the wake of World War I, however, the expansion of industry and the introduction of new mass production techniques brought inexperienced young workers into the labor force and at the same time jeopardized the situation of the skilled workers. For the first time drives toward unionization on the part of both skilled and unskilled coincided, and this had much to do with the war boom in Japanese trade unionism. Still, severe limitations continued to restrict the development of unions. Legal restrictions, though relaxed, continued, and police suppression shifted from trade union leaders as such to the radical ideologues among them. In addition the laborers from the countryside brought in a new infusion of attitudes of status acceptance that could be exploited by management, when the workforce became more stabilized to produce greater company loyalty and enterprise identification, especially in the 1930's and in the post-surrender period. But this was by no means the case in the early 1920's when it appeared that a pattern of voluntary contractual relations had begun to develop.

Such a new relationship was symbolized by what was called collective bargaining rights in Japan. The first note-

worthy instance of the Yūaikai (Friendly Society) making
a central issue of a demand something like this occurred during a strike in August 1919 at the Okumura Electric Company in Kyoto.[5] The next occurred in July 1920 at the Fuji
Gas Oshigami Spinning Mill (Fuji Gasu Bōseki Oshigami
Kōjō), which was followed by a clearer articulation of the
demand in the March 1921 strike that broke out at the Besshi
Copper Mine, led by the All-Japan Mine Workers' General
Alliance of Unions (Zen Nihon Kōfu Sōrengōkai) which was
affiliated with the Yūaikai. During June and July of that
year (1921) about forty instances of demands for the right to
bargain collectively occurred in the various cities of the Kansai region. The emphasis had shifted from ad hoc questions
of discharge and working conditions to what was felt was
more fundamental. But what was really meant by collective
bargaining is not clear. At times it was apparently only a demand for freedom to engage in union activity; again it
seemed sometimes to have meant the right of unions to affiliate with outside bodies.

Most of these attempts ended in failure on the part of the
union. Only in two or three instances did a company agree to
collective bargaining, but merely to the extent of being willing to listen when the union wanted to raise a question, not
in the sense we have discussed above. The causes for defeat
arose from management's extreme distaste for dealing with
any labor organization and from the workers' inexperience
in negotiating with management. Along with the frustration
felt by labor groups in agitating fruitlessly for the suffrage,
these failures to secure some orderly arrangement of labor-

[5] Along with the demand for higher wages was the demand that
the company "recognize the Friendly Society as the labor union, void
all individual contracts henceforth, and make collective agreements
(*shūgō keiyaku*) concerning all matters with the Kamohigashi branch
of the Friendly Society as the sole contracting party." See Matsuo
Takayoshi, "Dai Nihon Rōdō Sōdōmei Yūaikai no seiritsu," *Jimbun
gakuhō,* VIII (1958), 122. (All English translations are the present
author's.)

management negotiations made them receptive to anarcho-syndicalism, which expressed in ideological terms a simple, down-to-earth alienation from both workplace and politics and a consequent resort to "direct action."

The syndicalist surge waned in the latter part of 1922. After the great Kantō earthquake of 1923, the organized labor movement under the leadership of the former Yūaikai, now the Nihon Rōdō Sōdōmei (Japan General Federation of Labor), changed course to a more "realistic" direction. The government also revised its policy toward labor in 1924 by allowing the larger trade unions to take part in elections for the workers' delegates to the International Labor Conference. This encouraged union organization almost as much as if a trade union law had been enacted guaranteeing the right to organize. A doubling of union membership took place from 125,000 in 1923 to 254,000 in 1925.

With this limited recognition of the "respectability" of trade unionism, various managements and the government began to pay closer attention to the degree of radicalism of a union. They felt it better to encourage moderate union leaders in order to avoid the spread of extremism. The Sōdōmei responded to this by placing emphasis on "collective bargaining" and secured its recognition in an important case at the Tokyo Steel Company (Seikō Kabushiki Kaisha) in February 1926 (described below) soon to be followed by similar victories at ten other enterprises. By this time the Sōdōmei was aligned with the very moderate Social Democratic Party (Shakai Minshūtō). Its chief non-Communist rival was the Japan Labor-Farmer Party (Nihon Rōnōtō) whose main supporting labor federation was the Nihon Rōdō Kumiai Dōmei (Federation of Japanese Labor Unions). The latter's somewhat more militant labor leaders also emphasized collective bargaining with the result that their affiliate, the Awaji Kōjōkai (Awaji Uplift Society), in June 1927 gained acceptance of this demand from the Awaji Paper Company (Awaji Seishi Kabushiki Kaisha).

Even the politically nonaligned, still a bit syndicalistically tinged Nihon Rōdō Kumiai Sōrengō (General Alliance of Japanese Labor Unions) also began to demand collective agreements from 1926 on, especially its affiliates in the Kansai area. Five of its unions in Osaka and one in Nishinomiya won this demand from such medium-sized enterprises as those making electric cookers, iron, and glass. A less important federation had actively stressed this demand among pottery workers in Nagoya around 1923 to 1926 but apparently thereafter lost its vitality and became unable to exercise the rights it had been granted, as set forth in a short written "contract."

The prominent institute for studying social problems, called the Kyōchōkai (Harmonization Society), listed seventeen noteworthy instances in which collective bargaining agreements were concluded between the years 1919 and 1928.[6] Almost all of the employees in each case were unionists. Eight of the companies had 100 or fewer workers; three had between 100 and 200; three had about 500; and one had almost 2,000 (Tokyo Steel Company, mentioned above). Eight of these were located in or mainly in the Tokyo area; three in Kansai; and five around Nagoya. One was a special case, involving the organized shipowners and some 55,000 unionized seamen throughout Japan, which will be discussed in a separate section below.

Before examining more closely some of these agreements, it is necessary to make some general observations. A basic fact in the situation is that both collective agreements and bargaining rights had no support in law in Japan at this time. It is true that government recognition of unions for voting purposes for the ILO in 1924 encouraged unionism and, further, that abrogation of Article 17 of the Public Peace Police Law in 1926 removed certain handicaps to unions when on strike.

[6] Kyōchōkai, ed., *Saikin no shakai undō* (Tokyo, 1929), pp. 284–85.

That year also saw the enactment of the Labor Disputes Conciliation Law (Rōdō Sōgi Chōtei Hō), which provided for the establishment of an ad hoc conciliation committee whenever demanded by both sides to a dispute, except that it could be imposed in the case of public employees. This committee was to consist of nine members, three each from management and labor and three chosen by the former six from disinterested outsiders. As this committee would have access to the plants and all relevant materials, it would be bound to secrecy. The main points of its conciliation proposal would be made public only if the conciliation were not immediately successful. The purpose of such publicity would be to arouse the pressure of public opinion toward a settlement, since arbitration was not involved and the conciliation proposal could not be enforced.

Contrary to expectations, the law was seldom appealed to and practically no cases of the establishment of an ad hoc conciliation committee in accordance with the law were ever recorded. The reasons usually given for this were that there were easier ways to deal with the situation and that the parties involved shunned the possible publicity. But actually the kind of conciliation committee envisioned by this law could probably only have come into being in conditions where greater equality on both sides obtained or where a responsible union and collective bargaining were recognized by management.

The law nevertheless did have an observable effect in increasing the number of cases in which informal conciliation was resorted to in solving labor disputes. This was because the law assigned to certain local officials, usually police, permanent functions of conciliation which involved training and keeping abreast of labor events. Beyond that, for the first time, it convinced other officials (such as town and village mayors) that conciliation was condoned by the government. In the first two and a half years after the promulgation of the law the percentage of disputes solved by conciliation rose to

43 percent compared to 12 percent for the preceding four years.[7]

During the whole decade of the 1920's, agitation for a trade union law ebbed and flowed. Even the Kyōchōkai was convinced that it was only a matter of time before its enactment in some form. Nevertheless, efforts to pass such a bill through the Diet ended in 1931, and no further legislation along this line was realized until after Japan's surrender. The collective agreements listed above were thus purely voluntary arrangements between managements and unions.

While the exact meaning of collective bargaining differed with each situation, its general significance was that management would consult with the union and attempt to find some common consensus rather than one-sidedly determining each item of worker-management relations. Perhaps "collective negotiations and understandings" might be a better translation under these conditions. It did not mean the kind of negotiations that take place during a strike or other tense situations. But it did signify a recognition by management of an independent and permanent organization to represent the workers for the purpose of ameliorating labor conditions and compensation.

Three types of collective agreements might be distinguished: (1) Written agreements. More specifically, promises by management to do certain things, after negotiations with an organization representing some or all of the employees. In a fully developed situation, promises by the unions to carry out specific obligations would also be included, but no instances of this, other than general promises by the union or the workers to be "loyal" to the company, have come to my attention concerning this period in Japan. (2) Verbal agreements. The belief in the efficacy of verbal agreements depended probably on the degree of formality of the occasion a pronouncement was made and the events leading up to it. Verbal promises were routine in hiring workers and in explain-

[7] *Ibid.*, p. 812.

ing tasks and rewards. Yet hiring was a serious occasion even if no decor were associated with it. (3) Gradually accepted custom. This might also be called tacit agreements. An employer would always have to consider whether any particular benefit he might confer would be considered a precedent.

These three types rank in order from most "modernized" to least so in terms of rationality and specificity. Where conditions are written down, their meaning can be haggled over and negotiations can develop. When only verbal promises exist, it is easier for management to interpret them advantageously to itself. While custom and even verbal agreements can be tightly binding in a traditional situation, such as village life, they lose their strength where circumstances are in flux, such as with the rapid growth and collapse of shops and factories in a period of industrialization. Especially in a situation when a union is forcing a reluctant management to make concessions, the union would want to have them recorded and continue to be binding after the union has unserried its ranks. At this point it becomes clear how legal support for such agreements and for procedures to be used in reaching them constitute an element necessary to the process of developing fully contractual relationships.

In addition to these three types of agreements, one other kind of arrangement should be mentioned at this point— the formal setting up of advisory or consultative bodies, such as works councils. This will be discussed next, for only by doing so can we understand the whole context in which collective bargaining takes place.

To summarize regarding the question of collective bargaining as a dispute or strike demand, it can be said that the first noteworthy instances occurred in 1920. By the following year it came to be thought of by the progressive labor leaders as the most crucial demand. They reasoned that, if that demand were accepted by management in general, it would mean the recognition of unionism. Unions would grow and they would serve as a tool for the "liberation" of the working man. In the early part of 1922 at the peak of the anarcho-syndicalist appeal, disillusionment grew regarding the utility of the demand for collective bargaining. Better to frighten the capitalists with demonstrations and other forms of direct action, it was now felt. (Even after the ebb of formal anarchist thought, feelings of alienation have continued to lurk in the background of industrial relations in Japan.) Then in 1924 to 1926, as the inevitability of unionism began to be increasingly accepted, the basic demand for the right of collective bargaining—for recognition of the union by management—began to be superseded. It came to be taken for granted and referred to, if at all, in stereotyped phrases, while the operative demands became more specific and detailed.

Conversely, the actual working out of collective bargaining arrangements became more widespread with the increasing moderation of unions. By 1930 the Sōdōmei had 49 collective agreements, and by the end of 1937 (the year of the China incident, which proved to be a turning point), it reported 117. Such agreements, however, were hardly coefficients of trade union consciousness on the part of labor. Almost invariably they were concluded with a union leader and his immediate supporters in whom the company had full confidence, even though the unions had not originally been organized on company initiative. They were effective to the degree that the union cadres also had the confidence of the workers. Thus what was important was not the provisions of the agreements but the personal relations between management and the union staff and the latter's relationships with the union members. This led to a certain instability. If the union leader died or left his post, or if personal relations became embittered for some reason, the agreement would become ineffective. Given these characteristics of the collective agreements, it is not surprising to discover that they were found mainly in medium-sized industries which were closer to the mass of small shops than to the few large-scale industrial complexes in Japan.[8]

Works Councils as Substitute or Supplement

Coupled with the demand for collective bargaining the more progressive unions in 1920–1921 sought works councils (in Japanese, synonymously *rōdō* or *kōjō* or *sangyō iinkai* or *kyōgikai*, often with *seido* appended). This was more favorably received by management as a substitute or supplement to collective bargaining and had the blessing of the authorities concerned with labor problems.

The two demands were confused by labor groups at the time. They did not clearly comprehend that, while collective bargaining theoretically assumed negotiations between equals based on a balance of power if not social acceptance, consultation in the form of works councils implied that management had the prerogatives in running the enterprise but was willing to take into consideration workers' suggestions. In Japan at the time, among both labor and management circles, there were those who hoped or feared that works councils would lead to labor participation in management and then the workers taking over production control and the management function itself, which would in turn lead to revolution and the workers appropriating the means of production, as in the Soviet Union or in some ideal of an anarchist society. This was truly a frightening prospect to the capitalists and an exhilarating one to the convinced revolutionaries. But for both in the context of Japanese society at the time it was unrealistic.

Actually the idea of works councils was imported into Japan mainly from two highly unrevolutionary sources: the United States and Great Britain. The American works council was a device used to deal with labor relations problems in war industry factories after the government froze wages

[8] Morita Yoshio, "Dantai kyōyaku ni tsuite," *Shakai seisaku jihō*, CXXXII (Sept. 1931), 101–12.

and jobs in them during World War I and was widely and successfully applied by the government-created National War Labor Board. It gave management and employees a way to settle current emergency problems while side-stepping the issues of union recognition and jurisdictional disputes. In Britain the so-called Whitley councils received their initial impetus from the first report of the Whitley committee in 1917, which, unlike the situation in the United States, conceived the works committees and joint industrial councils as auxiliary organs for the trade unions and employers' organizations, for the purpose of facilitating collective agreements, preventing strikes, and improving working conditions.

In 1918 the Japanese government officially began to encourage the formation of voluntary works councils. This was a period of increasing labor disputes. In 1919 the Social Bureau of the Home Ministry drafted a bill for compulsory consultation. About the same time a managers' organization called the Tokyo Factory Round-Table Conference (Tōkyōfu Kōjō Kondankai) drew up a description of a model works council which it publicized in the hope it would be widely accepted.

In public enterprises, Tokonami Takejirō, then president of the National Railways (Tetsudōin) became convinced that this idea had merit, and he instituted a council system (*gengyō iinkai*) among the National Railway employees that went into effect on May 1, 1920. Other employers followed suit, but these initiatives were entirely from management's side and were purely for facilitating communication. The employers wanted to keep their ears to the ground, so to speak.

With the business slump in the latter half of 1919 labor problems increased, and demands for collective bargaining rights and works councils became especially prevalent in the Osaka-Kobe area, as mentioned. Since at this time management was disposed more in the direction of accepting or even proposing works councils, a number of them were set up.

Labor raised this as one of its demands in 25 disputes in 1921, and the incidence of the creation of works councils spread from the Osaka-Hyogo area to nine prefectures totalling 42 instances. If earlier cases are added in, the tally comes to 78 instances in 12 prefectures.

In this larger context of growing labor-management difficulties, the Kyōchōkai became especially interested in these works councils as a technique for promoting cooperation and preventing disputes. In October 1921 it presented a draft consultation bill to the Cabinet, the Home Ministry, and the Ministry of Commerce and Agriculture.[9] It held meetings with important industrialists and urged passage of this bill. In the Kansai area the Osaka Industrial Association (Kōgyōkai) bore the burden of this campaign, publishing an outline in August 1921 on how to organize works councils.

The movement did not make much headway thereafter, however, and from the following year both labor and management (except in the government-operated enterprises) gradually lost interest in the matter. The Kyōchōkai lists three basic reasons for this:[10] (1) The slump that had begun in 1920 gradually became worse, and workers' demands centered more defensively on discharge bonuses. (2) Both labor and management became disillusioned with the system, because both sides had expected too much from it without being clear as to what they expected. This idea can be expanded on by noting the labor leader Noda Ritsuta's observation that the workers had expected that if they engaged in collective bargaining and set up works councils their problems would be solved. These were hardly more than words to them in the light of their lack of experience. Noda even quoted one local labor leader who exclaimed, "Since we haven't had any preparation for it, if our right to bargain collectively is recognized at once, we might find ourselves in an

[9] A copy of the draft bill and a supporting letter may be found in Kyōchōkai, *Shakai undō*, pp. 524–25.
[10] *Ibid.*, p. 523.

embarrassing position."[11] The other union men hearing him became angry. For them, perhaps, the slogans were "amuletic"; they could not tolerate the expression of doubts about their talismanic efficacy.[12] (3) More realistically, in the Japanese situation where strong trade unionism had not yet come into existence, labor leaders began to believe that works councils would obstruct the union movement.

For about three or four years thereafter the works councils as a system of consultation seem to have been almost entirely forgotten. Then they again became a focal point of study for both labor and capital. This was occasioned by the introduction to the 51st Diet session in the spring of 1925 of a draft trade union bill. Management suddenly began to reexamine the works council system as an alternative to a bill which would give unions legal recognition. The Kyōchōkai was swamped with questions concerning its views on the system, requests for help in setting up councils, and for pamphlets on how to conduct them. Then in 1926 when revisions were made in the Factory Law of 1911, the Social Affairs Bureau of the Home Ministry issued a set of illustrative materials concerning employment regulations. Among them were some on the works councils, which could be made use of by employers.

The reexamination of the works council system by labor came in the wake of the "realistic" change of direction by the Sōdōmei and its subsequent split when the more radical elements left it in May 1925. The works councils were seen as sometimes useful in gaining recognition for collective bargaining. A few examples of this are discussed below.

In this way sections of both labor and management had come to the point of favoring works councils; but they soon also found themselves in agreement on opposing a compul-

[11] Noda Ritsuta, *Rōdō undō jissen ki* (Tokyo, 1936).
[12] Cf. F. J. Daniels, "Mr. Tsurumi–Syunsuke on the 'Amuletic' Use of Words: A Translation with Commentary," *Bulletin of the School of Oriental and African Studies,* XVIII (1956).

sory system of consultation. At the 56th Diet session in the spring of 1929, Representative Fujiwara Yonezō of the Kensei Isshinkai, after reaching an understanding with Seiyūkai members, introduced a bill for compulsory works councils. This was actually a revised version of the draft the Kyōchōkai had submitted in 1921. Vociferous groups opposed it with the following objections: (1) Conceding that if there were good will and understanding on both sides, the system would certainly be effective, it would nevertheless probably produce unnecessary evils were it made compulsory by law. (2) The system was likely to lead to presumptions on the part of labor for participating in enterprise management. Representatives of labor opposed the bill on the grounds that it would not be effective in situations where trade unions were not in existence and in fact might obstruct their development. Meeting such opposition from both sides, the bill did not pass.[13]

According to a study by the Kyōchōkai at this time, 112 works councils were in existence in January 1929.[14] One of them had a history of sorts going back to 1900, 14 had been set up in 1919, 21 in 1920, 16 in 1921, 29 in 1923 (all of them this year in government enterprises), 9 in 1924, 2 in 1925, 4 in 1926, and 3 in 1927. Of these, 29, the largest number, were located in the Osaka-Hyogo-Kyoto area and 20, the next largest number, in the Tokyo-Kanagawa-Chiba area, as might be expected, but a few were scattered, such as one each in Iwate, Okayama, and Ishikawa. Surprisingly, they were

[13] It is interesting to note that those favoring this works councils bill argued that this system would not hinder trade unionism but would replace collective bargaining. Promanagement representatives did not favor the bill because they opposed unionism. Prolabor Diet members argued that the recognition of trade unions meant nothing if the right to reach collective agreements was not simultaneously recognized. See Ōkōchi, "Nihonteki rōshi kankei," pp. 10–12. Also the same author's "Kōjō iinkai kō," *Shakai kagaku kenkyū* (April 1963).

[14] Kyōchōkai, *op.cit.*, p. 526; note slight contradictions with origin dates for the figures by the Social Affairs Bureau of the Home Ministry, *ibid.*, p. 524.

about equally divided between private (59), on the one hand, and government (43) and public (10), on the other. In the private sector the largest number was found in machine tools (27), then came metals (15), chemicals (6), dyeing and weaving (5)—all of which were highly mechanized industries. Only one was in foods. From location, ownership, and type of industry one might conclude that works councils were a concomitant of advanced industrialization. But to go much further with such an estimate, one must ask how they were organized, how they operated, and what their function really was.

In terms of organization, the works councils could be divided into two types: (1) the unirepresentational—composed only of workers, and (2) the birepresentational—that is, made up of representatives from management as well as the workers. In the first case, the workers would discuss among themselves until they had reached a decision and then approach management about it. In the second case, discussion would take place between two sides across a table. But even in the first case, management consultants (*sanyosha*), probably lower ranking staff, would be appointed by management to supply certain kinds of information the workers might need in formulating their proposals; very few councils had no consultants. In the birepresentational type, the two sides were usually represented by equal numbers, such as six from each. Of the 112 works councils in 1929, 69 were unirepresentational and 43 were birepresentational. Whereas most of the private enterprises had birepresentational councils, the public and government enterprises almost invariably had councils composed only of workers who would in turn have to send a delegation to the higher managers. Thus the unirepresentational type (but with consultants in attendance) was the more prevalent.

While the superior effectiveness of either type of works council over the other would depend on the individual situation, each had certain theoretical strengths and weaknesses.

The Kyōchōkai took no stand supporting one over the other, but it is interesting to note the kinds of considerations it raised in its discussion of the matter.[15] It pointed out that in the unirepresentational type the embarrassing (for Japanese) situation of face to face arguments (*tairitsu*) could be avoided and the workers would feel freer to express themselves (though the presence of the consultants might dampen this). On the other hand, without authoritative figures present, the workers' meetings might get out of hand, or else the workers might reach decisions simply by majority vote among themselves, without taking sufficiently into consideration the explanations of the employers. The birepresentational type apparently provided a setting more conducive to the development of fully contractual relations, if the difficulties of confrontation and the inhibitions of the workers in expressing themselves before some of the very people who supervised them in their daily tasks could be overcome. For then the employees' representatives could exercise their leadership for the first time on a plane of equality with the employers; they would be able to enter into fuller discussion; and more reasonable conclusions might be reached based on a sounder understanding of the needs of efficient operation of the company. The trend was apparently away from the more modern birepresentational type to the unirepresentational, because of difficulties encountered in confrontation. In one case the change was agreed to tacitly (despite written provisions to the contrary) and in another not, although it was the workers who wanted it.

Except for a very few cases, each works council had a chairman. He was almost invariably chosen by management from among the staff (*shokuin*) and only rarely was he co-opted by the council. The labor members were usually chosen by the employees as their representatives by secret ballot, voting by shop or office, whereas management was represented by

[15] *Ibid.*, pp. 526–27.

appointed staff members or higher company officers. Terms were usually for one year.

Eligibility requirements for voting and for election were generally made in terms of age and length of service, though sometimes there were none.

In only a very few works councils did trade unions as such participate. In one case, the Kubota Iron Works in Osaka, in addition to each plant constituting one election district, all those who were union members, no matter in which plant they worked, were to compose one election unit. But no one would come forward as a candidate for union representative on the works council. The actual union leaders preferred to be elected as representatives from their plant and not to be known publicly as unionists. This was true at Kubota as late as 1929, despite the fact that ironworkers in the area had first been organized by the Yūaikai in 1915. Since this was a situation in which the company had made a gesture in the direction of recognition of union participation on the council, one can get some insight into the extent to which unions were still suspect organizations.

The situation was different where the union leader and the head of the company had a special understanding. They would either confer directly or through others controlled by them. We are not here discussing "company unions" in the sense of unions which were completely the creation of the company, but something close to this. Instead of being a company man, the union leader had gained a name for himself in union activity elsewhere.

A good example of this was the situation at the Tokyo Steel Company in 1926. With headquarters located in Tokyo, it employed some 1,900 workers in three widely scattered plants in Kawasaki (Kanagawa), Kobe, and Kokura (Fukuoka), making wire rope. President of the board of trustees Akamatsu Hanichi became convinced that with the development of trade unionism it was better not to oppose the tide but to establish cooperative union relations. He came to know Matsuoka Komakichi (later to become one of the best known right-wing social democratic leaders in Japan), who at that time headed the Kantō Dōmei of the Sōdōmei. Under his influence the Kawasaki local of the Sōdōmei changed its name to the Steel Workers' Union (Seikō Rōdō Kumiai), and its right to bargain collectively was recognized by the company. On February 13, 1926, a memorandum was exchanged with the union which provided for a closed shop with the union responsible for unionists' misconduct.[16] The company promised increasingly better conditions in return for the union's help in promoting operational efficiency. While a works council as such was not set up, the union head, Miki Jirō, was given the position of secretary by the company and assigned all industrial relations problems. In addition, starting in 1929, a yearly conference on working conditions was held for the purpose of making agreements on wages, bonuses, holidays, and so forth.

Another example was the Okabe Electric Company (Denki Seisakujo) of Tokyo, which employed 100. It had been unionized by Local 6 of the Tokyo Iron Workers of the Sōdōmei. In April 1924 the union presented the company with nine demands including wage increases and dismissal of a foreman. With the company's refusal a strike ensued. After ten days, the owner, Okabe Sansuke, realizing the futility of ignoring the union, changed his attitude, probably at the behest of his son, and worked out an arrangement with Doi Naosaku (a *"deshi"* of Matsuoka), then a member of the executive committee of the regional federation (the Kantō Dōmeikai of the Sōdōmei), which was representing

[16] A copy of the memorandum may be found in *ibid.*, pp. 288–89. (See also Seikō Rōdō Kumiai, ed., *Dantai kyōyaku jūnen* [Tokyo, 1936].) Incidentally, this type of agreement is reminiscent of the pattern of Tokugawa village organization. In this case the union leader paralleled the *shōya* (village headman), who was responsible for the good behavior of the village but in return had the right to be heard by his superiors.

the strikers. Doi was made a "subcontractor" and given responsibility for all workers. But in order to be rehired, each had to sign an oath to Doi, written in stilted language difficult for the workers to read, pledging to work hard and agreeing to a number of conditions on which they could be fired, such as truancy over seven days and resigning from union membership.[17] However, since this appeared to be such a blatant example of an *oyakata* system, it was attacked by other unions and had to be changed. On August 20, 1928, a works council system was set up to take its place. Workers' representation would be through the union and the council would serve as a collective bargaining organ. It would be birepresentational with five members from each side plus one secretary and would meet once a month. The agreements it made thereafter were very much in line with the spirit of the earlier oath. Thus cooperation and better conditions for the workers were achieved, but at the price of strict union control and with the aid of "personal relations."

A third similar case concerned the Kawakita Electric Company (Kabushiki Kaisha Kawakita Denki Seisakujo) of Osaka. Originally this company took a laissez-faire attitude toward unions and as a result found itself not only involved in tense labor conflict in August 1922 but also witness to a jurisdictional dispute in its plants between the Osaka Iron Workers' Union and the Osaka Machine Workers' Union,

[17] A copy of the oath may be found in *ibid.*, pp. 289–90. In a sense Doi's position was a throwback to a common form of labor organization in the late Meiji period, especially among the semiskilled and unskilled trades where the labor boss that procured, and to varying degrees controlled, labor was often called an *oyakata*. My impression is that this system constituted a main enemy for the growing trade union movement from the time of World War I and that the creation of a union usually spelled the ouster of the former *oyakata* rather than his becoming the new labor leader (as was the case, for instance, in the New York docks), except where company unions were set up. Nevertheless, management's experience with the older form provided a strong temptation for the new labor leader to "compromise" and slide into the role of a de facto *oyakata*.

the former being opposed to the Sōdōmei and the latter affiliated with it. Gradually the latter won over about 800 of the 1,000 workers and expelled the former union. In March 1923 it set up five locals, two of which controlled the two Kawakita plants almost completely. At this time the Sōdōmei was still quite militant, and the company claimed to have suffered at the hands of the union.

Soon the president of Kawakita came to know one Yagi Shinichi, who had organized the more moderate Jun Kōjōkai (Genuine Uplift Society), after he had been expelled from the Kōjōkai (Uplift Society) when leftists had gained control in it. The Kōjōkai was affiliated with the Kangyō Rōdō Sōdōmei, which covered workers in government enterprises. Yagi, by contrast, attempted to spread his influence in private concerns. He was an advocate of what he called industrial constitutionalism (*sangyō rikkenshugi*) and, though a moderate, did not get along well with the Kansai Sōdōmei leaders, such as Nishio Suehiro. This may explain the relationship that developed between him and the company president, who with his help fought the Osaka Machine Workers' Union (the Sōdōmei affiliate) at Kawakita by firing 160 of those most active in the union. When it was dissolved, the company recognized the Jun Kōjōkai, which then organized all the workers at the two plants and after a month of negotiations was given the right of collective bargaining. The reason the negotiations took so long was that the Kawakita management was split on labor relations tactics. One group opposed any union recognition but eventually succumbed to the argument that it was better to have a cooperative union than to take the chance of having the workers infiltrated by a militant union again.

A comprehensive agreement was reached and notice of it was distributed to the workers on September 4, 1924.[18] According to this, the Jun Kōjōkai leaders were to have the right of entrance to the Kawakita plants whenever necessary. The

[18] A copy of the agreement may be found in *ibid.*, pp. 285–88.

company would first consult the union when hiring workers; thus a closed shop prevailed. Also when discharging, the company would consult the union on the selection and number. A works council was set up, composed of five employees chosen by the union from each of the two plants and an equal number of representatives from management. The council, however, would not be permanent but would be reselected whenever a problem arose. Decisions were to be made by unanimous consent, not by majority vote.

How did this system at Kawakita work out? A report made after a four year period showed that due to general business conditions the company steadily declined and was forced to discharge 144 employees in 1925, 59 in 1926, and another 171 in 1927. Yet the works council system of communication with the workers enabled the company to do this without running into labor trouble. It is interesting to note that in 1925 the company gave the union the choice of accepting a 30 percent cut in wages for all workers or countenance the dismissal of 144 employees and that the union chose the latter alternative. Finally, in January 1928 the union agreed that the workers would work temporarily without pay while the company reorganized to get back on its feet again!

It seems almost pathetic that the Sōdōmei (and the Kyō-chōkai) should present these, as it did, as examples of using works councils for gaining rights to collective bargaining. Yet the Sōdōmei rationalized support of them by insisting that they could be utilized to develop modernized attitudes on the part of the workers. That is, in cases where workers had little or no experience with labor organizations, they could learn about collective bargaining at first hand.

In contrast, the radical, Communist-inspired Nihon Rōdō Kumiai Hyōgikai (Council of Japanese Labor Unions), which had split off from the Sōdōmei in May 1925 only to enjoy a short but eventful life until suppressed by massive police arrests and brutality in March 1928, expressed contempt for the works councils. Its leaders saw them as strongholds for right-wing labor leaders or devices for increasing worker exploitation, as at times many undoubtedly were. In some cases, however, Hyōgikai unionists supported works councils and infiltrated some of their own men into them in order to expand unionization and their own strength.[19] Their line was to insist on the independence (*jishusei*) of the works councils in order to shut out the influence of management and of rightist union leaders.

They also developed another technique which had a similar name but a very different function. A short description of this phenomenon may help enlighten us on the councils we have been discussing. It was called the factory representatives congress (*kōjō daihyōsha kaigi*). The first of these was formed among the printing factory workers in December 1925 in Osaka. For the brief period of the next three years they spread quickly and then were snuffed out by concerted police action.

The first objective of these congresses was to mobilize aid for disputes that were in progress. Another aim was to organize the unorganized, and a third to serve propaganda purposes for the spread of revolutionary ideas.

More specifically, toward the end of 1926 they became the form in which a campaign was launched against the way health insurance premiums were to be collected partly from workers' pay. Quite a number of them were organized on this issue in the beginning of 1927, and in May the Hyōgikai at its annual meeting developed a policy with regard to them. They were to be organized as common fronts on particular issues and to represent both the organized and the unorganized and gain representatives from as many different unions as possible no matter what their affiliation or political color. The purpose was to utilize the issue that agitated the groups in common to develop "struggle consciousness" and "class

[19] Watanabe Masanosuke, *Sayoku rōdō kumiai no soshiki to seisaku* (Tokyo, 1930), p. 141, and Taniguchi Zentarō, *Nihon Rōdō Kumiai Hyōgikai shi* (Tokyo, vol. 2, 1954 edn.) pp., 308–10.

neous.")[21] The overwhelming emphasis on welfare was undoubtedly in line with management's desires and reflected a kind of paternalism. Still the very presence of the other items cannot be ignored.

During meetings the workers' representatives would ask management questions and in so doing express the employees' feelings on certain subjects. Management would usually reply within the limits of not disclosing confidential company matters. Only in a few instances had the council's right to be consulted been stipulated in writing. For instance, in one such case (Hatsudōki Kabushiki Kaisha) it was specified that if the company found it necessary for business reasons to discharge workers, the management would state the reason and the number to be laid off at least one week in advance, but in emergencies it could ask the council to agree to immediately effective dismissals. In another example (Fujimoto Paper Factory), it was agreed on June 5, 1922, that any changes in wages or working conditions would only be decided upon after consultation with the works council. At the same time it was agreed that: "Items concerning enterprise management should be decided upon after consultation with the council." The Kyōchōkai cited this as the first instance of concrete negotiations by a works council concerning industrial control in Japan, and while this agreement seems not to have been abrogated during the next five years or so, the Kyōchōkai could find no other such agreements.[22] In another instance at the same time (Tantō Kabushiki Kaisha), it was agreed to negotiate wages for the coming three months at every council meeting. Finally, in yet another case (Kubota Iron Works), the works council, it was decided, could be used to conciliate disputes among workers, if both factions agreed and where management was not directly involved.

Convinced that the works council system supplemented

[21] Kyōchōkai, *Shakai undō,* p. 528.
[22] *Ibid.*

collective bargaining and that these developments constituted an opening wedge in modernizing industrial relations in Japan in an orderly fashion, the Kyōchōkai attempted to diffuse knowledge of foreign practices during the critical years of the importation of these concepts.

Concerning the true intent of the Kyōchōkai, my impression from working with the materials is that the staff was genuinely interested in "Westernizing" Japanese industrial relations in accord with appropriate Western experience, appropriate in the sense of being close to Japanese conditions and therefore applicable and also in the sense of being attainable with the least social dislocation and the least damage to the interests of management. The latter sense was probably uppermost in the minds of the trustees and those who contributed large sums to the development and maintenance of the Kyōchōkai.

An examination of the journal it published, *Shakai Seisaku Jihō* (*Social Policy Report*), reveals how the works council system was supported particularly between 1920 and 1926, with the peak years in terms of frequency of relevant articles being 1921–1922. About two thirds of them concerned works councils in England, the United States, Germany, France, Belgium, Austria, Czechoslovakia, and other foreign countries, and only about one third dealt with these matters in Japan.

Despite the availability of foreign materials, it must be admitted that the works council movement touched only a small segment of Japanese labor and that the closed shop situations discussed in some detail above constituted only a handful of cases. As mentioned earlier, only 112 works councils were reported as operating in 1929. Some 37 others had been formed earlier but had been disbanded for a number of reasons such as collapse of the company, its merger with another, or a deterioration in industrial relations.

No further attempts after 1929 were made to provide legal support for the works councils system. Big business in Japan had favored them for purposes of resisting the intrusion of unionism and encouraging greater harmony in industrial relations. Even before the onset of the world depression, however, big business turned to more direct means to effect these ends. More attention was paid to labor problems. Enterprise identification was engendered by means of wages based on seniority, retirement bonuses, and welfare provisions. Workers were hired directly from school and trained within the firm. This developed into expectations of permanent employment for those accepted for that status and the concomitant growth of the temporary workers (*rinjikō*) category. These policies broke down the previously achieved horizontal nature of the labor market and brought about greater variations in labor conditions from enterprise to enterprise even within the same kind of industry. The worker's whole life became more and more wrapped up in the well being and survival of the company. The Patriotic Labor (*Sangyō Hōkoku*) movement after 1938 only intensified the idea that the firm was "one big family." In these circumstances the works council mechanism became superfluous and collective bargaining unthinkable.

These subsequent trends (with their legacy in present-day Japan) are all too likely to overshadow the roles, limited though they were, that collective bargaining and works councils did play in the 1920's unless we also examine the exceptional success achieved with these innovations in an important segment of Japanese labor, namely, the merchant marine.

The Exceptional Case of the Organized Seamen

The picture of collective bargaining and works councils systems in Japan in the 1920's cannot be complete without a discussion of the seamen and the shipping industry. This involves not only industrial unions but also a nationwide employers' association, namely, the Japan Maritime Officers' Association (Nihon Kaiin Kyōkai), the Japan Seamen's Union

(Nihon Kaiin Kumiai), and the Japan Shipowners' Association (Nihon Senshu Kyōkai). A unique feature to begin
with was the long history of the first and last of these
organizations.

The Maritime Officers' Association traced back to 1896
when the Maritime Officers' Club was organized for the purpose of increasing welfare facilities and bettering ship conditions. Its new name dates from 1907 when it was incorporated as
a legal person. Then its main objective became the study of
the arts of seamanship. But in 1919, caught in the rising tide
of the labor movement, it developed into a trade union. This,
as will be remembered, was the year following the Rice Riots,
the year when the Yūaikai changed its name and strikes
were breaking out all over Japan, the most startling of which
was that of the Tokyo Arsenal. Even Premier Hara the year
before had expressed the opinion that it was proper and legal
for labor to organize on its own behalf.

In these circumstances a dispute arose within the association, which was made up of ship officers such as captains,
pilots, engineers, radio operators, chief clerks, and ship doctors. The question turned on whether such personnel were to
be characterized as workers and whether the organization
should be considered a trade union. It was finally decided
that even the officers were, after all, employees and in this
respect similar to the lowest crew members. They should,
therefore, organize and fight to protect their positions and
at the same time cooperate with the shipowners for peace and
prosperity in the shipping business. On the basis of this policy the association decided to participate as a labor organization in the election of labor delegates to the International
Labor Conference. Accordingly, the articles of association
were revised in January 1925. In August an understanding
for cooperation with the Japan Seamen's Union was reached,
and then together with the Japan Shipowners' Association a
move was made to establish a Joint Maritime Board (Kaiji
Kyōdōkai), modeled on the British National Maritime Board.

This was achieved in December 1926, and the right of collective bargaining was recognized. By the beginning of 1927 the association boasted a membership of about 10,800.[23]

The Japan Seamen's Union, which was composed of crew members, was organized later than the Officers' Association. Its official date of formation was May 7, 1921, but it gained from its being joined in October 1926 by the Kaiyō Tōitsu Kyōkai (Ocean Unity Society), founded in 1920, and in July 1927 by the Nihon Sempaku Shichū Dōshikai (Japan Brotherhood of Ship Stewards), founded in 1923. By the middle of 1928 the union claimed to have some 80,000 members.[24]

The Japan Shipowners' Association was incorporated in July 1920, though it had long been in existence as the Nihon Senshu Dōmeikai. By 1928 some 150 companies belonged to it, together owning 940 ships totaling some 3 million tons. This included all of the famous shipping lines, making it a truly national organization. Its objective was to aid shipowners to reach agreements among themselves concerning shipping matters, such as schedules, use of harbors, and types of cargoes. It did not concern itself with labor problems. However, due to the development of a labor movement among seamen and most specifically due to the ratification of the treaty for establishing Seamen's Employment Exchanges which had been drawn up at the International Labor Conference, the association began to be concerned with labor problems. With governmental blessing, the association, as representatives of the employers, together with the Marine Officers' Association and the Japan Seamen's Union, as employees representatives, became the three constituent members of the Joint Maritime Board.

Originally the Joint Maritime Board was only an agency for managing the employment exchanges according to the Seamen's Employment Exchange Law promulgated in April 1922, but then it took upon itself the discussion and settlement of conditions of work for seamen; that is, it was rec-

[23] *Ibid.*, p. 247.   [24] *Ibid.*, p. 263.

ognized as an agency for ameliorating working conditions through collective agreements. Thereafter the board functioned with increasing success. It dealt with such questions as (1) employment exchanges, (2) agreements on working conditions for crews, (3) the prevention and conciliation of disputes between the shipowners and ship personnel, and (4) recruitment of crews and management of seamen's homes.[25] A set of by-laws was decided upon on December 24, 1926.[26] An examination of this shows that meetings were held once a month with twelve members, half chosen from the owners and half from the employees. When agreement could not be reached, the matter was to be decided by an arbitrator or group of arbitrators (*chūsainin*) to be chosen by voluntary agreement between both sides. The board was to decide on rules governing allowances to be paid to crew members who had suffered accidents, and on standard monthly minimum wages. Along with the arbitrator, another item seldom seen in labor agreements at this time was the provision for conferences on wages and grievances.

This whole arrangement came to the test in the strike of May 1928, in which the Japan Seamen's Union was pitted against the Japan Shipowners' Association over a demand for setting up a scale of minimum wages.[27] More specifically the strike was directed against the owners of tramp steamers (*shagaisen*), that is, the smaller shipowners, most of whom had ships that carried cargoes on nonscheduled sailings. The larger companies (Nihon Yūsen, Kinkai Yūsen, Ōsaka Shōsen, and Mitsui Bussan) had already made collective agreements with the salmon and crab boat workers in Hokkaido concerning wages, hours, and treatment.

The Seamen's Union had brought up the subject of a scale of minimum wages and better treatment for the workers on tramp steamers. The Joint Maritime Board had been study-

[25] *Ibid.*, p. 736.
[26] The by-laws may be found in *ibid.*, p. 292.
[27] *Ibid.*, pp. 369–71.

ing the subject since October 1927, the year befo
only collected materials and come to no conclusio
the union sent an ultimatum to the Shipowners' A
and the Joint Maritime Board on May 7, 1928, de
reply in four weeks.

Nevertheless, on May 9, the Seamen's Union began
ations with the Kawasaki Steamship Company
Kaisha) and distributed leaflets at the docks. As a result
ships of that company at Yokohama and Nagoya began
stop. After three days of further negotiations the union's d
mands were pretty well met and the strike was settled.

But this was not the end of the story, because the union felt
that at the moment it was in an advantageous position vis-
à-vis the Shipowners' Association and wanted to press its demands for the establishment of a general scale of minimum
wages throughout the shipping industry. Such a thing had
not yet taken place in Japan, and there was great hesitation
on the part of the shipowners because they felt it would have
widespread repercussions in Japanese industrial relations.

But the union was headed by capable, energetic, and experienced men, who got the union behind them and forced
the association to set up in the Joint Maritime Board, a new
special committee of six, three from the shipowners and three
from the union. As the deadline approached, the special committee met daily but finally negotiations collapsed. Then
when this news came out, crews left their ships here and
there and by June 6, 241 ships were still.

Already by the fifth both sides decided to utilize the previous agreement and form a group of arbitrators, whose decision both sides promised to abide by. On the seventh the
arbitrators committee was chosen, composed of five men
(one union leader, one union advisor, one former Japan Seamen's Union president, the chief of the Hyogo prefectural
police, and the chief of the Osaka Communications Bureau).
On the evening of the eighth, they arrived at a proposed scale
of minimum wages for various ranks of workers on different

s. A meeting of the Joint Maritime Board was
the agreement was accepted unconditionally by
, bringing the strike to an end, with a precedent-
eement.

rike, which was settled in a few days, provides a
contrast to the Noda Soy Sauce strike which caught
ention of the country the same year and lasted an un-
edented seven months, ending in utter defeat for the em-
led workers.[28] The shipping industry was far more vul-
erable to concerted action than the semiagricultural workers
of Noda. The shipping industry was competing against the
advanced Western nations and required experience and skills
less easily come by. Shipping was far more important to
Japan's survival, and thus the government was seriously concerned with the situation. The government's prestige was
also involved, since an international treaty had been ratified.
Thus it can be concluded that the seamen, even those working for some of the smaller enterprises, enjoyed a special position in the working force.

The strategic importance of shipping for Japan with its
various implications probably also had much to do with the
"moderate" character of the Seamen's Union, which constituted the strongest affiliated support for the conservative
Sōdōmei. Almost everywhere else, except in Japan, the seamen as a group have traditionally tended to be on the fringe
rather than at the center of the organized labor movement
and have been marked by strife and radicalism. Yet historically they have also been one of the first groups to gain
special recognition of their rights, even internationally. The
Japanese seamen were the beneficiaries of this earlier struggle
by others. The separate organization of the Maritime Officers'
Association, made up of highly skilled personnel, played a

[28] For an analysis of this strike in terms of the theme of modernization, see George O. Totten, "Worker Protest in Prewar Japan: The
Great Noda Strike of 1927–28," 32 pp. mimeo., prepared for the March
1961 meeting of the Association for Asian Studies, available from the
author on request.

buffer role. A sense of skill and distinctiveness pervaded many of the seamen, too (as novels about their life by such a leader as Yonekubo Mitsusuke show). Communications developed through the mixing of crews, and solidarity grew by the very confinement of life on board, not easily amenable to distant supervision. Nevertheless, this very distinctiveness could help insulate what trade union consciousness existed among the seamen from readily spreading to the rest of organized labor. And this was also one of the reasons why the innovations and precedents achieved in the shipping industry did not produce serious repercussions in Japanese industrial relations as a whole.

Summary and Conclusions

Industrialization had reached a stage in Japan in the decade after World War I in which industrial techniques developed in the more advanced Western nations became increasingly applicable. Both organized labor and management were groping after new institutional arrangements. Initiative usually came from labor in the form of almost unpremeditated strikes which managements were equally poorly prepared to cope with. Then a small but highly self-conscious and politically oriented labor movement developed, taking its cues from Europe, America, and the Soviet Union without clear ideas of the implications involved. Gradually a number of concerns worked out arrangements with moderate unions, prompted both by the government and such pressure groups as the Kyōchōkai, while cooperating with the police and ultra-rightists to crush leftist labor organizations.

Especially in the early post-World War I years, when a dispute occurred, management's first reaction was usually of shock and disbelief that the workers could be so "disloyal" and "disrespectful." They claimed that they had thought of their workers as their "children." It was in fact true that at this time apprentices to skilled workers might be no more than nine years old when they came to a firm and that management often helped in the search for suitable brides for employees. Even the workers felt this paternalism and were aware that when a dispute occurred the employers became angry at their "bad behavior." Often after the settlement of a strike workers would apologize to their employers, saying, "Please excuse me, I shall never do such a *bad* thing again."[29] As the decade wore on, however, some advance in trade union respectability took place.

The situation differed greatly between pigmy and giant enterprises. The larger the firm the more attenuated were the employer-employee relations and the more anonymous the mass. A new kind of worker camaraderie and class consciousness could come in to take the place of traditional ties. Specifically, outside agitators could be more effective here. When a dispute occurred, the workers felt a need for psychological and material support from other worker organizations. This provided the basis for the development of the Sōdōmei, the Hyōgikai, and other federations, limited in scope though they were in the total context of labor relations. By contrast, organized labor could make little headway in the small shops, which constituted the overwhelming number of enterprises. Only in medium and large industry, including government and public enterprise, did organized labor achieve some stability in industrial relations.

It was thus mainly in medium and some larger-scale industry that the demands for collective bargaining and works councils were first raised by labor around 1920. The two demands were then often confused. Actually the collective bargaining demand initially meant a demand for union recognition. As unions achieved wider acceptance and at least a limited respectability, that element in the collective bargaining demand became less important. Another relevant

[29] Nihon Kōgyō Kurabu, Chōsaka, ed., *Saikin ni okeru rōdō sōgi no jirei* (*Chōsa hōkoku gōgai 6*, October 1930), p. 47, but also see pp. 7, 72, 116, and 143. This, incidentally, is a fascinating discussion by a group of factory owners and managers from the Tokyo area about their experiences with strikes.

factor was the gradual decrease in labor mobility, especially among craft and skilled workers as mass production techniques enabled employers to recruit younger workers without apprenticeship background at lower wages, train them in the firm, and pay them on the basis of seniority and bonuses. The more permanent workforce, combined with a new employer paternalism, did not at first so much affect the existence of already established unions as their orientation. As outside influences gradually diminished, labor and unions became more enterprise-centered.

Management and the government had become interested in works councils earlier than labor, then became somewhat frightened of them when labor demanded them, since management suspected labor saw them as a path to ultimate participation in management. Managers as well as labor leaders became disillusioned with their first experiences with works councils, because they had expected too much from them as a way of producing labor-management harmony, but leading employers expressed renewed interest in them whenever prospects of the passage of a trade union bill appeared, since they saw works councils, along with conciliation (legally provided, as mentioned, in 1926), as preferable substitutes to a trade union law. As it turned out, however, the more successful works councils appeared in medium-sized enterprises where strikes and labor troubles had destroyed the traditional personal paternalistic relations. The new relationships were either more truly contractual, based on the autonomy of the labor union, such as with the seamen, or else took the form of turning the union into a form of personnel management department, as in the cases of Matsuoka, Doi, and Yagi. A new "class consciousness" had appeared in the larger enterprises; the moderate federations could help keep it in check.

While works councils in Japan did not achieve more than a modicum of success—only a little more than a hundred were going concerns by the end of the decade—it must be remembered that they were not prospering elsewhere. In

Britain most of the post-World War I works committees and joint industrial councils were disbanded during the slump of the early 1920's. They were not revived until World War II, when in a slightly altered form joint production councils were organized. In the United States as well, many were dissolved after 1919, though a number were continued to secure employee cooperation and hedge against unions. In the 1920's some took the form of "employee representation plan" committees, which grew until the start of the great depression in 1929. But this was all prehistory to the triumph of industrial unionism which was only made possible by a sympathetic New Deal in the 1930's. Undoubtedly the ineffectuality of works councils in Western countries of the 1920's, where unions were already powerful, was due to entirely different causes. But that in itself dampened any Japanese success. The Japanese were as sensitive to failures in foreign social techniques as they were to new developments. At home, too, it could be seen that the councils had had no measurable effect on reducing the incidence of labor disputes, which reached 2,500 in 1931, twice their number in 1929. Generally, labor conflict rose and fell not as a result of the adoption of a technique, but in accordance with economic cycles and changes in the political climate, such as followed the Manchurian incident.

In specific cases, probably, evaluations could be made to the effect that works councils, with or without attendant union participation, reduced or prevented strikes. Their main function, it turns out, was to facilitate communication between labor and management at any particular enterprise. But which side was being more "enlightened" by the other? A greater flow from labor to management would presumably signify greater equality and wider participation in decision-making. A flow in the other direction might mean no more than an additional device for preserving the traditional ethos, though perhaps in a new form.

Apparently a few extreme cases of flow in one direction or the other existed, but usually labor was able to make proposals, as well as hear explanations, with regard to working conditions and welfare facilities. By and large, however, an intuitive reading of the materials convinces me that the councils were more effective in persuading the workers not to make trouble or to pull in their belts for the good of the enterprise than in convincing management to share the determination of working conditions, much less any other matters. It also seems to me, however, that management could not help but be made more aware of employee needs through the periodic formal council meetings. But to the extent that the establishment of works councils systems hindered local unions from linking up with others along industrial or craft lines, they played a role in shoring up the pattern of enterprise identification that has subsequently characterized Japanese industrial relations to a singular degree.

CHAPTER VIII

Postwar Trade Unionism, Collective Bargaining, and Japanese Social Structure[1]

SOLOMON B. LEVINE

VIGOROUS and widespread collective bargaining is a manifestation of pluralism in an industrial society. By providing for a mutual sharing in decisions vital to the participants in industry, it is a mechanism that can have a profound affect upon a society's system of interpersonal relations. Collective bargaining may serve to underpin individualism and equality by circumscribing authority and setting impersonal standards of behavior in circumstances where authoritarianism and hierarchical ordering have always been the rule. For, as industrialization extends and proceeds, behavior at work is increasingly subject to rules which must be followed with greater and greater precision, else the industrializing process falters. Hopes for democratic relationships in industry thus may easily be dimmed unless institutions for wide participation in the inevitable rule-making are firmly established. Traditions of this sort are now rather well anchored in certain Western industrial nations, notably some of the Western European countries, the United States, Australia, and New Zealand. Elsewhere, they have only begun to take shape, if at all.

No doubt one of the most dramatic instances of the attempt to achieve industrial democracy has been the transplantation of the collective bargaining institution into postwar Japan. Among the Occupation reforms that directly

[1] I am indebted to Mr. Yasumitsu Nihei for his assistance in preparing this paper. I also wish to thank Professors Bernard Karsh and Masumi Tsuda for their helpful comments.

challenged ingrained Japanese values of hierarchy, authoritarianism, harmony, order, subservience, and loyalty, none was more pathbreaking than the guarantee for all industrial workers of the right to organize autonomous unions, to conduct collective bargaining with employers, and to engage in disputes and strikes if union and management failed to agree. Although these rights have been somewhat modified from their original form (denial of the right to bargain and strike for government civil servants, of the right to strike for employees of government-owned enterprises and corporations, and strike restriction on workers in certain key private industries such as coal mining and electric power), they have remained essentially intact, and at present there is no serious attempt to destroy their legal basis. Today, because of widespread response of industrial employees to join unions, a network of institutions exists to exercise these rights—obviously in great contrast to the prewar arrangements.

This paper reviews the results of these changes, first, in terms of the extent to which the collective bargaining institution has grown, the structure the institution has taken, the process it represents, and the scope of subject matter it deals with, and then with respect to their implications for Japanese social structure in the industrial sphere. The conclusions appraise the future prospects of collective bargaining in Japan. At the outset, however, it is necessary to summarize certain hypothetical propositions against which the recent Japanese experience may be assessed.

The Prophecy of Pluralism

Following Kerr and his associates,[2] we start with the assumption that wherever industrialization begins, it sets into motion an unending process of further industrialization. Once a nation goes down this road there is no turning back.

[2] Clark Kerr, John T. Dunlop, Frederick H. Harbison and Charles A. Myers, *Industrialism and Industrial Man: The Problems of Labor and Management in Economic Growth* (Cambridge, 1960).

Further, the journey engenders its own "logic," so that all such journeys share certain universal characteristics or imperatives. A primary example is the elaboration of an industrial "web of rule" that defines the relationship between the managers *of* and the managed *in* industrial operations (the very nature of the production system requires both types of actors, it is assumed). Unless the "web" evolves, industrialization would stop dead in its tracks, impeded by lack of incentives and coordination.

Moreover, the rules become increasingly complex, formal, and specific—"the industrial system creates an elaborate 'government' at the workplace and work community"[3]—far more so than existed in earlier agrarian systems. Since technology, work organization, scales of operation, economic structures, etc. incessantly change, the web of rule cannot stand still. There is a continual restructuring of compensation systems, discipline, work allocation, workforce utilization, performance standards, and so forth. Further, in order to effect these "substantive" changes, it is necessary to develop "procedures" that assure consistency in the substantive rules. Rule-making procedures themselves become part of the rule system.

Two central hypotheses emerge from this depiction of the industrialization process. First, however the process is initiated, whether by narrow elitist group control or through broad open-market pricing, rule proliferation grows at such an increasing rate that opportunities for broader participation in the rule-making procedures multiply. The growth may come in fits and starts, but it surely comes, for the basic reason that increasing industrialization demands more and more functional specialization. Beyond the initial stages of industrialization, no small group has the omniscience or expertise to plan every detailed rule in the increasingly complex set of relationships; and, in fact, as groups are driven into greater and greater specialization, they become less and less capable of this task.

[3] *Ibid.*, p. 41.

This development lays the basis for collective bargaining. Certainly occupational differentiation, based on specialized knowledge, skills, and functions, requires bureaucratic co-ordination by professional managers; but coordinating decisions are tied to negotiations with each of the occupational groups (or with sets of them) that comprise the managed, since exact specification of rights and duties lies in an indeterminate range which only formal, and usually regularized, negotiations can resolve. Government, too, is unable to lay down all of the rules, although it no doubt will set forth universal minimum standards, generalized benefit systems, and procedures for the various groups to follow in working out their bargains. Thus industrialization which begins with unilateralism gives way to bilateralism and eventually to multilateralism. "In the fully developed industrialized society, regardless of the relative balance and roles of enterprise managers, workers, and the government in the transition, all three tend to have a significant part in the establishment, adaptation, and administration of the rules of the workplace and work community."[4] Collective bargaining, as a crucial (although not exclusive) technique for decision-making, gains in importance as the industrialization process unfolds.

The second hypothesis deals with the nature of the substantive rules themselves. Such rules turn more and more upon universals that industrialization must come to stress if it is to move forward. They must be geared to permit a high degree of flexibility and versatility for the workforce. They must allow growing emphasis on education, research, and innovation which nourish the ever-advancing, changing technology and call for new skills, recombination of old skills and proliferation of specialized skills. "The industrial society requires continual training and retraining of the workforce; the content of an occupation or job classification is seldom set for life. . . . Its occupational mobility is associated with a high degree of geographical movement in a workforce and with

[4] *Ibid.*, p. 42.

social mobility in the larger community both upwards and downwards."[5] Accordingly, rights and duties of each occupation must be made highly visible or "universal." Substantive rules applying to each occupation, and the changes in these rules, have to be spelled out. (Occupational wage rates especially must be systematized and formalized.) They cannot long remain particularistic and personal, but are depersonalized through detailed written collective agreements and grievance settlements, arbitrations, and the like, in addition to legal enactments (laws, court decisions, administrative rulings, etc.).

Universalistic collective bargaining links labor markets and rule specification. Institutionalized rule-making becomes an unending process as groups haul and tug with one another to preserve or alter their respective positions in the dynamic occupational complex of the labor market. Although certain rules may be universal to all occupations (for example, minimum wages and social security benefits), alongside will develop subsets of rules specific to certain occupations, thus giving birth to a number of interconnected industrial relations subsystems in an industrializing society.[6]

What are the implications of these propositions for interpersonal relations and social structure in the industrializing society? First, since bargaining presumably becomes a necessary technique for decision-making, superior-subordinate distinctions in industry presumably decline. Workers achieve a relatively independent position vis-à-vis managers principally by developing autonomous bargaining agencies which circumscribe employer authority. Second, control over the workforce is achieved largely through the application of impersonal rules, laid down by detailed marketwide agreements geared to occupational qualification, rather than to particularistic qualities based on birth, seniority, family, or clique.

[5] *Ibid.*, p. 35.
[6] See John T. Dunlop, *Industrial Relations Systems* (New York, 1958).

Third, workers enjoy increasing freedom of choice both in attaching themselves to the production process and in following consumption patterns; reference to one's own well-being or that of certain other specific individuals gains ascendancy over reference to the well-being of some group on which he is dependent and to which he owes loyalty. In short, industrialization produces an ordered fractionalization of society, in which the individual pursues his goals through a pluralism of group attachments, no one of which exercises final control over his behavior.

To what extent may this prediction apply to contemporary Japan? To what degree is the bargaining process becoming rooted in Japanese industry? How has it been structured and with what does it deal? What are its prospects for further evolution in terms of the above hypotheses? The answers to these questions may shed light on what may be happening to the Japanese social structure, at least in the industry sector.

The Extent and Vigor of Collective Bargaining

A considerable network of formalized collective bargaining machinery has come into existence in Japan since the end of World War II. There are, of course, no exact figures on the extent of genuine collective bargaining in Japan (in fact, we have none for any country). Mere existence of formalized machinery is no guarantee that bargaining is carried on, nor is the absence of such machinery a sign of the lack of bargaining. Despite these limitations to empirical investigation, it is useful to plumb for two practices—formal agreement-making and visible disputes—as indices of the extensiveness and intensity of union-management bargaining. We approach these first by summarizing the extent of union organization, wherein formal collective bargaining may occur.

The industrial complex of Japan embraces some 4 million nonagricultural enterprises, which employ more than 35 million persons, of whom about three-fourths work for wages and salaries in the employ of others (the remainder are self-em-

ployed or unpaid family workers) and thus are considered organizable. Between 10 million and 11 million workers actually are members of unions (an organizational rate, incidentally, which compares favorably to the United States and is not much less than Britain's); but, while organizable workers are found in almost 300,000 enterprises, those actually organized work in only about 15,000. It is not known exactly how many of these firms have written collective agreements, but a reasonable estimate is half.

To look at the bargaining potential from the union side, in 1965 the 10.1 million organized workers were embraced by more than 52,000 local organizational units (counted in terms of the smallest formal organizations that possess sets of by-laws and officers, presumably in conformance with legal requirements). This number of local units (*tan-i kumiai*) has shown a steady growth over the past decade, increasing between 1,000 and 2,000 each year, mainly in the smaller enterprises; but there is considerable turnover among these units (in 1965, for example, 3,774 were newly established and 3,282 dissolved[7]).

About one fourth of these units—the national and local civil servant unions with a total membership of 1.5 million —are excluded by law (since 1948) from collective bargaining. (The national and local personnel authorities established by law unilaterally determine the work rules for these workers.) Thus there is a maximum collective bargaining potential for about 45,000 of the basic union units, totaling a membership of more than 8.5 million. At present, about 30,000 of these units are covered by written collective agreements, either of the type that applies to a single unit alone or on a multiple-unit basis. They embrace approximately 6.5 million members, or close to 80 percent of those legally eligible for coverage.[8]

[7] Japan, Rōdōshō, *Rōdō hakusho 1965* (the Ministry of Labor's annual survey).
[8] *Idem.*

In light of the very limited collective bargaining experience in prewar Japan, this achievement, on its face, is impressive. With one fourth of all Japanese industrial workers employed under the terms of written union-management agreements and with two thirds of their union units eligible to bargain actually covered, it appears that the collective bargaining institution has been substantially rooted in the Japanese industrial terrain.

Unionization has penetrated both large and small enterprises, but in highly varying degrees. While almost half the firms that have organized workers employ fewer than 29 workers, less than 3 percent of these small enterprises are unionized. As the scale of employment increases, however, there is a remarkable growth in union coverage. Unionism has saturated the large enterprises. For example, virtually all of the approximately 450 manufacturing enterprises in Japan that employ 1,000 workers or more have organized workers. (In all of Japan, there are only slightly more than 1,000 enterprises of this size in both manufacturing and nonmanufacturing.) Much of the steady growth of the Japanese labor movement since 1950, however, has been concentrated in the smaller firms.

As would be expected, the larger union units have obtained the most extensive contract coverage. The larger the union unit, the more likely it will have concluded an agreement with the employer. Moreover, since the union unit in the vast majority of cases (about 90 percent) typically embraces all the regular workers in a plant or enterprise, when an agreement is made it will in all likelihood apply to this entire workforce. Thus, virtually all enterprises with 1,000 or more employees have contracts, accounting for perhaps at least 50 percent of the total worker coverage; while probably not more than half the unionized enterprises with smaller workforces have agreements.[9] A mere handful of seven or eight

[9] Japan, Rōdōshō, *Rōdō kumiai kihon chōsa hōkokusho* (1960), p. 35 (the Ministry's survey of labor unions).

huge enterprises, in fact, each with union memberships of more than 50,000, appears to account for as much as one fourth of the worker contract coverage.

The skewed distribution of union organization among large and small enterprises is reflected in wide variability of contract coverage by industry. In transportation, communications, electricity, gas, water, and similar public utilities, industries which are composed almost entirely of large-scale enterprises and whose regular employees are fully organized, at least 90 percent of the 2.1 million unionized workers are covered. But in other sectors where there are mixed patterns of large and small enterprises, contract coverage varies widely. In manufacturing, which employs almost 10 million wage earners, the rate of union organization is around 40 percent, and contract coverage is close to the general average of 85 percent. High rates of both organization and contract coverage are found in mining; but industries such as forestry, wholesale and retail trades, and finance and insurance, which have extremely low rates of organization, have high rates of contract coverage for those organized. Other sectors—such as agriculture, construction, real estate, and the services— have relatively low rates of both. Among the services, however, education is almost fully organized (as is true among most government employees) but because of legal restrictions has a low rate (20 percent) of contract coverage, as is also true of government employees in general.[10]

These figures reveal a somewhat jagged pattern of contract-making. Where unionization has taken place, making of written agreements has followed in the majority of cases. Where enterprises are large and industry concentrated, unionization and contract coverage are virtually complete, except of course in the case of civil servants. On the other hand, there are important instances of contract-making throughout all the major industrial sectors, so that it cannot be said that

[10] *Ibid.*, p. 45, and Japan, Rōdōshō, *Rōdō tōkei nempō 1965* (the Ministry's yearbook of labor statistics), pp. 10–12, 298–99.

bargaining in Japanese industrial relations is exclusively a phenomenon of the large-scale enterprises and concentrated industries. The bargaining institution appears to have taken root at least to some degree at all levels of the industrial structure.

But how active is agreement-making? Bargaining intensity appears highly variable. First, although by law agreements are supposed to expire within three years, it is quite commonplace to have automatic renewals of labor contracts, so that many of them in effect have been indefinitely extended without serious negotiation. On the other hand, since it is general practice to conclude a series of separate agreements on different issues, some of the bargaining relationships are considerably more active than others.

One indicator of collective bargaining intensity is given by the frequency and incidence of labor disputes. Although occurrences of disputes do not necessarily mean that the end result is the concluding of agreements, nor does the absence of disputes indicate a lack of vigorous bargaining, nonetheless, because they represent known confrontations over the nature of the industrial rules, they are useful to examine. Japanese dispute statistics are helpful for this purpose because they cover "all known disputes" not only those which involved "dispute actions" (strikes, lockouts, slowdowns, "production control," etc.). These are usually known because of the presence of conciliators and mediators from the various labor relations commissions provided for by law.

Despite impressions gained from the Japanese press, it cannot be said that an exceptionally high rate of disputes has accompanied Japanese collective bargaining on the whole. From 1946 to 1965 known disputes in progress each year have numbered well over 1,000 (the highest, in 1965, 3,051 disputes, involving more than 8.9 million workers). Of these, about two thirds have usually involved some type of dispute action. While manufacturing accounts for about half of the outbreaks, mining, transportation, and communications provide

a disproportionately high percentage compared to the proportion of unions and workers organized.[11] This probably means
that the incidence of disputes is highly concentrated, with
certain unions and enterprises involved in such conflicts more
than once each in a given year. In other words, while dispute
incidence is generally low in Japan, where they occur the
frequency is relatively high. Moreover, this high frequency
takes place where there is a high degree of unionization, a
high rate of contract coverage and frequent negotiations.
Vigorous contract-making and disputes, therefore, appear to
go together.

There has been little or no slackening off of dispute activity
in postwar Japan, further indicating the vigor of collective
bargaining in certain sectors. This is accounted for by at least
two reasons. A few industries, as mentioned, have remained
rather highly dispute-prone. In addition, as unionization has
spread from the larger to the smaller enterprises, disputes
have been increasing among the latter. More than 40 percent
of disputes in recent years have involved fewer than 100
workers each; and enterprises with less than 100 employees
each have been involved in at least a third of the disputes.[12]

Dispute figures support the general conclusion that while
collective bargaining has spread in Japan, so far it is still
practiced on a spotty basis. Where it occurs, it appears to be
relatively intense, but there are considerable gradations of
intensity. The reasons for this will be explored further in the
sections that follow. To approach the explanation, it is first
necessary to examine the nature of the bargaining structures,
for they become a vital clue to the type of subject matter dealt
with in the Japanese collective bargaining machinery and, in
turn, the viability of the collective bargaining institution
itself.

The Structure of Bargaining

Collective bargaining structures in Japan are not as varied

[11] Japan, Rōdōshō, *Tōkei nempō 1965*, pp. 300ff.
[12] Japan, Rōdōshō, *Hakusho 1965*, p. 404.

as those found in some Western nations. In the United States, for example, bargaining units (the worker jurisdiction which a labor agreement covers) include such types as industry-wide units, multiple-company units, company-wide units, plant units, craft units, regional industry and craft units, and numerous other varieties, which are not necessarily coterminous with the local union structure of American labor organizations. In Japan, however, the bargaining unit is virtually identical to the basic union organization. The complexity of defining appropriate collective bargaining units led to enactment of special legal procedures in the United States for their determination; but in Japan, because of the simple one-to-one relationship of union and bargaining jurisdiction, this has not been a serious problem, except in cases of union splits.

The chief reason for this lack of complexity of Japan is the great predominance of the "enterprise" union, a structure which includes as its members all nonsupervisory employees of a given plant or enterprise (frequently the latter when an enterprise has more than one plant establishment). As many as 90 percent of all union organizations are of this type, including a like proportion of the total membership.[13] Other structures—craft, industrial, general, regional, etc.—do exist, but are of so little importance for the collective bargaining activity, except in a few instances like the seamen, that we omit discussion of them here.

This does not mean that the enterprise union structure is unique to Japan. Unions in Western countries often attempt to organize their constituents on an enterprise basis both to enhance their bargaining power and to achieve more effective internal administration. There are, however, certain notable features about Japanese enterprise unionism that set it aside from the counterpart Western notion of one union for one plant or company.

In general, Japanese enterprise unions mainly stress the

[13] See Okōchi Kazuo *et al., Sengo rōdō kumiai no jittai* (1950), and *Rōdō kumiai no kōzō to kinō* (1959).

protection of workers' interests *only within the enterprise per se*. They are not market oriented and comparatively little concerned with the members' relative position in the industry or in the national economy. In contrast, Western movements have usually stressed the stake of the local union beyond the enterprise as a member of an industrial group, or craft, or of the whole working class. Enterprise unionism may be said to be another example of the "particularistic" pattern so often found in Japanese social structure. There is, for example, a striking resemblance between the enterprise union, or the plant-level branches of a multiple-establishment enterprise union, and the typical *buraku* organization of rural Japan, in the sense of what Dore has called hamlet solidarity.

We have a fair understanding of why Japanese unions took the enterprise structure.[14] In the chaos following the war, despite the democratic "universals" pushed by the Occupation, the forces of particularism remained especially strong. Workers took refuge in organized entities that afforded what measures of security could be obtained. By 1946 no longer could industrial workers flee back to the security of villages and farms, from which they had cut themselves off a generation or two earlier, and where, as the result of land reform prospects, uncertainty also was at its height. Further, large masses of evacuees and veterans were returning home to reestablish themselves in this distraught nation. Given the ingrained habits of group solidarity and particularism that had been fortified by wartime devices such as the Sampō (Patriotic Industrial Association), the primary motivating force for industrial workers was the desire to belong to organizational entities that had promise—or at least some likelihood—of weathering and outliving the crisis. The enterprise was the logical haven, and unionism an added assurance of continued attachment to the enterprise.

Paradoxically, ideological appeals probably helped to

[14] *Idem.*

strengthen this particularizing force, rather than weaken it. Every opportunity was given in the early years of the Allied Occupation to permit the industrial workforce as a class to challenge and thwart reemergence of the elites that had controlled Japan's polity and economy. Released from jails, left-wing leaders were, until the outbreak of the cold war, unrestrained in their attempts to develop working-class solidarity, primarily through the building of industrial union structures. But they had to work upon a Procrustes bed of particularism, and their efforts probably did more to stimulate and sanction the establishment of enterprise unionism rather than to achieve industrial unionism, which they then advocated and still do. Other groups, notably identified with the revived Sōdōmei, recognized the intractability of enterprise unionism and were willing to pursue a more gradualistic course. After all, enterprise unionism had produced Japan's first widespread organization of workers. Had the Occupation had any doubts about the efficacy of this organizational structure in its efforts to promote a collective bargaining, these were soon shoved aside when it reversed its liberal policies of encouraging worker organization and left-wing agitation. As a result, union particularism has remained a dominant structural theme of the Japanese labor movement. With it emerged a particularistic bargaining system.

Even with this base of union organization, the practice of writing labor agreements at the enterprise level quickly spread. By 1948 more than 20,000 unions with two thirds of all the union members were covered by contracts—or really "codes" recognizing their legitimate place in the enterprise. Even though occupation labor restrictions and deflationary economic measures destroyed some of this bargaining activity in the next two years, after 1950 contract-making quickly revived and spread, but primarily at the enterprise level.

One major accompaniment of this collective bargaining structure was the tendency to limit union membership only to the enterprise's "regular" workforce and at the same time to define the union's jurisdiction to include both white collar (*shokuin*) and the blue collar (*kōin*) workers together. (About 60 percent of all basic unions are of this "combined" type.) Union shop provisions, which most Japanese contracts include, further strengthened these arrangements.

As a result, collective bargaining drastically altered the formal status system *within the enterprise*, and thus displayed a tinge of the "new democracy." The earlier sharp status distinction between *shokuin* and *kōin* now was eliminated, as labor contracts were applied equally to both categories.

At the same time, each union *limited* its bargaining jurisdiction in most cases (and hence their membership as well) only to the regular or permanent workforce within the enterprise. Temporary employees, casual workers, subcontract workers, day laborers, and so forth were not as a rule included. They were left to fend for themselves, either to attempt on their own to secure permanent employment status or to develop their own self-defense organizations. In neither respect have they been overly successful, despite their growing number, and in most cases the enterprise unions have not sought seriously to widen their respective jurisdictions to embrace them, despite the frequent proclamations of the central labor federations and national industrial union organizations exhorting them to do so. The enterprise unionists thus have been elitist.

It is fairly clear why the unions took the "combined" form where they could. *Shokuin* and *kōin* needed one another's support to assure their continued attachment to the enterprise. Both groups equally felt the ravages of the rampant inflation and dire shortages—their economic interest in sheer subsistence became identical. Also, the sweep of democratic ideology promoted equalitarian unification.

However, of equal importance was that in order to assure their own status within the enterprise group the *shokuin*, who usually had enjoyed permanency of employment, had to demonstrate visibly that they were still the leaders among all the regular enterprise employees. Unionism was a ready answer; to be elected officers of the new unions was a mark of this leadership. Similarly, since the *kōin* had developed very little enterprise-based leadership of their own, the *shokuin* were invaluable to them in support of their own permanent employment status. To become attached to those who already had achieved the status of permanency was an important motivation.

The two groups thus went together as a collectivity. Under the circumstances of the time, had either group gone it alone (had there emerged separate white and blue collar movements), it is doubtful that either movement would have survived, or at least attained anything like the present extent of Japanese unionism. The *shokuin* would not have been able to draw upon *kōin* strength to gain management recognition; they would have been easily played off one against another. The *kōin*, too, relied upon the *shokuin* for access to management and intimate knowledge of enterprise conditions. Separate *kōin* movements would have suffered from inept leadership, lack of expertise, and above all little support from and approval of a high status group. In short, combining together further legitimized unionism. The coalition that Western labor movements often have disdained in their history because of its potential divisiveness was perhaps in the Japanese case the only way for quick achievement of bargaining power, perceived as so necessary in a perilous period of economic and social insecurity.

By the same token, moreover, the exclusion of the temporary employees symbolized the permanency of the unionized regular workers. Since it was easily established who had achieved which type of status—by pay rates, career progression, access to welfare benefits, etc.—the outer boundaries for the enterprise union were abundantly clear. The only major problem on this score came after the revision of the Trade Union Law in 1947 when "supervisory" employees were excluded from union membership. Here, there were difficult problems of drawing the line between supervisory and non-supervisory regular employees. On the other hand, temporary workers presented no important legal question over their right to join enterprise unions or to be covered by agreements they conclude—temporary workers were clearly on their own. Not only did the exclusion of temporary workers serve the economic purpose of providing a buffer against the ups and downs of business activity, but also it fortified the joint interest of regular *shokuin* and *kōin* in remaining together as the workforce core permanently identified with the enterprise. The existence of a temporary employee cadre thus not only reinforced enterprise unionism but also sustained its combined nature.

In light of these factors it is no surprise that Japanese collective bargaining structure largely follows the enterprise structure and, therefore, is highly decentralized. In 1960, for example, of the close to 21,000 union units (90 percent plant-wide or enterprise-wide) covered by labor agreements, about one third were subject to contracts covering the entire basic unit and most of the remainder, multiple units within a single enterprise.[15] In total, 11,000 unions made agreements. Supra-enterprise bargains—at the industrial, regional, or craft level—have been rare. Splinter-group bargaining within an enterprise is also infrequent. Only a small handful of contracts are made to cover jurisdictions beyond the enterprise level. Even though there are more than 3,000 supra-enterprise union structures in Japan (including at least 120 national unions), in 1960 merely 173 such organizations concluded labor agreements.[16] While these include some of the most important—such as the seamen, coalminers, textile workers, private railwaymen, etc.[17]—they are far too scattered and, as

---

[15] Japan, Rōdōshō, *Kumiai chōsa*, pp. 47, 51.

[16] *Idem.*

[17] Before the law eliminated collective bargaining for civil servants in 1948, the teachers union also had concluded nationwide and prefecture-wide agreements.

will be seen, limited in bargaining scope to escape the conclusion that Japanese bargaining is enterprise-confined.

Moreover, there has been no discernible trend away from this pattern of contract-making. While contract coverage has steadily increased, it has been almost invariably on an overall enterprise or plant basis, the only point of note in this development being that there has been an increasing tendency to conclude agreements on an enterprise-wide or multiple-plant (within the same enterprise) base. Moreover, the single plant unit contract has grown apace. During the past ten years there have been only limited instances of widening the agreement-making base up from the enterprise or its plants to the multienterprise or industrial level.

The Bargaining Process

That enterprise contracts characterize Japanese collective bargaining means literally what it says. Despite attempts to coordinate and direct bargaining efforts on the part of Sōhyō and of national industrial unions, the enterprise unions do most of the actual planning and execution of negotiations with little outside participation. There are notable exceptions, such as the small machinery shops in Kawasaki, the construction trades, and small shops in certain regions where labor mobility is relatively high; in the maritime trades, where the seamen have long been treated as a special unified national labor force resource because of the critical role of international trade in the Japanese economy and succeeded in establishing stable trade unionism back in the 1920's; in coal mining, where there had been acute industry-wide problems of inefficient production and where virtually a new labor force was recruited (a good many from urban and intellectual backgrounds) into the industry after the war; in the major cotton textile spinning companies, where the majority of workers are young females, temporarily employed, but led by permanent male employees.[18] Although negotiators fre-

[18] Where there has been supra-enterprise bargaining, management

quently compare their own situations to those at leading enterprises, the idea of multiple-enterprise bargaining has not been contagious. In cotton spinning the multiple-company bargaining system is incomplete with many of the key decisions actually made at the enterprise level. Moreover, there have been reversals. The major coalminers union, Tanrō, itself suffered a stunning reversion to enterprise bargaining in 1960 following the Miike Mine conflict. After 1952 centralized bargaining in the electric power industry collapsed and returned to the enterprise level.

The absence of national or other "outside" union participation in the formal bargaining process at the enterprise level is but one side of enterprise unionism. These unions themselves, let alone management, are reluctant to admit "outsiders" to the bargaining table, for their main reason for existence is to cater exclusively to the demands of the regular workforce members of the enterprise for assured status in the enterprise. They tend as a result to believe that outsiders are less able to understand the problems peculiar to the enterprise. To some enterprise unions, so few seem to be the advantages of affiliating with national unions that as many as one third with as much as one fourth of the total membership have remained "neutral."[19] Also, even though national union organizations have gained legal rights to represent their constituents at the bargaining table, except in cases where the national union itself is equivalent to the enterprise unit (National Railways, Telecommunications, Japan Express, etc.), they have not pressed to be present out of fear of causing disruption and disaffection at the enterprise level.[20]

---

associations have usually bargained on behalf of their employer members.

[19] Japan, Rōdōshō, *Tōkei nempō 1959*, p. 386, and *1965*, p. 300. However, a recent development has been the formation and growth of a loose-knit confederation of "neutral" unions (Chūritsu Sōren).

[20] Recently the Synthetic Chemical Workers Union (Gōkarōren)

That the enterprise union is usually an organizational carbon copy of the management hierarchy[21] is still another facet of the "closed" nature of the bargaining process. Branches and subunits of the union correspond to the subdivisions of the enterprise, and decision-making tends to become centralized at the top as in the case of management, where a small group of leaders share responsibility for policy-making. To be sure of their information, a network of union functionaries, supported by *habatsu* (cliques), typically is established down through the enterprise branches to keep track of proposals and ideas that will filter their way to the top. Democratic practices, as required by law, tend to be formalities. The top leaders rely upon "felt" consensus of the rank and file to make their decisions on bargaining issues, with union meetings serving primarily as plebiscites and not for determining bargaining strategies and positions.[22]

This close organizational correspondence facilitates continuing informal contact prior to the actual bargaining process between union and management. A usual device is the *kyōgikai*, the union-management conference, held at various levels of the enterprise hierarchy, which does not undertake negotiations but is used for exchange of information and opinion. In addition, the personnel or labor departments of a company often promote numerous informal meetings with union representatives in each section. No doubt these activities do clear away various issues, but they also help to clarify

---

tested the right of a national union to participate in enterprise level negotiations in an unfair labor practice case before the Central Labor Relations Commission. That right was upheld, but Gōkarōren has not heatedly pressed to be seated at the bargaining table. A serious internal split within one of its major enterprise union constituents may have "scared off" the national union.

[21] See Okōchi *et al., Rōdō kumiai no kōzō to kinō.*

[22] Kichiemon Ishikawa, "The Regulation of the Employer-Employee Relationship: Japanese Labor Relations Law," in A. T. von Mehren, ed., *Law in Japan* (Cambridge: Cambridge University Press, 1963), p. 461. However, there are considerable variations among unions. The *Tanrō* units, for example, have a large interlacing of local union divisions to provide wide opportunities for rank and file participations.

what will become the key bargaining demands. Their main significance, however, is to restrict attention to the enterprise itself and to confine the eventual bargaining to enterprise-level problems.

For example, among the companies in the synthetic chemical industry, organized for the most part by enterprise unions affiliated to Gōkarōren, bargaining at the top enterprise level prevails. As in most other industries, formal bargaining takes place at least three times a year (for a general wage increase, or "base-up," in the spring, and for bonuses at midyear and year's end). In addition there may be negotiations at other times over such matters as retirement allowances and writing the entire contract. Typically prior to and interlaced with these bargaining activities, however, are the on-going *kyōgikai* meetings and numerous informal discussions held at the various shops and departments to provide information on production, sales, profits, safety, welfare, mutual aid, discipline, and the like and to hear out complaints and grievances. But no union-management agreements are made on the basis of these discussions, although there may emerge informal understandings. Furthermore, issues unresolved by bargaining are often put aside for deliberation in the *kyōgikai*.[23]

When it comes to actual bargaining, however, each side at the outset tends to present a highly rigid position. There is likely to be little give-and-take in the formal bargaining sessions, which usually are confined to the mere presentation of demands and counterdemands. In the negotiations, the parties tend to avoid face-to-face argumentation or even analysis of the issues. The process therefore lends itself to sporadic displays of strength, in the form of demonstrations, strike waves, and lockouts. To break or avoid impasses, there is need for considerable behind-the-scenes maneuvering—informal meetings, third-party conciliation (especially the labor relations commission), and in some instances negotiations

[23] See Japan Productivity Center, *The labor relations in the integrated chemical industry in Japan* (Tokyo, 1961).

that often feature reciprocal concessions and indulgences by management and union leaders. Centralization of both management and union in all likelihood contributes to this formal display of solidarity and inflexibility. Each leadership group strives to manifest its power not only to impress the other but also its followers and inside and outside rivals. As a result, in the formal bargaining the immediate objective does not appear to be the making of an agreement, but to display strength. To take the synthetic chemical industry again as an example, despite the widespread development of informal and conciliatory devices in most companies, over the years open disputes have been frequent and regularly resorted to in advance of serious negotiations. The form of the disputes ranges from "quickie" partial strikes to longer-term enterprise-wide shutdowns.[24] Such displays of strength usually mean that the parties become even more rigid in their initial positions, requiring especially heavy dependence upon the use of intermediaries for reaching settlements.

The typical bargaining relationship at the enterprise level in Japan, therefore, contains elements of close cooperation and sharp hostility, no doubt reflecting unevenness between management and union in both power and status. On the union side this combination makes for organizational fragility, seen clearly in the instances of union splits. Rigidity in the union's bargaining position, coupled with weak mechanisms for broad participation in union policy-making and with management's informal cultivation of the union's subunits, may invite fragmentation. The splits, moreover, are usually not breakaways of occupational or special interest groups (although it is notable that *shokuin* frequently take the leadership), but rather are struggles for control of the entire membership centering around rival leaders and ideologies they happen to embrace, which the competing national labor federations eagerly exploit.[25]

[24] *Ibid.*
[25] See Fujita Wakao, *Daini kumiai ron* (Tokyo, 1955).

Under these circumstances the role of the national unions in the Japanese collective bargaining process is oblique and indirect. Enterprise unions do look to them for legal, research, educational, and propaganda services. The nationals also furnish a locale for joint consultation and strategy-making for the enterprise constituents, and in some cases they provide financial assistance in strikes. But for the most part the national organizations are left to devote their energies to political strategy and to the "ideological struggle," and the more they concentrate upon these activities, the less qualified they become to handle bargaining issues at the enterprise level. One simplified way to put this is that the national unions and centers perform universalistic political functions of the labor movement; the enterprise unions, particularistic economic functions. However, the two functions, while separated, closely interrelate with one another.

The widespread system of enterprise bargaining probably sustains political action as the primary orientation of the national organizations. Not only is this political emphasis a major means for challenging the conservative government, but also it serves as an antidote to the "enterprise consciousness" of the workers. So far, however, success in the latter respect has been dubious. Yet as long as union members fail to display a high degree of union-consciousness, the national unions feel that they must keep the ideological pot boiling, an approach that no doubt goes a long way toward explaining the inevitable opposition Sōhyō will display toward almost any government policy, domestic or international.

For their part, enterprise unions do not perceive the role of the national organizations as competing with their own, for as long as the latter concentrate upon political strategy, especially without actually succeeding to political power, the enterprise unions remain relatively free to carry out particularistic bargaining at the enterprise level.

Nonetheless, national union-centered political activity has its impact on the bargaining of the enterprise union. The national unions provide plentiful opportunities for rank and file participation in political and ideological action. A prominent example is the "workshop struggle" promoted by national unions.[26] While often lukewarm to this outside intrusion, enterprise union leaders are not likely to oppose these activities openly, and many, in fact, utilize them in displays of strength during bargaining. Such action helps to compensate for the relatively limited role the rank and file plays in the central bargaining process and, especially the workshop struggle, substitutes as a "grievance procedure." In themselves, workshop struggles cannot be said to be a bargaining procedure, for there is a little intention to achieve agreement on the rules of work, but are chiefly designed to keep the workers aroused and in a continual state of protest—useful to the enterprise union leadership when the time is ripe to make bargainable demands, and to the national unions when mass political action is applied.

Displays of force, moreover, are carefully timed or "scheduled," perhaps as much to place the union membership on notice that struggle is legitimized as it is to notify the management, government, or public for the purpose of meeting certain legal requirements. The implication for the bargaining process is that the strike, as a rule, is not carried out because negotiations have broken down; rather it is a signal that negotiations have begun, and, as such, it is considered a "normal" part of the bargaining process. A large proportion of all disputes, for example, especially those accompanied by dispute actions, occur at the beginning of or during the negotiations over the springtime base wage increase or the summer or year-end bonus.[27] However, while this strategy serves momentarily to produce a coalescence between the national organizations and the enterprise unions, the underlying di-

[26] The workshop struggle attempts to promote active rank-and-file militancy and class consciousness at the site of work by insisting upon resistance to any management steps, however minor, that might be considered contrary to worker interests within the given shop.

[27] Japan, Rōdōshō, *Hakusho 1965*, p. 402.

vergence between the two usually appears early in the course of the bargaining as the enterprise unions tend to abandon the national demands and to concentrate only on enterprise-levels issues. National unions, by attempting to gain control of the finances and instituting union welfare programs, hope to exercise greater discipline over the enterprise unions, but except in a few instances, already mentioned, this has remained only a hope.

As a result, in the bargaining process there is an asymmetrical relationship between the two levels of the union movement. National unions often see enterprise units as an obstacle to achieving their objectives, but not vice versa. Probably this is because the national unions serve the enterprise organizations more effectively than the other way around. For the economic issues that the enterprise units seriously pursue, which are discussed below, national union political activity enhances the strategy and tactics of bargaining at the enterprise level, especially when sentiment can be whipped up for both economic and political demands simultaneously. The threat of joining in with the national unions in the demonstrations, strike waves, and other tactics they sponsor, just as the enterprise unions are making their economic demands upon management, becomes a powerful bargaining weapon. In a sense, then, the enterprise union often may attempt to play company off against national union to gain bargaining strength for its own demands.

Thus the enterprise unit frequently turns its support for the national union's activity on and off—seen in their enthusiasm for political issues at the time of wage bargaining and in their relative political apathy between negotiating periods. Many enterprise unions, however, are far from quiescent; there is a constant ferment of issues and planning of strategy to meet them. Although large differences exist from union to union, this activity represents a modicum of worker independence that was not permitted before the war; and there is no reason to conclude necessarily that most enterprise unions are nothing more than a variant of company-dominated organizations. Nonetheless, particularism continues to pervade the industrial rule-making scene; and the bargaining structure and process have been fitted to it. This particularism may be seen even more clearly in the subject matter of the bargaining itself.

The Scope of Collective Bargaining

Enterprise-based bargaining translates itself into an emphasis on a certain set of select enterprise-oriented bargaining issues. As alluded to earlier, the bargaining usually revolves around rules particular only to the enterprise's regular workforce. This is not to say that in other nations bargaining is unconcerned with the rules applying solely to the enterprise employees as a group, but elsewhere bargaining attention usually extends beyond this group. A basic underlying reason for this particularism is the relative compartmentalization of labor markets in Japan compared to other industrial countries. In collective bargaining, a chief manifestation of this is the almost complete absence in Japan of negotiating occupational wage-rate structures. In Western countries the firm's internal wage rate structure, especially as it is related to external occupational rates determined through labor market operations, is the grist of much of the day-by-day bargaining activity. In contrast, even in instances where managements in Japan have introduced features of job classifications and evaluations (usually in the spirit of "modernizing" their management practices), these have yet to become major bargaining issues.[28] Although the Japanese central labor federations, like their counterparts elsewhere in the world, insist upon "equal pay for equal work," a universal minimum wage, and promotion of temporary workers to permanent stature, little except lip-service heed is given to these universalistic principles in enterprise-level bargaining.

[28] For some recent notable exceptions, however, see Nihon Rōdō Kyōkai, *Shokumukyū to rōdō kumiai* (Tokyo, 1962).

Instead, Japanese bargaining takes two major concepts as its major referents: the guarantee of permanent employment for regular members of the enterprise workforce (*shūshin koyō*) and compensation for these employees based chiefly on length of service within the enterprise and level of formal education (*nenkō joretsu*). Again, these are factors that are not entirely ignored in other countries, but, rather than being the central criteria for rules of work determined by collective bargaining, they are likely to be peripheral to other concerns such as relative skill levels. This "inward" bargaining so far has been subject to only two important outside influences: (1) the competitive entering wage for the labor force regulars (usually a competition confined to companies hiring new school graduates) and (2) legally determined minimum work standards (the Japanese have been singularly resistant to the enactment of universal or other broad-based minimum wage rates, so that the application of minimum wages required by law has been relatively limited). In general, however, neither legal enactments nor labor market pressures have as yet exerted an important direct impact on the scope of collective bargaining.

Most argumentation in bargaining, rather, is over the enterprise's "ability to pay" as a total entity, premised on the acceptance of the twin principles of the employment relationship. (Here is another reason, incidentally, for the almost exact duplication of union and management structures; top union leadership needs such an organization to keep close track of the entire system of internal personnel administration.) With this focus, bargaining demands tend to deal only with general improvements for the entire regular workforce and little attention is paid to detailed differences within the workforce. A closer look at the money and nonmoney issues usually dealt with in collective bargaining supports this point.

First, there is the annual across-the-board "base up" issue, usually in the form of a demand for a permanent increase in the payroll of the regular workforce to be apportioned in accordance with the individual's monthly base pay. In most cases, the demand is made in the spring, just at the time the fiscal year customarily begins for most private and government enterprises. This demand, of course, makes no or little alteration in the internal wage structure.

Perhaps next in importance, if not more important, are the seasonal issues for single wage payments or bonuses, timed as a rule with the gift-giving seasons of *Obon* and New Year. Typically, the bargain over these *teate* is for a single-payment, lump-sum amount for the entire regular workforce, with the total again divided up in proportion to each regular worker's monthly base wage. A bonus payment equal to one or two month's salary for regular workers has been common in recent years. Although management often insists upon parceling out the bonus according to performance, ability, or merit, by and large the formula for division is mechanically related to the basic length-of-service pay, and there is little disturbance to the wage hierarchy. In some cases the union takes over the function of distributing the bonus in order to assure such a division, or it is done through the device of the *kyōgikai*, where there is little overt bargaining and enforceability.

A third wage issue of importance is the periodic increase each regular worker is entitled to as his length of service accumulates in a company. Here the problem is how large the increases should be and how often the increases are to be made. Again, this item is not usually treated on a worker-by-worker or job classification basis but usually deals with the entire regular workforce as a whole with age, education, years of service, and number of dependents as principal criteria. In addition, there are usually a number of other *teate* that are bargained, such as cost of living allowances, productivity bonuses, and family-size payments, also essentially based on length-of-service criteria.

Beyond these issues, interest in money bargaining wanes. Few of the money welfare arrangements provided by the enterprise are important subjects of bargaining, although in some cases management has relinquished administrative control to the unions. The major exception is provision for retirement payments. These, too, are usually based strictly on the wages received by the time the worker reaches retirement age and therefore are little related to the job performed. Some other welfare items, such as travel allowances, lunch payments, etc., are also bargained, but do not loom large in the negotiations.

Individual wage progression thus is almost entirely dependent upon achieving permanent status in the enterprise in the first place. Sizeable individual wage differentials relatively unrelated to worker productivity or to the content of jobs performed have grown up within the companies due to this practice. It is not unusual, for example, for a worker close to retirement to receive a monthly wage five or ten times that of a new entrant, although the jobs they perform and the skills required may be similar.

Equally central to bargaining are nonwage issues related to the permanent worker's attachment to the enterprise. While the unions rarely control recruitment and training of the new entrants, they conduct the most intense "struggles" should management attempt to discharge regular workers. (Japanese unions almost unanimously refuse to accept any type of lay-off system for regular workers.) Next to the base-up and seasonal bonus, opposition to discharge, even for cause, is the chief issue in Japanese labor disputes[29]—and if economic conditions in recent years had not been so favorable, it likely would have been the chief one.

The enterprise union's dedication to the permanent attachment of its members to the enterprise also takes the form of insistence upon union "security." Union shop and automatic dues check-off provisions are nearly universal in agreements. Since in most cases only the regular workers are union members, these provisions symbolize their permanent status in the

[29] Japan, Rōdōshō, *Hakusho* 1965, pp. 306–307.

enterprise, and the infrequent management attempts to relax union security clauses have been met by fierce union opposition.

In addition, preoccupation of enterprise unions with employment security for their members, especially in view of the tendency of large firms to employ more and more temporary and "outside" workers, to subcontract work, and to speed up technological change, has recently led to increasing demands for reducing hours of work. This spread-the-work principle, however, is probably viewed by the enterprise unions also as a means for increasing wages of regular workers who would benefit by overtime payments.

This about concludes the list of substantive matters usually dealt with in Japanese collective bargaining. As a result, contracts usually are not large arrays of detailed negotiated rules covering the vast gamut of control of hiring, training, seniority, promotion, transfer, worksharing, layoffs, work-scheduling, work assignments, subcontracting, technological change, health and welfare, wage incentives, safety, retirement, and so forth. Much of this is left to the law—to be dealt with in very general terms—and to work rules unilaterally put into effect by management. In fact, 12 percent of the unions covered by collective bargaining have contracts that merely repeat items already found in the Labor Standards Act[30]—an affirmation that the law of the land actually does apply! Most written agreements are relatively simple documents, according recognition and security to the union, drawing its jurisdictional lines, providing for bargaining and grievance procedures and consultative machinery (*kyōgikai*), promising observance of the labor laws, and exhorting industrial peace. Even the substantive wage issues that engage most of the bargainers' attention are not as a rule written into these agreements, although they may take the form of supplemental memoranda. The labor contract becomes in effect part of the union constitution, with the implied guarantee of

[30] Japan, Rōdōshō, *Kumiai Chōsa* (1960), p. 49.

permanent attachment, rather than a detailed specification of the work rules.

Very few disputes have arisen over the meaning of these agreements; there are even relatively few over their establishment. And, as the earlier figures show, a sizeable group of enterprise unions do without them entirely. Beyond these simple documents, the unions prefer to deal with substantive issues on an ad hoc basis and through constant rounds of negotiations. This may be partly due to ideological and economic factors, but also in part to the enterprise union's principal and almost exclusive preoccupation with assuring security and advancement of the permanent workforce at every turn. As a result, contract administration has little place in Japanese industrial relations. Although most agreements provide for grievance procedures, they are relatively little used and there is almost no resort to grievance arbitration, since few issues of concern to the enterprise union in its bargaining revolve around individual workers. Such matters are likely to be referred to the *kyōgikai*.

Where attempts have been made to shift the basis of employment relationships from the permanent attachment and length-of-service criteria to job classification, which ordinarily would require much fuller involvement in work rule detail, the two basic concerns have usually reemerged. For example, in the National Railways, largely as the result of Occupation pressure, a job classification system was introduced by the government more than a decade ago and, along with position classification in the civil service (both utilize examinations for selection and promotion), has been a model for many of the private enterprise managers seeking to change the basis for wage payments. In all, some six railway job groups were identified and rated in terms of minimum and maximum monthly wage rates. In turn, each job group was broken into the three categories of clerical workers, station and depot personnel, and workshop employees. The lowest job group, for example, included eleven clerical occupations (including, curiously, cooks, chauffeurs, boiler attendants, and custodians); eleven station and depot job titles; and eight railway workshop jobs. The other four job groups have similar numbers in each category. The National Railways Workers Union accepted this classification system reluctantly; but, rather than focus its bargaining attention on factors that differentiate the classifications, it has continued to stress issues affecting the workforce as an entity. In part, this was due to the fact that the classification system as it was structured actually demanded little such attention, since the entering wages for most of the jobs were virtually similar, with only relatively small differentials in the minimum wages paid in each of the job groups, even as between the three categories of clerical, stations, and workshop jobs. (A sharp break in the minima comes, in fact, only as one moves from the conventional *kōin* to the conventional *shokuin* categories.) But, also, union pressure has been primarily for general wage increases and wage supplements regardless of classification. In dealing with the classification system itself, the union has focused on widening the minimum-maximum wage spread within each job group and its component job categories to give room for guaranteed periodic payments that increasingly reward length of service rather than job values. At the same time, the union insists on a freeze of the number of classified workers by law, which since the great reductions in force of the early 1950's has been accomplished.

Thus, despite the apparent establishment of a job classification system, within it the union has succeeded in reaffirming the two basic principles of permanent employment and length-of-service payment. It is probably correct to say that in most other instances where there has been an attempt to substitute job evaluation criteria for wage payment in unionized enterprises, they have either been bargained back to the length-of-service criterion or have turned out to blend the two sets of criteria, with length-of-service retaining major weight. Despite technological, economic, and at times po-

litical pressures, *shūshin koyō* and *nenkō joretsu* have remained obdurate.

Impact on Social Structure

The limited scope of Japanese collective bargaining, related
as it is to bargaining structures that have been erected, has
meant that while relatively large numbers of workers are covered by labor agreements, they are covered only with respect
to a few major rules of work. In terms of the expectation that
collective bargaining in an industrializing society becomes a
major decision-making mechanism for detailing the vast
complexity of rules governing industrial relations, the Japanese experience so far has fallen quite short.

Nonetheless, even these limited accomplishments have produced a significant change in Japanese industrial relations.
Bilateralism, although limited, has been established. Bargaining, supported by egalitarian ideology, now permits frank,
open, and direct confrontation of different value systems to a
degree not tolerated before. Public policy sustains this, and
failure to do so would be at the peril of worldwide ridicule
for the government and nation—a highly sensitive point in
view of Japan's precarious and ever-shifting position in international trade markets.

For the workers covered by collective bargaining agreements, in all probability there also has been an impact upon
interpersonal relations at work. Some of the major rules of
employment are now visible and standardized. There are the
beginnings of introducing new criteria such as job classification and evaluation. No longer is there a great dependence
upon the whims of superiors as there used to be, nor as great
a need to resort to as elaborate a labyrinth of interpersonal
connections to attain security in the enterprise as there once
was. The sharp distinctions between *shokuin* and *kōin* have
weakened. That the workers have ready and frequent resort
to protest, legitimized and institutionalized, is further evidence of the breakdown of insistence upon personalized har-

mony and loyalty demanded by the employer. No doubt the trend toward self-dependence of workers will continue to strengthen as the influence of the new educational system takes hold, as urbanization embraces larger and larger proportions of the population, and as consumption expectations continue to rise, especially among the younger workers. In all of this, the practice of collective bargaining in Japan probably has made an important contribution to elevating worker status in the industrial society.

Yet there is little evidence so far to show that despite the spread and intensification of collective bargaining, there has been a wholesale revolution in the criteria determining relative status in industrial organizations. Collective bargaining by and large has continued the criteria of length of service and educational background as the main determinant of status so that the previous social distinctions have been carried forward with considerable force.

Certainly the rise of unions and collective bargaining represents institutions that circumscribe authority. Enterprise unions have in some respects sharply limited the discretion of management. National labor organizations have had some similar effects upon government. But what has occurred thus far has been the formalization of certain rules regarding continued employment and income progression that are usually particularistic to given enterprises. In terms of the rule-making that collective bargaining has dealt with, therefore, it may be said that the behavior of the individual participant in industry remains structured mainly with reference to his enterprise group rather than to his own well-being or of that of other specific individuals.

The past seventeen years in Japanese industry have been mainly a process of redistributing power, rather than the spinning of a new "web of rule" that, it is predicted, comes into being with economic and industrial development. The problem of power redistribution has meant on the one hand a preoccupation with stable political relationships, especially at the national level, and the establishment of unimpaired economic security at the local (or enterprise) level. In order to have paved the way for a new set of rules relating worker and manager and worker and worker, in all likelihood this process of power redistribution had to come first.

Collective bargaining in Japan has dealt with compartmentalized segments of the workforce and has yet to contribute directly to workforce flexibility. Its seeming inability to shift from a particularistic enterprise focus to the wider reaches of the economy invites gradual reemergence of unilateralism in the inevitable rule-making, either on the part of management or government—and with it the gains made in social relationships in Japanese industry could also easily go down the drain.

Prospects and Dilemmas

If it is true that the Japanese economy is now in the midst of extremely rapid structural and technological changes, there is a serious question whether collective bargaining in the structure and scope thus far developed is capable of playing a significant role in devising the many new rules of work such changes will necessitate. Bargaining in Japan since the war has been built around a set of rules concocted for an earlier period of economic development. *Shūshin koyō* and *nenkō joretsu* are rule systems that were aimed at securing and committing a stable and reliable workforce to industrial work in certain key enterprises at a time of rapid transition from agrarianism to industrialization. The immediate postwar periods, passing through phases of economic chaos and reconstruction, revived these rules and extended them to large numbers of workers who had become permanent members of the industrial work community. No doubt the singular achievement of Japanese unionism in the postwar period has been to secure these guarantees through collective bargaining for those it has organized. Bargaining and trade unionism assured that these rules of employment would not be violated without a desperate struggle.

Management, by and large, seems to prefer the enterprise bargaining system, at least as against any supra-enterprise arrangements. Under it, management has been left free to utilize the workforce, with relatively little union interference, within the confines of the enterprise. There are few restrictions upon its methods of recruiting, training, and allocation of workers to tasks. Although the periodical and constant wage demands are rankling, and although enterprise unionism invites outside political and ideological appeal that at times is disruptive, it is comforting to management that the quarrels are not likely to get outside the enterprise family and that enterprise unionism stands in the way of "outside" participation. Labor administration, while exacting, is relatively uncomplicated.

A growing number of managers, however, see this position as wishful thinking that relies too much on the cultural pulls of the past and not enough on the economic and technological pushes of the future. They would prefer to rely more on market prices and more universalistic rules. Organized firms have paid a heavy price for maintaining enterprise worker solidarity and loyalty, and suffer as a result from top-heavy and inflexible labor costs. They have devised expensive recruiting and training programs, which it is feared may eventually serve only to furnish other expanding firms with skilled labor. In face of rapidly changing economic and technological conditions, long-range planning schemes based on rigid organization and personnel commitments may prove to be costly investments. These managers appear willing to sacrifice enterprise unionism and enterprise-level bargaining if necessary to take advantage of greater flexibility in their operations.

Management's internal organization itself, however, remains a serious impediment to such an adjustment. Japanese managers have built their own subempires; it is difficult to root out the cliques (*habatsu*); responsibility and authority chains become blurred. Consequently, while it has become

highly inviting to some managers (usually the younger professionals) to throw out the whole set of mechanisms that
have been developed in the past for structuring the labor
force and to resort to a system of open labor markets with
greater and greater reliance on public institutions for training in the skills that will be needed, such an enormous shift
in all likelihood would cause serious dislocation within management. Thus, in part, the transition to a broader bargaining system is an internal management problem not easily
resolved.

Government also shares many of the same fears and con-
tentments of management. As a major employer of a large
segment of organized labor, its dealings with unions often
sound the themes for industrial relations in the private sectors of the economy. With conservatives holding the reins of
power, government is under considerable pressure from private management (one of its principal supporters) not to
enter into arrangements with the unions that would widen
the role of bargaining in industrial decision-making, disrupt
management organizations, and break down the closed enterprise systems.

Perhaps this has been no better dramatized than by the
recent issue over ratification of ILO Convention 87, which
guarantees organized workers the right to select their bargaining agents without restriction. Inasmuch as the Public
Corporation and National Enterprise Labor Relations Law
provided that union leaders must be elected from among the
employees of a government-owned enterprise (or basic union
unit), adoption of this convention conceded their right to select leaders from the outside. Although the government, as
early as 1959, agreed at Geneva to ratify, it in fact managed
to drag out the issue and to hold out on actual adoption until
1965. The issue of outside leadership, of course, is symbolic for
trade unionism and collective bargaining beyond the public
employment sphere; explicit recognition of the principle could
mean an opening wedge for national unions to participate in

enterprise-level negotiations and thereby open the way for enlarging the scope and structure of bargaining. Thus the issue is a heavily tinged political one, despite the legal and constitutional guarantees.

In addition to the specific ILO question, that the government deals with some of the most militant unions on the Japanese scene casts much of the present collective bargaining practice in a political context. Virtually all government employees at the national level and a sizeable majority at the local level are organized. Cut off as they are by law from full collective bargaining rights, they have been especially prone toward political activity and, accordingly, since most of these groups are affiliated with Sōhyō, exert a heavy influence in the policy decisions of this major federation. Defiance of the government on a broad scale by rank and file governmental employees is a new phenomenon in Japanese history. Led by and centered mainly around intellectual white-collar workers, the government unions harass the government as much to demonstrate that traditional authority may be challenged as to protect their own job interests—perhaps especially because the tenure of their members is highly secure. To grant full rights of bargaining to them (including, in the case of the public corporations, the right to strike) would not only admit a larger role for the national unions within the governmental sphere, but also within the private sector, thus opening up a whole Pandora's box of disarrangements in the present industrial relations system. The government fears that the resulting instability and militancy would upset its plans for rapid economic growth.

The government's policy of containment thus seemingly thwarts the development of the collective bargaining system. However, to continue to discourage broadening of the bargaining system as pressures mount for participating in decisions that affect labor force utilization and mobility invites further politicalization of the labor movement. The inability of enterprise structures to handle these issues by bargaining increases the political efforts of the national unions among the rank and file, especially since they are largely excluded from the bargaining process. As the opposition parties gain strength, there is likely to be greater reliance upon governmental enactments of the industrial rules rather than upon collective bargaining. Basically what is at stake is whether the government will give full recognition to the collective bargaining institution as a major decision-making mechanism in the unfolding Japanese industrial life—or invite the increasing use of governmental machinery.

Finally, any transition to a broadened bargaining system poses serious dilemmas for the labor movement itself. Aside from the lack of experience with a wide bargaining scope, there is deep reluctance among the segments of the union movement to shift roles. At the grass roots level, deep fears of being cast adrift in the labor market and the almost exclusive focus upon guarantees and symbols of permanent attachment deflect the enterprise unions from any major concern with the detailed rules of work. To broaden the scope of bargaining could invite self-destruction of well-established enterprise union entities.

For their part, too, the national union organizations are geared to a primary interest in gaining influence in the new political structure, especially in supporting parties which have had to be built almost from scratch in a hostile conservative context, a formidable task requiring most of the energy of these organizations and complicated by their own internecine in-fighting. At the same time, the fact that the enterprise unions have dealt with a limited scope of collective bargaining has meant that there are many issues for the politically minded national unions to feed upon—the remaining impress of management authoritarianism and paternalism, the gross income inequities between workers in large and small industry, the lack of social security safeguards, including the minimum wage, the plight of the underemployed and unemployed, and so forth (not to mention, of course, government domestic and foreign policy). Theirs has been a dramatic political role in postwar Japan, which the leadership would not easily give up to concentrate upon collective bargaining.

The new stage in Japanese industrial development, however, appears to be making this role-mix for the unions obsolete if collective bargaining is to be the prevalent instrument for rule-making. Rules will be made, and there is, as already noted, considerable temptation and pressure, particularly from progressive managers and the skilled younger workers, to shift the basis of the employment relationship to job classification and job evaluation. Unless the enterprise unions widen their bargaining interests and unless the nationals enter the negotiating process, worker representation in the devising of rules that will be made is likely to remain minimal, and increasingly so as the old employment criteria phase out and new ones phase in.

Thus, in addition to employer and government ambivalence toward broadening the bargaining system, the labor movement itself is its own obstacle. Sōhyō, sensing this dilemma, has recently announced that it will begin to concentrate more and more upon economic issues and, after considerable soft-pedaling, now is advocating "preconsultation" at the enterprise level on management plans for technological change. Presumably, even though direct bargaining may not be immediately involved, the aim is to widen the range of issues that the enterprise unions would consider and to increase participation of national unions in the bargaining planning and negotiations. This effort represents a rather fundamental shift in the federation's policy, which heretofore had refused support for "productivity drives" (especially since Sōdōmei and Zenrō Kaigi support them) and would brook no infringement of the two basic principles of employment security that the enterprise unions embrace. Apparently the present Sōhyō leadership, now rather firmly established after a number of years of internal struggle, has concluded that existing bargaining arrangements will lead to an increasingly restricted role for trade unions in the making of the industrial rules. However, it remains to be seen whether this approach actually will materialize, for left-wing opposition groups within the center see this as an abdication of the labor movement's political and ideological mission, while enterprise union leaders also tend to see this as another attempt at "outside" intrusion.

In view of the present ambivalence within all three major groups, it is likely that Japan will continue to see considerable conflict between and among them for some time to come. The past fifteen years produced a collective bargaining system for the first time in Japan, but the institution is too restricted in extent, too truncated in structure, and too narrow in scope for the new stages of economic development. In its wake has been left a series of dilemmas as to how to reconcile particularistic and universal values. As earlier inferred, however, just because the reconciliation of the two sets of values has yet to be achieved, this does not necessarily mean the triumph of "traditional" Japanese culture in adapting to technological and economic change. The presence of unionism and collective bargaining in Japan, however deficient by Western standards, has probably accelerated Japan toward equality and individuation and away from hierarchy and group reference. Without these institutions, in the extent and depth to which they exist, it is dubious that the conflicts would have been so sharp as they are or that change toward social "modernization" would have been so impending.

Patterns of Belonging

PART FIVE

Patterns of Belonging

CHAPTER IX

Organization and Social Function of Japanese Gangs:
Historical Development and Modern Parallels

GEORGE DE VOS AND KEIICHI MIZUSHIMA[1]

Introduction

ONE of the features of Japanese culture and social structure least known to the West is the nature of the Japanese underworld. Western social scientists in attempting to describe Japan have paid very little attention to deviant, or "out" groups. The *burakumin*, discussed elsewhere in this volume, have been similarly neglected. The functioning of professional criminal groups within Japanese culture is almost totally unknown in the West, though it has been treated by some Japanese writers.

It is our general thesis that to understand the total social structure of any modern culture, one must understand not only forms of behavior conforming to cultural norms but also those of morally or legally unsanctioned behavior. Not only are officially unsanctioned illegal activities an organized part of every complex society, but there are romanticized and openly condoned legends making heroes out of past outlaws, deviants, or innovators, which serve to orient deviancy in the present. In complex societies heroic legends about the in-

[1] This research report, at various stages of preparation, was made possible through support from the Center for Japanese and Korean Studies of the Institute of International Studies, University of California, and the Asia Foundation. Our present research investigations are being supported by a P.H.S. research grant MH-04087 from the National Institute of Mental Health, Public Health Service. Gratefully acknowledged are the counsel and additional background material supplied by Mrs. Sachiko Aiba and Hiroshi Wagatsuma.

novator, the rebel, or the deviant are parts of common lore which can be drawn on as justification for contemporary deviant behavior. To better understand the nature of present social function the social scientist can learn much from these legends with their ambiguous attitudes toward legitimate authority.

Knowledge of the underworld and its legends is of special pertinence in understanding the foci of present power within the political structure of the society. The overt exercise of power is often closely, though covertly, related to officially illegal groups. The American big city boss at the turn of the twentieth century as described by Lincoln Steffens does not appear too different in social function from his Japanese counterpart, the so-called *oyabun*.[2] What differs is the degree of loyalty demanded of the *kobun* or followers.

Delinquent and criminal gangs within a culture are also a reflection of the type of social conflicts generally going on in the society. This is especially true in times of social change. Socially deviant individuals may act either as innovators in helping patterns of change come about, or they may act as conservative forces attempting to hold back and maintain older forms of behavior. Robert Merton has well discussed the respective roles of the deviant and conformist in respect to innovation.

Viewed from this standpoint, it is interesting to note how the Japanese outlaw gangs have acted generally as a conservative force within the society, rather than being in any way facilitative of political or social change.[3] Gang traditions still

---

[2] In American vernacular, "boss"; directly translated, "parent part" or "role" in a gang relationship. *Kobun*, or follower, directly translated, means "child role." See Ishino, Iwao, "The Oyabun-Kobun: A Japanese Ritual Kinship Institution," *American Anthropologist,* LV (1953), 695–707.

[3] Nevertheless, at the time of social revolution occurring with the restoration of the emperor in 1868, these gangs were found operating on both sides. Some assisted the feudal shogunate, while others backed the clans and other forces that were seeking to overthrow the Tokugawa regime and establish the emperor as head of a modern

influential today had their origin within the feudal structure of the preindustrial society. These gangs drew their cohesiveness and strength from being organized on the quasi-familial lines of loyalty that were so characteristic of Japanese society generally during that period.

Conservative traditions both on a legitimate and outlaw-racketeering level are found residually operative in present-day industry. Such traditions help maintain marginal operations that would disappear if more subject to modern labor-management operations. For example, the coal industry of the southern island, Kyushu, is in large part economically marginal. Smaller mines are kept in operation by labor *oyabun* who keep groups of workers together on an *oyabun-kobun* basis. These gangs resort to violence against one another with the aim of controlling "territory." The workers can be forced to continue to work on a level of marginal existence as "loyal" *kobun*. Unionization would put these marginal mines out of business.

Today new forms of gangs termed *gurentai* are becoming established and consolidated around recently more stringently outlawed activities related to prostitution. Even in this new type of organization built less on traditions of continuing personal loyalty, older traditions maintain some force, and these newer groups are still more congenial to the holders of a conservative political ideology.

In addition to professional gangs a newer phenomenon—that of the *chimpira* or juvenile gang—is noticeable in the modern industrial city. These juvenile gangs, mostly of a shifting impermanent nature, are only most indirectly related to the professional adult gangs. They draw their models from Western, mostly American, sources. Nevertheless, the *yakuza* tradition still gives some content to the thinking of masculine "heroics" through which one demonstrates and validates his masculine "tough guy" identity.

---

state. Their purpose was not modernization, but indirect political advantage.

The Gang Tradition: Romance and Actuality

GANG ACTIVITIES DURING THE TOKUGAWA ERA

The feudal period of Japanese history has become part of the sufficiently distant past to be used by present-day Japanese for the construction of legends. It is now far enough away to be exploited in a romantic fashion much as the American opening of the West has become a focus for American romanticism concerning heroes and villains. There are curious parallels between Japanese society and American society in the formation of legends around outlaw heroes. In the American tradition of the Western hero, he is a man who lives by his wits, and although given to being a law unto himself, he often fights for the forces of good against corruption and evil in his society. In a similar vein, certain types of Japanese outlaws have been turned into heroes fighting against oppression and misrule on the side of the underdogs. In both countries the type of violence expressed by modern delinquent youth is influenced by this legendary past. In America the fast draw and the ability to handle a weapon in all circumstances have crept into the delinquent picture. In Japan the tradition of violence is more focused on the sword as a weapon and symbol of masculinity.

The Tokugawa period (1603–1868), the subject of so many modern legends, was quite radically different in social organization from the open frontier West. But in each instance the outlaw has been used as a symbolic example of individual against society. Again in each instance the actual facts are quite different from the developed legend. Groups which came to be called *yakuza* were in actuality organized gangs involved either in shady activities as itinerant merchants (*yashi* or *tekiya*), or gangs whose chief occupation was gambling (*bakuto*). To understand how some of the leaders of these gangs of gamblers or petty racketeers and confidence men were turned into legendary heroes, one has to examine in some detail certain features of the feudal Japanese society.[4]

The origin of Japanese gangs in the form they were to take during the Tokugawa period can be traced back into the period of chaos preceding the establishment of the rigid social structure which was to last for 250 years. Prior to the Tokugawa period there had been many confused years of continuous civil war. The samurai, members of a retinue of one feudal lord or another, very often became unemployed when changing fortunes caused one of these decentralized governmental units to be defeated. Thus apart from the more organized forms of feudal warfare, there was a great deal of violence and looting of the ordinary farmers and townspeople by dissolute gangs of individuals who became organized into roving bands in the best tradition of banditry.

[4] Today, in common parlance the collective term for both *tekiya* and *bakuto* is *yakuza*, but this is not quite appropriate historically. Originally, according to Tamura (Tamura Eitarō, *Yakuza-kō* [Tokyo: Yūzankaku, 1958]) the word *yakuza* or *ya-ku-sa* (eight-nine-three) was used among gamblers to denote something "no good" or useless, because eight, nine, and three sum up to twenty—a losing number in gambling. Later the word *yakuza* came to be used outside the gambling world by the general public to denote people who are useless and good-for-nothing. The word gradually came to designate outlaws generally. At present the word is used collectively to designate *bakuto*, *tekiya*, *gurentai*, and other professional and semiprofessional outlaws.

The word *tekiya* is relatively new; in the past *yashi* was the more common term. According to one theory, *yashi* derives from *no-bushi* (*no-bushi—Noshi—Yashi*; the same character is pronounced both *no* and *ya*). *Nobushi* were bandits, mostly warriors serving defunct feudal lords, who had lost their jobs. Bandits were very active in Japan during the Sengoku period of continual warfare (around 1500 to 1575). The origin of the word *tekiya*, according to one theory, was a reversal from *ya-teki* ("arrow" and "mark"). The word "mark" had the same meaning as used by American confidence artists. Usually *tekiya*, when selling small commodities on the street or at a fair, cheated the customers by using many of the techniques still practiced by confidence men today, including the use of decoys or shills.

With the consolidation of political power under the Tokugawa shogunate, this period of political confusion came to an
end, but private violence continued in the interstices of the
new, more tightly regulated society. The earliest of the
groups still celebrated in legend were the samurai *yakko*.
These were in the main young men who, at the beginning
of the period, failed to adjust to the new peaceful Tokugawa
world. They might be called (like right-wing groups today)
reactionary protagonists of lost warrior values. They looked
on the easy luxury of their fellow samurai as a sign of de-
generacy, trained themselves in swordsmanship with strict
discipline, adopted a distinctive dress, and bound themselves
to each other with oaths of loyalty.

Some of these, the *hatamoto-yakko*, developed into gangs
of young—often adolescent—terrorists. Direct servants of the
shogun, they sought compensation for the loss of their function as loyal protectors of their lord in battle—and for the loss
of opportunities for plunder—by roaming the streets of Edo
seeking an excuse to vent their aggression on innocent
commoners.

In response, commoners organized groups of equally aggressively inclined youths for their own self-protection: the
so-called *machi-yakko*, whose battles with the *hatamoto-
yakko* as protectors of the commoners are celebrated in folk
tales and songs. A typical *machi-yakko* leader, still a heroic
figure, was Banzuin no Chōbei, a labor contractor who had
been the foot-soldier servant of a samurai until he married
into the labor contracting business. The pool of tough laborers whom he kept at his house were at once construction
workers, gamblers, and *machi-yakko*.

The Tokugawa government stepped into the battles between the *hatamoto-yakko* and the *machi-yakko,* and by the
end of the seventeenth century both groups had disappeared.
Their legends and their style of protective heroics were inherited by other groups, however.

Of these there were two main types: the *yashi* or street

traders and the *bakuto* or gamblers. The *yashi* were men who ran small portable stalls in the market fairs held at shrines and temples in accordance with the religious calendar —men who had a well deserved reputation for shoddy goods and trick methods of selling. For mutual protection they formed tightly knit groups usually under the dominance of a single *oyabun* leader. The group might be spoken of as the oyabun's family—his *kobun* or children—and the territory (*niwaba*) within which it moved would be fixed. The leader would control the allocation of stalls, collect rents and protection money, and pocket the difference between what he collected and the lump-sum rent to be paid to the temple or shrine. (Though with the growth of towns in late Tokugawa, *yashi* were able to organize additional independent fairs of their own, often resembling carnivals with show booths and side shows.)

These groups were bound by formal rituals as well as by social and economic ties. The yashi's patron god—perhaps because patent medicines were a staple fair commodity— was Shinno, a Chinese god of agriculture who was credited with discovering medicine to help the sick and the poor. A ritual exchange of *sake* cups cementing *oyabun-kobun* would take place in front of an altar to Shinno and the *oyabun* himself might be called Shinno. Such altars are still to be found in the houses of *oyabun* of the *tekiya*—the modern descendants of the *yashi*.

The authority of the *yashi oyabun* was greatly reinforced— indeed it may even have been largely created—by some official recognition of their status by the feudal authorities. Between 1735 and 1740, in order to reduce sharp practices and prevent brawls over territory, the government appointed a number of these leaders as "supervisors" and allowed them the dignity of "a surname and two swords," symbols of near-samurai status. As supervisors the authority of the *oyabun* was greatly enhanced.

The *bakuto*, men who organized gambling establishments

in the towns and more especially in the post stations of the great trunk roads such as the Tōkaido, were organized in a very similar way. They were pledged, *oyabun* to *kobun*, by fictive kinship ties of loyalty, and often a blood oath bound them to a code of behavior which could not be broken with impunity.

Though less formally than in the case of the *yashi*, the *bakuto* too had their authoritarian structure reinforced by official action. After a reorganization of the criminal police system in 1805, a central office was established for the whole of the Kanto plain. The eight traveling marshals who operated out of this office made a practice of cultivating protected informers among the *bakuto* outlaws, men who would promise to keep their own band's illegality within certain limits and help the police against rival bands. A leader who had this kind of informal relationship with the police was able readily to enhance his own power.

One of the chief functions of both *bakuto* and *yashi* organizations (apart from their value as an income source to their leaders) was to limit competition in the interests of those who were already in the game, and to protect territory or income it was necessary to maintain an aggressive military attitude. Factional conflicts over territory were constant, resulting in bloody brawls, violence, and death. Sometimes professional swordsmen were hired, but usually the *bakuto* and *yashi* did their own fighting.[5] As specialists in violence they developed other functions too. They might be called on as private police by otherwise respectable pillars of society. Their disciplined organizational loyalty made them usable for the deliberate and controlled application of violence.

It was these military activities which bred the "outlaw temperament" of the legends, the so-called *yakuza-katagi* (*yakuza* being a word used sometimes just for *bakuto*, sometimes for both *bakuto* and *yashi*). Their code[6] was a parody

[5] Ōhashi Kaoru, *Toshi no kaso shakai* (Seishin Shobō, 1962).
[6] Some of these groups did in fact have formal written charters. A

of the samurai's *bushido*, and their hero ideal was drawn on samurai models. Their preoccupation with violence and controlled aggression could be romanticized as manliness, and like the samurai a *yakuza* might have to prove his manliness by stoic endurance of pain, hunger, or imprisonment. Violent death, for the *yakuza* as for the samurai, was a poetic, tragic fate. Wealthy *oyabun* might even cultivate the same kind of cultural attainments as the samurai, training in literature and the arts as well as swordsmanship, and eventually achieving —sometimes through personal connections with the more dissolute members of the nobility—a position of some prestige in the community at large.

An essential part of the romantic legend of the *yakuza* is that in his battles with authority he stood up for the common man. In this sense he was the heir of the seventeenth century *yakko*, from whom he may well have derived in part his self-image. It is unlikely that the *yakuza* would have been so romanticized by the commoners of the Tokugawa period if there had not been so little opportunity in Tokugawa society for the legitimate criticism of governmental authority. People needed a symbol of resistance and of the free spirit, and they found one in the *yakuza* outlaw.

The *yakuza* played up to their legend. There was an emphasis on *noblesse oblige* toward the poor. (Charity can be a means to social mobility in modern society too;[7] it also dis-

---

modern one, quoted by Berrigan in Berrigan and Durrel, *Yakuza-no-sekai* (Tokyo: 20-Seiki-Sha, 1955), has the following rules:

1. Do not touch the wife of another member.
2. Do not do anything other than the regular "business" (that is, gang activities), even under the pressure of poverty.
3. Do not reveal the secrets of the organization to the police if caught.
4. Keep strict loyalty in the *oyabun-kobun* relationship.
5. Do not use ordinary language; practice the gang's special terminology, or argot.

[7] See L. W. Warner and Paul S. Lunt, *The Social Life of a Modern Community* (New Haven: Yale University Press, 1941).

tracts attention from the source of one's income and helps others to "forget.") At the same time *yakuza* leaders, just as the modern big city bosses described by Steffens[8] were prone to justify their activities as necessary for the good of society. Thus the *yashi oyabun* might claim that he not only provided the means whereby the small helpless trader could protect himself, but that he also ensured, in the interests of society at large, that the worst sharp practices would be kept under control. A Japanese sociologist has found similar self-justifying arguments in a handbook circulated among the *tekiya* today.[9]

Yakuza *in Modern Society*

RECENT ACTIVITIES IN THE UNDERWORLD

The traditional forms of *yakuza* continue to exist since the industrialization of Japanese society, though they have somewhat changed their financial activities as well as their morals in order to accommodate to new conditions and opportunities. The *bakuto*, or gamblers, could not continue their fairly open activities in the new state. Police control became more severe, and their open brawling and territorial disputes were no longer tolerated. Open gambling was forbidden, so that the gambling bosses had to camouflage their sources of income by carrying on certain respected economic, social, or political activities as a façade. In a number of instances that have been documented, the gambling boss maintains protection from the police by a direct donation of money to police chiefs, so that subordinates are discouraged from observing any gambling activities in their area. In certain situations where there has been some disruptive violence, the direct relationship between the police chief and the gambling boss is used to "solve" the problem. It is easier for the gambling boss

[8] Lincoln Steffens, *The Autobiography of Lincoln Steffens* (New York: Harcourt Brace and Co., 1936).

[9] See Maeda Shinjirō, *Hanzai-shakaigaku no shomondai* (Tokyo: Yashindo, 1955), pp. 33–34.

in certain situations to give up one of his guilty subordinates than it is for the police to find out the guilty party directly.

The *tekiya*, or former *yashi*, have shifted with modern times. The amount of trickery or extortion possible from small street stalls or itinerant selling became less and less lucrative with the development of modern commercial and entertainment activities. To keep up with the times, *tekiya* bosses have tended to go into modern industry themselves, and in certain cases actually end up managing companies. Some *tekiya* going into large scale activities have become "legitimate." (In the confused period after World War II, when businesses were conducted on a shoestring, *tekiya* appeared in their more traditional form for a brief period.) The *tekiya* existing today, having become semi-legitimate, are in a stronger position than the *bakuto* who have not adapted themselves as much to changing times.

The façade of "knightly spirit" appropriate to the feudal period has disappeared to a great extent from *yakuza* groups. Since World War II it has been very difficult for any of these organizations to cloak themselves with any form of social purpose. It must be noted that previous to this period these *yakuza* groups played a considerable political role on the far right. Such ultranationalist parties as the Genyōsha, and later the "Black dragon" (Kokuryūkai; named after the Amur River —the "Kokuryūkō" in Japanese) included some *yakuza* leaders, and in the 1920's and 1930's the violence or terrorism they commanded was used as a means of achieving political or economic ends. *Yakuza* acted as mercenary strike-breakers and intimidators, and by engaging peripherally in politics as enthusiastic antisocialist and anti-Communist militants the *yakuza* leaders were able to claim legitimacy for their violent activities. As Japanese politics in the late 1920's became more and more militaristic, *yakuza* groups cooperated with the militarists by going out to Manchukuo or China as part of "land development" programs. This was the heyday of the *yakuza*, a return to the good old days of feudalism, but when war itself broke out, the *yakuza* were suppressed by the military government, no matter how willing or cooperative they were. Many of the *yakuza* were brought into the military system under military discipline and others were imprisoned.

In the postwar period of confusion, *yakuza* appeared in rather open fashion, sometimes as contractors providing materials for the American military, who were not aware of their background and the sources of procurement. The postwar *yakuza*, however, never recovered the power they had been able to maintain during the prewar period. The ultra-rightists today are a strongly disparaged group.

Iwai[10] notes that the old-time *yakuza* are much concerned with the changing conditions of today. He quotes one of the traditional bosses as stating, "What is happening today has never happened before. The traditional *yakuza* used to fight among themselves and sometimes steal, but as such, it was only a matter of living in underworld society. If a *yakuza* caused some injury to ordinary people, we used to immediately punish him. It was not permitted by our rules to hurt the weak; however, today, force is used against weak people indiscriminately, and there is no longer any sense of order in the *yakuza* world."

Iwai observes the increasing competitive encroachment of the *gurentai*, or modern mobsters,[11] into the traditional areas of the *bakuto*, or gamblers. These *gurentai* are more directly expedientially or instrumentally organized.[12] They attempt

---

[10] Iwai Hiroaki, "Hanshakai shūdan to shakaiteki kinchō," in Nihon Jimbun Kagakkai, ed., *Shakaiteki kinchō no kenkyū* (1954), pp. 81–122.

[11] According to some, the origin of the word *gurentai* is supposedly a combination of a slang verb, *gureru*, to turn bad, and *rentai*, a unit of military organization. Also, the prefix *gu* usually suggests stupidity or foolishness.

[12] See definitions of instrumental vs. expressive role behavior in Talcott Parsons, and Robert F. Bales, *Family: Socialization and Interaction Process* (Glencoe: Free Press, 1955). The *yakuza* have pretensions that their behavior has expressive as well as instrumental elements.

no self-justification through avowal of a mystique of fictive kinship, loyalty, and social protection of the innocent.

The *bakuto*, in order to maintain themselves, have also spread out into newer practices, such as extortion or blackmail, as major sources of finance. Where the *bakuto* have sought to stick mainly to gambling, it is reported that they have often been pushed out by the *gurentai*. In a number of instances the *bakuto* groups have had to accommodate themselves and form some kind of liaison with *gurentai* to continue to exist.

The prohibition against injuring ordinary folk in any way is less true for *yakuza* today. The traditional *bakuto* used to feel some responsibility for protecting his own territory from the encroachment of thieves and other forms of crime within their own district. Modern urban districts today cannot be as well controlled, and such practices are no longer much in evidence within the increasingly impersonally organized modern city.

Hence, today's criminal boss tends to establish a fairly impersonal relationship with his underlings and feels very little responsibility for their well-being. On the other hand, several cases have been reported in which the subordinates of a boss have ganged together and attacked him for one reason or another. The unquestioning authority or control of the boss is losing force. If the boss shows any weakness, his underlings tend to take advantage of him. In one minor youthful gang, for example, one of the underlings stole his boss's bicycle and sold it. Such insubordination would have been unheard of in the past.

The *gurentai*, without any sense of continuity with the past, are more modern organizations which bear little resemblance to the traditional *tekiya* or *bakuto*. These organizations received a great deal of impetus after the new laws made traditional forms of prostitution impossible. Such new organizations quickly developed to take over pandering and protection of less traditional forms of sexual traffic.

Traditionally the business practice of running a house of prostitution could be maintained with considerable status; it was not run by underworld figures directly but by families who had some pretensions to social acceptance. As late as 1955 the wealthiest brothel in the city of Nagoya held "open house," an occasion when the owner (a graduate of Tokyo University), who inherited his profession from his father, showed off the architectural riches of the house and entertained pillars of the local community to formal tea ceremonies conducted by some of the best tea masters. But with the de facto end of previously legal prostitution in 1957, and the enforcement of prosecution, the underworld, which had control over street girls, took over more completely and became the dominant force in the operation of this vice.

Gurentai gangs have become increasingly more powerful in pleasure resort areas. They are used to protecting houses of prostitution both from minor criminals and from official detection by the law. They are also employed to prevent runaways on the part of certain prostitutes. Some are managers of night spots or are employed by cabarets and bars as bouncers and strong-arm specialists. As was true for the *yakuza*, there are certain acknowledged territorial areas which are controlled by each *gurentai* group. In certain districts where the *yakuza* have been more powerful, the *gurentai* sometimes function as a type of suborganization under the jurisdiction of a *yakuza* boss.

In general, the *gurentai*, without the formal patterns of *oyabun-kobun* relationship, are the form in which modern underworld organizations are shaping up in Japan. They function in pleasure resorts and places where business is operating on the fringes of the law. They are intermediaries in these areas, largely dependent on personal negotiations for protection, and use violence and threat as effective modes of control.

The tendency to limit violence to individuals within the underworld—an attitude derived from gang activities in the past—is still apparent within organized gangs even today, even though the activities of those outside the gang itself are not controlled. This tendency has the present social function of not stirring up unnecessary attention, hence trouble with the police.

In most instances, assaultive crimes occur principally in areas frequented by the gangs—pleasure resort areas, houses of prostitution, cabarets, dance halls, and around racetracks. As in the United States, the people from the nondelinquent world who have most contact with these gangs are usually unskilled laborers or members of the lower class, not for the most part white collar or blue collar workers. Fringe groups in the society such as street merchants and street musicians, having no well-defined social role, continue to have a great deal of social contact with the criminal element, for reasons already stated.

Even among the *gurentai* effort is made to prevent any of their members from attacking individuals who are not considered a part of the delinquent world. Most of their aggressive activities are directed against other gangs or individual delinquents. Casual stealing may be tabooed.

In our empirical research with the TAT[13] it is most noteworthy that in the fantasy stories constructed by delinquents, violence, when depicted, occurs among members of a delinquent gang. In stories made by American delinquents, no such distinction appears; rather, the delinquent activity is usually seen as taking place against some person who himself is not cited as being criminal or delinquent. There is evidence that a strong tradition in the Japanese underworld still tends to keep aggression directed toward members of the delinquent groups as much as possible. It seldom spills out in at-

[13] "Thematic Apperception Test," originated by Murray and Morgan. We have developed a Japanese modification of this series of pictures designed to elicit spontaneous fantasy. See paper now in preparation for publication, Eiji Murakami and George DeVos, "Fantasies of Violence and Aggression in American and Japanese Delinquents."

tacks on the outside population. There are special prohibitions, for example, in ordinary gangs against any rape of nondelinquent girls. The inference would seem to be that only girls who are demonstrably delinquent are fair game.[14] While part of the criminal code served as functional protection from possible reprisals by an aroused society, such restraint also served, formerly, as a means of self-justification allowing professional *yakuza* to maintain an attitude that their activities were simply a "business" and that they were social "benefactors" to those innocents who found themselves within the territorial boundary of a particular group.

In the American free-lance criminal conscience of the present day, there is no similar tradition of a protective attitude toward the square John, although such "humanitarian" tendencies are to some degree attributed by legend at least to outlaw figures such as Jesse James. One must note, however, that present day organized crime in the United States provides an interesting parallel to this traditional "business" ethic of the *yakuza*.[15]

In spite of some continuity in this tradition, public concern regarding the increase of violence results not only from a possible rise in the absolute number of assaultive crimes, but also from the fact that the violence seems to be spreading from within the delinquent groups themselves into indiscriminate attacks on the public in general.

POLITICAL ACTIVITY OF JAPANESE GANGS

Before the recent war, there were numerous instances in

[14] There are sometimes instances cited that former outcastes do not limit themselves as readily to these rules.

[15] Reports on the "Syndicate" indicate that violence is used fairly systematically more as a threat than as an actuality. Indiscriminate acts of violence are considered disruptive to the smooth operation of gambling and other recognized activities. It is the threat of violence more than violence itself which is the controlling force of the criminal world. It must be noted that the "Syndicate," as such, or "Cosa Nostra," is a derivative of a tightly organized Sicilian society and in actuality is a transplant onto American soil.

which right-wing political parties were directly or indirectly related to *yakuza* groups. In the postwar period, similar indirect liaisons continue. There are also cases today in which certain gang activities are actually camouflaged behind a political right-wing ideology, that is, the gangs disguise themselves and their operations as a minor political party.

Iwai did a study of seven cases of criminal activities by gangs to see in what way they affected the ordinary populace. These activities are well illustrative of the type of violence and fighting that occurs today between gangs.[16]

Case 1 cited by Iwai occurred when an arrest was made of two *bakuto* groups who were struggling with each other in the vicinity of an American Occupation area to gain jurisdiction over the entertainment district that serviced the American soldiers. Case 2 involved a *tekiya* group who were picked up by the police as a result of some struggle with a group of Korean nationals. Case 3 illustrated a conflict between two policemen over their "pay" relationships with a *tekiya* group. Case 4 involved a somewhat different type of *tekiya* group which functioned around a coal-mining area. In this case the police picked up a gang which, acting as strike-breakers, had gotten into a fight against the labor union. The conflict between the labor union and the gang resulted in the murder of a local policeman and hence came to the specific attention of the authorities. Case 5 became public due to the publicity that the *Asahi* newspaper gave a particular *yakuza* group working in the vicinity of an American military base. As a result of the publicity given this gang, action was taken both by the American Occupation and the Japanese to stamp out their violence and extortionist activities. Case 6 is an example of the right-wing political activity of *yakuza* groups. A *bakuto* group sponsored a physical attack on a famous Communist leader in an attempt at assassination. Case 7 occurred in a similar fashion when some younger members of the *yakuza* group organized strike-breakers in the coal mine area and tried to kill a union secretary who was considered a

[16] Iwai, "Hanshakai shūdan," pp. 104–105.

Communist. These particular cases are illustrative of features of gang function we have previously noted. First is the tendency to support a conservative political ideology and to function against unions and other organizations, partly on account of the leftist ideology of these organizations, and in some cases partly because the gangs are paid mercenaries of conservative business interests. Second is the tendency for a great deal of the violence in cases of gang function to be directed against other groups like themselves. At times, conservative politicians have made blatant, overt mention of the support they have received from a *tekiya* group.

We can quote a statement found in a weekly news magazine, *Shukan Asahi*, in 1952, made by a right-wing politician. The particular law to which he referred was fought very bitterly by liberal elements in the government since the law had to do with the suppression of meetings which could be construed by the police as being in some way "potentially destructive" of the country. The law was a very vague one and was reminiscent of some of the prewar totalitarian edicts. To quote the politician:

> One of the greatest successes of our party was to have enacted a law which is strongly resisted by socialist forces. When the bill came to the Diet, many left-wing students appeared to make a petition. I was warned of this by the police beforehand and I was personally asked by the Minister of Justice to try to do something to take care of the situation. I called a *tekiya* boss, and approximately 100 members of his group got together around the Diet. I am one of the bosses of the *tekiya* in Tokyo so that my order was carried out smoothly by every one of our groups in this area. Thus the students as well as the other left-wing forces were unable to make this petition and to disrupt the discussion of the law, which went on smoothly in the Diet resulting in its enactment. The Minister of Justice as well as some cabinet members gave me many thanks for my assistance.

GEORGE A. DEVOS AND KEIICHI MIZUSHIMA

Another characteristic of the *yakuza* groups is their anti-foreign activities, that is, they have been antagonistic to any underworld activities of either the Chinese or Korean minorities in Japan. After the Japanese defeat, the Korean and Chinese minorities reacted very violently in many cases against the Japanese authority that had so long exerted severe pressure on them, and some Chinese groups profiting from the weakness of the government became extremely provocative, openly aggressive, and heavily involved in underworld activities. During the occupation, they, and also Formosan and Korean groups, could make use of their privileged status as foreigners in smuggling and black market operations, and in this manner had an advantage over their Japanese counterparts. The *tekiya* felt themselves pushed by the Chinese and a great deal of tension developed, with Japanese gangs seeking to gain lost power. On one occasion, for example, a member of a *tekiya* group attacked a Chinese, and the Chinese group, in retaliation, forced its way into the *tekiya* headquarters and killed the individual who had committed the assault. A regular battle broke out with the *tekiya* counterattacking the headquarters of the Chinese group with drawn swords. A number of Chinese gathered in the open space by the emperor's palace, almost in battle formation, to launch an attack on the Tokyo *tekiya* groups generally. A main boss of the *tekiya* ordered all his organizations to cooperate and armed them with swords and other weapons. Ordinary individuals in the vicinity cleared out so as not to get hurt. The police were unable to cope with the situation and the American occupational military police were brought in. It was rather ironic that this action by the *tekiya* against the Chinese underworld focused attention on what was becoming a growing problem. This event, as well as others, caused the American military to restrengthen the Japanese police so that they could cope with underworld activities.

The Japanese professional criminal gangs have informal relationships with professional groups elsewhere, notably

307

Hong Kong, the Philippines, Hawaii, and the mainland United States. While gambling is the most prevalent activity of these groups, smuggling of narcotics, guns, and illegal currency is also quite common. Japanese gangs previously were quite active in narcotics trade with China, but there seems to have been relatively little attempt to push narcotics into Japan itself. Whether this relative lack of narcotics activity in Japan is due to the absence of receptivity of the Japanese to narcotics use or whether the Japanese criminal element has some traditional reluctance in pushing these drugs cannot be clearly determined.[17]

JAPANESE JUVENILE GANGS

The juvenile gang, as such, was not a characteristic of pre-World War II Japanese society. While recruitment patterns into the adult criminal world were always present, the large-scale appearance of highly organized juvenile gangs having indirect relationships with criminal adults is something new to the Japanese scene. Such gangs are in varying degree a symptom of modern industrial urban societies throughout Europe as well as in the United States.

The basis on which some of these juvenile delinquent gangs are related to adult professional groups seems to be an extension of the symbolic *oyabun-kobun* relationships that still exist in the adult criminal world. An adult subordinate of the criminal boss may develop around himself a small gang of juvenile members toward which he acts as boss. These minor gangs are not formally affiliated with the adult gang in any way, but they assist the activity of their adult sponsor.

Juvenile gangs today are called *chimpira*.[18] Not all *chimpira* have any direct or indirect connection with adult criminal

[17] In 1960 in all Japan there were approximately 2,000 police cases involving narcotics. Most of these involved stimulant drugs.

[18] Etymology of this word is considered obscure. We suspect it partially derives from a Japanese word for penis.

308

gangs. Some are groups of aggressively oriented high school students who hang around a pleasure resort area and engage in minor bullying of one sort or another. When their activities become more properly delinquent, they most often come in contact with the adult group in whose *nawabari*[19] they are functioning. Sometimes the *chimpira* will attack a member of a *yakuza* group without knowing his identity, only to be confronted with the formal organization. There are as yet few instances in which the *chimpira* or juvenile groups find themselves strong enough to cause the type of disruption of the adult organized gangs that has been reported in the American setting.

There are two routes through which members of the juvenile gang establish contact with the adult professional group. One mode of contact occurs when a subordinate member of the adult gang meets with the leaders of the juvenile gang and recruits them as loyal but loosely attached subordinates. This is considered quite an honor by the juveniles so considered, and they gain higher status in the eyes of rival groups when their affiliation becomes known. In many instances a young *yakuza* who is officially a member of some gang group and has exchanged *sake* cups with its boss, acts as a leader of a delinquent group, whose members sport a common badge as a symbol of their group membership. Out of such delinquent groups, the more promising "tough boys" are later recruited as full status members of the adult gang organization.

Another mode of recruitment is on an individual basis. When some juvenile gang members become notorious in one way or another in respect to the police or community, and at the same time handle themselves well, they are occasionally contacted by the adult group and taken in. There are numerous occasions when this incorporation into a gang takes place after some form of conflict. Sometimes members of the juvenile gang who have been disturbing the area are taken

[19] Literally, "roped off area" or jurisdiction.

to a room on a quiet street and are beaten up by adult *yakuza*. If the juvenile survives this ordeal in a manly enough fashion and shows himself to be tough and "takes it," the adults may suddenly change their attitude and suggest that the youth become a member of their gang. The juvenile, thereupon, is expected to swear loyalty to the adults and become a member. This method of recruitment is not unknown to the juvenile gang itself as a means of taking on new membership. Sometimes one gang will defeat another delinquent group and as a consequence form an amalgamation.

Quite young groups often fight at shrine festivals. These groups are considered too young to meet at ordinary pleasure resort areas, such as dance halls, cabarets, and gambling houses, but will seek an occasion for gang activity at some particular shrine festival. Preoccupation with territory, in a manner very similar to that described for American gangs, is one of the main characteristics of these groups.

Starting at a relatively early age within the gangs and throughout the process of recruitment into the adult criminal world, there is an emphasis on hierarchy. An individual has to show allegiance through these various stages up into the adult world. It is relatively rare today that an individual is recruited into the adult criminal world without going through some prior apprenticeship, in one form or another, as a juvenile. There are exceptions when an individual of extremely high intelligence and better social background is able to shortcut his way into the professional criminal world, but such individuals are a distinct minority.

In a manner similar to that of Cavan,[20] Junkichi Abe[21] has described four stages of the delinquent's alienation from his own society and attachment to that of the criminal. These stages have geographic as well as psychological distance. At

---

[20] Ruth S. Cavan, *Criminology* (New York: Thomas Y. Crowell Co., 1948), pp. 120–25.

[21] Abe Junkichi, "Hikō no shakai shinrigaku," in Togawa Yukio *et al.*, eds., *Seikaku no ijō to shidō,* vol. 4 of *Seikaku shinrigaku kōza* (Kaneko Shobō, 1960), pp. 179–227, especially pp. 204–225.

the first stage the delinquent activities occur in the individual's own family and social setting, either at home, school, or at work. In this stage the normal frame of reference is dominant. In the second stage of development of a delinquent identification, the delinquent acts are performed outside the home, usually at a place of amusement or in some other appropriately questionable area. The delinquent usually frequents this area while living at home. In the third stage, the individual has shifted his main activities and relationships outside the home, and his major contacts are now in the geographic area of delinquency itself. They are characteristically with others who are also engaging in delinquent activities. In the fourth and final stage, delinquent identification has become complete and the individual has become an integrated member of a professional delinquent group, in which he finds his major role behavior.

To illustrate the process of alienation, we will briefly describe such a development. The author, Mizushima, cites the first case out of his own experience in a juvenile detention home. It illustrates a typical development from juvenile gang relationships to adult professional crime.

Kazuro, as a boy, had a very poor school record in primary school and took part in some minor delinquent activities, such as stealing, with his play group. This group itself was never defined by anyone as particularly delinquent in nature. When he graduated into secondary school at age twelve, the group with which he associated gradually became increasingly delinquent in their activities. At first the group would play truant together, walking around the neighborhood and sometimes engaging in some minor stealing of iron or steel from a nearby company yard. Since he was above average in strength, he frequently fought with his friends and readily dominated those boys with whom he came in contact. He was continually disobedient at home, but the family was rather indulgent with him and there were no serious overt conflicts with family members.

By the time he had finished nine years of compulsory education at fifteen, he had developed a reputation in his area as a "tough guy." He seldom would commit actual delinquent acts, but rather he would threaten and dominate his friends; and through fear of him they would often turn money over to him which they would have to replace by going out themselves and stealing. Older boys who had graduated from the same school heard about him, and one of these youths invited him to a nearby amusement center and proposed that he join their delinquent gang. Such a "pickup" by an older group is not accidental, but as in this case is done on a somewhat systematic basis. Every year the new recruits are looked over much as university graduates are picked up by major companies. Thus Kazuro became familiar with the amusement area and became acquainted with other boys who had already left school and were now gang leaders. Nevertheless, he continued his contact with the previous group in his old school, and in turn sought to introduce some others of his friends to his new associates. He needed the money he could draw from his old school group for his own amusement in the pleasure resorts and also because he, in turn, was required to give money to his new associates.

At this stage he sometimes ran away from home for considerable periods of time. He could stay over with many of his associates during these periods of absence from home. He manifested considerable bravado in his new group and took easily to drink, gambling, and found it not difficult to establish his domination over others among his new associates. He gradually gained in stature in his new group. He was arrested by the police and brought to court several times, but was never put in any institution because the police could not cite him for any major offense. After some time he became personally acquainted with a member of an adult *gurentai* group which had jurisdiction over this particular amusement area. It was not long before this man invited him to join the adult group with whom he was eager to swear allegiance. His contacts with the group in the minor amusement area permitted him to go to the larger resort area more central in the city.

By this time he had broken completely with his family and lived most of the time with his adult companions in a *gurentai* group. He gave up a minor job which he had held since graduation from school, and instead was given a task by *gurentai*. His duty was to get acquainted with managers of pinball establishments and find ways of buying back from the winners who preferred cash, the prizes of cigarettes, candy, and cake they did not want. These articles, bought cheaply from the customers, could then be sold at a profit to an ordinary store. This is one type of petty business activity through which minor *gurentai* obtain funds. However, when such business did not go well and the group lacked money, they would go out on the street and extort money from passers-by, threatening them with violence.

He was arrested, finally, for extortion, and put into a reformatory. He showed no regret concerning his arrest because his time spent at the reformatory was one indirect means of gaining status in the underworld. When interviewed at the prison, he asserted with pride that having now obtained sufficient status within his group, he would no longer have to occupy himself with such minor activities, but instead would have subordinates working for him when released.

Berrigan describes the life history of a rather well-known *yakuza* boss and the manner in which he entered the world of crime. Oza was born in the family of a small manufacturer who belonged to the lower middle class. The father loved to an inordinate degree a stepmother who was a prostitute. He ignored his clever son, while the stepmother was cruel to him and used to beat him. Oza in turn became a bully at school and caused much trouble with his associates there. At last he ran away from home and became a vagrant, begging from adults in a Tokyo park. He slept in the park at night. Sometimes he was beaten up by other vagrants or criminals in the area, but at last an older boy came to him and picked him as his *kobun* (subordinate). From that time Oza was trained under the supervision of his mentor as a member of a pick-pocket group. Later, through the pickpocket group, he became acquainted with the *tekiya* operating in his area, and because of his violent, strong, "masculine" personality, he rapidly rose within the ranks of this group until he himself became an *oyabun*.

These two cases illustrate the gradual mobility taking place within the hierarchy of the Japanese criminal system. However, there are individuals who, coming from a different class background, sometimes move along more rapidly in the re-cruitment system.

Berrigan cites also a case of the son of a doctor who was forced by his father to follow the father's own career, so that he was sent to medical school. Tsutomu hated his studies and looked for some opportunity to quit. One day he went into a restaurant where two young men were fighting. When the fighting became so furious that the tables and chairs of the restaurant were being broken, an old gentleman came in, intervened, and with a mild smile was able suddenly to stop the fighting. The witnesses in the restaurant were amazed at this man's personal force and wondered what the source of such control and presence could be. The old gentleman said something to the young men and left the restaurant, still smiling in a gentle way. The medical student was most im-pressed by this old man and asked the bar girl who he was. He was identified as the famous "boss" of that area. The medical student, Tsutomu, wanted desperately to meet the old man, and although the bar girl insisted that he would never gain an interview, he persisted in locating the old man's residence and followed him around. Tsutomu aban-doned the study of medicine. At last he met a subordinate of the old man and told him his wish to meet the boss. The *kobun* was impressed by the seriousness of the young man's attitude and introduced him. Thus the student became a member of the *yakuza* group and was given quite high status from the first because of his serious attitude and good social background.

It must be remarked that cases of this kind are very rare. They illustrate, however, many of the Japanese virtues, such as intensity of allegiance and seriousness of purpose. Recruitment into professional gangs out of the middle class is in itself a fairly rare phenomenon.

The author, DeVos, interviewed Masao, a young man of nineteen in prison who well illustrates another type of recruitment based on quasi-familial ties. One must acknowledge that part of the appeal for the young Tsutomu of the old man was the value that this man had for him as a father symbol. In the case of Masao, a need for some type of familial tie was also most evident.

Masao was the son of a wealthy upper-middle-class family. The father was killed during the war, and at an early age Masao was sent to live with his grandparents while his mother became the mistress of a wealthy industrialist involved in oil. Eventually Masao's mother married the industrialist. Masao, at age nine, was brought to live with his new stepfather and mother. The boy became highly resistive in this relationship and did poorly in school, opposing all efforts of his parents to send him to special schools to obtain a better education. Finally, Masao, in adolescence, took up with delinquent groups and spent much of his time in amusement areas. Unusual circumstances brought him into contact with the wife of a *yakuza* leader, who became maternally attached to him. As a result of this relationship, Masao became a courier for the *yakuza* group, acting as a messenger delivering stolen commodities. He was eventually caught and institutionalized. The story that he tells indicates that his fantasy now is to go straight and open a barber shop, a trade which he has been learning in the reformatory. However, one may speculate whether, upon release, Masao will not rejoin his *yakuza* group and take up his favored position as

315

not only a *kobun* of the chief, but a favorite "son" of the chief's wife.

Conclusion and Discussion

An historical perspective on Japanese gangs affords, as does any historical approach to groups of individuals in Japanese society, a view of both continuity and change with modernization. Some supposed changes, however, upon closer scrutiny often turn out to be mere surface phenomena rather than symptoms of basic shifts in group behavior. History teaches that one must exercise great caution in assuming that any form of social behavior is without precedent in the past. Yet however critical we may be of attempts to define that vaguely felt social ambience we call modernization, we cannot escape an awareness of its presence throughout today's world. In discussing the underworld, as any other feature of Japanese culture today, it is necessary to make as careful an effort as possible to delineate how the past continues into the present so as to assess with some degree of cogency what is "modern" about what we observe.

ALIENATION AND THE ADOLESCENT SOCIAL WORLD

One basic conceptual change seems to differentiate delinquent and criminal behavior today from that noted in the past. Industrial urban society in its need for increased specialization in all class segments has been changing the definition of adulthood. Adulthood is now preceded by a less socially responsible, transitional, preparatory period called adolescence. Adolescence has become so universally recognized as a definite period in social maturation that it is difficult for many to conceive of a culture in which it does not exist. A careful study of Western culture as well as of Japanese culture, however, reveals it to be an essentially modern concept.

Adolescence, as a separate, legally defined, "age-graded" period in the technical usage of anthropology is socially visible in deviant as well as in conforming behavior within Japanese society. As a reflection of the modern age it seems apparent that there is a proneness for what is termed personal or social alienation to occur within this adolescent period in forms not as directly visible or as easily defined in the past. Amorphously structured juvenile gangs are a new feature of Japanese society at least insofar as they are defined as distinct from the adult world.

The gangs of *yakko* that appeared in a previous unsettled period in Japanese history could possibly be considered as parallel phenomena to youthful gangs today. But their social function and definition by society were quite different. Delinquent gangs today conform neither to the majority society nor to the professionalized world of crime. They are essentially an expression of alienated social behavior without any clear definition of purpose.

The social definition of adulthood at approximately age fifteen in the premodern Tokugawa period did not allow for any recognition of a distinct period of adolescence. In Japan as in other modernizing societies this preparatory training period was first recognizable historically in the professional and commercial segments of the society and only subsequently became universalized and applied to all social segments, including the laboring class. It is to be noted how in European countries such as Austria or Germany where a strong apprenticeship tradition is still retained the concept of "delinquency" is coming into usage only recently.

Before the Meiji Restoration youths when apprenticed into varying occupations were essentially treated as adults as far as legal responsibilities were concerned. Their delicts were adult crime, their self-concept was essentially that of a young adult, inseparable from the adult world. The samurai, most given to formal ritual, recognized a direct transition from childhood to adulthood in a ceremony called *genpuku*, when for the first time adult clothing was worn. It was no different for youths who sought a career in the outlaw segments of society. They perceived themselves as young adults who had chosen to live outside the ordinary prescribed patterns. They in no way identified themselves as part of a transitional age group.

ALIENATION AND THE LOSS OF FICTIVE KINSHIP

A second major change noted in Japanese gang behavior is a shift from adherence to a system of personal, pseudo-kinship loyalties to a more overtly expediential, less formal, more impersonal structuring of relationships. While ties between outlaws in the past were often in actuality expediential, motives had to be cloaked in the garb of personal, family-type relationships, virtuously expressed through the exercise of a system of mutual obligations. The criminal world reflected the value system of the majority society in this respect.

In the modern period the breakdown of this formal system of loyalties is to be found also in the changing structure of the underworld. The old *yakuza* "*katagi*" is breaking down. Members of this segment of society are consciously bemoaning the fact that no such ties seem to inhibit or guide the behavior of the newer gangs. Before accepting, however, that this shift in ideology represents an actual shift in behavior within the underworld, considerable caution must be exercised. As we have indicated, some dispassionate studies of the past would show that the influence of outlaw codes or behavior can readily be exaggerated. Nevertheless, the shift from personalized ties, whatever may have been their breach in behavior, to impersonal expediency in the underworld must be considered a symptom of modernization.

THE FUNCTION OF OUTLAW LEGENDS IN MODERN SOCIETY

In our discussion of the Japanese outlaws of the past we have briefly noted how they serve as heroes of legends. The function of these legends, however, has shifted somewhat with modernization. Today outlaws are no longer direct symbols of revolt from arbitrary political oppression. The more recent use of these legends in Japan we would suggest fulfills the same sort of need that is so apparent in the American concern with the cowboy. Legendary outlaws become symbols of unfettered masculinity and freedom of initiative, even violence, within societies in which such outlets are less directly available for most. The sense of confinement has become more internalized, in a sense more psychological.

Today both Japan and the United States comprise highly complex, commercial-bureaucratic social organizations. They are "service" societies in which one must please his clients and superiors for self-advancement. Attainment of social status within an acceptable position in the dominant class demands a sustained commitment to a long-range career. The direct expression of aggressive feelings is severely inhibited lest one irreparably damage his chances in a society with a well-organized memory file that records even inconsequential events throughout one's career. In other words, the romanticized cowboy figure which has become a fantasy outlet for an increasingly conformist American society has a parallel in *yakuza* legends which serve as a similar expressive outlet in Japan.

Legends of undomesticated, untamed outlaws of the past, or of the present, uncaptured by commitment, have a particular appeal to youth during adolescence since these echo their own desires to remain uninvolved—to escape from what appears to them to be a confining, unrewarding, continuity of adult existence.

PERSISTENCE OF THE GANG MEMBER AS A PERSONALITY TYPE

Case histories suggest that certain patterns tend to appear in the family histories, both of famous *yakuza* of the past and of modern delinquents. Although materials are sketchy and unclear, we can gain from such histories an impression of some selective features in the family which would seem to be conducive to delinquency formation in the present-day society just as in the past. Repeatedly mentioned are experiences such as running away from home at an early age, rejection, or some form of alienation from parents and a social environment during childhood filled with sexual irregularities or preoccupation with sexual activity on the part of parents or other close figures. Such material suggests that whereas the overall social structure may be changing in Japan, underlying personality variables orienting an individual toward deviant behavior are less changed by modernization.

A perusal of personal descriptions of *yakuza* in the past as well as of delinquents in the present leads one to infer continuity in those personality factors and social attitudes that selectively lead an individual to enter upon a career of crime. In the literature of the Japanese concerning the *yakuza* one is repeatedly impressed by descriptions of certain characteristic aggressive personalities found in the criminal world. "Masculinity," as an exploitative aggressiveness, and a concern with either dominance or submission are much emphasized.

There is some continuity in the *oyabun-kobun* relationship of the Japanese criminal world because it is emotionally satisfying. This formal structure not only is a means of organizing or controlling criminal activity itself, but also allows for types of dominant-subordinate relationships in which personal expression of aggressive masculinity, and at the same time a strong dependent relationship on a dominant figure, are part of the rewards to be gained. Even though these organizations are diminishing, today's juvenile delinquents in Japan seem to want to belong to something which might provide such a relationship. We are finding evidence in our empirical data of such concerns in adolescents.

There seems to be, in delinquent as well as in nondelinquent youth, the need to find a suitable father figure with whom to identify, in either an active or passive sense. By itself, such concern has no specific relatedness to delinquency. However, once this preoccupation in individual cases becomes intermeshed with pressing, ill-controlled needs for self-gratification at the expense of society, without tolerance for delay, or in a context of violence, the deviant society of the underworld becomes an attractive arena for personal activity.

POLITICAL IDEOLOGY AND THE PERSONALITY OF THE GANG MEMBER

Perhaps the most interesting aspect of the organized *yakuza* gang member's ideological adaptation to recent social change is his ready adoption of conservative nationalist philosophies and his periodic appearance as a force in the political arena. This affinity with right-wing attitudes may well be partially explicable in terms of the personality factors we have just mentioned, namely his concern with dominance and subordination as well as a propensity of violence. Some types of personality structure cannot well tolerate types of association demanding mutual internalized self-control and self-discipline. One type of delinquent cannot express aggressiveness through intellectual channels; he is more likely to employ physical means. Such a modern institution as a give-and-take political discussion is somewhat alien to his makeup.

Rightist organizations in Japan give an outlet for a more physically aggressive type of expression and allow for certain political-social rationalizations of this aggressive behavior. A need for some form of strong external authority, also a part of the criminal personality in many cases, puts emphasis on the virtues of manliness and bravery in a manner harmonious with a rightist ideology but basically antithetical to a more liberal approach to public affairs. Hypernationalism goes well with the caricature of the romanticized warrior's code that is used in *yakuza* groups even today. More immature personality types with incomplete control systems feel more at home in situations of officially tighter social control. Attempts at implementing a challenging, emotionally difficult democratic social atmosphere bring forth uneasiness and a tendency toward the outer expression of physical aggression. The *yakuza* gang today in Japan in many instances has become a group of bully boys who are found useful to others

321

in situations such as labor-management conflict or in political demonstrations of the extreme right. They have little else to recommend them in spite of the legends of humanistic activity to which they have supposedly subscribed in the past.

In one sense the personality predispositions of the *yakuza* "fit" better in the past. They are ill-suited to the modes of egalitarian, nonaggressive behavior now predominant in modern society. Such individuals are now perceived as delinquent rather than "hot-blooded" youth.

In the present age, however, we have seen frightful throwbacks to barbarism with such shifts in the control of power as occurred under the Nazis and the Japanese militarists. These reversions struck the unprepared modern conscience as somehow unreal atavisms until it was too late to control them. The fact that modern society generally condones only less direct forms of aggressive behavior does not change human nature and its proneness toward violence, nor does it put an end to its lust for activities and releases not overtly countenanced by the legal codes reflecting majority consensus. The Japanese underworld, both in its recruitment of professional personnel, as well as in its providing for the periodic indulgences in unsanctioned activities on the part of otherwise conforming citizens, performs apparently inescapable social functions today as it did in the past.

MODERNIZATION AND CHANGES IN INSTITUTIONALIZED SOCIAL SANCTIONS

It is not possible to determine objectively the validity of the lament of present-day *yakuza* about an increasing absence of self-control in youth which would serve to delimit the perpetration of haphazard delinquent acts. The *yakuza* today tend to see themselves as being able to exercise less control not only over other criminals operating in their own territory but also over the tendencies for their younger members to victimize innocent outsiders. Such acts are seemingly part of a general tendency on the part of uncommitted segments of the modern younger generation toward more "impersonal," less socially inhibited attitudes. Police reports suggest that robbery and rape committed by individuals under age twenty have increased radically in recent years. Youth now comprise a notably larger proportion of offenders brought to the attention of the police. While the concentration of reported criminal acts still is heaviest in entertainment areas, their surrounding vicinities as well are no longer considered as safe for the casual visitor. Public awareness seems to indicate concern over an individual possibly meeting with some attack to a degree unheard of in the remembered past.

What one could gather from reports of this nature is that the adult criminal organizations seem to have less direct contact with or control over alienated delinquent youth. These youth, motivated by their own interests, are detached from direct influence of sanctions applied to them either by legitimate society or by the underworld itself.[22]

In discussing changes in crime rates in the context of modernization it is perhaps best to end with a caveat concerning any too ready conclusion that available statistics represent actual proportionate increases or decreases in any form of behavior within a society.[23] While the present authors accept the

[22] In this context there is a report that the operation of juvenile gangs in a particular district of New York was so disruptive that members of the organized underworld moved to a new location after unsuccessful attempts to prevent disturbances drawing police attention.

[23] The use of criminal statistics in themselves in modern times is more sophisticated, but they are still compiled by individuals representing agencies dealing with recognized social problems. Statistics only indirectly reflect behavorial incidence. They sometimes reflect shifts in vigilance or relaxation toward various forms of deviant behavior. For example, when any particular behavior becomes seriously recognized as a social problem, statistics may be compiled with greater vigilance. Some problems are legally ambiguous, and available statistics have no direct relationship to incidence, i.e. arrests for homosexuality in the United States. Arrests for any type of behavior may increase as a consequence of social pressure on police. One cannot

statistical evidence as indicating a greater incidence of aggressive behavior in youth, they do not feel the issue of what it indicates about the overall incidence of violence in Japanese society as a whole is closed. Such behavior in youth is in effect part of a larger issue concerning the relationship of modernization to the socialization of violence, namely, how, when, or where is potential aggression vented by youth or adults in modern societies when traditional avenues for the expression of violence have become blocked; when political tranquillity has replaced civil unrest; when peace has replaced the havoc of war; when "pacification" and colonization of overseas regions have become impossible; or when more open arenas within the society such as the American frontier have become "civilized"? Is it that violence in modern societies in such cases became detached from ready causes and hence becomes instead more readily visible as socially disruptive or criminal in nature?

It is not easy to ascertain that changes in the amount of reported violence do not in actuality represent greater vigilance of policing agencies especially in respect to lower-class behavior. For it is only with "modernization" as a universalization of privileges and expectations throughout society that social attention is drawn directly to problems or elements of so-called disorganization already prevalent in the less privileged levels. The lower-class population is not only expected to achieve, but to conform and to behave like the professionalized segments of the society. When some fail to do so, they become problems for all.

There is no doubt that the forms of social control are changing in the more stable modern societies. Not only are police agencies encouraged toward increasing impersonal and systematic exercise of justice extended to all levels of society, but other newer welfare agencies are increasingly instituted

---

easily determine whether increased public clamor represents actual increase in incidence, whatever its effect on police statistics.

to "treat" the deviant or criminal offender as well as control him through punitive sanctions. With the lessening of the harshness of punitive sanctions more deviant behavior is readily visible and perhaps, earlier in the life cycle. Less concealment due to the lessening of repression does not indicate a greater degree of potential for deviancy in the society but a greater awareness of these suppressed elements in human nature.

Without further discussion, what we are trying to say is that modernization in Japan, to an extent difficult to assess, is represented not only in some changes in the structure and functions of criminal gangs which we have examined in this chapter, but more generally in the way social sanctions are institutionalized, by what agencies they are exercised, and to what degree they partake of what we may call a modern professionalization and depersonalization of social facilities through special training of agency personnel. Modernization as it affects the expression of deviant behavior, singly or in groups, may result more in a change in the institutionalized social perception of behavior in some instances rather than in gross changes in the total incidence of specific deviant behavior itself. Nevertheless, changes in social perception in turn strongly influence the openness, the group context, and the social circumstances in which behavior can be expressed— so too with gang behavior within modern Japan.

CHAPTER X

Giri-Ninjō: An Interpretation

L. TAKEO DOI

IF ONE wants to study changes in the nature of interpersonal relations in Japan since 1870, one should ideally compare the material prior to 1870 with the material of succeeding periods up to the present day. My discipline being psychiatry, I have no dearth of contemporary clinical material, but comparable evidence from earlier periods is totally lacking. My alternative is to look at the history of certain concepts which my clinical experience has shown to be crucial, notably *amaeru* and *sumanai, giri* and *ninjō*. I propose to show the relation between the first two, expressions of states of mind, to the last two, descriptive of types of interpersonal bonds, an examination of which is essential to the understanding of changes in interpersonal relations since 1870.

Amaeru and Sumanai

I have described elsewhere[1] the central importance of the concepts of *amaeru* and *sumanai* for the understanding of Japanese patterns of emotion. To summarize the argument briefly:

Amaeru can be translated "to depend and presume on another's love," "to seek and bask in another's indulgence." It is an expression of what the British psychoanalyst Michael Balint calls "passive object love,"[2] a basic ingredient, in his theory, of all psychopathology. Though sometimes translated as "wheedling," note that the object of this behavior is to re-

---

[1] See L. T. Doi, "*Amae*: A Key Concept for Understanding Japanese Personality Structure," in "Smith and Beardsley, *Japanese Culture* (Chicago, 1962).

[2] M. Balint, *Primary Love and Psychoanalytic Technique* (London, 1952), p. 69.

ceive love itself, not to manipulate a relationship for some other end.

The word is typically used of the behavior of a child toward its mother, but it may also be used of the behavior of lover to lover, of subordinate to master. The word is only rarely used for the behavior of a social superior to a social inferior. The social superior may, however, have an *amaeru* type of emotional dependency on an inferior; in fact he often does. But as a rule he has to guard against revealing it either to himself or to others.

Balint notes that European languages have no word for this passive object love. Japanese has, and the availability of the word makes it easy for Japanese patients to express the wish to be loved and to become aware of it, and also for the therapist to detect that wish. By contrast, according to Balint, although Western patients may have the same passive desire to be loved they come to accept and gratify it only after a lengthy painstaking analysis.

The linguistic difference does reflect a difference in social relations. In Japan the dependency of children on parents is fostered even beyond the nursing period and institutionalized. It is not the case, however, that the desire to be loved is always gratified. The variety of phrases to describe distortions or frustrations of that desire is evidence enough.[3] They do, however, serve to reinforce the impression that the Japanese are preoccupied with this desire.

Sumanai, more politely *sumimasen*, caught the attention of Ruth Benedict[4] because it is used on occasions when English speakers would use three different expressions: "I feel guilty," "I am sorry," and "thank you." Apart from its use as an expletive, the same word, as the negative form of the verb *sumu*, may be used to say that a debt is "not paid off" or that a task "is uncompleted."

[3] See the analysis of *suneru, higamu, hinekureru, tereru, toriiru, tanomu, kodawaru,* and *amanzuru* in Doi, "Amae."

[4] *The Chrysanthemum and the Sword* (Boston, 1946).

Benedict, noting these other uses of the word and the parallel they implicitly draw between financial and moral debts, explained the use of this word to mean "thank you" by saying that it expressed one's sense of indebtedness accompanied by a painful realization that repayment is required some day.

She may be right that there is this ambivalence, but my analysis of Japanese neurotic patients has led me to suspect an ambivalence of a different kind related to the feelings expressed in *amaeru* behavior. If one has caused another person real harm or trouble, then the expression *sumanai,* standing for "I am sorry" or "I feel guilty," is a natural expression of a sense that one has not done as one ought to have done. But I have observed neurotic patients to use the word in this sense when the harm or trouble they have caused is imaginary. In these cases they secretly harbor hostile feelings toward the other which have been caused by frustration of their wish to *amaeru.* To say *sumanai* wards off such feelings; it implores the other not to drop one from grace despite one's fault (i.e., one's hostility). As such it is a disguised expression of the desire to *amaeru.* Likewise, *sumanai* where an English speaker would say "thank you" is an acknowledgment that one has indeed caused the other trouble inasmuch as the favor received is at his expense, and simultaneously a request that the other should not drop one from grace in spite of his loss.

Ninjō and Giri

When Benedict spoke of the concept of "human feelings" in Japanese culture and included in it all the natural impulses and inclinations of man, she was presumably referring to the word *ninjō,* which etymologically means "human feelings." But *ninjō* to the Japanese means a much more specific constellation of feeling and one which is looked on by Japanese specifically as Japanese. (Hence comments to the effect that Westerners "do not understand" or "also have" *ninjō.*) In my interpretation *ninjō* means specifically knowing how to *amaeru* properly and how to respond to the call of *amaeru* in others. Japanese think themselves especially sensitive to these feelings, and those who do not share that sensitivity are said to be wanting in *ninjō*.

Giri, by contrast, refers to a bond of moral obligation (whether or not of a kind specific to Japanese society is a controversy which need not concern us here). Thus, whereas *ninjō* primarily refers to those feelings which spontaneously occur in the relations between parent and child, husband and wife, or brothers and sisters, *giri* relations are relations between in-laws, neighbors, with close associates, or superiors in one's place of work. However, there is an inner connection between the two. Family relations also have an aspect to which the term *giri* can be applied, and at the same time *ninjō* can be extended to *giri* relations. In other words *giri* relations are pseudo-*ninjō* relations in which one may—and ideally always seeks to—experience *ninjō*. One may never, or only seldom, succeed, and usually one is left only with the semblance of *ninjō* and frustration of one's desire to *amaeru,* yet nevertheless the ideal is worth striving for. Interestingly enough, it is in *giri* relations that one would experience the feelings expressed as *sumanai* very frequently. This, I think, nicely illustrates the point that has been made above, that is: *giri* relations are pseudo-*ninjō* relations, since *sumanai* indicates the frustrated desire to *amaeru* seeking to express itself.

In this connection I would like to point out a few misleading remarks made by Benedict and shared by others; for instance, the notion that "the circle of human feelings" and "the circle of duty" are mutually exclusive. At times they may appear to be mutually exclusive, but *giri* relations are really there in order to be pervaded by *ninjō*. In this regard, Dore's assertion[5] that, for the male, the family belonged to the circle of "duty," and male friendships to the circle of "human feelings," also obscures the psychological interrelations of

[5] *City Life in Japan* (London, 1958), pp. 175–76.

giri and *ninjō* by making the same assumption of mutual exclusiveness. What is more, I think that if one were to ask a modern Japanese to label family life and male friendships according to *giri* and *ninjō*, he would rather reverse Dore's classification. This again does not mean that the family never freezes into mere *giri* relations devoid of *ninjō* or that male friendships never flourish into *ninjō*. Such possibilities clearly suggest that the circle of *giri* and that of *ninjō* are not fixed, but fluid; also that these two concepts refer to states of affairs rather than to kinds of personal relations. Finally, Benedict's statement[6] that "these old tales of times when *giri* was from the heart and had no taint of resentment are modern Japan's daydream of a golden age" is quite misleading. It is true that many *giri* relations are just a semblance of what they are supposed to be, but this fact does not prevent some *giri* relations from being entirely satisfactory to each partner because they are suffused with *ninjō*. It is such satisfactory *giri* relations which the Japanese usually understand by the term of friendship.

Historical Changes and the Traditional Patterns of Behavior

Modern Japan underwent two critical transformations, the Meiji Restoration and the defeat in World War II, which had immense effects on traditional patterns of interpersonal relations. At the time of the Meiji Restoration the emperor system or *kokutai* was formally established and came to constrain the traditional patterns of behavior—those centered upon *giri* and *ninjō*. Because the emperor was now a deity,[7]

[6] *The Chrysanthemum and the Sword*, p. 139.

[7] I believe that the national myth of the emperor as "God" was really created at the time of the Meiji Restoration, even though it appeared on the surface that this was only an official restatement of a Japanese myth about the emperor's being *kami*. In other words, I would like to stress the point that the form of emperor worship we held after the Meiji Restoration would possibly never have been established were it not for the impact of Western civilization upon

dedication and loyalty to him (loyalty was originally a feature of personal *giri* relations) became an absolute duty
(*gimu*) that should take precedence over *giri* and *ninjō* in
ordinary human relations. This emperor system, I think,
served a double function in terms of individuation in modern
Japan. On the one hand, it apparently promoted the individuation of the Japanese, inasmuch as it gave a rallying point
for every individual, irrespective of social status, family, sex,
or education. But on the other hand, and this was more important, it hindered individuation since it subjected every individual to the emperor by a spiritual bond and did not allow
him to establish his independent self apart from this bond.

Now thanks to the defeat in the last war, the emperor system has been abolished. Being freed from the mysterious
bond that tied them to the emperor, people also began to
question the validity of all traditional morals, especially the
morals of *giri* and *ninjō*. With this questioning, however, it
seems that people have become even more acutely aware of
the frustration of their desires to *amaeru,* since previously
their personal conflicts were supposed to be absorbed into
personal dedication and loyalty to the emperor. The follow-

Japan. It is well known that Western civilization became the model
for Japan to copy from, whether this civilization was introduced in
the form of science, technical skills, religion, individualism, democracy,
or communism. The establishment of the emperor system was a special
case in the Westernization of Japan. In fact, there is good historical
evidence that the nature of the authority which Meiji statesmen invested in the emperor was really borrowed from their image of
Western civilization, especially Christianity, in order to cope with it.
(See Maruyama, Masao, *Nihon no shisō*, 1961, pp. 28–31.) At any
rate, at the Privy Council in 1889, when the draft of the first constitution of Japan was introduced, Prince Ito had this to say: neither
Buddhism nor Shintoism could play the role which Christianity was
playing in Western countries as the basis for their constitutional governments. He then proposed that in Japan only the emperor could serve
as the basis of the constitution, thus fulfilling the role of religion in
Western countries. It was for this reason, I believe, that the emperor was officially held as sacred by the first constitution.

ing example is particularly interesting in this regard. One of my patients said that he would like to have somebody who would take the responsibility of doing *hohitsu* with him. *Hohitsu* is a special legal term which was used for the act of assisting the emperor with his task of governing the nation, and in this task his subordinates took all the responsibility, leaving none to the emperor. In other words, the emperor's position, psychologically speaking, signified the absolute gratification of dependency wishes. Of course, prior to the abolition of the emperor system, nobody thought that way or envied the emperor for that matter. But now the emperor being no deity, my patient intuitively sensed the psychological meaning of the emperor's position and used the word *hohitsu* to reveal his deep frustration of the desire to *amaeru*.

Removing the strait jacket of *kokutai* had definitely made people more vulnerable to internal conflicts. Also, without the support of *kokutai* for one's identity, the onslaught of various ideologies in Western civilization has to be faced individually. Thus we have in modern Japan the chaotic influx of various "isms" and faiths superimposed on the intricate entanglements of *giri* and *ninjō*. There is, for instance, increased self-assertion or pursuit of self-interest emerging out of the conflicts over *giri* and *ninjō*. This new trend is usually associated in the minds of the Japanese with individualism, one of the Western ideologies imported into Japan. It seems to me, however, that this trend amounts in most cases to what I would describe as an extreme pursuit of the desire to *amaeru*, accompanied by another emotion, that of suspicion and mistrust toward others. I do not mean to say in this regard that such individualism is only a peculiarly Japanese phenomenon and does not exist in the West. I also cannot discuss here how it compares with the original spirit of individualism as it developed in the West. At any rate, the postwar trend has made one crucial conflict manifest, that is, the conflict over *amaeru* or that of whether one is loved or not. I say this conflict is crucial because one's self-respect in the final analysis hinges upon its successful solution. Only when one is certain on this score is one able to stand as an independent individual.

In this connection it is interesting to recall a recent comment by Masao Maruyama that almost all Japanese leaders in all walks of life are convinced that they are always surrounded by hostile critics, a consciousness which Maruyama calls "an ever-present sense of being wronged by others (*higaisha ishiki*)."[8] This fact clearly indicates that all of these people harbor the desire to *amaeru* and feel frustrated in it. If the leading representatives of Japanese society are like this, how would the rest feel, not to speak of those patients who come to seek help from psychiatrists. Perhaps if there was anything defective in the working of the traditional patterns of behavior centered in *giri* and *ninjō*, it was the fact that it did not solve the conflict over whether one is loved or not, rather perpetuated it, since *giri* by its nature binds people in dependent relationships and *ninjō* only encourages dependency. The fact, then, that the Japanese are blessed with such a word as *amaeru* may not be a measure of their satisfaction after all, but rather of their preoccupation with it because of dissatisfaction. But then the question remains: how does one solve the conflict over one's dependency wishes? Would it be by acquiring the inner certainty of being loved once for all or by dispensing with dependency wishes altogether? I cannot discuss this matter any further, since it touches upon a more philosophical question of how individualism developed in the West in the first place and of what is the nature of individuation. At any rate, if Japanese society should proceed toward more individuation, I should think that it will not be simply by dint of industrialization, but by searching deeply into the foundations of Western culture.

[8] *Nihon no shisō*, pp. 141–44.

Group and Individual: Burakumin as a Special Case

PART SIX

Group and Individual: Functionalism as a Special Case

CHAPTER XI

Individual Mobility and Group Membership: The Case of the Burakumin

JOHN B. CORNELL

IT IS an assumption implicit in my title that the Japanese individual is somehow always powerfully subject to the supra-individual concerns of his group, the group concerned being usually a relatively small and localized segment of the whole society rather than a major subdivision such as class. How, if at all, is the situation of the *burakumin* different in this respect from that of other Japanese; how different his scope for individuality or the expression of self-interest? In trying to answer these questions, we must examine the social forces which account for the differences which exist and show how these forces act to set the boundaries of outcast society, to cause the individual *burakumin* to choose between identification with, or categorical rejection of, his group. Finally, we must discriminate the patterns by which *burakumin* personal goals—for their personal ambitions and striving are in many ways typical of those of all Japanese—are sublimated, or reinterpreted, by those openly identified with *burakumin* subsociety who accept accommodation within it.

"Individuation" as a process[1] appears to operate under far more restrictive limits in Japan than in the United States. The capacity of the Japanese individual to conduct himself with resolute independence in the face of group constraints, to entertain private ideas contrary to the group's, guided

---

[1] I follow R. P. Dore's usage, namely, "certain characteristics of behavior and motivation, and not a consciously held politico-economic philosophy." See Dore, *City Life in Japan: A Study of a Tokyo Ward* (Berkeley: University of California Press, 1958), p. 357.

mainly by the gyroscope of conscience, is always limited, for life is hazardous without collective support or the personal patronage of a senior. It is particularly hazardous for the minority individual who cannot even count on the neutrality of society once his family origin has become known. For, as Wirth asserts, "to the individual members of such a group the most onerous circumstances under which they have to labor is that they are treated as members of a category irrespective of their individual merits. Hence it is important to recognize that membership in a minority is involuntary; our own behavior is irrelevant."[2]

Many cases to the contrary notwithstanding, the conviction dies hard among social scientists that Japan tends to cling to "the concept of group duty, rather than individual rights or privileges, [as] the basis for action and behavior."[3] But individuals may remain tradition-directed with respect to the overt modes of behavior while yet developing other "value orientations" concerning the goals of life. The *burakumin* individual is in fact usually individuated in his aims; the things he wants *are* "things he wants for himself or for specific individual others, not for some group . . . to which he belongs."[4]

Noninstitutionalization of "Difference"

For the most part Japan does not face the dilemma of race, nor has she had a long history of admission of foreign elements in which to develop a "melting pot" tradition. Minority phenomena are regarded only as transitory or as problems to be obliterated as rapidly as possible for the health of the society, ideally without residue. Therefore, no conscious

[2] Louis Wirth, "Problems of Minority Groups," in Ralph Linton, ed., *The Science of Man in the World Crisis* (New York: Columbia University Press, 1945), p. 349.

[3] Yoshiharu Scott Matsumoto, *Contemporary Japan: The Individual and the Group* (*Transactions of the American Philosophical Society*, new series, vol. 50, pt. 1, 1960), p. 7.

[4] Dore, *City Life in Japan*, p. 357.

polity of toleration of minorities, no genuine policy of pluralism, may be said to exist, but only various attempts to solve
a particular minority problem.

Uncomfortable with the problem of what to do with any
minority, Japanese society is especially uneasy about the
burakumin. This is not because they, the *burakumin,* really
desire to be treated differentially; not at all. But by being
forced in effect to live apart in segregated *"buraku"* communities they are willy-nilly exposed to discrimination. In
Wirth's terms again, "Though not necessarily an alien group
the minority is treated as regards itself as a people apart."[5]
It is particularly disquieting to most thinking Japanese that
there should be such people in contemporary Japan, for in
culture, as well as in race, the *burakumin* are virtually indis-
tinguishable from other Japanese. And yet they are so effectively segregated, at least in the critical respects of residence,
marriage, and—frequently—occupation, that Japan might almost be called a dual society. In a land where pluralism is
anathema this situation is disturbing to the majority. It is
even more resented by the minority.

Let us disregard for the moment the question of how far
factors within the minority itself encourage and, in fact, necessitate the persistence of their isolation. Let us consider that
such obstacles to intermarriage and to intimate social inter-
course as currently exist are the products of processes affecting the whole society, desirable neither to the minority nor to
the majority. The present stalemate rests upon quite unique
conditions not taken into account in the general theory of
minorities but which have created, unexpectedly, the tendency toward another type of situation posited by Wirth,[6]
secessionism. By being in fact thwarted in their effort to remove the barriers to free interaction in the society, the *burakumin* have developed a conscientiousness of kind, a community of purpose throughout the country which solidifies

---

[5] Wirth, "Problems of Minority Groups," pp. 347-48.
[6] *Ibid.*, p. 358.

"caste" unity and which thereby increases the gulf separating them from *ippan* (majority) society. To achieve their avowed goal of complete assimilation, they have brought upon themselves in the last forty to fifty years a sharper delineation of the boundaries of the group through nationwide organization and collective political action.

The Rise of Minority Group Consciousness and Exposure of the Individual

Looked at in a historical perspective, it is clear that despite the growing pressure for uniformity of social structure, administration, law, and ideology which begins with the centralization of feudalism in the Tokugawa period, regional and even local colorations of outcast culture dating from the premodern period, persisted strongly well into the modern period. The pattern of life of the *semmin* (the "base people" as the groups variously called *eta* or *hinin* were collectively designated) was essentially a deviant version of the regional subculture. There was no general *semmin* culture apart from the similarity of their popular status image and the identity of their legal position everywhere prior to the Meiji Restoration and the Emancipation Edict in 1871.

While economically as well as politically their ghetto-like villages began to change profoundly in the early Meiji period, newly achieved civil equality seems to have induced little immediate change in the lives of the outcasts within these villages.[7] Their *buraku* communities offered a refuge against the bewilderment of this freedom and for at least the first thirty years of the period, the meaning of "emancipation" (*kaihō*) did not penetrate the ethical concerns of the slowly coalescing *burakumin* minority.

[7] See Shigeaki Ninomiya, "An Inquiry concerning the Origin, Development and Present Situation of the Eta in Relation to the History of Social Classes in Japan," in *Transactions of the Asiatic Society of Japan*, second series, x (1933), 110-11.

Living in their isolated *buraku*, the outcasts characteristically exhibited coarse, unruly behavioral traits associated with the depravity believed natural to people of their status. Under the impact of the "self-help" values prevalent in the first few decades of Meiji, literacy, community cooperation, thrift, diligence, cooperation with law enforcement officers, and similar values were advanced among them in the name of social improvement (termed *kaizen*), calculated to raise the minority to the general Japanese level.

The ferment over popular rights and democracy, which climaxed in the Taisho period, came at a time when *burakumin* individuals were finding increasing opportunities for self-expression—for individual emancipation—but were also being exposed to new situations where hostility of the majority had to be faced, for instance, as a conscript in the army barracks. The founding of the national union of *burakumin*, the Suiheisha ("the Levelers"), in 1922 stemmed mainly from a growing awareness of the idea of popular rights. It shifted the focus of outcast attention from the *kaizen* ideal of closing the moral gap between themselves and others to the goal of assimilation on their own terms irrespective of their moral acceptability. In effect, the creation of the Suiheisha and of its state-sponsored counteragency, the Yūwa ("Conciliation") program in the Interior Ministry,[8] at once exposed the closed *buraku* to large new external pressures. They also offered to the *buraku* intelligentsia new paths to individual achievement and power. Further, by weakening the authority of the local entrepreneurial elites, who had taken control of the traditional outcast craft economy in its early adjustment to the modern national market, these forces probably also made it easier for the individual to take the ultimate "quantum" step—to pass into *ippan* society.

The circumstances of the Japanese *burakumin* after 1922 may be compared to those of Jews in Germany of the same

[8] By this time all *kaizen* activities tended to be styled "*yūwa*."

341

period. As Kurt Lewin describes their predicament,[9] in the "ghetto period" of their history the social boundaries of the Jewish community were made sharp and clear by the physical limitations of the ghetto itself. However, "as a result of disintegration of the group, the individual was much more exposed to pressure as an isolated individual." He became "a separate whole." Diminution of pressure against the group itself was "accompanied by a development which shifted the point of application of [the same] external forces from the group to the individual; . . . the strength of the conflict situation [increased] with the weakness of the boundary between groups concerned."[10]

Like the Jews released from ghetto life, the position of the *burakumin* has become far more complex in the past several decades of conscious striving for "emancipation" (*kaihō*). From Edo times down to the upsurge of social awareness in the 1920s, the tight, collective parochialism of their segregated communal life had served to defend the people against often harsher oppression applied to *heimin* peasantry who were not so cloistered. Moreover, there is good reason to believe that the *eta* in the Tokugawa period were frequently better off than their *heimin* contemporaries through their monopolies over certain crafts and public functions in preindustrial Japan. Because their "defensive wall [the *buraku*] safeguarded them from external force, they lived a surprisingly serene existence inside their area."[11] Now there are no barriers cutting them off from the education of the outside world, from wage employment, and the political responsibility of citizenship. More external relations have engendered more occasions for overt discrimination, which has borne more directly on the individual or on his family. Discrimina-

[9] Kurt Lewin, *Resolving Social Conflicts* (New York: Harper, 1948), ch. 9, *passim*.

[10] Lewin, *Resolving Social Conflicts*, pp. 153-56, *passim*.

[11] Nishimoto Sōsuke, *Buraku mondai to dōwa kyōiku* (Sōbunsha, 1960), p. 163.

tion is now more often personally experienced, and therefore the individual's sense of it is deeper. Greater sensitivity to discriminatory affronts is not just because the *buraku* person is in fact still unfree after so long a period of theoretical equality; rather it is because his perception of the minority problem is much sharper and more penetrating.[12]

Persistence of the Buraku "Ghetto"

The persistence of the modern *burakumin*'s social dilemma is generally seen to be rooted in his special kind of economic handicap. It is a common assumption of both the government's "*yūwa*" line of conciliation and the outcasts' own *kaihō* position that the root cause of discrimination is poverty and the lack of employment opportunity in the *buraku*; this circumstance regenerates by "feedback." Latent discriminatory attitudes are aggravated by the attendant characteristics of *burakumin* poverty and so limit employment opportunities and so make poverty more certain. Such conditions as "overcrowding; lack of higher education; limited range of occupations; unkempt and careless appearance; bad morals; unsanitary conditions; thriftlessness; limited mental outlook and prejudice; irreligion and fanaticism"[13] are still typical of contemporary *buraku* life.

Efforts to improve living conditions and economic opportunities have merely taken the edge off the immediate complaints, alleviating the side effects while leaving the locus of the infection—the *buraku* slum—intact. Their main effects have been both to increase the population of those places where governmental subsidy programs have been most bountifully applied and to engender resentment among their *ippan* neighbors who have not been similarly subsidized. In a word, the primary therapeutic device of public programs

---

[12] Nishimoto, *Buraku mondai*, p. 164.
[13] Nobutaro Yoshikawa, *Suihei undō* (*Japanese Outcaste Movement*), unpublished M.A. thesis, Northwestern University, 1929, p. 56; quoting *Yūwa jigyō nenkan* (*Yearbook of conciliation*) (1928).

of amelioration, special economic assistance, had helped to rebuild social walls around the *buraku* by giving special advantages to its residents and thereby perpetuating the alleged economic causes of its isolation.

Except in the larger cities, it is not easy to lose sight of the presence of *buraku* districts. There usually remains in place over time an undiluted core of outcast families who are completely immobile. Some, as Nishimoto found in Kyoto, wish to break out but cannot do so for economic reasons; others, a local elite with in fact better economic opportunities, may not wish to do so.[14] Only very rarely are *buraku* wholly new. For instance, in two cases of large-scale wartime dispersal, one in Tokyo and one in Kyoto, the residents later regrouped to form a new *buraku* in a slum area.

In crowded urban areas, high mobility alone may ultimately obliterate effective discrimination. Suzuki has recently commented: "Tokyo authorities . . . seem least concerned about improving the *burakumin*'s living conditions, partly because the ghettoes in the capital are already well integrated with the surrounding districts, and pose no particular problem. Very few people in Tokyo are aware of the exact location of the city's ghettoes. The inhabitants of fairly well-integrated ghettoes tend to be satisfied with partial assimilation, and wish to maintain the *status quo* by not drawing further attention to their needs."[15]

Where there are no powerful outward manifestations of outcast society and culture synthesized in a unique complex of traits attributed to poverty, ignorance, and ill-breeding, it is not impossible that discrimination will quietly disappear. But there are also persistent and deeper factors—beliefs in preternatural customs of the *burakumin* and in concepts of ritual pollution (i.e. untouchability) through personal contacts with them—which live on in rationalized modern guise.

[14] Nishimoto, *Buraku mondai*, pp. 168–69.
[15] Jirō Suzuki, "Burakumin: Japan's Untouchables," *Orient-West*, VI:vii (July 1961), 5.

Experience has shown the *burakumin* that however much he desires to live unrecognized away from the *buraku*, it is often hazardous to his livelihood. To live outside usually means to discard family and community ties and to exist under the constant threat of exposure to the full effects of discrimination as an isolated individual.

Burakumin in Okayama

The situation is somewhat different in provincial Okayama, where blurring of the loosely demarcated boundaries of urban outcast districts through "creeping" assimilation often tends to result more in *ippan* anxiety than complacency. To illustrate the effect of group membership on the individual, I shall concentrate on a large but reasonably typical rural *burakumin* community called Matsuzaki on the outskirts of the city of Okayama, which was the subject of my own field research.[16]

To a much higher degree than in comparable *ippan* communities, residence in the *buraku* is impermanent. For a majority it is a home base rather than a place of regular livelihood. Matsuzaki is especially attractive to its large migratory segment because it lies within the shadow of the city labor market. In general, the drift is from outlying communities where job opportunities are relatively scarce to the urban cn-

[16] Matsuzaki is one of six administrative districts (*ku*) of former Yokoi Village, since 1959 part of the amalgamated entity Tsudaka Town (*chō*). Its population is variable but ranges between 800 and 1,000 at all times (resident population in December 1958 was 842). Matsuzaki was intensively studied by the writer and by sociologists under Professor Yamamoto Noboru of Osaka Metropolitan University from October 1957 to January 1959. Research was supported by a Fulbright research grant with supplemental funds from the American Philosophical Society. An earlier report on this field work may be found in the writer's "Outcast Relations in a Japanese Village," *American Anthropologist*, LXIII (1961), 282–96, and in various publications by Yamamoto, especially "Sabetsu ishiki to shinriteki kinchō—mikaihō burakumin no ishiki ni kansuru kenkyū," *Jimbun kenkyū*, x, no. 12 (1959), 25–59, Osaka Metropolitan University.

virons where more commuting jobs are available, and from which one may again move on.

The adjacent city integrally contains three distinguishable districts of outcast concentration.[17] The *burakumin* of the largest of these, Mikado in northwestern Okayama, have gradually infiltrated surrounding *ippan* areas since the war; while certain key features of the status survive there—for instance the only *burakumin* temple in this part of Bizen—Mikado lacks the cohesiveness of *buraku* outside the city.

The economic advantages of Matsuzaki's position near Okayama—within the urban network but not corporately or legally of it—is offset by its comparatively impermeable caste isolation. At a number of other places in the prefecture studied by Yamamoto and myself, we found that even where the *buraku* had a reasonably viable relationship to the local economy—where, for instance, the *burakumin* divided their time between farming and factory work like everyone else—a corresponding residential and social assimilation had not begun to develop.

What such *buraku* communities have in common is the unacknowledged but impermeable shield of status isolation. In the Okayama hinterland the physical mobility evident in the creeping assimilation of the city *buraku* is probably very rare, for the boundaries of the suburban satellite *buraku* remain well defined. Mobility here is lateral; rural people more commonly move between established *buraku* rather than from the *buraku* into undifferentiated areas. Marriage tends to displace individuals in the same fashion. Such lateral movement, when the *buraku* limits are clearly delineated and maintained, is not a source of intercaste tension, as movement under conditions of creeping assimilation can be.

[17] These town districts, *chiku*, are less clearly delineable than *buraku* in the suburbs which remain basically agrarian, movement in and out of the *chiku* being prompted more often by needs of shelter than concerns of social status; boundaries of the districts are now ill-defined.

The Buraku as the Minority Image

Any answer to the question "Why is physical segregation and social discrimination vis-à-vis residents of a *buraku* like Matsuzaki kept alive?" involves a consideration of the image the *buraku* represents to other Japanese.

I found a regular pattern among *ippan* informants in the village when referring to Matsuzaki. By and large it was difficult for them to regard the *burakumin* other than collectively, not as individuals, as when they thought or spoke of other *ippan* villagers. Attitudes toward *burakumin* individuals tended to fall back on the character configuration ascribed to the entire *buraku* unit and were based, at that, upon the behavior of the lower-class mass of *burakumin*. Observers were prone to think of all Matsuzaki residents as rough in speech, crude or brutal in relations with each other, having a low boiling point, quarrelsome, highly sensitive to insult, born traders, and relatively much more cohesive than any other community.

Even when an adult informant was well acquainted personally with someone from Matsuzaki, it was usually an age-group friendship formed in school or in the *seinendan*, which was not very actively maintained after assumption of adult responsibilities. Associations with *burakumin* adults were reported from formal contexts, much of the time in meetings on village business at the village office or the agricultural cooperative; however, these never seem to warm to the point of frequent home visiting, nor do other members of the families become involved. In any case, these village matters affect comparatively few persons in each hamlet,[18] usually only the elected officials or members of the village public service committees for public welfare, or maternity aid, or on the com-

---

[18] I use the word "hamlet" for the nucleated rural settlement (part of an administrative village) usually called *buraku* in order to keep *buraku* for its other sense (an abbreviation of *tokushu-buraku* or, currently, *mikaihō-buraku*) as an outcaste settlement.

mittees of the PTA, or irrigation cooperative, or producers cooperatives, or on the panel of poll watchers at the voting place Matsuzaki uses with an adjacent *ippan* community. The fact that these suburban hamlets have closer ecological and social ties to the city than with each other has the effect of intensifying the basic ideological isolation of these *burakumin*.

Most usually the rationale behind this *apartheid* is expressed in terms of *burakumin* being "different," "strange" in an uncomplimentary sense, or because they are cleverly "shrewd." Virtually no informant, not even a very candid one, can say exactly why he feels so, except that this complex seems to arise from a variety of cognitive bases, never just one. It is very common for a genuinely cooperative informant to begin by saying "It's very difficult to explain . . ." before going on to cite things in *burakumin* behavior he does not admire. In the main it is only by attributing to the *burakumin* some characteristic or practice which would be accepted as "dirty" (read: unhygienic, immoral or antisocial) in judging any Japanese that a man is able to account for his own feelings about the *burakumin*. While he may employ words which convey a quality of ritual disgust, such language is openly discriminatory and, perforce, proscribed. Generally this feeling is disguised in complaints of offences against good taste or society which could be leveled against anyone.

The common intuitive perception of the *buraku* is that it is darkly disreputable, mysterious, and substantially unknown. The perception can be maintained in part because very few Japanese have ever knowingly entered a *buraku* or associated with *burakumin*. The folklore substantiating this pejorative image of the *buraku* is thematically consistent in attributing behavior to them which ranges from the extraordinary through the morally scandalous to the unnatural. A salacious interest is often sublimated into hearsay theories

348

about the remarkable beauty of *buraku* women or the uncommon devotion of its men to hard drinking.

Peculiar dietary practices are one of the most resistant justifications for popular odium against the *burakumin*. My own survey of Matsuzaki suggests that in fact the only food peculiarities are that they eat poorly and cheaply; some men of the *buraku* still engage in taking loaches in the paddies but more because there is still a fairly steady market among the public for them than because they themselves have a taste for this food. However, the fact that they do catch loaches may be used as one more indication of their depraved character. While less commonly than in the past, some Japanese will still refuse to partake of food they know has come from a *burakumin*. In an incident related by a prefectural official of a school in the Kojima Peninsula, Okayama, children happily shared the lunch of a generous fellow until they learned he was from the *buraku*, whereupon all pointedly refused to take any more.

Passing: The "Quantum Leap" Out of Caste

The *burakumin's* aspirations of interclass mobility are generally more restricted than those of other Japanese. He is aware of the opportunities open to the average person, but is also acutely aware of being one of a distinctive minority with a heavy body of social restraints to which this membership subjects him—more particularly if he lives in the *buraku* but even if he lives elsewhere, too, as long as his connection to it can in some way be established.

For the *burakumin* the true upward movement, to which he may aspire as a matter of principle but which is seen as a realistic objective by relatively few, is "passing." I call this the "quantum leap" out of caste, for to be truly successful it must be a complete and final break. While many linger at the edges of caste, gradually sundering their ties, they usually find that only a total break is worth the physical and emotional cost.

349

To become a member of *ippan* society, essentially without trace, it is not enough simply to move out of the *buraku*, vote in an *ippan* electoral district, or cut cold all one's relatives and former friends. It is normally a process which to be effective should be done in a series of planned steps, which take a generation and perhaps more. Physical removal from the *buraku* only signals firm intent. The final, crucial act seems often to be an effort by a descendant, a child or grandchild, to make an honorable marriage with a member of *ippan* society.

I doubt, therefore, that the benefit of a quantum vertical change can realistically be expected by the individual who initiates passing; while he himself may experience some immediate improvement in his latitude for private action, particularly by release from the collective obligations of *buraku* life, he is also confronted with increased anxieties over being found out in his new milieu. The major aim in passing appears to be to leave a legacy of private emancipation—*kaihō*—to one's descendants.

A good measure of serious intent to pass is transfer of *koseki,* the legal registration of address. This may come before or after physical removal, for it is necessary first to acquire a reasonably secure economic position for the family outside before any physical move can be contemplated. In his study of *burakumin* districts in Hiroshima city, Suzuki has found that several successive transfers of *koseki* from one neutral *ippan* district to another might be tried to disguise ultimate origin.[19] About half the resident households in the *buraku* were registered in *ippan* areas, so that their legal residence cannot reveal their true origin.[20] Since without influential connections it is virtually impossible to succeed in making a false transfer, over 70 percent of these transfers

---

[19] Suzuki Jirō, "Hiroshima-ken, 'O'-gumi no chiiki-sei shokugyō kekkon ni tsuite—Buraku mondai shiryō sono ichi," *Philosophia,* xxxiii (1952), 151–55.

[20] *Ibid.,* p. 153.

were to *ippan* areas in the same city, where, presumably, they could work through friends and relatives. My impression is that although the number of transfers are fewer in Matsuzaki, the majority are similarly limited to the Okayama metropolitan area.

We might suppose that the numbers passing should have increased with more positive individual freedoms and with some improvement in general mobility since the war. This does not seem to be the case. Again, in Suzuki's Hiroshima *buraku*, by 1951 the volume of registration transfers had actually noticeably declined from prewar and wartime rates. Earlier, a large share of the work of the *rimpo-kan* (block officer) had been processing *burakumin* requests for transfer. Bribery was certainly involved in getting the cooperation of such officials. One of the services of the Christian (Methodist) settlement house in the area was to advise those who could not afford to pay a gratuity how they might manage *koseki* transfers. The statement of the chief of this settlement house illustrates the intensity of desire to do this.

> Nowadays the number has very much declined, but in the old days there was lots of counselling about registration. This was mainly for legitimizing children born out of wedlock, and transferring registration. It was not limited to discussing their problems. The entire procedure was requested; at the beginning most were interested in choosing a place to transfer their registration. Many wanted to move out of the city and then there were also quite a few who hoped to change their registration into [*ippan* areas] of the city. Still, the biggest part of them only transferred their registration and lived on in the district.[21]

In sum, passing—the private solution—would seem never to have been practicable as a truly individual action. When it occurs most probably it is the effort of a whole family group. There is general agreement among Japanese most familiar

---

[21] Suzuki, "Hiroshima-ken, 'O'-gumi no chiiki-sei shokugyō," p. 152.

with the problem that individuals who are well educated and intelligently motivated have the best chance of success. This may be an unconscious motive behind the eagerness of many Matsuzaki families, even those of very modest means, to maximize their children's education. We may think of education, then, as a new and not altogether clearly perceived method of accelerating private escape.

Mobility Aspirations and Burakumin Self-Image

The problems of mobility for *burakumin* differ from those of other Japanese in that they turn on the awareness of being subject to discrimination. Freedom from discrimination itself becomes the goal, either for the *burakumin* himself or for his minority group as a whole. Unless he elects to pass,[22] he must sublimate his mobility goals to achieving status within his minority, largely in fact within the microcosm of his own *buraku*.

For most *burakumin*, then, the issues of personal ambition and achievement must operate in quite narrow limits, and there are few alternative categories of achievement. The problem is quite clear-cut: life outside is almost unanimously the more desirable because ideally it offers the minimal freedoms of residence, occupation, and marriage. The path of attainment of these freedoms is hard, however, requiring great cost in personal effort, and success has heretofore depended upon great strength of purpose, unusual advantages plus considerable sheer luck; on the average a *buraku* person meets obstacles that are more than a match for his determination. There is a time in life, before family responsibilities are set, when he may learn of these barriers at first hand by sojourning outside. The adult *burakumin* is chastened by the knowledge that passing is a tense, often perilous adventure into the dubious freedom of personal marginalism which strips him of the support of kinsmen and intimates which

[22] Comparatively few do, according to Nishimoto Sōsuke, perhaps 20 percent. Personal communication, June 13, 1958.

Japanese usually need to get a start. He is understandably reluctant to try more than once. For practical purposes he prefers the easier security of the minority group, although he does not thereby relinquish his image of the "emancipated" good life as an ideal, nor does he regard cloistered *buraku* existence as an adequate substitute.

To test the general level of satisfaction with life in the *buraku*, let us look at some questionnaire results. Studying urban *burakumin* in Hiroshima in 1951, Suzuki found that of 82 householders picked randomly from the rationing list more than half (61 percent) expressed preference for living in this *buraku* district.[23] When asked "If you were to live elsewhere (i.e. outside), can you think of any sort of undesirable conditions you might face?" most thought of the personal hardships this would entail.

> "Personal relations would be difficult."
> "I would face discrimination."
> "Because I am a shoemaker, everyone would know of my *buraku* origin."
> "It would be hard to get acquainted and people wouldn't help me out."

And so on. Similar, and even more nearly unanimous results were obtained in studies of a *buraku* district in urban Saitama prefecture[24] and in a *buraku* district in the city of Nara.[25] The belief that *ippan* people are at least cold, if not openly hostile, would seem to have become for the minority a "self-fulfilling prophecy" for which the proof of experience is only incidental to its general fitness to their image of this

---

[23] Suzuki, "Hiroshima-ken, 'O'-gumi no chiiki-sei shokugyō," p. 157.

[24] Jirō Suzuki, "Burakumin no chiiki-sei shokugyō, kekkon—buraku mondai shiryō sono ni," in Nihon Jimbun Kagakkai, ed., *Shakaiteki kinchō no kenkyu* (Yūhikaku, 1953), p. 387. 82 percent of 97 respondents said they preferred to stay in the *buraku*.

[25] Nara Minsei Rōdōbu, ed., *Mikaihō buraku no jisshōteki kenkyū* (1953), pp. 60-61. 77 percent of 331 respondents said they preferred to stay put.

other life. At any rate very few respondents are conscious of having experienced discrimination personally (in seven studies at hand, negative replies average over 70 percent). One cannot help but agree with the evaluation of a school principal in my own study in Okayama that only those few with initiative of their own truly want to get out.

In the countryside, where the opportunities for association with *ippan* persons are ordinarily less and the *buraku* is patently more distinctive, there is perhaps less realization of the stresses and loss of security that living like *ippan* can bring. Living just at the edge of the city but predominantly still rural, Matsuzaki residents agree that *buraku* life is easier but accept this less overwhelmingly than in Nara or Hiroshima (about 54 percent of 125 respondents).[26]

When the interviewer asked why living in the *buraku* is easier, he got more unequivocally positive responses from the majority preferring to stay where they were than from the minority (23) who opted for the outside. While some of the former showed singular complacency,

"It's my home."
"You live where you can."
"I'm used to living here."

the bulk of them stressed the emotional and economic security the *buraku* affords.

"You know these people."
"It's easy to associate with these people."
"I have my acquaintances here, know life here very well."
"People are kind."
"People are hospitable and help each other."
"There is no need to feel tension."
"I would feel uneasy [outside], afraid lest they find me out."

Again, keyed more to practicalities,

[26] Yamamoto, "Sabetsu ishiki to shinriteki kinchō," p. 45.

"We can always make a living here."

"It's more expensive outside."

"Economically more stable."

"The basis of my living is here."

A little over 59 percent of those queried stated they intend to continue living in the *buraku*, content there or not. Following are some representative reasons given.

"This is land inherited from my ancestors."

"I think I cannot move outside because I have real estate here; I will not be able to dispose of it and move elsewhere unless I am definitely sure of my future life outside. However, I am intending to make my children move out of here."

"I don't have enough money to move out."

"I am old."

"It can't be helped."

Reasons advanced by the minority hoping or expecting to leave (just over 27 percent) include:

"We will be set free [*kaihō*]."

"I would like to have a broader outlook to my life."

"If we stay here, we will feed on each other and be ruined."

"It's better for the children to leave the *buraku*."

"[I'd leave] if I could make a go of it."

"It is better for the children to live in a place where they would not know of their birth. I don't want them to go through my sorrows."

Evident in the foregoing is that so far as personal aspirations are concerned, many have permanently cast their lot with the *buraku* who feel little satisfaction with it. Should conditions permit successful departure from the *buraku*, however, Matsuzaki respondents strongly desire to leave (by just over 70 percent).[27] As Yamamoto sums up the results of

[27] *Ibid.*, p. 47.

these conflicting sentiments: "Most believe that it is better to dress poorly, eat poorly, live with relatives, do any sort of work, but still be able to live, and to be able to avoid the feeling of inferiority in being known as someone from the *buraku*."[28]

In answer to other questions Matsuzaki people showed that they accepted the principle of assimilation. Above 67 percent favored intermarriage with *ippan* society whenever possible.[29] But at least 80 percent responded that they had never considered such marriage for themselves.[30] Yamamoto obtained similar results in four other outcast *buraku* in central Japan.[31] The affirmative replies expressed marked idealism on the principle of intermarriage.

"It is only natural because we are the same human beings."

"It will lessen discriminatory feeling."

"All men are equal."

"[It is a good idea] in order to avoid consanguineous marriages."

"[Through intermarriage] discrimination will disappear spontaneously. However, it cannot be done at present."

"Whatever our ancestry, discrimination will disappear by mingling of bloods."

"There will be much more chance for 'love' marriage."

On the other hand, respondents who disapproved did so basically for reasons of personal security.

"There's no need to feel restraint if [one marries] within the *buraku*."

[28] *Ibid.*, p. 46.

[29] This survey was conducted by Yamamoto Noboru and staff of the Sociological Research Center, Osaka Metropolitan University, in December 1958 and January 1959. Some of its results have been published in Yamamoto, "Sabetsu ishiki to shinriteki kinchō," and in Cornell, "Outcast Relations in a Japanese Village"; most of the following material is appearing for the first time.

[30] Yamamoto, "Sabetsu ishiki to shinriteki kinchō," p. 47.

[31] Yamamoto, "Sabetsu ishiki to shinriteki kinchō."

"I still can't help feeling inferior [with outsiders]."

"Both sides get along better [by not intermarrying]."

"I would feel ill at ease toward people in the *buraku* [were I to marry an *ippan* person]."

The sense of these reactions is reluctance to take the step personally while favoring it in principle.

From their perspective, Matsuzaki respondents' image of their own *buraku* society evokes a mixture of pride and embarrassment. By some moral criteria they consider themselves superior to outsiders, by others inferior, as is shown by Table 1, a summary of the results obtained by asking the sample to make a point-for-point comparison of the *buraku* people and their *ippan* neighbors on a series of twenty value aspects.[32] The table lists the fourteen of these twenty points on which the *burakumin* self-image differs sharply from their image of *ippan* people. As for the other six, there was a notable failure to see clear differences in matters of family (*iegara*) and lineage loyalty, in the relative position of the spouses in the household, or in the degree of deference shown to authority at either the hamlet or village levels.

Of the sources of pride, it is interesting that Matsuzaki people think of themselves as adhering more closely to the conservative tradition of arranged marriages, since in fact the incidence of "love" marriages is higher there. In contrast, they recognize as a moral flaw their propensity to coarse, crude, even violent behavior. The *burakumin* regard their stealing and reputation for acts provoking fear in others as another serious character flaw.[33] Equally serious, in their sight, is their association with occupations which *ippan* people will not do and which are regarded as morally unclean (*kitanai*).

[32] Also included in this discussion are response data to another question in the survey, asking what aspects in their behavior they feel tend to perpetuate *sabetsu* (discrimination).

[33] Yamamoto, "Sabetsu ishiki to shinriteki kinchō," p. 53 (table 12).

TABLE 1

COMPARATIVE VALUE RATINGS OF BURAKUMIN IMAGES OF SELF AND IPPAN
NEIGHBORS ON CERTAIN ASPECTS OF COMMUNITY RELATIONS
AND CASTE CHARACTER

Question	Percentage of the sample[a] answering		
If one compares *burakumin* with *ippan* people, which:	"Burakumin"	"Ippan"	"No difference"
1. Are more filial?	28.0	5.6	66.4
2. Are more respectful to ancestral dead?	55.0	4.0	41.0
3. Prefer arranged to love marriage?	19.2	2.4	78.4
4. Are more cooperative with neighbors	89.6	0.0	10.4
5. Are more deferential toward person with status?	37.6	8.8	53.6
6. Are generally more cooperative in collective enterprises?	48.0	9.6	42.4
7. Work harder?	87.2	0.8	12.0
8. Are less selfish?	32.0	21.0	47.0
9. Have higher (more standard) speech habits?	8.0	53.6	38.4
10. Are better reared and educated?	2.4	46.4	51.2
11. Observe proper relations between the the sexes better?	4.0	16.8	79.2
12. Have more hygienic habits?	13.6	20.8	65.6
13. Plan their daily lives more rationally?	3.2	31.2	65.6
14. Are better, more tastefully dressed?	13.6	23.2	63.2

[a] N = 125

In summary of the *buraku* self-image, we can see that not only are there hazards, real or imaginary, for the *burakumin* in associating with the *ippan* world, but in addition the psychological burden of maintaining self-respect would seem on balance to be a serious deterrent to the individual venturing alone into outside society. Perhaps, too, he has a sense of loyalty to his group which, though widely deprecated on moral grounds, he feels has many moral virtues worthy of his respect.

However, loyalty may be ambivalent and partly compounded of resigned acceptance of a fate which cannot ever be expected to be a happy one. One of the younger, firmly committed leaders of the Matsuzaki community, for instance, observed that "everyone hates the place," though he saw no immediate solution but to improve living conditions inside the *buraku.*

The resentment accompanying this resigned acceptance of the *buraku* is never, when it is expressed, against any specific feature of the community but against the whole entity construed as a complete, if miniature, social universe. Nevertheless, the one thing the residents feel most keenly is the lack of economic opportunity, and the fact that since few have enough land to make a living from the respectable calling of agriculture, they are forced into occupations which brand them as *burakumin.*

Itinerant peddling (flower selling is a common form), for example, can furnish a better living with less investment than all but about 12 percent of the households make by farming alone. By buying cut flowers on credit from an Okayama auction house, a peddler can clear about one thousand *yen* a day in the peak summer season. Such business is seasonal and unstable, of course, but a more serious objection to the socially conscious seller is often that it is repugnant. One very successful young man in this line reacted to it in this way: "I can't stop peddling, but I don't want my children to do the same thing. Customers often say, 'It's a nice job, you're always seeing and handling beautiful flowers. Besides, it's a clean job.' But I don't think it's respectable work. I sometimes feel ashamed that people see me doing it."

Typically the occupational structure of Matsuzaki is very complex. Of the 62 occupational categories represented in our census at least 22 may be thought in some degree directly "traceable" to the minority role. While classic "untouchable" callings have now almost disappeared, residual discrimination has by extension adhered to any menial work that becomes economically popular among *buraku* residents. Today such activities are mostly of the itinerant variety associated with a floating labor force. Seasonal peddling, the commodity varying with time of year, and construction labor under labor contractors are the more important ones. The embarrassment of being identified with these occupations is softened somewhat by going far off where the minority connection is not known. Even so, employment in these lines usually depends on some sort of collective organization based in the *buraku*. Purchasing and sorting flowers, for instance, is frequently done cooperatively through a group of neighbors; hiring of young men for construction jobs, usually in one of the large cities, always occurs through arrangement with a local labor recruiter. The poorest segment of the outcasts, therefore, is purely dependent on the community to exploit their only marketable asset—themselves.

The Buraku as the Minority Individual's Focus of Dependency Relations

Whether he works only as a farmer or a shopkeeper within the community or whether he normally works as a peddler or laborer outside, the individual in Matsuzaki is a member of certain social structures of the *buraku*. These comprise his meaningful dependency attachments, and it is evident that over the past century there has been a shift from a predominance of *Gemeinschaft*-type relationships, such as family and lineage (*kabu*), to a greater emphasis on *Gesellschaft*.

More than a century ago, probably no one resided in the *buraku* unless he belonged to one of its five great lineages. Today the influence of the *kabu* has shrunk to a vague recollection of common descent and a weak feeling of kindredship indifferently maintained by rites to an ancestral *ujigami*; for most this is no more than a very minor feature of social grouping. Comparatively few continue to keep the festive days of the god, many do not know the location of its shrine, and some younger persons are not aware that their family ever had a *kabu* relationship. Insofar as they survive in the present day, *kabu* seem to be assuming the character of a unit of common residence instead of descent.

Kabu-uchi (*kabu* members) help each other by allocating functions within the group incidental to conducting death rites and disposal of the dead; the *kabu* may act defensively to protect a member in trouble with the law. But, as one older informant put it, "*kabu-uchi* help each other but they are not so important as 'relatives' [*shinzoku*]. Unlike blood relatives or neighbors, they do not offer mutual aid in everyday life."

However, the ties of immediate kinship are not overwhelmingly strong, either. It holds true in general that rules of inheritance in Matsuzaki are weaker than in neighboring *ippan* communities. Perhaps two thirds of the households do not possess sufficient tangible property for its division to be a source of much friction or rivalry. (Holdings averaged about eight tenths of an acre in 1959, and only some 40 to 50 households are classed as independent farmers.) Primogeniture tends to be modified by the principle that the parents live with the son they get along with best or who most needs their continuing support after marriage. One form this takes may be termed ultimogeniture, that is, a younger son inherits the house and the largest share of whatever farmlands there is. Or it may result in a reverse sort of branching, the parents with or without a younger son breaking away to establish a new household, leaving the eldest in possession except perhaps for a small "retirement allotment" of land. Reasons given by informants for this practice are couched mainly in interpersonal rather than clearly economic terms; for instance, the parents may be seeking to avoid in-law tensions with the first son's wife, which is frequently cited as a very worrisome family problem. The implication for the individual's dependency relationships of this tendency to fragment into separate conjugal family units is that extended family ties often carry little more weight than those of *kabu*.

In default of strong family ties, one turns to associations

with friends of similar interests and to close neighbors, especially those whose houses face on the same narrow section of alley. This is particularly so in the crowded, indigent slum neighborhoods, especially in the eastern and southern portions (into which hillside shanty dwellers were resettled with government funds some twenty-five years ago). There is frequent visiting and much casual loitering in chattering groups in the alley; where a neighbor operates a tiny street stall there may be found spontaneous work-bees and knots of baby-sitters. The warmth of these neighbor ties is suggested by the answers to inquiries about what are the closest of one's kin ties. In the solidary neighborhoods (where family continuity is correspondingly lowest) people are ambiguous about connections with true kin but express a positive preference for intimate neighbors, whom they think of first as "our relatives."

As an agricultural community, Matsuzaki, like any other hamlet, possesses a formal structure of several kinds of instrumental associations, such as *fujinkai* (women's associations), the *seinendan* (youth association), the *hōgyo-iinkai* (agricultural liaison committee), and the *PTA-kai* (PTA). Because of their external sponsorship, it is known that they will go on however unenthusiastic the *buraku* is. They enjoy no great popular support.

On the other hand, truly voluntary associations comprise a sector of active, popular community relations. Predominantly, these are of the type known as *kō* (in the vernacular, *kōai*). Membership in them is often hereditary in a family. Most *kō* operate basically as religious-ceremonial groups, being as a rule offshoots of popular Buddhism; typical are the Daishi-kō (worshiping Daishi-sama), a healing cult, and the Himachi-kō (worshiping Sendatsu-sama), a syncretistic sun-worshiping belief. Other *kō* combine a financial purpose with pietism; the Ise-kō, for example, is a mutual aid society which provides travel expenses for pilgrims to Ise. The familiar *tanomoshi-kō* is the only type which is completely secular, serving as a cooperative credit society. There are reputed to be 20 to 30 of these *kō* in existence at any time with 30 to 60 members apiece. Each such *kō* meets one or more times a month to bid for loans from a common fund. This style of *kō* has a particularly weighty effect on community solidarity; unlike the religious-ceremonial *kō*, however, participation in them is largely limited to families who are able to bear the 300, 500, or 1,000 *yen* contribution required at each bidding session, that is, families of at least the middle stratum of the *buraku*.

The poorer, indigent stratum of families, often dependent entirely on day labor and peddling, lacks the means to join such *kō*, but turn instead for support to the more informal assistance of neighbors and other kin. They also rely on the tolerant attitude of village authorities toward squatter's rights on unused public lands adjacent to the settlement, and they reap the most benefit of public welfare and public works programs.

For all residents of the *buraku*, but especially for those who are dependent on nonagrarian pursuits, the fact that Mat-suzaki is favored by special public subsidies as a minority community is an important stimulus to its collective solidar-ity. Originally intended to offset the inequality of *buraku-min* living standards—in line with *yūwa* and *kaizen* "com-munity development" goals—they have become a permanent part of the fiscal structure of the community. In our survey a majority of the sample (53.6 percent) enthusiastically ap-prove continuation of these subsidies, while only a small dis-senting group (15.2 percent) see it as a way of aggravating discrimination. When equally as needy *ippan* communities in the village do not receive such subsidies, it is recognized by those few that a feedback of jealousy and resentment may result. Overwhelmingly, though, the bad effects of preferen-tial treatment are felt to be morally offset by the proportion-ately more desperate need of *buraku* people. Not even the dissenters doubt the justice of the *buraku* receiving this open charity—one more piece of evidence that chronic, ineluctable poverty occupies a central position in the *burakumin* self-image.

Buraku Solidarity and the Kaihō Dōmei

One focus of comparatively intensive solidarity is the *burakumin* community itself. Irrespective of family and lineage, of occupation, or of personal aspirations, a man's physical presence in the community exposes him to serious collective pressures to conform; and the points of conformity are to be found in the articles of faith of *kaihō* dogma which are preached and enforced by the Kaihō Dōmei, the national organization which seeks to represent the interests of all *burakumin* throughout Japan. The Matsuzaki chapter of the Dōmei exercises effective political control in the *buraku,* and the Dōmei is one of the primary areas into which individual ambition and initiative is easily channeled and sublimated. The other, as we shall see, is the practice of modern agriculture.

When in our survey we asked about the presence of a chapter of the Dōmei organization in Matsuzaki, most thought it essential to the well-being of the community (39.2 percent as against 24.8). Most affirmative respondents regarded it as the only effective advocate of their minority cause and the single best means of uniting them in the struggle for emancipation. Yet there were more who approved its goals than its methods; for example, a common complaint was that it is too radical, too much given to using violence. And some also felt that the very aggressiveness of the Dōmei tends to heighten discrimination by publicizing and reviving such feelings at a time when they should soon cease to be a serious problem.

It has been suggested by Yamamoto[34] that a smaller minority in Matsuzaki support the Dōmei program than in other *buraku* he investigated. More than half of his respondents in eastern Okayama and in Kōchi prefectures supported collec-

[34] Yamamoto, "Sabetsu ishiki to shinriteki kinchō," pp. 58–59.

tive action for emancipation, whereas in Matsuzaki more than 40 percent were opposed. In Matsuzaki, as both Yamamoto and I feel, there has been some disillusionment with the Dōmei's head-on approach because of the tensions and hostility it aroused a few years ago when it vigorously attacked the proposed merger of the village with Okayama city. The motives in this case were fear of losing the privilege of cultivating public lands under a lenient village administration and of losing the balance-of-power position which the *buraku* enjoyed in village politics.

The headman (*kuchō*) of Matsuzaki and its village councillors (*sonkaigiin*) are simultaneously also officers of the local Dōmei branch. Very few respondents alluded to this fact. Some adverse comments were obtained about one or two councillors who were said to use their position for personal profit, but the consensus seems to be that these are the best men for the jobs. Outstripping all others in popularity is the headman himself, who is the chief of the *buraku* Dōmei and also an important prefectural functionary of this organization. Almost 95 percent named him as the man they most admire.

This central figure is surrounded by a small and close group of intelligent, usually better educated, and generally more worldly younger men who hold effective control in the community. Such individuals may be thought of as an elite. However, as one of these men made plain to me, the elite do not think of themselves as the headman's *kobun* ("henchmen"); they claim to be united by mutual concern for the *kaihō* movement, not by simple loyalty to the man. These are the men who might be expected to attempt private escape by passing, but once committed either economically or socially, or both, such persons are bound more tightly to the community than the average. There is a paradox here: those who are leaders, either for or against the Dōmei, are by personality and intellect more susceptible to the lures of individuation within the larger society; but when the emancipation of the *burakumin* is at issue, they are morally more bound to work with the group.

Individuation among the Leadership Elite

The average person, the mass type, in Matsuzaki seems to have no individualistic goals. I refer to the mentally inert, usually economically harassed bulk (perhaps above 60 percent) of the community. These residents have almost no conceptualization of their social dilemma as *burakumin*, nor of what they personally might do to overcome it. Their vision is limited to the immediately personal problems of getting along day by day. As one informant expressed it, the mass are like frogs in a well who think that the whole universe is the water in which they live.

The elite, though, are mainly a group apart in thought and action, men who are aware in the abstract of the broader social implications of their status. They fall into two groups, the Dōmei leaders and their chief opponents, but both are of the most rational, self-assertive, and aggressive members of the community. They would seem equally personally qualified to become officials of the *buraku*, but it is their respective positions on the emancipation question and their attitudes toward the Dōmei which has given power to the one group rather than the other. The pro-Dōmei elite, who are our primary interest, are able by virtue of their Dōmei connection to exercise a more effective leadership than derives simply from their official functions at the village and *buraku* levels. The anti-Dōmei faction, though smaller and relatively impotent currently, comprise the only really independent voice raised against the stewardship of the Dōmei.

Politics and public service through the Dōmei is one of the principal ways an individual can serve his own ambitious purposes while devoting himself to collective objectives. In a *buraku* community where solidarity is strong this offers a route to prestige and power. This situation represents a change in patterns of leadership. In the past, power was concentrated in the hands of the entrepreneur-leaders who traded in special *buraku* products, or in powerful landlords; but now, since the destruction of these elites, the baton has passed to a coterie of political activists who ride the Dōmei to power. The volume of elite authority has diminished with this; informants recognize that in prewar days there existed what amounted to an *oyabun* ("boss") here, but since the war no single leader has attained this role.

The Dōmei is not an obtrusive feature of the *buraku* structure. It was largely dormant during the time of my study; only once during the village elections of March 1958 did its cadre appear to take open control of political affairs. Even then there were no meetings called specifically by the Dōmei or any demonstrations. But its influence through the dual or "shadow" role of its officers, as elective public officials, can be felt at all times.

While our findings are inconclusive, it seems quite probable that a new set of values, of a secular, rational character, has come to hold sway in the past several years, during which the Dōmei has enjoyed a return to postwar power. Through the mechanism of the Dōmei, and reflecting the tough-minded rationalism of its leaders, many of the moral values espoused by the prewar *kaizen* and *yūwa* programs, plus plans for rationalization and secularization of family expenditures, are being effectively propagated in the *buraku* for the first time. They include exhortation against conspicuous waste in private spending for funerals, weddings, and the like, against the idle habits of gaming and drinking, for family planning, for community rather than family sponsorship of periodic Buddhist memorial services for the dead (also as an economy measure), and for maximizing community services primarily for the benefit of the underprivileged stratum. For example, the Dōmei stresses that everyone, even if he has a bath in his home, should patronize the community bathhouse. Sanctioned norms in the community, then, tend to favor the viewpoint of the Dōmei, and their most vocal advocates are its leaders.

Those persons of influence who are thus committed are nine times out of ten numbered among the sixty to seventy substantial farmers (claiming agriculture as the only gainful occupation) of the *buraku's* upper class. These same individuals form the nucleus of the so-called *sengo-ha* (postwar generation) clique of progressive farmers. A core group of these young men—in fact, today three of the most modern-thinking, respected citizens, and dedicated Dōmei activists—began as early as 1948 to participate in a village-wide Good Farming Society (*Kō-no-kai*). Attracted by the society's interest in experimental farming methods which would increase output, they were the main agents in bringing about a minor agricultural revolution. It was through their pioneering interest that the possibilities in hothouse culture of grapes captured the imagination of fellow farmers, many of whom, thanks to the land reform, were just experiencing the exhilarating incentive of being landowners for the first time. By 1954 their pioneering efforts in converting former dry fields to hothouse use had induced about half of the community's full-time farming families to build hothouses of their own on borrowed capital.

In commenting on the effects of this pioneering, one of these men recalled: "Around 1951 we were beginning to consider that if we could borrow money on a cooperative basis to start hothouse grape culture we might have a very good business thing for Matsuzaki. We began to look into it. Before the war nobody had even thought about it. . . . At first we got a group of six people together and got started with a loan from the cooperative. Somehow, we succeeded in making a go of it and this gave us confidence in our own ability."

Agriculture has generally declined in the postwar economy of Yokoi village, but quite the opposite trend is to be noted in Matsuzaki. Not only has the land reform had a beneficial effect, as it provided numbers of former tenants with land of their own, but the impact on the livelihood of each household of this redistribution has been still more revolutionary.[35] Farmland, which had previously been transmitted to heirs only as a customary tenancy right, now has become private property outright. The post-reform cultivator is thus more free to vary the use of a specific plot, and most often this is done to take advantage of new agricultural technology and the changing demand for agricultural products. There has been a decided movement away from the established sequence of summer paddy rice and winter wheat or barley to dry-field growing of special or luxury crops, including grapes, melons, and strawberries.

As a vehicle of private ambition and advancement, modern scientific agriculture is not exceeded today in Matsuzaki. The *buraku* elite, as we have observed, are nearly all farmers of this stamp; they exhibit to the interested observer more independence of action, more initiative, and more individualistic motives in farming activities than in any other. The potential economic advantage of technically modern farming is felt to be high, while there is no concomitant deflection of the solidary common interests of the *burakumin* as a whole by striving in this area. Quite the contrary: informants recognize that it has been through the collective efforts of this small group that new techniques and the capital wherewithal to convert fields became available at all. Loans of up to 50 percent of the cost of a 300,000 *yen* hothouse were secured through pressure of the *sengo-ha* clique and were authorized because of the sympathetic interest of their sponsor in the Good Farming Society, the chief of the village agricultural cooperative.

We should not lose sight of the fact that this clique shares a strong sense of collective obligation to the whole farming element of the community to encourage adoption of these

---

[35] Total land in private ownership in Matsuzaki was a little more than doubled by the land reform, from approximately 54 acres to 108 acres.

new agricultural practices as well as to help arrange loans for others. They feel, however, that their obligation to the group tapers off just beyond the point of cooperating to get new producers started and working together to process and market the crops. The minute details of grape culture are matters the individual producer must learn for himself through experience and by careful record-keeping. The usual feeling is that these are competitive secrets (*hiden*) with which the clever, resourceful person may outstrip his fellows without social disapproval.

A rather forceful illustration of this occurred during my study in Yokoi. Led by a ranking member of the *sengo-ha* clique, who is a village councillor and an officer of the Dōmei, a few of the most progressive farmers approached me with the proposal that I help them master a difficult production trick; it was a secret process of quick-freezing muscat grapes so they might be stored in a fresh condition for up to six months beyond the harvest, when, of course, prices could be expected to rise to a peak. This spokesman pointed out it was rumored that such a process was currently in use in the United States; I was asked to seek information on it from the Department of Agriculture and other sources in this country.[36] The intelligence that a grower in the northern part of Yokoi had already mastered the secret, which he was said to be guarding closely in order to cash in on off-season demand, prompted this somewhat dramatic request for technical assistance.

Discussion and Summary

Such enterprise typically seems to result when dependence on full-time farming is combined with above-average educa-

---

[36] My American sources did send helpful information, but it turned out that (as of 1958) the quick-freeze process had only been tried experimentally with mixed results; the technical papers sent me were eventually translated and placed in the hands of the Matsuzaki growers.

tion and relative youthfulness. As was suggested at the outset, the personal ambition of the *burakumin* individual is
largely confined to achieving minimal freedoms within the
group. For the elite individual especially, goals of individuation are on two levels, that of individuation within the
group, private, practicable, and minimal, and the other, general and idealized, associated with emancipation of *burakumin* in society. Unless he is able to effect the quantum leap of
passing, at best a risky business for all but the most highly
qualified in terms of native ability and education, he cannot
expect to realize the freedoms of emancipation himself,
though he may well continue to enunciate them as desirable
objectives. There exists, in fact, a great discrepancy between
these idealized goals and those he knows are reasonably attainable. The nonheir, the marginal cultivator, or any other
sort who is tenuously committed to the community does in-
cur a liability of insecurity. But unlike the elite person, such
economically unstable *buraku* residents are at least much
freer to move from one outcast *buraku* to another, usually
freer to seek romantic attractions, and freer to achieve the
highly valued ideal of intermarriage with an *ippan* person.

The *burakumin* elite individual, on the other hand, rarely
can afford such freedoms. Such a person's circle of obligations to the community and the caste, which commonly
stems from the fact that his livelihood is inseparable from the
buraku, militates against the minimal freedom of relative
physical mobility which is enjoyed by the nonelite person.
The typical member of the elite can be regarded as more a
prisoner of his caste than his less-favored proletarian fellow.
Descent and inheritance patterns also favor the economically
less secure individual; characteristically, inheritance practices
are least consistent and loosest in the lower social strata; more
consistent, tightly lineal, and prescribed in the highest
stratum.

This commitment causes the elite member to channel and
to modify his private ambition and adapt his personal striv-

ing for economic advantage to the restraints of *buraku* life. Modern agriculture, as we have seen, is currently a major area of private ambition. Another area of personal attainment which is actually more closely keyed to total, or lifetime, commitment to the community is leadership under the banner of Dōmei activist policy. While the motives of personal achievement in this channel seem to reflect close kinship with the general values, the spread of which has promoted individuation in Japanese society as a whole (gaining recognition through one's own efforts, maximizing one's freedom from group control, and increased reliance on a rational and tough-minded approach to situations), the consequence of the elite's efforts to realize these valued things is in fact an intensified identification with the *burakumin* group, an identification expressed in their commitment to the Dōmei organization.

Perhaps this may be summarized by observing that the elite individuals who are the nucleus of the Dōmei would seem personally to embody the hopes and goals of the larger universe of *buraku* coresidents. Or, to put it in another way, our data seem to say that what the elite favor, what they do, sets the tone of individualism as it is visualized and such as it is permitted amid the restraints of outcast society.

CHAPTER XII

The Outcaste Tradition in Modern Japan: A Problem in Social Self-Identity

HIROSHI WAGATSUMA AND
GEORGE DE VOS

Introduction

THE present paper is an exploration of the general and specific consequences on the individual of a social situation in which assimilation from a socially defined minority group is blocked by strong social prejudices.[1] There are striking functional parallels between the social problems encountered by the *burakumin*,[2] or, as the group is known

[1] The material in this chapter appeared in modified form as part of a more general theoretical and descriptive work. (George De Vos and Hiroshi Wagatsuma, *Japan's Invisible Race*, Berkeley: University of California Press, 1966.) The research was supported by grant #MHO 4087 of the National Institute of Mental Health. Additional financial assistance has also been provided by the Center for Japanese and Korean Studies, University of California, Berkeley.

The authors would like to acknowledge their deep appreciation for the assistance afforded by various informants, who courageously cooperated in spite of the delicacy of the subject matter. Special acknowledgment is given to one of our friends, who shall remain anonymous, who assisted us in taking our work beyond mere superficiality. Father Diffley, a Catholic priest working in Kyoto, also deserves appreciation both for his warmth of understanding and his personal dedication to a difficult cause. For obvious reasons, we have structured our illustrations in such a way as to disguise and protect privacy. Our materials are drawn from urban communities in the Kansai area of Japan (Kobe, Osaka, and Kyoto). The authors are also appreciative of the able help rendered them by Mrs. Sachiko Aiba in organizing the field notes.

[2] The word derives from the Japanese expression *tokushu-buraku* (special communities) or, with leftist connotation, *mikaihō-buraku* (unliberated communities), both of which can be abbreviated into

pejoratively, the *eta*, in Japan and the problems faced by the American Negro in the United States. These parallels are obscured first by the fact that the *burakumin* are not physically discernible and, second, by the fact that a major "coping" technique of Japanese society in respect to the general problem of discrimination concerning this group is avoidance or tacit denial that any problem exists.

The problem of finding a satisfactory sense of personal identity has been difficult enough for all Japanese in the period since 1870, with a rapidly changing society constantly offering new roles and new means of self-definition while former concepts of social status and group identity still retained some force. The problem has been even more poignant for the individual coming from a segment of the society long considered subhuman and incapable of more refined human attainments. His choice is limited but, whether consciously or not, he must choose in essence between three alternatives: the first, and easiest, path is that of maintaining an overt and direct identity with his minority status and what it implies. So doing, he may either be passively receptive and resigned to the past definitions of society; or if actively oriented, he may seek to gain increased advantages for himself through concerted action with others sharing his status. Second, he can go into a selective disguise in which he maintains family affiliations and group membership within the

---

buraku. Eta is another Japanese term for outcastes. It means literally "full of pollution" and as a highly charged insult could not be used in polite Japanese society today.

There are variations in the names the *burakumin* give to the outside community. The word *ippan* (general) cited by Cornell does not seem to be used in Kyoto and Kobe. Instead, words like *kotchimae* (or *kotchi*)—"this side"—and *uchi*—"inside,"—are used for themselves, and the corresponding *atchimae* (or *atchi*)—"over there"—and *soto*—"outside"—for the majority society. These particular words are not affect-laden, but there are also aggressively contemptuous words for the outsider such as *dabusuke* or *sukemae*, much as the American Negro uses the term "ofay," derived from pig Latin "foe."

buraku community, but for occupational and other purposes he may lead a life of semidisguise among members of the majority population. A third choice open to a *burakumin* is an attempt to "pass" completely, to move out from the community and cut off overt contacts with his family, to forge for himself an entirely new identity and in some cases to fabricate a new past. The psychological cost of this third course will be discussed in detail later. To become individuated and at the same time maintain a secure social self-identity is no easy task for the *burakumin*.

It is a challenge to psychological understanding to define the processes involved. They are unlikely to be unique, for many complex societies have parallel situations in which the process of assimilation to full status within a majority culture is likely to be similar. In this paper we will explore aspects of *burakumin* minority status and its psychological consequences in a social-psychological framework. Much that has been said by Erik Erikson[3] about the nature of identity formation affords excellent theoretical background for our discussion. We will also draw heavily on other concepts fairly general to social psychology and to culture and personality theory.

Some Ethnographic Features of Urban Buraku

THE SOCIAL STATUS AND OCCUPATIONAL STRUCTURE OF AN URBAN BURAKU COMMUNITY

Of the 19 identifiable *buraku* communities in Kyoto, Takagamine will serve as an example. It lies in back of one of the largest Buddhist temple compounds (the Daitokuji), is located most closely to the Kyoto suburbs, and shows most strongly the characteristics of a well-defined rural outcaste community; that is, members of the community are almost exclusively of outcaste background, and they retain a very

---

[3] Erik Erikson, *Childhood and Society* (New York: Norton, 1950); and Erikson, "Identity and the Life Cycle: Selected Papers," *Psychological Issues*, 1 (1959), 1–171.

strong in-group feeling. In-migration and out-migration are minimal, so that the community shows a great deal of social stability. It has approximately 500 households with a total population estimated between 1,700 and 2,000. Most of the inhabitants are unskilled day laborers in construction or similar work. A number work for the city, often on a daily or temporary basis for street cleaning, garbage collecting, or night-soil collection. Some of the members of the community become supervisors of work gangs and thereby achieve what Lloyd Warner would call "upper lower-class" status within the community.[4] There is also a group of leather workers under the direction of a local *oyabun*, or boss, producing materials for the shoemaking industry. They occupy a status somewhat below that of the supervisors of daily laborers.

Three "general stores" within the community mainly sell fried tripe, a favorite *buraku* snack, the taste for which is considered by other Japanese as a repugnant habit. The two butcher shops within the community also sell more tripe than anything else, hence their slang name *iremon-ya* (literally a "container"—i.e. "stomach"—shop). The owners of these shops are also "upper lower-class," perhaps because the scorn of merchants typical of Tokugawa Japan has persisted longer in *buraku* society, but the proprietors of the only other establishments—a barber shop, a public bathhouse, and a dyer and cleaner—are accorded somewhat higher prestige.

There are ten or twelve officials of the Kyoto city office in the *buraku*, all with a high school education. One is head of the transportation bureau and enjoys high social status. There is also a superintendent in a construction firm who is of middling status. It seemed apparent that these white-collar workers had the strongest motives to try to pass.

There are a good number of women among those employed in small stores and in some cases as factory workers.

[4] See W. L. Warner, and Paul S. Lunt, *The Social Life of a Modern Community* (Yankee City Series, 1; New Haven: Yale University Press, 1951).

If the husband works in a store or factory, generally the social status of the family seems to be classifiable as upper lower-class. If, however, the father works as a day laborer or casual construction worker and his wife or daughter works as a factory hand, the family is considered of lower lower-class position. This is true also if the father or the household head is dead or an invalid.

Occupying a unique position is a family that still engages in the manufacturing of *geta* (wooden clogs). This particular family used to head the community. After the death of the last head of the house, however, the house as a unit went into a financial decline. Although present income seems to be limited, this family nevertheless still enjoys high prestige derived from its previous position.

There are a few families within this community who own land and rent out houses. They are the "upper upper" group, ranking just above four other families who own shops outside the community and also, perhaps, above the person who is head of the transportation bureau in the city office.

Traditionally the "upper-class" families have been in firm control of the so-called *buraku* industries of shoemaking, dyeing, slaughtering animals and handling their skins, providing laborers for crematory or graveyard work, and scrap collection of all kinds.

There are two Buddhist temples, the Renshō-ji and the Shōkaku-ji. Almost every member of the community, including those who have moved out and are now more or less successfully "passing," maintains strong religious affiliation with one of these two temples. There is also a kindergarten, but unlike the temple this is not universally patronized; middle and upper families send their children to a kindergarten outside the community.

MOBILITY PATTERNS AS A SOURCE OF INSTABILITY
AND INTERCOMMUNITY TENSIONS

Only one other of the Kyoto communities is as homogeneously outcaste in composition. As an example of the others, Uchihama, near the station, has numerous shoemakers and shoestores, but the community also contains a sprinkling of Koreans, a group of in-migrants from Amami-Oshima, and a number of poor day laborers and garbage pickers of nonoutcaste origin. Similarly, Iwamoto-chō, a new community, also near the station,[5] has only 70 percent *burakumin*,[6] mostly people who came from Osaka and Kobe during and after the war. It is now a general lower-class slum, rather than a typical *buraku,* including some Koreans, some poor Japanese of non-*buraku* background, and a mixed marriage group who have married outcaste men or women and comprise a marginal minority group within the minority population itself.

The population tends to be mobile, for as soon as an individual becomes financially better off, he tends to leave. Many go back to Osaka if they have family there. They are people who do not accept being classified as outcastes—so much so that they will call people of neighboring Uchihama—a *buraku* of long traditions—by the abusive word for outcaste, *eta.* For their part, the people of Uchihama consider the people within this "new" area as tough, rude, and criminal and

[5] Very often it is a characteristic of Japanese cities to have a low-status residential area to the rear of the railroad station. The station fronts on department stores, commercial businesses, and recreational entertainment establishments. Public transportation radiates out from the station front, and the main roads of the city often converge there.

[6] Suzuki, in a study of 802 rural and 381 urban households in 12 areas clearly defined as *buraku* (3 in Kyoto prefecture, 3 in Hiroshima, 2 in Okayama, 2 in Nagasaki, and 1 each from Saitama and Saga), found that 13 percent of the total population in the urban and 5.2 percent in the rural *buraku* areas were entirely or partly of nonoutcaste background. Nearly all the rural and about a third of the urban outsiders had married outcastes, and the others (73 households with no outcaste member) were uniformly poor. "*Burakumin no chiiki-sei; shokugyō, kekkon,*" in Nihon Jinbun Kagakkai, ed., *Shakaiteki Kinchō no Kenkyū* (Tokyo, Yūhikaku, 1953), pp. 381-94.

largely responsible for the bad image that people have of out-caste communities.

It is true that the people of this new area, although mostly destitute, are heavy drinkers of *shōchū*, a poor-grade rice brandy. But although some violence occurs in the context of drinking behavior, generally speaking this neighborhood does not live up to the reputation of toughness and criminality ascribed to it by neighboring *buraku*. Nor is there evidence of juvenile gangs. The disorganization apparent in this community does not seem to be focused particularly on youth, nor has it resulted in organized gang behavior.

Fragile family ties and unregistered common-law marriages are fairly frequent and so is wife-beating. An informant acquainted with the area has an impression that casual liaisons occur in this community more readily than among the lower-class people without *buraku* background,[7] and there are few sanctions to be invoked against the wife who deserts her husband.

In- and out-mobility in Iwamoto-chō contribute heavily to social and personal tensions and to the fact that family relationships are more fragmented and sexual mores even more relaxed than in the more stable *buraku* communities. The Iwamoto-chō community is rather disorganized; community sanctions are not operating, and the force of tradition is almost absent. In the older communities with less mobility, community pressures remain sufficiently strong to discourage complete casualness in human relationships.

It is in the new community particularly that there is greater evidence of intrapersonal conflict over one's *buraku-min* identity. Internalized self-hate is displaced as hostility

[7] Father Diffley, personal communication. His interpretation is that the individuals living in Iwamoto-chō have no opportunity to develop any sense of pride in themselves. They have perceived themselves in a degraded role. "Unless you have pride in yourself, you cannot be very ethical or moral."

toward others of *buraku* status who can be somehow differentiated from oneself. Rather than concerted group action, individuals in this area tend to face their problems alone without much social support or solidarity to bolster them.

DISTINCT CUSTOMS WITHIN THE URBAN BURAKU

Food. Eating meat was formerly exclusively a *buraku* habit, disapproved by other Japanese in accordance with Buddhist teachings. Since the end of the nineteenth century it has become general, though most butchers are still thought to be outcastes, and, except for a growing consumption of liver and kidney among the younger postwar generations, a taste for the internal organs of animals remains an abhorred *buraku* characteristic.

Dress. Within the *buraku* community itself, dress is extremely informal and can be described as careless, however well off the family. A university graduate of *buraku* background said that a conscious distinction is made between what one wears inside the district and outside. The community itself is "home," where one does not have to dress up. Children under the school age of six usually run about completely naked when weather permits.

One specific article of dress in the Kyoto *buraku* is a special sandal, *setta zōri.* This is a somewhat self-conscious tradition, and there are indications that the continued use of this form of *zōri* evokes some feeling of belonging and self-enhancement. One informant remembers that as a child he very much disliked seeing his own father walking in such *zōri* because he had become aware by that time that this was an easily identifiable characteristic of a *buraku* person.

Speech and comportment. Those familiar with the intricacies of local dialects agree that *buraku* people have speech patterns of a more "informal" and "less refined" nature than the general society. There are distinctive definable characteristics in vocabulary and in pronunciation.[8]

[8] Thus certain words like *kotchimae* and *iremon-ya* are used only

Although there are economic differences among members of the *buraku*, these special culture patterns of speech, dress, and comportment are shared by all individuals, though individuals of the wealthier families may also learn to comport themselves in a style acceptable to the outer society. This sharing in the patterns helps maintain a strong sense of in-group social solidarity.

Within the *buraku* it is very difficult for individuals with higher incomes to isolate their children from the rest of the community in the way in which middle-class or upper-class individuals in the outside society, through separation of residence and schools, are able to impose isolation from "unacceptable" lower-class children and therefore encourage their children to play and to develop only those modes of comportment acceptable to their own class. Although, as noted above, children are sometimes sent to schools outside their community, the speech patterns and modes of behavior are generally shared whatever the economic means of the family. Emotional alienation occurs in individuals deciding to pass. But if they desire, they can easily reassume language patterns and other gestures of communication spontaneously, since they have had ample firsthand experience growing up with peers within the community.[9]

Group Solidarity within Buraku Communities

Group solidarity within *buraku* communities has three as-

---

among Buraku people, and "z" sounds tend to become "r"—*yukuro* for *yukuzo* ("I will go").

[9] For instance, one of our informants, a governmental officer in the correctional field who is successfully passing, once told us of his intention to live right in the outcaste community in order to "know better the delinquent children of the community." Answering our question how he would disclose his hidden identity (background) to *buraku* people so he would be accepted as a boarder at some house, he said, "I would say that although I am now boarding at *atchimae*-person's house, I feel uncomfortable. The use of the single word *atchimae* would be enough to disclose my background to *buraku* people."

pects: first, the type of security one gains from belonging and maintaining cohesiveness with group members; second, the nature of the hatred and the sense of enmity toward the outside; third, the problems of individual and group identity related to passing into the majority society. These attitudinal patterns have to be seen in the context of the general question of individuation in Japanese society.

IN-GROUP SOLIDARITY

In order to live in the face of strong social discrimination and prejudice, the ordinary *burakumin* has to rely heavily upon his own group. He cannot easily take a job in the majority society unless he has the capacity to successfully pass, and few succeed in getting into the big firms.[10] Most of the *buraku* individuals have to stay within the community and make their living there. A considerable number of individuals living in *buraku* communities are on some form of public relief, having little opportunity for self-support.

[10] The occupational handicap of *buraku* youth is demonstrated by Mahara Tetsuo, "Buraku no shakai," in *Buraku no genjō* (Kyoto: San-itsu-Shobō, 1960), pp. 131–79. In his study of 249 graduates of a junior high school in Kyoto city in 1958, Mahara reports that only 1.5 percent of *buraku* youth found employment with factories of more than 1,000 workers, compared with 15.1 percent of youth from the majority. On the other hand, 29.8 percent of *buraku* youth found work in firms employing less than 10 workers, contrasted with 13.1 percent of non-*buraku* youth.

He also found, "Buraku no kodomo to shinro shidō," *Buraku*, xiii:ix (1961), pp. 55–59, that the average starting monthly salary for *buraku* youth is 4,808 *yen* ($13.36), compared with 5,196 *yen* ($14.43) for non-*buraku* youth. According to Ishida Shin'ichi, "Shinro shidō to kōkō zennyū mondai," *Buraku*, xiii:ix (1961), pp. 51–55, in a study of districts outside of Kyoto, non-*buraku* youth in almost all cases after finishing junior high school find employment by the end of May. By the same period, however, only 39 percent of *buraku* youth have become employed. It takes until about September of the same year for most of the others to find some sort of employment. The impression is that they are the last chosen, after others have been picked over, in the employment market.

Those who work within the community depend upon their employer. Usually the relationship with the employer is a very paternalistic one, the traditional pattern of mutual obligation involving financial protection and income security.[11] Occupations within the communities studied in Kobe and Kyoto were mainly in the leather industry, shoe-making, animal slaughtering, metal or rag picking, and the handling of corpses and burying the dead. Each of these occupations is controlled by a few bosses. The working conditions and income may not be very acceptable for the individual employee, but when dissatisfied he has almost no alternative choice. Jobs outside are hard to come by, and if he is "disloyal" to one employer he risks the possibility that his attitude will be conveyed to other bosses so that he will have a hard time getting into another occupation. Therefore, obedience and passivity toward bosses are strongly sanctioned. As long as an employee remains passively loyal and hard-working, he can enjoy a modicum of emotional and financial security; if, for instance, he or his family members get ill, the boss will protect him and help defray medical expenses. As far as the poor are concerned, individualism is discouraged.

Social solidarity is reinforced within the community by a feature which in itself creates caste status, namely, enforced endogamy. In-group marriage is still the rule. Only occasionally will an individual make a "love" marriage with a person of nonoutcaste background in the face of the difficulties engendered. As in the case of relations between Negroes and whites in the United States, differences in caste position do not prevent sexual relationships between men and women, even though unhappiness rather than marriage often results.[12]

[11] Cf. Donoghue, "An Eta Community in Japan: The Social Persistence of Outcaste Groups," *American Anthropologist*, Vol. 59, No. 6, pp. 1,000-1,017.

[12] In Suzuki's survey (cf. above, note 6), nearly 5 percent of households contained a mixed marriage, and they were rarely arranged mar-

As in all endogamous groups, the number of eligible individuals of proper age is limited by the size of the community as well as by relative status within it. This allows relatively little room for individual choice, particularly in wealthier families. In most *buraku* there are certain individuals, usually middle-aged or older women, who take on the role of matchmaker. Such a person needs to be one that people can especially trust.

A sense of family solidarity or family relatedness within the *buraku* is certainly in part based on the fact that in actuality most of the individuals are related in one way or another due to the high rate of endogamy. According to one of our informants, expressions such as "we are like one family" are much used. Everyone knows everyone else. Children are accepted in every house. When a child is afraid of an angry father, he will simply flee into a neighbor's house and will at times sleep or eat there on a very casual basis. Parents do not worry, even when the child does not show up at home for two or three days, as long as they are sure that the child is within their community.

The social solidarity of the *buraku* is also partly reinforced by participation in services and worship at a segregated Buddhist temple. In the middle of a *buraku* community, one will characteristically find a very well-built large Buddhist temple, which often makes an impressive contrast to the shabby-looking houses in the vicinity. There is some indication that the *burakumin* tend to maintain adherence to

---

riages; in fact, they often involved conflict with one or both sets of parents or relatives. Of the nonoutcaste wives, about 30 percent worked before marriage as waitresses, geisha, or other kinds of female entertainers. In any case, most of these love matches sprang of necessity from contacts outside the outcaste district. After the war the number of such marriages increased and is increasing. When one such marriage takes place within a family group or within a lineage, other members of the group seem to be encouraged to take a progressive step toward marriage across the caste line.

their Buddhist religion with a greater tenacity than that now noted generally in Japan. A number of the individuals are seemingly very pious and devoted and donate a considerable amount of money to their temple so that it can be kept in good repair. Most of these temples belong to the Shinshū sect, which may be partially due to the fact that Shinran, the founder of the sect, taught that, with Buddha's intercession, outcastes would receive full-fledged social status, if not in this life then in a later incarnation, though few, perhaps, hold this traditional belief today. There is also evidence that in the Tokugawa period the government at one time decided to have all the *eta* belong to the Shinshū sect so that there may have been people at this time converted by force from their own sects to Shinshū.

Ambivalence toward the meaning of achievement outside of the community plus a concern with the psychological and marital security of their children can lead parents to enforce children's continued participation in *buraku* life. The primary family in this way can maintain continuity and social solidarity and sanction the necessity for endogamy within the group.

OUT-GROUP ENMITY

People too readily assume that the problems caused by social discrimination can be soon resolved if the majority society changes its attitudes and becomes more accepting of the discriminated individual. This overlooks the fact that there are often strong forces in the socialization pattern of discriminated individuals which make the maintenance of their minority status important to them in their psychological integration. Hatred of the outer society and hostility toward the majority society become a part of the individual's total personality structure; they are not simply angry reactions to prejudice and discrimination. Some of the reputation of the *burakumin* for being aggressive seems to have a basis in fact, and the relation between this and out-group enmity and patterns of socialization in the *buraku* will be considered below in the section on socialization.

Methods of passing. The outcaste in Japan is not physically different. Only his place of residence identifies him with any degree of certainty. Passing, therefore, requires moving. As a first step, a man might work in a store or factory outside of the outcaste district and try to conceal his home address—perhaps getting off the bus one or two stops early and walking home to avoid discovery. A second step is to move out of the outcaste community itself. A third step to insure security against revelation is to change one's legal "place of registry" —the address on one's "family register," a copy of which has normally to be provided in every application for a job. The procedure is complicated, however, and when a registry is changed, the previous address is recorded; therefore to be secure one must make at least two changes. Generally speaking, the poor majority of *burakumin* are too concerned with ekeing out their everyday existence to think seriously of passing, particularly since it requires such cool long-range planning to be ready with nonrevealing credentials when applying for a job. They are mostly, moreover, bound to bosses within the community by both psychological and economic ties, and since they have little direct social contact with outsiders, they are not continuously exposed to feelings of rejection.

In the case of the upper-class family, the motivation for passing is not compelling for other reasons. First, their sources of income and prestige lie within the community itself. Second, if they are particularly wealthy, they can afford to take a trip to a hot-spring resort and be treated as ordinary guests in good hotels. In effect, they can pass when they wish in their recreational activities.

The pressure to pass is felt most strongly among the middle-class families who are sufficiently well-off to provide the education and financial support for their children necessary for them to become established as white-collar workers. The motives of the children themselves become stronger for, working continually with people on the outside, they are exposed daily to the disadvantages of being recognized as *burakumin*.

The attempt to pass is not easy, however, since a person must cut himself off from his meaningful primary ties and the friendships of childhood, or else run the danger that some curious individual among his new neighbors will discover the area that he visits so often to see his relatives and friends. The psychic cost is considerable, for the *burakumin* share the Japanese emphasis on family interdependence. They are not socialized for independent individualism and the "passer" is therefore particularly prone to an anomic sense of marginality.

Should a man manage to maintain himself economically outside the community and break his emotional bonds to his old community, he still must reface his problem at the time of marriage of his own children. It is particularly on the issue of intermarriage that the caste feeling toward the *burakumin* remain strong. Neighbors may be friendly and sociable although suspicious of the *buraku* origin of a family until the family seeks to establish marital liaisons in their new neighborhood. Then latent suspicions will come to the fore and deliberate investigations might be made. A frequent solution is for a boy of a passing family to marry an eligible girl of another passing family. Even in this case the go-between's task requires great delicacy, for normally passing families try to avoid each other, in much the same way as homosexuals trying to pass as normal may avoid each other lest suspicions may be magnified by their contact or some unconscious word or action reveal their common bond. The role of the passing deviant in society is always fraught with danger.

One solution to the passing problem has been migration to the United States, but this is by no means a final solution.

Numerous matches between American-born *nisei* have been broken off when one family's "register" is found to record a *buraku* address. A Japanese student recently at the University of Chicago was astonished to find that several *nisei* who took her out volunteered the information at the beginning of their acquaintance that they were *not* of *eta* origin.

Some psychological barriers to passing. Many outcaste individuals succeed in passing as far as the external conditions are concerned. Nevertheless, the intrapsychic tensions and difficulties over self-identity make it impossible for them to continue their passing role. Even someone without an outcaste background going from a rural area to a big city like Tokyo has various difficulties in adjusting himself to a strange environment. He may feel alone or awkward and that people of the city are cold and disinterested or even unkind. However, new arrivals can usually endure such an adjustment period and gradually become accustomed to city life; the few who fail and return home usually attribute their failure to their own inability to adjust to the requirements of city living.

A migrant from a *buraku*, however, is likely to react differently. He is more prone to attribute difficulties which in reality are common to all rural migrants specifically to his *buraku* background and to imagine that city people are indifferent or hostile to him because they know his origin. He may return home disappointed and resentful and tell members of his own community that prejudice and discrimination in the city make it impossible for him to live there.

Socialization, Social Self-Identity, and Burakumin Status

DIFFERENTIAL SOCIALIZATION WITHIN THE BURAKU COMMUNITY

The *burakumin* are considered to be somewhat more impulsive and volatile than other Japanese and, as a related trait, hostile and aggressive to individuals from outside society. We have discussed above the relationship of hostile behavior to in-group solidarity. There is in fact some evidence that in socialization practices the *burakumin* tend to be less restrained in the expression of aggression toward their children. According to some informants, parents, especially fathers, do not hesitate to resort to physical punishment in handling children. Not only shouting loudly or wildly but also slapping and hitting on the head or cheeks are common expressions of disfavor when provoked. Counteraggression on the part of the child toward either parent, especially the father, is not permitted. Children within the *buraku* community often fight one another. When such fighting becomes too serious, however, it tends to be discouraged.

These patterns may be related to the perception of the outside community by the *burakumin* child, as well as the adult. Hostility, hate, aggression developed within the family or peer group by these aggressive control methods are readily displaced toward people of the outside community, who are judged to merit it in terms of their prejudice and discrimination. At the same time it is not implausible to explain the father's physical aggression toward his own children as a partial displacement of hostility induced by his relations to the outside community. One must quickly qualify and say that there is no valid quantification of the alleged greater aggressiveness of the *burakumin* child, particularly as compared to the non-*buraku* lower-class child, but the evidence does point in that direction.

The *buraku* child is probably also more sexually aware than is general for the total Japanese society. There is less hiding of sexual relationships, and the children seem to develop less of a latency period than in the more restrained Japanese household. In general there would seem to be less stringent impulse control demanded of either sexuality or aggression of the *buraku* child. The adult relationships he sees also illustrate for him the fact that adults do act impulsively and can give vent to their feelings when they are under the influence of strong emotions.

DIFFERENTIAL ROLE EXPECTANCIES IN RELATION TO BEHAVIOR
RELATED TO SEX, PROPERTY, AND AGGRESSION

As we have indicated, in certain *buraku* communities, at least among the lower strata of the community, there is considerable casualness about marriage ties and sexual fidelity. A husband who goes to a distant place to work for a year or two is likely to find another partner in the place where he lives and works and his wife may take another man if the opportunity occurs. In the majority society, such a situation would provide a good subject for gossip and criticism. In the *buraku*, however, it is taken more as a matter of course if the person who forms the temporary liaison is of their own community or a neighboring one. It is considered necessary for a woman to have someone to rely upon for income and training of children, as well as for her own pleasure, which is an acknowledged part of the relationship of the sexes.

According to the opinion survey by a Japanese sociologist quoted by Cornell,[13] *burakumin* consider themselves to have "inferior" sexual morals compared with people of the majority society. The chief difference seems to be that whereas casual infidelity by a man was taken for granted in both the *buraku* and traditional majority society, especially if the man is a good hard worker and supports his family, the *buraku* was also lenient toward women. The stringent double standard of majority society did not apply in the *buraku*. Unmarried girls were not expected to be innocent. Should a girl become pregnant, the general attitude, while disapproving, is protective. The baby is usually registered as its mother's younger brother or younger sister, or a marriage is quickly arranged either with the father or somebody else.

However, relative sexual freedom does not seem to imply general equality of status between man and wife. Women among the *burakumin*, as in the traditional society, are required to be subservient, docile, and nonaggressive, at least

[13] See p. 358 in this volume.

toward their husbands. Husbands beat their wives but wives do not hit back. Mothers are also less violent with their children than fathers, but probably more than mothers of the majority society, certainly more than middle-class mothers. And fights between women are known.

Upper-class *buraku* families in respect to aggression seem to be closer to the majority middle-class society, which acts as a more compelling reference group for them. General *buraku* identification, however, makes for some feeling of vulnerability about inability to control one's passions even among the middle-class families of the *buraku*.

SELF-DISCOVERY AS A BURAKUMIN

Perhaps the most poignant material that we have gathered concerning the social self-identity of the *burakumin* has to do with early experiences by children when they discover themselves and their families to be members of a disparaged group. It is not only the majority society's rejection that he learns about; if he is at all permeable to the majority's role expectations he has to cope with an image of himself as potentially aggressive.[14]

One informant describes how once, at the age of four or five, as he wandered out of his own community, children of a neighboring village ran away at the sight of him shouting "*Yotsu!*" ("four-legged")[15]—an abusive term for outcastes which he had heard of as a dreadful word never to be spoken.

[14] Horace Cayton and Richard Wright and others have documented the similar situation of the American Negro who has to handle within himself a complex patterning of fear of the majority's stringent sanctions and sense of power springing from his awareness of the majority's definition of him as aggressive and sexually potent. See H. R. Cayton, "The Psychology of the Negro under Discrimination," in A. M. Rose, ed., *Mental Health and Mental Disorder: A Sociological Approach* (New York: Norton, 1955), pp. 377–92, and R. Wright, *Black Boy* (New York: Harper, 1945).

[15] I.e., "animal," though *yotsu* ("four") is also associated with an unrealistic fantasy that these "subhuman" people have only four fingers on their hands.

He chased them and beat them, and remembers them as defensively passive with fear. Later, at the same spot, he tried repeating the incident reversing the roles, himself crying "*Yotsu!*" at another boy from his own community and then running away.

Two other memories emphasized the sense of shame. Once he was scolded by his parents for having drawn at a school art class a picture of his father at work as a cobbler; living as they were outside the *buraku* his parents hoped that at school the child would pass. (The poignancy of the experience was all the greater in that he was fond and proud of his father, and the art master had praised his drawing.) Once, when he delivered shoes, the money was given him tied to the end of a bamboo pole—an ancient way of avoiding "unclean" contacts. Another painful memory included the discovery of aggression in his mother, a fearful occasion when his mother, normally a calm, gentle woman, wildly hit out at the wife of another shoemaker (like themselves partially passing) who had shouted "*Eta!*" and "*Yotsu!*" at the boy. The incident recalled fights between women he had seen in the *buraku*; it destroyed his idealized picture of his mother and simultaneously undermined the ego-identity of himself as a non-*buraku* person which he had tried to create.

THE BURAKUMIN'S SELF-IMAGE

A very difficult aspect of minority status is a continual need to cope with a negative self-image automatically internalized as one becomes socialized within the context of a disparaging majority society. A self-image is not always conscious. Sometimes, under a situational stress, one comes face to face with attitudes toward oneself that have been consciously repressed, as we will illustrate below.

Conservative, passive, and intrapunitive elements in conscious self-images. Some revealing materials have been gathered by Japanese social scientists concerning the *burakumin's* conscious self-concepts.

Koyama illustrates the mixture, in *burakumin* attitudes, of active resentment against the majority society and a passive sense of personal inferiority.[16] In a questionnaire survey in an Osaka *buraku* he asked: "What do you think is the best way to abolish social discrimination against *burakumin?*" He classified the answers in seven categories. Of 97 persons approached, 18.5 percent gave what Koyama terms "ignorant" responses or "don't know" answers. The second group, or 11.3 percent, gave what are termed "no solution" answers, or "I know something must be done, but I don't know what to do." The third group, 6.2 percent, gave what Koyama called "avoidance" answers, such as, "I do not want to think about it, I want to be left alone," etc. These three groups, consisting of nearly half of the individuals approached, reveal a general attitude of passive resignation, helplessness, and avoidance toward the problem of discrimination. The fourth group, 29.9 percent, gave what Koyama terms "self-reflective" answers. These attitudes reflect, though not completely passive helplessness, a great deal of intrapunitive thinking, such as "we should behave better; we should give up our slovenly behavior and keep our houses and clothes clean; we should seek more education; we should cooperate with one another; we should move out of this dirty area; we should change our occupation to more decent and respectable ones," etc. In contrast with these passively oriented attitudes, the fifth group, 15.5 percent, gave what is termed "extrapunitive" responses, which put all the blame on the majority society: "We should destroy discrimination; we should make them learn that we are all equally Japanese; those who have prejudice should be legally punished," etc. The sixth group, 10.3 percent, also militant, is termed "passionate" by the author because, in their attempt to answer the interviewer, they were too much overwhelmed by their own emotions of anger and resentment

[16] Koyama, "Buraku ni okeru shakai kinchō no seikaku," in Nihon Jinbun Kagakkai, ed., *Shakaiteki Kinchō on Kenkyū* (Tokyo: Yūhikaku, 1953), pp. 395-410.

toward the outside society to verbalize adequately their opinion. The last group, 8.2 percent, was considered by Koyama the most objective or realistic. Their answers pointed out the necessity of both the enlightenment on the part of outside society and actual improvement in the *burakumin*'s life situation.

Men tended to be either intrapunitive or extrapunitive in their attitude, while women tended to "don't know" or "avoidance" answers. Self-reflective and objective-realistic answers were found most often among the people between thirty and fifty-five years of age. People older than fifty-five tended to be extrapunitive, and those younger than thirty tended to fall in the "passionate" group.

Unconscious and suppressed negative self-images. We have illustrated already the difficulty experienced by a passing *burakumin* in freeing himself from his own concept of himself as an outcast person. We will note here briefly examples describing the presence of negative self-images on less conscious levels of awareness.

One *buraku* resident has a responsible post in the Osaka city government, an hour's train ride away from home. He has adapted to his double life apparently without strain, but one day, discussing the question of passing, he maintained that he could always tell when someone he meets has a hidden *buraku* background. The terrible physical conditions of *buraku* life, he said, leave the *burakumin* "with something vicious, something dirty, something like a bad body odor." It was not clear how much of this negative feeling was consciously directed toward himself.

A teacher, now successfully passing in outside society, told us of harrowing experiences of his own youth. Both he and his brother had been sent to good private schools and eventually to a university. His father, who came from a *buraku* upper-class family, constantly urged him to study hard in order to get ahead and become a success in the majority society. Achievement and passing became identical words. He had done well at school, but when he first went to Tokyo to the university he began to lose confidence. He was lonely; the academic competition was more intense, and one day after a particularly bad classroom experience when he was unable to answer the teacher's questions, he began to imagine that people were staring at him and that his face was becoming distorted into a strange ugliness. Recounting his experience recalled to him an earlier childhood incident when he had nightmares for a month after seeing a Dracula movie which showed ugly close-ups of the transformation in the faces of the vampire's victims.

The interpretation is fairly obvious. The ugly face symbolized for him one of his self-images as an outcaste person, similar to the image held by the passing public official. The man who passes may maintain the common prejudice of the majority society toward his own people, seeing them as dirty, ugly, full of vice and violence. But though he consciously thinks that he himself is free of these characteristics, unconsciously he has internalized these attributes as part of a disavowed self-image. When he is under stress and his sense of achievement becomes threatened, his security about his successful passing also tends to become shaky, and anxiety over failure may be experienced in a symbolic way—in the fear that his face will reveal his ugly identity and show him up as a vicious vampire character who hates and preys on ordinary good folk—even, perhaps (for do not the *burakumin* have abhorrent eating habits?) showing his cannibalistic designs on them.

These interpretations were suggested by himself, and he added a further possible reason why he should see himself as having such a Jekyll-and-Hyde potentiality. He had seen his own mother change personality. Outside of the *buraku* in the middle-class neighborhood where they lived his mother had become fully proficient in adopting the behavioral patterns of the traditional majority society and was genuinely spontaneous in the company of the middle-class ladies with whom she associated, restrained in speech, dress, and gesture. Yet when they occasionally visited relatives in the family house in the *buraku*, she automatically reverted to the "ruder" *buraku* forms of speech and behavior. He felt as if he had two different mothers, one within the outcaste community and one outside.

Deviant Attitudes of the Burakumin toward Formal Authority in Educational, Legal, Medical, and Welfare Matters

The social role expectations of the adult *burakumin* do not induce as strong a conformist identification with prevailing social authority as is found in middle class Japanese. One basic means of expressing discontent with discrimination is through concerted political action. The more educated *burakumin* find outlets for discontent through leftist political organizations which seek to change social attitudes by changing their society's pattern of political-legal sanctions. Such political movements, usually on the far left, while they may show questionably realistic assessments of their possible influence and may in some cases be characterized by an overly emotional approach, are psychologically mature at least insofar as they seek to find means of effecting change without a denial of self-identity or a resort to deviant mechanisms of expressing hostility to authority through extralegal or unsanctioned behavior. The individual who takes political action is mobilizing his energy toward a cause rather than falling back from it in either resignation or apathy.

In others, social discrimination tends to induce deviancy in individual behavior. Minority group members are not only relatively impermeable to conformist attitudes toward the law and fail to internalize them, there are also active inducements to flout the rules of the majority society either symbolically or actually. A basic defensive maneuver is to find methods of trickery to "outwit" the authorities. By so doing the minority-group member salvages some of his self-esteem and "gets back" at an authority structure which is perceived as operating to maintain his degradation or to hinder his freedom rather than to benefit him in any way. He may become a deviant from the standards set by the dominant groups in the society, hostile to the school and the legal system, using a distinctive language of his own and refusing to conform to patterns of marriage stability set by the majority society. He is less likely to exercise the control over aggressive feelings or sexual urges that are maintained by individuals more motivated by conformist needs, seeking to keep their social status in the majority society.

The majority society is less likely to exercise police powers over expression of impulses, sexual or aggressive activity, among minority-group members, since in its pejorative perception of a socially degraded group such behavior is expected and covertly condoned. It is more liable, however, to be sensitive to assaults on the persons or property of the majority group. Legal sanctions are likely to be interpreted as more severe toward minority members in the latter situations, deepening a sense of expected injustice on the part of minority-group members.

Experience of American society suggests certain hypotheses concerning social deviancy in the *burakumin*. First, we would anticipate a high incidence of apathy and nonreachableness in regard to education and to official public health and sanitary activities. Second, we would anticipate some deviousness and dependent opportunism in respect to welfare programs. Third, we would anticipate a higher incidence of antisocial attitudes expressed in behavior defined as delinquent or criminal in nature.

RELATIVE PERMEABILITY AND THE EDUCATIONAL
 EXPERIENCES OF THE BURAKUMIN

The "double bind" in the buraku community. One strik-

397

ing parallel between the value systems of American and Japanese culture is the emphasis of both on occupational and educational achievement. Yet while a minority member, a Negro or a *burakumin*, is well aware of the fact that he "should" apply himself to his own training and education, he also knows he will be faced with a highly problematical situation when he applies for a job in the profession or skill for which he has trained himself. He has to be willing to face a number of situations of self-deflation and rejection. The stimulus is there and also a potential negative shock, if the stimulus is responded to. In the case of simple psychological experiments with animals, it very readily can be demonstrated that such a reward-shock situation brings about experimental neurosis. The easiest solution is not to try, or to discredit the goal. A protective self-identity with a submerged group makes the necessity for trying unnecessary. Although a number of individuals from minority groups nonetheless have the strength of purpose and the ego capacities to survive in spite of discrimination, a goodly number react with general apathy and lack of involvement with the educational process. In other words, they become relatively impermeable to the educational experience afforded them in public schools.

There appears to be evidence of this. As one indication, although confirming statistics are not available, according to one of our community-worker informants, the truancy rate among *buraku* children is very high, as is that of Negro and Mexican-American children in California. There is also a comparative study of I.Q. test results by Nomura carried out in Shimane prefecture in northwestern Japan.[17] The scores of *buraku* children were significantly lower than those of

[17] Nomura Nobukiyo, "Tsukimono no shinri," in Oguchi Iichi, ed., *Shūkyō to shinkō no shinrigaku* (Tokyo: Kawade, 1956), pp. 247–57. The situation was complicated in this instance by the presence of another minority group of "fox-possessed people" whose children did only slightly better than the *buraku* children in the tests.

other children.[18] Similarly, in junior high school achievement tests Mahara found that a sample of 83 *buraku* children scored, depending on the subject, from 10 to 15 percentage points lower than the 164 non-*buraku* children.[19]

DEPENDENCY, DEVIOUSNESS, AND APATHY IN RELATION TO HEALTH, WELFARE, AND POLICE AUTHORITIES

In members of a minority group who have experienced a long tradition of discrimination, a combination of a defensive hostility toward the dominant group with attitudes of economic dependency is common. These dependent feelings are given an expediential flavor by finding means of being devious in how one "takes." Deviousness is a balm to the ego and allows the individual to maintain his self-respect by not having his needs make him feel completely helpless. Individuals in majority culture sometimes are angered when they discover some form of "relief cheating." It confirms their prejudice concerning the worthless nature of the individuals who are being helped through the efforts of the more humane elements within their community. American society today expresses considerable division of opinion concerning the effects of its relief policy in this regard.

The *burakumin*, too, have developed certain expectations that they are due economic assistance from the majority society. They see it as a right that goes with their minority status.

[18] That what is being measured here are not differences in "biological intelligence," but rather in the use of intelligence and the amount of motivational cathexis given to intellectual tasks determined by social differences, is suggested by the fact that both Mexican and Negro children in American schools have been found to have progressively lower I.Q. scores as they grow older, and the average I.Q. in Northern states is higher than in the South, for both Negroes and whites.

[19] Mahara, "Buraku no shakai," Buraku Mondai Kenkyūjo, ed., *Buraku no genjō* (Tokyo and Kyoto: San-itsu-Shobō, 1960), pp. 131-80.

SOME INDIRECT EVIDENCE REGARDING THE RELATIVE INDICES
OF DELINQUENCY AND CRIME

Informal impressions by members of the Kobe family court
when interviewed suggest that although the *burakumin* are a
small minority of the population of Kobe city, they do indeed comprise a disproportionate number of cases of both
family problems and delinquency coming before the court.[20]

We have subsequently made a study of the Kobe Family
Court records.[21] From this study we estimate that the children
with *buraku* background have at least three and a half times
the arrest rate of children of ordinary background within the
Kobe area.

There is also court evidence from Kobe, that, as in Kyoto,
burakumin inspire fear in the rest of the population. A number of *buraku* children have been brought before the court for
intimidation; for demanding money or other property from
children frequently a good deal older than themselves. Sometimes all a child has to do is to say that he comes from Banchō
(a fairly large outcaste district) and the children threatened
will turn out their pockets for him.

Community control seems to deflect delinquent activities
outside the *buraku* community. It is widely agreed by our
informants that violence, acts of stealing, or other forms of
antisocial behavior rarely take place within the outcaste com-

[20] In regard to delinquency, the American evidence strongly associates delinquency problems with the social dislocations of mobility
and migration and ethnic minority status. In California, for example,
in our research we have documented the fact that the Mexican-American is sent to Californian correctional institutions five times more, and
the Negro four and a half times more, approximately, per population
than is the white of European background. It must be noted that other
minority groups have escaped the negative self-identity through the
effects of cohesive, well-integrated communities that do not bring
them into conflict with the majority society. In California the Japanese-
American and the Chinese-American minority groups have the lowest
delinquency rate of any distinguishable group.

[21] Cf. G. De Vos and H. Wagatsuma, *Japan's Invisible Race*, Chapter 13.

munity itself. Although children will be verbally aggressive toward one another, if physical aggression seems to be in the offing, an adult will quickly step in to make peace.

The *burakumin* do not support outside authority should a child be accused of delinquent behavior. They stand behind the child and support him against the authorities. What is important, seemingly, is that the children obey their parents rather than show any allegiance to the outside. In court, the fact that children are obedient to their parents is cited as a mitigating factor when the parents talk to court officials.

When children are put on probation, they are usually put under the supervision of a voluntary "supervisor"[22] within their own community. But since *buraku* children do not indulge in delinquent activities within their own community, the *hogo-shi* actually does very little in the way of supervision and seems not to be active in preventing the individual adolescent from committing delinquent acts elsewhere. The recidivism rate is disproportionately high for *buraku* children on probation.

The community is not at all supportive of court decisions to place a child in a correctional institution. When children have been committed to such an institution there have been hostile demonstrations at the court building and appeals to put the child on probation instead so that he does not have to leave the community.

A general attitude of hostility is directed toward the buildings that house the prefectural offices, police, and court. These institutions represent for the *burakumin* the legal authority of the majority society, but also, in the case of the prefectural office, the place where the family registers are kept—the records which tie them to their *buraku* identity.

The police come in for considerable criticism. Policemen, it is implicitly understood, can only marry with the permis-

---

[22] These voluntary *hogo-shi* supplement the work of the professional probation officer under one of the two Japanese systems of probation. They are often schoolteachers or small businessmen.

sion of a superior officer which is given only after a careful scrutiny of the girl's family background. When the police were brought up in conversation, informants would often cite instances of policemen being refused permission to marry *buraku* girls they were in love with, because of their "unfavorable background."

A criminal career may be one method of passing for members of the *buraku* community. If a *buraku* youth is successful in becoming a member of a criminal gang or *yakuza* group, his outcaste background is discreetly forgotten. Therefore, the *buraku* youth may feel more readily accepted in this career activity than in attempting to face the more overt discrimination that occurs in other occupational pursuits. In the same manner, *buraku* women who become prostitutes find it an easy way to pass and to remove themselves from the *buraku* community.

Conclusions

The foregoing materials outline the social-psychological problems faced by the *burakumin* in present-day Japan. Individuation among the *burakumin* is a more difficult challenge than among ordinary Japanese, for to become a mature adult, one needs to overcome the need to have ready acceptance from members of the majority culture, on the one hand, and one must avoid a regressive acquiescence to a debased self-image, on the other.

Our presentation of these materials may not be acceptable to many. It may be thought inadvisable to make overt a situation which many are attempting to handle by covert means. Some may consider this chapter as placing undue emphasis on the prevalence of prejudice in Japanese society. Conversely, the paper may be considered by others as a confirmation of the majority's stereotype of the *burakumin*.

Those familiar with reactions to research related to the caste status of the Negro in American society know what strong feelings an attempt at a dispassionate analysis of prejudice can call forth, both from the prejudiced and from the victims of prejudice. We believe that for issues to be resolved they have to be faced squarely and overtly in all their ramifications, psychological as well as political. We cannot avoid being misinterpreted except by complete silence.

It has been our intention to present the *burakumin* problem in as dispassionate a manner as possible. We do recognize, however, that in writing of it as a "problem" we may have given more emphasis to the negative aspects involved than to those constructive solutions that may have been worked out by many. It has not been our intention to suggest that all urban *burakumin* are manifestly suffering from social or psychological problems or, on the other hand, that all Japanese are prejudiced toward members of the former outcaste group. Like many American Negroes, many former *burakumin* outcastes have sustained themselves through great difficulties to make noted contributions to their society and to live felicitous lives.

Nevertheless, without cavil, a good many members of the *buraku* minority do suffer, as do members of discriminated minority groups in other cultures. We have attempted to point out throughout our paper the functional similarities of the treatment of the Japanese outcast to that of the American Negro. Racial visibility seems to be of secondary importance when one considers the psychological mechanisms involved. Various different characteristics may be stressed as criteria of differentiation, but their functions are congruent. Particular language forms and manners, just as much as mere physical differences, can come to be interpreted as "unrefined" or "ugly" if they differ from the standards set by the majority. Equally, prejudice overlooks individual differences within the outcaste groups.

MODERNIZATION AND INDIVIDUATION IN THE BURAKUMIN

The question arises of how the situation of the former Japanese outcaste relates specifically to the social change going on in Japan today. How does it relate to questions about authority, inequality, individuation, and identity, as they are affected by modern trends in Japan?

The picture is a complex one. First, discrimination causes different reactions on the part of those *burakumin* who maintain their identity in contrast with those who seek to pass and become lost in the majority society. For the former, the tendency is toward extremes. Many remain more conservative than the general trend in Japanese society today—more concerned with hierarchy in authority and the necessary subservience of the individual to his group or family role identity. It is as if they cling to the moral maxims and the traditional customs of arranged marriage and the like which were propagated by the nineteenth century schools at the time of their legal enfranchisement, and in so doing can pride themselves on being more truly "Japanese" than the majority with their modern laxity. Others, by contrast, join movements of the extreme radical left as a means of forcing a form of social change from which they presume they would benefit. In contrast to these extremes, the white-collar official or office employee who passes faces in a more poignant way the same problems as personally alienated members of the majority culture, namely, an enforced individuation in which he must cut past ties and develop a form of self-reliance in an impersonal environment, at the sacrifice of any dependent or affiliative feelings he may maintain toward his family or group.

In further answering the question how being a member of the outcaste group prevents a person from becoming individuated, two points can be made. First, on the level of social relations, because of the strong discrimination against *burakumin*, the *buraku* person who remains identified with this group is obliged to depend more strongly upon other members of his own group than do members of the majority society, especially in the sphere of occupation and marriage. A more intense group solidarity prevents him from becoming more individuated. Second, on the level of thought and feeling, he reacts to the negative attitudes held toward *burakumin* by the general society by wanting to remain different from this outside life, and to maintain the separate features of behavior thought to characterize his *buraku* identity.

A last aspect of the effects of modernization on problems of discrimination is the change in government policy. Today the Japanese government, in its official policies at least, is eager not to discriminate among its citizens; it is "universalistic" rather than "particularistic." Law enforcement seems to be, generally speaking, nondiscriminatory. (In the United States, in contrast, the Negro today still has to fear the reality of condoned violence on state levels. In Japan today the general public is in fact more in fear of the *burakumin* than the *burakumin* is in fear of members of the majority society.) The government also seeks to alleviate the position of the *burakumin* by general welfare programs, providing relief for the unemployed and the destitute in the manner of any modern welfare state. Some observe a "demanding" attitude on the part of *burakumin* toward the government as a result of these programs and suggest that they have encouraged greater attitudes of dependency. It may be that "modernization" does lead in certain cases to greater dependency as well as to the more individuated independence fostered by a capitalist money economy, but it seems certain that for the *burakumin* the *nature* of dependency has changed. They turn for help now less to the personalized institutions of family and community and more to the impersonal institutions of the state.

Modern Japanese society no longer supports either the economic base or the rationale underlying the caste system of Tokugawa times. The rigid hereditary hierarchy has given place to a fluid industrial class structure in which occupational adjustment is subject to the market place and social standing depends largely on occupational function. Lineage is less emphasized. There are no hereditarily prescribed behavior patterns, deviation from which can make one an outcaste and there are in principle no unclean occupations.

Yet we see that as in the case of the American Negro,

where caste status developed out of the feudal plantation system of the South, remnants of former attitudes continue into the present day. The question arises, therefore, of what the functions are of a continuing caste attitude in Japan. We might ascribe the persistence of these attitudes to conservative beliefs concerning hierarchy and biological continuity in talent. But there are other functions of the outcastes that, once established, become a continuing part of the society, and we have to explore these as well.

CLASS VERSUS CASTE DIFFERENCES: IMPLICATIONS FOR A
THEORY OF SOCIAL EXPLOITATION

It is obvious that purely economic explanations of caste in the Marxian manner are inadequate. Man's behavior has "expressive" as well as "instrumental" aspects,[23] and every culture defines certain forms of expressive behavior as highly valued while others are reprehensible and disavowed. In the case of caste differences the disavowal is accompanied by abhorrence—the abhorrent activities having to do with oral, anal, and genital functions all initiated as well as responded to with the autonomic nervous system. It is these aspects (which ensure the endogamy of caste groups and their hereditary perpetuation) which find no explanation in Marxian theory. Just as the economic exploitation of the Negro within a plantation economy is no full explanation of the attitudes toward the Negro in modern America, so we must look for deeper psychological feelings that maintain the "untouchable" status of the *burakumin*.

The outcaste, whether Negro, *burakumin*, or witch,[24] is in

[23] The distinction is elaborated in Talcott Parsons and Robert F. Bales, *Family: Socialization and Interaction Process* (Glencoe: Free Press, 1955).

[24] The witch is distinguishable from the outcaste not only insofar as the outcaste is a scapegoat group rather than a specified individual, but also in that disavowed activities or forces tend to be related to the supernatural, rather than simply a disavowed aspect of human nature. Also, the outcaste group is a permanent structure within a society,

one sense a scapegoat, and the kind of scapegoat he is depends on the particular kind of expressive behavior which the culture is most concerned to "repress." Thus, as Dollard has shown in his now classic work,[25] a predominant element in the southern white's stereotype of the Negro is his potent and primitive sexuality. "Dirtiness" and "aggressiveness" are also components of the stereotype, but less emphasized. In the case of the *burakumin* the emphasis is reversed. Although there is ample evidence that the sexual behavior of the *burakumin* is "looser" than allowed in the majority society, it is rather their "unclean" habits in reference to language and manners, as well as a supposed tendency to be inordinately violent and aggressive, which are emphasized. Within Japanese society sexual experience is more tolerated if exercised at the right time and place, but there is a great need to disavow the appearance of direct aggression in everyday relations and to emphasize specific rules of propriety.[26]

There is no doubt that "caste" prejudice may involve feelings of economic competition; nevertheless, the main psychological factors maintaining prejudice with any force in society are deeply expressive of intrapsychic conflicts over internalized social values and expectations. A thorough understanding of these, as well as of the society's cultural history and the economic functions of discrimination, are necessary if we are ever to understand the nature of prejudice in modern society.

---

whereas the role of a witch may be the result of some form of individualized selectivity.

[25] John Dollard, *Caste and Class in a Southern Town* (New Haven: Yale University Press, 1937).

[26] W. Caudill, "Patterns of Emotion in Modern Japan," in R. J. Smith and R. K. Beardsley, eds., *Japanese Culture: Its Development and Characteristics* (Chicago: Aldine Publishing Co., 1962).

PART SEVEN

The Pattern of the Future

CHAPTER XIII

Japanese Economic Growth: Background for Social Change

JOHN W. BENNETT[1]

Introduction

IN THIS paper we shall take the position that contemporary rapid growth in the Japanese economy is exerting an unprecedented impact on many important sectors of Japanese society; that is to say that a kind of breakthrough has occurred which for a time has permitted change to move in a fairly consistent direction, especially at macroscopic institutional levels. This direction may be defined as that associated with high industrialization and the development of a consumer economy in the European and North American nations. The principal characteristics of this general pattern of change, in contemporary Japan and elsewhere, are as follows:

1. There is a growing cooperative rationalization of the entire economy, with the standards of efficiency and cost-profit ratios associated with industrial production being felt in all other sectors (e.g. in agriculture). That is, a common frame of reference tends to be adopted for all economic effort, and "dual economies" of the type often described for underdeveloped countries tend to disappear.

2. Employment in the secondary and tertiary sectors of the economy tends to outstrip employment in the primary (i.e. industry over all others).

3. A tendency develops toward integration of many separate smaller enterprises under the leadership or control of a few

[1] The writer wishes to acknowledge the advice of Glaucio Soares and David Carpenter in the preparation of this paper.

larger enterprises. Private ownership of smaller businesses may or may not persist, but in any case their productive effort tends to be geared to the larger companies.

4. Universalistic standards of competence and employment are preferred over particularistic criteria as maximum efficiency of the labor force becomes a goal. This is also associated with growing competition among enterprises for the most desirable personnel.

5. A major effort to maintain production at a high, and increasing, level by utilizing the entire population as a market (i.e. a "consumer-goods economy") begins to accompany whatever other productive effort exists (e.g. manufacture of export goods).

Social changes which appear to be associated with these economic developments are as follows:

1. The society recognizes the legitimacy of aspirations for financial and status enhancement on the part of all individuals and groups in the society; that is, sanctioned deprivation for certain groups tends to disappear.

2. Freedom to change jobs and to change residence in order to improve the individual's social and economic position is accepted and even encouraged. Thus social and spatial mobility tends to increase, other things being equal.

3. These changes seem always to be associated with a growing "middle class," consisting of white-collar, managerial, and professional groups who are provided with a life style defined by the cultural climate of the large organization. Security of business operations or of employment becomes a dominant concern of this class.

4. Cultural attitudes and preferences tend to be closely associated with the outlook of consumer industries and their advertisements, and social status tends to be defined in terms of consumption patterns in addition to whatever else may be involved.

412

The *political forms* associated with industrialized societies of this type tend to be those subsumed by the term "democracy," which signifies at least moderate freedom for business enterprise and for the individual to determine his own life chances. Within this broad pattern there is room for considerable variation in the degree of state control, especially over industrial enterprise and production. In societies with democratic institutions, centralized economic control may take the form of a complex partnership between business and government. This may be particularly true for countries like Japan, which lack natural resources and where consequently the balance of exports, imports, and internal consumer production must be maintained with great care.

In the sections to follow we shall examine some current Japanese economic indices in the light of their possible significance for the changes noted above.[2] In most cases the conclusions are tentative, since there are little available research data which would permit us to relate social changes to specific economic developments with confidence. We assume that if the economy has acquired the importance for social change which we shall attempt to show, studies of micro-

[2] A variety of materials from Japanese and Western sources have been consulted in the preparation of this essay. However, references have been confined to the most readily available publications. These sources, and their abbreviations, are as follows: United Nations, *Statistical Yearbook*, 1961 (UNSY); United Nations, *Economic Survey of Asia and the Far East*, 1961 (UNEA); *United Nations, Report on World Social Situation*, 1961 (UNRS); Japan, Economic Planning Agency, *Economic Survey of Japan*, 1961 (ESJ); Japan, Bureau of Statistics, *Annual Report on the Family Income and Expenditure Survey*, 1961 (FIES); Japan, Bureau of Statistics, *Statistical Yearbook of Japan*, 1961 (SYJ). The paper was written in 1962, and therefore the cutoff point for most statistics was 1960 or 1961. Its late publication therefore makes some conclusions obsolete. However, after a five-month stay in Japan in 1966–67, including some research on social change, I feel that all error is on the conservative side; that is, that the effect of economic growth has continued very strong in the ways indicated or hypothesized in the paper.

cosmic social change by sociologists and anthropologists will need to use the economy as an essential point of departure.

Economic Magnitudes: Comparisons with Other Nations

Some general observations on the scope and pace of Japan's economic transformation in the post-World War II period are desirable by way of introduction.

The term "boom" is commonly used to describe this phenomenon, although the care with which Japanese government and business leaders have guided and controlled the postwar economy suggests a deliberately planned expansion and not a free-for-all reminiscent of the U.S. in the 1920's. This distinctive Japanese synthesis of boom and plan was exemplified in Prime Minister Ikeda's proposal, announced in 1961, for the doubling of the national income within ten years. The objective was not offered in a spirit of wild optimism, but rather as a sober possibility in light of the current annual rate of economic growth, which was reported between 7 percent and 8 percent in the late 1950's and early 1960's. Gross national product showed a record 19 percent increase in 1961, but declined to about 5 percent during 1962 as a result of the deliberate imposition of import and internal credit controls, mainly designed to curb heavy investments in foreign-made equipment by Japanese companies eager to tool up for sustained production. Despite these planned slowdown measures, industrial output in late 1962 was running 6 percent higher than the previous year, and consumer expenditures had climbed 10 percent over the 1961 level. Moreover, the controls worked so well by the end of 1962 that a favorable trade balance was restored, and in early 1963 practically all the controls were removed.

A few international comparisons will give an indication of the relative level and pattern of Japan's industrialization. In 1960 her total gross national product was the fourth largest outside the Communist bloc (in the 91st percentile). In terms of per capita GNP she comes much lower down the scale (the 48th percentile), but in terms of rate of increase in per capita GNP she led the Western world in the late fifties, even if one makes the usual generous allowance for error in such figures.[3] The 1960 figure represented a 67 percent increase over 1953, which compares with Canada's 2 percent and the United States' 5 percent, and is even better than West Germany's 48 percent (UNSY, 1961). This rapid growth reflects the full use being made of Japan's productive capacity, the very low rate of unemployment, and the very high rate of investment. (Only 65 percent of GNP went into personal consumption in 1960, compared with, say, as much as 80 percent in Honduras. UNSY, 1961.)

A standard index of industrialization is, of course, the declining share of agriculture in the economy. It is difficult to offer international comparisons of Japan in this respect by recourse to figures for the distribution of the labor force, since the great recent increase in the part-time employment of farm families in industrial wage work or domestic industry makes accurate classification impossible. The following table, however, offers the next best thing, a comparison of sectoral shares in GNP (UNSY, 1961). How far Japan has moved from, say, the Indian pattern will be apparent.

TABLE 1

| | Percentage of GNP provided by: | | |
Country	Manufacturing	Trade and Commerce	Agriculture
Germany	39	13	8
France	38	12	15
United Kingdom	35	14	6
United States	30	19	4
Japan	30	12	15
Canada	29	14	15
India	16	18	49

[3] The percentile figures are based on the 1955-56 data from N. Ginsburg, *Atlas of Economic Development* (Chicago: University of Chicago Press, 1961). In 1967 Japan moved up to the fifth largest in the world (GNP), including the Communist countries.

415

Other indicators show interesting disparities. United Nations' statistics group countries into a number of categories in terms of various indices. There are six graded categories for per capita GNP, six for levels of infant mortality, and six for school enrollment. In terms of per capita product, Japan comes in the fourth category (medium to low), but on the other two criteria she comes quite high up the scale, in the second category, with high school enrollment and low infant mortality. Education, of course, was one of the earliest and most efficient institutions in Japan's modern era, and health and sanitation was an especially successful program of the Occupation period. But whatever the reasons, it is apparent that a highly educated and sanitized population has not been provided for at the level of income to which it might aspire, and in fact underemployment of college youth has been a major social problem of contemporary Japan.

These various international comparisons do not permit us to place Japan in an all-inclusive category. However, the historical growth pattern is clear: she has moved from an agrarian to an industrial society in her century of modern existence, and this movement has been especially rapid in the years since World War II. She resembles Germany and France in the latter respect, and in terms of most of the indices and problems of highly industrialized societies, Japan resembles the Western highly developed nations more than any other. Finally, in the high and "unbalanced" development of particular social services like education and population control, Japan might be considered to exhibit the effects of the unique centralization of her early modern government, with its emphasis on efficient public education and other institutions. Continued economic growth in Japan hardly could fail to have the effect of intensifying her industrial-consumer economy and further eradicating the traces of her agrarian past, with its inequality of distribution.[4]

[4] In a paper published since the above was written, Leon Hollerman ("Japan's Place in the Scale of Economic Development," *Eco-*

J O H N   W .   B E N N E T T

Urbanization and Industrialization

Most of Japan's industrial expansion since World War II has taken place in the large cities, where it had been located before the war. By 1960 this "overconcentration" (ESJ, 1960–61, p. 44) had created a shortage of land, industrial water, and severe traffic congestion and housing problems which reached a point where major remedies were required. One of these was the decentralization of industrial production, a move made possible by improved roads and railroad services, and also by the increasing reliance upon oil as a fuel. Japanese industrialists were developing small, specialized plants, adapted to the labor supply in particular localities and placed so as to cause minimal social disturbance. This movement will of course expose ever-larger numbers of rural people to industrial culture.

DEMOGRAPHIC ASPECTS

Accompanying this concentration of industry and its services in large cities has been a movement of population from

---

nomic Development and Cultural Change, xii [1964], 139-57) finds that Japan is "backward" in a number of characteristics as defined by Harvey Leibenstein, and "highly-developed" as defined by N. Ginsburg. Many of the "backward" criteria are simply those associated with large and dense population and the undeveloped agricultural base. The "highly-developed" characteristics are those mostly associated with intensive utilization of all resources, including labor and capital.

A general characteristic of the imbalance is the low per-capita figure in various categories; e.g. Japan has a high gross GNP but a low per capita GNP. Japan thus emerges in Hollerman's analysis as a busy, industrious, growing, but overpopulated and therefore relatively poor country. This may be true, but it is aside from one point of this paper, which concerns the gain in prosperity since World War II and its effects upon social life and cultural patterns. Hollerman's conclusion, like others which evaluate wealth or poverty on strict per capita figures, needs to be qualified by cultural patterns of living. Thus in Japan both cheap consumer goods and widespread standards of aesthetic order and cleanliness modify the Western-type consequences of low income status.

rural areas to urban centers.[5] Some of the demographic results can be seen in this tabulation of data from the 1960 census of Japan:

TABLE 2

Age bracket	Percent living in the most densely populated areas of all prefectures
15 and under	24.5
15–44	43.3
45–64	15.4
over 65	4.0

The most significant percentages are those for the 15–44
and over-65 age groups: the large plurality of the former and
the very small percentage of the latter indicates that the
urban centers received a great many more young people in
the productive age range, whereas the very old stayed in the
smaller communities; that is, the less densely populated countryside. Also indicative of migration is the fact that the 1960
census figures reported that the number of births per 1,000
persons in the 15–44 age group was one-third greater in the
least densely populated areas than in the most densely populated, indicating that much of the increased population of the
urban centers was due to in-migration and not to natural
increase.

Japanese census officials reported that before World War
II the rural population was about 60 percent of the total, a
figure which tended to put Japan in the general demographic
category of agrarian Asian nations. Since boundaries of administrative districts have been changed, comparative percentages are difficult to interpret (though the consolidation
of administrative areas which has taken place since 1953, an-
nexing villages to town centers, does in itself sociologically
imply urbanization). For what the figures are worth, however, Japanese demographers in 1961 stated that the percent-

[5] See Minoru Tachi, "Regional Income Disparity and Internal Migration of Population in Japan," *Economic Development and Cultural
Change*, XII (1964), 186-204.

age of the rural population had fallen to 45 percent and was declining at a rate of 2 or 3 percentage points a year. With the rural population becoming a minority, Japan is rapidly approaching a population distribution pattern similar to that of the industrial nations of Europe and North America. The reasons are similar: population flows where income is available, which in turn helps to make adjustments in income disparities between the "poor" and the "rich" districts, a process which becomes possible when a nation evolves common standards and effective transportation.

Urbanization of the modern type has changed a basic feature of the Japanese city: its close relationship to rural culture based on the fact that the migrated rural population tended to seek out urban neighborhoods where relatives and friends from the old communities resided. The contemporary rural in-migrants have seemed to be a more urbanized group to begin with, due to the spread of consumer culture and improved communications, and in comparison to their predecessors more clearly motivated by financial considerations. Hence labor unions and other urban organizations and employment security measures can replace the old communal and kin ties, and informal welfare institutions would appear to lessen the historic influence of rural life on the urban in Japan; and along with it goes an end to the long dependence of Japanese urban economy on rural capital.

URBAN PROBLEMS

The city of Tokyo had in 1962 about 14 percent of the total national population of about 94 million. This population shared Tokyo's streets with about 800,000 automobiles, which in 1962 were increasing at a rate of 10,000 per month. The streets constituted about 9 percent of the city's area, which may be compared with 43 percent for Washington, 35 percent for New York, and 23 percent for London. The Tokyo layout has remained largely that of a medieval city—a medieval city inundated with thousands of cars, buses, trucks, and smaller vehicles. The traffic death toll in 1961 was 16 deaths per 10,000 vehicles, the highest among the world's major cities. In 1960 there were 60,577 injured victims in 140,000 accidents, including 179 persons killed. In 1961 the city appropriated 200,000 million *yen* to build eight new four-lane highways, and a loop route and additional highways to handle the Olympic Games traffic were also under construction, though local politics and the absence of a law of eminent domain have made it extremely difficult for the city to obtain right of way. The city also has lacked the governmental apparatus to impose a uniform system of traffic control throughout the metropolitan area. These difficulties have however been overcome about as effectively as the American metropolis has dealt with its obstacles to renovation. Actually the road problem was nationwide; the Japanese government developed in 1962 a 3 billion dollar program of highway construction to handle the increase in truck traffic associated with industrial decentralization. The goal of this program was specifically acknowledged to be a level of efficiency comparable to that of the U.S. road system.

The traffic situation is simply one example of the many problems which have beset Japan's cities in rapid economic growth. The expansion of industrial centers and the growth of population in them has come so quickly that Japan's governmental organs simply have not had time to respond to the need to accommodate them. City planning and basic changes in governmental authority proceed slowly and have been impeded by the vested interests and shortage of public capital that have affected American urban centers, but in Japan the situation has been worse because of the less developed base and the lack of legal precedent. Private enterprise has of course been responding to the needs in its own way, by vastly expanding the subsidiary urban centers around rapid transport terminals and shuttle stations, but these measures have often served merely to intensify the traffic problem by increasing congestion and adding new barriers to the flow of traffic. Housing needs have been met in part by government construction of high-rise apartments and by private developments, but these have been located wherever land is available and thus have an unplanned character which often intensifies the maldistribution of population.

Such pressures have generated a mood of rational planning for Japan's urban society and economy. While the phenomena noted were continuations of trends under way before World War II, their greatly increased magnitude in recent years has made it obvious that industrial relocation, extended public services, increased authority of governments, and a more rational taxation base must be instituted in order to preserve some degree of order. Developments of this kind project an image of a new type of Japanese city, one more nearly approximating the Western. The Japanese city has, until recently, preserved much of its preindustrial character; industry and other modern urban facilities existed within the matrix of what was largely a federation of independent neighborhoods. While some features of this prewar Asian-Western pattern will undoubtedly survive and adapt, there are powerful forces at work molding the large Japanese city in the model of the organized, centralized, self-conscious Western type.

Industrial Enterprise

"One of the peculiar features of our industrial structure is the existence of large enterprises surrounded by hordes of small, poor enterprises, with little room left for medium enterprises. However, the recent high rate of economic growth has resulted in an increase in the number of medium enterprises, particularly those in machinery and chemical fields. The role played by these enterprises in technical innovation and in the consumers' revolution is not small."

ESJ, 1960–1961, p. 353

SELECTIVE EXPANSION

The number of manufacturing enterprises[6] in Japan increased by 9,500 during the 1954–1957 period; by 2,600 during 1957–1960. However, the number of workers increased by 350,000 and another 400,000, in the same two periods. Enterprises with less than 4 workers *declined* by half during the two periods; a similar decline was noted for the number of employed persons in such enterprises. During 1957–1960, large enterprises of more than 500 employed persons had 37 percent of the total of all workers for all classes of enterprises (16 percent in 1954–1957), and medium enterprises 35 percent (27 percent in 1954–1957) (ESJ, 1960–1961, p. 276). Thus smaller enterprises were declining and medium and large enterprises increasing.

The causes of these trends were familiar enough: labor shortages in the younger and more productive age classes, rising wages, improving working conditions, technological change, and general increases in prices and production costs. These factors are felt in the economies of all industrial societies; Japan's experience thus has been typical and of a kind to be expected given the speed of her development. It would appear on the basis of current trends that the typical pattern of Japanese industry established in prewar times—"large enterprises surrounded by hordes of small, poor enterprises"— may have been a transitional phase and not necessarily a permanent adjustment to industrial conditions.

The small, family-operated enterprise has been hard-pressed as prices and wages increase, and its employees, including family members, have sought jobs in larger companies. Labor shortages in younger age groups, felt in all industries including the largest, were due partly to the reduced crop of babies during wartime and partly to the insatiable demands for workers in Japan's rapidly growing economy.

[6] The Japanese reports use the following categories: very small, 4 workers or less; small, 29–99; medium, 100–499; large, 500 and above.

The influx of rural population was not sufficient to meet these demands; smaller, poorer industries were also supplying labor to the larger and more prosperous concerns. The increased costs also made it much more difficult for older persons to start small businesses with retirement money, hence this important resource for small trades and industry was cut off. Banks did in 1963 liberalize loan policies with respect to small business, but they tended to favor companies with good prospects of subcontracting from large industries, or new service trades which emerged in the expansion of consumer production.

The rise of medium-sized industries has been a direct reflection of the development of large industries in that the typical medium-sized company is one which subcontracts from large firms.[7] The standard arrangement involved free blueprints and certain materials. The medium enterprise paid wages only slightly below those in the large organization; this wage gap, while small, was still large enough to reduce the cost of manufacture of many small, often precision parts. The technological level of these new medium enterprises was generally high, and the large companies have encouraged experimentation with new processes and materials.

CONSEQUENCES

Many of the rising medium enterprises were former small companies which had been able to modernize or to attract the support of large companies. Their movement into the medium class signified an abandonment or modification of traditional management procedures, employer-employee relationships, and craft production methods. Moreover, this "se-

[7] The reliance of large companies on subcontracting from medium-sized enterprises rose from 20 percent in 1957 to 50 percent in 1960, and was approaching 65 percent in 1962 (measured by number of working hours devoted to specific manufactures in parent and offspring factories). In the average large enterprise in 1961, 2.5 times as many workers as in the parent plant were employed in the subcontractor factories.

lective expansion" of Japanese industry has meant a rapid disappearance of many traditional products and services. Medium industry was strong in machinery, electronics, processed food, chemicals, plastics, synthetic textiles, furniture, and ready-made clothing—products of this type were replacing such items as bamboo containers, wooden clogs, hand-tailored clothing, locally made ceramics, wooden ware, hand-made interior house fittings, and the like. Each year fewer of the famous "cottage industry" products have been seen in the cities; they may persist mainly in the smaller rural communities.

Likewise, many neighborhood merchants were going out of business as the new service industries, another category of medium enterprise, took over. The independent grocery business has retained much vitality, but supermarkets were beginning to appear, and were predicted to spread by reason of their lower costs, which enabled them to operate at retail margins of 10–15 percent compared with the 25–30 percent of the small family stores. Some neighborhood merchants have tried to meet this competition by banding together in co-operative retailing schemes under one roof, but this pseudo-supermarket has not achieved the economy of chain operation, volume buying, and sales. In Tokyo even the retail bookselling business has been giving way to large companies with branch stores.

Some examples: the baking industry and wooden packaging: The small village and neighborhood bakeries were declining in 1961 and the big commercial bakers increasing. In Tokyo 10 new large automated bakeries appeared between 1954 and 1961, and employed over 500 workers each in 1961. Capital from the private railways and commercial fisheries were behind these endeavors—such capital can purchase the needed equipment for automatic ovens, assembly-line trimming and wrapping, slicing, and preservation. The last-named is a critical factor in the disappearance of small retail food enterprises of all kinds; they were not able to handle volume business because they could not afford expensive freezer equipment. The big food catering companies also were coming to dominate the institutional field—school lunches, small hospitals, and the like—where formerly there was reliance on small local suppliers.

Japanese wooden packaging was not only a utilitarian enterprise but was an intimate feature of the craft atmosphere surrounding small manufacturing. The rapid replacement of wood packaging by paperboard is indicated in the fact that the national production of corrugated board rose from 9,100 million *yen* in 1955 to 41,000 million *yen* in 1960. Citrus fruit packers, for instance, have virtually given up wooden boxes, and many small box makers, caught between the competition of a cheaper product and a shortage of workers, have been forced to close down. Wood packaging has survived mainly in the self-conscious arts and crafts industries which cater to sophisticated or tourist trade, or in sectors of the market which preserve craft methods, like part of the toys and novelties business.

Sociologically, these various changes might predict the modification of two important sectors of the Japanese economic structure: (1) the small family enterprise, with its kinship-dominated organization; and (2) the traditional hierarchal, paternalistic employer-employee relationship system. The former has declined, but slowly; the latter is changing, but retains its strength wherever skills are low or labor a seasonal or migrant factor. However, the economic reports have spoken of a growing "rationalization" of management centering on efficiency, technological improvement, the equalization of wages, upgrading of workers by technical training and skills, and a generally heightened concern for commercial goals and procedures. The hordes of young girls with abaci have been giving way to machine processing of records; business decisions are beginning to be made on the basis of linear programing rather than personal deals and ties. These influences were being felt by the new medium enterprises as well as in the larger companies, since the former were becoming more closely tied to the latter's production standards.

A medium-sized optical firm in Tokyo well known to the writer was founded and operated for many years by a traditional old-school businessman with all the expected virtues: adherence to authoritarian-paternalistic practices and the values of Ben Franklin and Ninomiya Sontoku. In the 1958–1962 period this firm expanded its production threefold and began to sell expensive specialized optical equipment to U.S. and European customers. A new modern factory was under construction in 1963 in a satellite city of Tokyo to replace the several ramshackle wooden sheds scattered through an old Tokyo neighborhood. The owner planned to retire soon and hand on the business to one of his top young engineers, trained in modern management and labor-relations methods. The new man has already declared his plans to expand the output of mass-produced small optical articles which have larger returns, and curtail or modify production of the expensive, specialized equipment now being made. The paternalistic methods of hiring and firing, and generous support of workers' families through differential wages are to give way to a higher standard wage and a more competitive system of promotion according to skill. This transition appears to be typical of the changes under way in various Japanese industries. The picture of Japanese industrial social organization presented in such books as James Abegglen's *The Japanese Factory* is seriously out of date, or at least not representative of many sectors of the economy.

INDUSTRIAL INTEGRATION

Japanese industry has been rapidly approaching a state of high integration in which productive units are tied together in a massive national structure. The automobile industry, which used to be dominated by many small alley-garage assembly shops, has been converting to General Motors style mass production, with parts manufacture subcontracted to hundreds of smaller companies linked to the larger corporate structure. This type of integration is leading to a standardization of working conditions and business philosophy, a shift from hand work to the machine, and the emergence of substantial investment in precision and labor-saving equipment.[8] This further reduces the importance of small family enterprise and, even in cases where family control may persist, accelerates the trends noted in the example of the optical firm.

All this has been accompanied by a shift in the identity of the enterprise. The rate of issue of stocks and debentures has tripled in the past seven years, and the small-scale purchase of securities has reached a point where even department stores have a stock counter, to catch the investing housewife. Banks have become less important as sources of financing, as the Japanese company enters the stage of public financing. The citizen to an increasing extent has saved to increase his income, via investments, and thus has come to have a stake in the economy which contrasts with the prewar picture of large, autonomous, remote, semimercantilistic corporations tied to a stratospheric political elite.

Labor

WAGES

Equalization of wages within industry by 1962 had progressed much further than in prewar and wartime Japan, although there was still some distance to go. We have spoken of the wage gap between the three classes of industry, and how this wage gap was still large enough between medium and large enterprises to encourage the growth of the former as adjuncts to the larger firms. While no one can predict that this gap will eventually be closed, it is currently becoming smaller, as competition for workers, something new in Japan,

---

[8] 65 percent of all enterprises in the Tokyo area invested in new equipment in 1960-61, including enterprises of only 30 workers.

leads to an upgrading of wages and working conditions. The high quality work turned out by the new medium enterprises has led inevitably to wage increases, and the owners and managers of some of the medium companies are introducing working conditions which are better than those in the big plants, in order to preserve the wage differential but also retain workers.

Equalization of wages had, up to 1962, primarily affected the younger workers (ESJ, 1960–1961, pp. 354ff.). Older people were experiencing greater difficulties in getting new jobs and in securing pay rates equal to the younger workers. In some cases older workers were forced to take pay cuts in order to permit management to increase wages for younger people so as to ward off raiding operations by the big firms. The large firms may have been selecting young people for their trainability, on the assumption that they would remain on the job for life, in the traditional Japanese pattern: or they may simply prefer younger workers for their greater productivity. In either case, older workers were disadvantaged. The result of this hiring differential was a high rate of public relief and unemployment payments among older people. Some 600,000 Japanese families in 1961 were receiving relief payments and many of these cases were related to the differential.[9] The number of day laborers who received work through public employment agencies was rising (550,000 in 1961, an increase of over 100,000 in one year), and a majority of these were in the older age brackets. In 1962 economic planners were advocating extensive minimum wage legislation and government investments in retraining facilities.

[9] These 600,000 families receiving relief obviously do not share in the great gains made by consumers described in the next section. While this helps to modify the impression of prosperity given there, the gains have still been massive compared to prewar years, or to any other Asian nation. The failure of some groups in the population to share in the unprecedented prosperity has its dangers, as is suggested in a later section in connection with the emergence of a number of new religious cults which stress achievement and gratification themes.

MOBILITY

In Japan labor mobility has traditionally been low: the inability or lack of desire of a worker to change his job has been regarded as a symptom of traditional social relations and obligations, and of a class system in which labor lacked some of the "rights" of the individualistic "free" worker of the West. Before World War II it had become fairly common for workers to leave their jobs in the big companies and get new positions in smaller firms, but the reverse was extremely rare. Employment in the large firms was defined as a permanent lifetime role.

The employment needs in the larger firms and their satellite companies seem to have modified these practices in the direction of greater mobility of workers from the smaller enterprises into the larger. Formerly most workers recruited into the big firms "in mid-career" from smaller firms or from agriculture were "temporary workers" hired at lower rates than the "permanent workers" recruited straight from school and with no guarantee of security. Recently, however, a slowly rising percentage of these mid-career recruits have been recruited directly as permanent workers (21 percent in 1960–1961), and in the same year the number of temporary workers promoted to permanent status tripled over the previous year in enterprises of 5,000 workers or over, and increased by 80 percent in the 1,000–5,000 category (ESJ, 1960–1961, p. 181). The reasons suggested are that the big firms are being forced to offer permanent status to older workers in order to secure labor, while the simplification of tasks in the larger industries means that specialized training from youth is no longer required. If this is true, it provides an example of technological impact on an important social aspect of the labor force. Whether or not the increased mobility has any far-reaching consequences for social relations and personality, it does imply changed expectations on the part of the younger members of the labor force.

In the early 1960's the most employable person in the Japanese labor force was the younger worker with a high school education. As already noted, these people had the best opportunities for employment, and their place of origin, family background, and even specific skill level did not matter as much as formerly. Their popularity was great enough to produce a "labor shortage" in firms with poorer working conditions, especially the smaller enterprises. The older workers were found to be less flexible: they expected special and differential treatment, they expected jobs suitable to their interests and needs, and they expected personalized responsibilities due them by virtue of their senior age status. These traditional practices were of course not dead, but whatever their frequency, a note of revulsion against them has been evident in Japanese business literature: one of the economic reports referred to them as "confusion."

Union policies were ambiguous or complex on this issue of traditional practices; they supported the seniority wage system, but at the same time protected the interests of their many new and ambitious members, and often certain features of paternalistic job security and union goals coincided.

The rise to influence of the Japanese labor union has been one of the best-known consequences of the Occupation reform program, although the rapid and efficient response of the Japanese to the new right to organize was indicative of their sociopsychological readiness and of the existence of a social need for the union system. The union system was itself subject to some of the particularistic social arrangements found elsewhere in Japanese public life, and observers of the labor scene in the early 1950's were careful to define union organization and labor-management relations in terms which included the "curious" obligations of the union to the paternalistic employer (which seemed, from the American point of view, to violate the very spirit of the labor movement). Reports on the situation in the 1960's suggested that the Japanese labor union and its relations with management was more closely approaching the industrial pattern of struggle, competition, and bargaining, and that the admixture of "preindustrial" social patterns was less evident. In any case, the union movement constitutes a break in the policy of conformity and loyalty imposed on all Japanese organizations during the militarist era. The fact that the Japanese Council of Dock Workers Unions could appeal in 1963 to similar unions the world over for help in their long-drawn-out fight for better working and hiring conditions is a sign that the climate has changed. It, along with other things, is a symptom of a change in the monolithic consensus; Japan is experiencing the emergence of genuine interest groups.

The Revolution in Consumption

CONSUMER HABITS

The expansion of the Japanese economy has been based on a vast growth of the internal market. Whereas at the beginning of the century a good proportion of manufactures was for export, now the domestic market is all-important. At the same time the vastly expanded import bill has come to include a greatly increased proportion of consumer items, especially of foodstuffs and recently, as domestic industries have become able to withstand competition, of such items as automobiles.

According to the Government's household income survey there has been a steady rise in incomes since the turning point in 1953 (FIES, 1960). By 1960 it was 10.9 percent higher than in 1959. If one discounts the effect of the "nagging inflation," as one commentator has called it (retail prices rose 3.7 percent in the same year), this still represents a spectacular gain of 6.9 percent in real income, and the increase was of a comparable order in the following year.

Food measured a real increase of 2.6 percent in household expenditures over 1959, with the greatest increases in dairy products, processed foods, Western-style baked goods and

431

sweets, fruit, and beverages. Fuel and lighting expenditures increased by 17.3 percent over 1959, and payments for services in connection with powered appliances increased similarly. Clothing registered an 11.7 percent increase over 1959; preliminary reports for 1961 indicate an increase in the neighborhood of 15 percent. Furniture and household utensils showed a real increase of 9.6 percent, which was slightly lower than the 1958–1959 increase, suggesting that a plateau was reached, possibly due to price rises. However, the greatest increases in expenditures in this category occurred in the lowest income bracket, with television sets indicating the largest gain among all items. In other words, the style of life of the lower income groups in Japan has been changing more rapidly than that of any other group, demonstrating the revolution in aspirations which has affected this segment of the population.

The Tokyo Metropolitan District led all the rest in changes and increases in consumption. The consumption of meat and butter in 1960 was double the average level of prewar times. In 1959, 465 households out of 1,000 possessed electric washing machines, as against 9.4 in 1954. Similar rapid increases were reported for other household appliances and types of consumer goods, although yearly fluctuations can be noted, and in 1962 the increase had leveled out.

Table 3 provides additional details for four key consumer appliances. Refrigerators are expensive and therefore help to suggest the tendency for consumers to save for such expenditures and interests. Refrigerators, washers, and rice cookers are labor saving and therefore suggest changes in the household, i.e. in the woman's role. Television signifies contact with mass culture and the international entertainment media.

While these 1959 figures are considerably out of date, they illustrate the trends. The lower income groups and the poorer prefectures like Iwate have shared to a considerably lesser extent in the consumer revolution than the middle and upper groups. Since, however, consumption gains in 1961–

TABLE 3

Income Group (monthly income in yen: ¥ 360 = $ 1)	Number of appliances per 1,000 urban households, 1959			
	Electric refrigerators	Electric washers	TV sets	Automatic rice cookers
Lowest (less than 9,999)	1	40	23	83
Next lowest (10,000–19,999)	10	97	79	205
Low-middle (30,000–39,999)	65	408	420	404
Middle (40,000–49,999)	109	535	532	404
Highest (80,000 plus)	392	834	808	569
Average for Japan	69	334	323	334
Tokyo Metropolitan District	60	465	556	294
Hokkaido prefecture	19	337	275	293
Iwate prefecture	14	140	163	157

Source: SYJ 1961, pp. 382–83

1962 seem, from preliminary reports, to have been greatest in the lower income brackets, the average for all Japan will probably move closer to the level shown for the middle-income category. This is not to say that large numbers of poor and unemployed will continue to lack many of the important or more expensive articles.

Improved transportation has been one of the more spectacular developments of the postwar period. Automobiles had been manufactured in Japan for a long time, but production in prewar times was overwhelmingly in favor of commercial and work vehicles. The private citizen rode bicycles, taxis, or occasionally rented a car. Japan was called a "bicycle society" in prewar years, since the bicycle was within reach of every citizen, whereas an Asian country like India was a generation or so away from even this level. The end of the war found Japan still at this level, since the disruption of automotive production by the war had reduced powered vehicles to a minimum. By 1954 the production and sales of motor scooters had almost caught up to bicycles, and by 1957 motorcycles had passed scooters and bikes. By 1960 three-wheeled automobiles had begun to catch up to motorcycles, and by 1962 the four-wheeled passenger automobile was beginning to compete with the smaller vehicles.[10] Import quotas for passenger cars were exactly doubled for 1963. Reports indicated that the bicycle industry was "depressed" and was becoming dependent upon export sales, especially to Asia and Latin America.

A PARENTHETICAL NOTE: DIET AND PHYSIQUE

The changes in food habits noted previously have had implications beyond the cultural and economic. The traditional rice-and-fish diet has been supplemented by a Western diet with emphasis on dairy products, meat, wheat, and sugared desserts.[11] Rice was being sold in 1962 on the black market at prices below the official level, since Japan had a slight surplus. Production of rice reached a high of over 12 million tons in 1955, then dropped, but regained this figure in 1959–1960 (JSY, 1962). In 1962, according to official reports production was 1 percent higher than demand. In contrast, the demand for meat and dairy products was one-third higher than domestic production, and imports, as already noted, were sought in order to control the price situation.

The impact of these dietary changes on the Japanese physique was reported in a 1961 government physical anthropological survey. This survey used a comparable study made sixty years ago as a base for comparison. The data in-

---

[10] Although Japanese had to work an equivalent of 21 months as against the U.S. 3 months (on average wage basis) to earn the purchase price of a car (ESJ, 1960-61, p. 268).

[11] UNEA 1961, p. 19, reports that among the following Asian countries—Japan, Ceylon, Taiwan, India, Pakistan—Japan's diet had the highest per capita caloric content during 1957-1960, although it was in the middle range for 1948-1951. Japan had the highest animal protein intake of all these countries for both periods.

dicate that fifteen-year-old boys averaged 4 feet 11 3/4 inches sixty years ago; they were in 1960 over 5 feet 3 inches. Girls of the same age went from 4 feet 9 inches to 5 feet. In the weight categories the average for men went from 117 to 125; women, from 106 to 112. In general, average gains for the women were greater than those for the men, which is explained in the study by the proportionately greater changes in female behavior: sports, the use of chairs instead of mats for sitting, riding of bicycles, and the like. General gains in height and weight are explained mainly by dietary improvements, however, and this is confirmed by the fact that the greatest changes—in many categories the *only* changes over the sixty-year period—were registered by the post-World War II generation. The findings concerning the children about ten years of age in 1962 indicate that many of them will exceed the increases shown for teenagers, many of whom had begun life under early postwar conditions of deprivation.

Physical well-being, symbolized by new values placed upon robustness, bulk, and height, especially emphatic in the "new middle class," contrasted with the much-remarked prewar Japanese values of ascetic leanness and Spartan deprivation and endurance. Thus the new diet and its effects took their place in the general shift of values toward prosperity and an expanding level of living.

CONSUMER PRODUCTION AND ITS EFFECTS ON THE ECONOMY

The expansion of consumer industries and the diverting of former export commodities into the domestic market has had its multiplier effect on the national integration and technical level of the Japanese economy.[12] The 1960-61 *Economic Survey* has the following to say of the car industry, which was beginning a rapid expansion of private car production in that period:

[12] A case study: K. Nakagawa and Henry Rosovsky, "The Case of the Dying Kimono: The Influence of Changing Fashions on the Development of the Japanese Woollen Industry," *Business History Review*, XXXVII (1963), 59–80.

The phenomenal increase in production by the machinery industry strongly reflects the present stage of technical advancement and changes in consumption. Mass-produced items such as automobiles and durable consumer goods not only create multifold demand effects as items produced by comprehensive assembly-line industries but also demand a high level of production technology. An automobile is the crystallization of the power of various industries—iron and steel, nonferrous metal, machine tool, synthetic rubber, plastics, synthetic fibers, glass and paint industries. Compared with the production of TV sets, the demand effects and technological effects of automobiles are far more multiple and far-reaching. (p. 77)

An important effect is the great expansion of research and technical training. Scientific research by industry and by universities and government in the interests of industry was rising sharply, as efficiency was sought in order to maintain quality in volume production at low prices. In 1960, 586 million dollars were spent on scientific research, in the previous year 480 million dollars. Private enterprise alone spent in 1960 some 110 million dollars in salaries for research personnel. In terms of a percentage of the national income, Japan spent 1.8 percent for research; Germany 1.6 percent; the United Kingdom 2.6 percent; and the U.S. 3.1 percent. Much of Japan's rising research budget represents a process of catching up after the years of isolation and imperialism, but the steep rise in the 1959–1962 period was more a direct reflection of the efforts to create an efficient mass production plant.

Consumer industries have bred hordes of new service trades and the educational facilities they require. Private trade schools have become proportionately almost as numerous in Japan as in the U.S. Installation, maintenance, and repair of the new appliances have given some staying power to the smaller entrepreneur who, as already noted, has been losing out in his traditional pursuits to the larger and more efficient industries. Figures on service trades for recent years are difficult to obtain, but all reports agree that their importance is rising, and in 1960, *service industries throughout Japan for the first time provided a portion of the national income in excess of agriculture*: a typical index of a society in the stage of high development.

Rural Economy and Society

MIGRATION

The historic movement from country to city, which played such a vital role in the building of a modern economy, is still under way, as data discussed earlier appear to show. The migration has reached the point where the shortage of farm labor, in spite of drastic wage increases (a 29 percent rise by 1960 over the 1950 level), was so serious that farms were being driven toward machinery and new forms of management such as cooperative arrangements and large-scale commercial farming. The rise in prices forced farm owners to take part-time jobs in order to increase income, hence a drastic rise in this type of activity occurred: 65 percent of all farm households in 1961 had side incomes derived from various service-trade and industrial jobs. This was of course a continuation of certain old patterns, but its sheer magnitude reflected a considerable movement away from the old rural virtues and cultural habits. It was also facilitated by the movement of factories into the countryside.

The rural outgo was measured principally in the younger age groups and was particularly heavy among persons with a secondary school education, the same segment which registered the greatest gains in wages and promotions in industry. However, many people in their twenties and thirties, and middle-aged farm people, also moved away from rural areas, the latter often because they were discouraged by the difficulty of maintaining traditional small-scale farming in the face of steeply rising costs. An especially interesting trend, because of its social-historical implications, is the reported tendency for eldest sons to migrate to the city in numbers approaching those of the younger sons. Japan's modern urban-industrial labor force was built mainly out of the latter, due to primogeniture and the closure of economic opportunity in a highly populated countryside. Eldest-son migration reflects both the legal abandonment of primogeniture after World War II and the decreased popularity of farming as an occupation. Sociologically, it is related to a general loosening of the restrictions and rules of the extended family system of rural areas, and also of the reduction in size of this family toward the nuclear family core type. Multiple inheritance, made the legal form in the postwar Family Code revision, is not working, however, and single inheritance, though not necessarily primogeniture, is still the dominant mode.[13]

CHANGE IN FARMING PATTERN

The reports have emphasized the uneconomic position of the small holder in the face of rising costs and labor shortages; that is, the small family farm, for generations the mainstay of Japanese agriculture, was seriously disadvantaged and larger enterprises were emerging. The available figures on size of holdings do not clearly show all the factors at work, but one unambiguous trend is for an increase in the number of larger holdings, over 1.5 hectares (made possible by modifications in the postwar land reform legislation).

Most of these larger holdings are still family farms, but their owners were buying their own machinery in quantity. Reports pointed out, in fact, that many of these purchases were unnecessary and resulted in passing up economical sharing arrangements, a trend excessively familiar to North

[13] See ESJ, 1960-1961, p. 248; also Y. S. Matsumoto, "Notes on Primogeniture," in Smith and Beardsley, *Japanese Culture*, and T. Koyama, "Changing Family Structure," in the same volume.

American rural economists. Farm machinery has been enjoying an intense vogue in many rural areas, and competition among farmers over ownership of the latest models has developed. These signs of intensified individualistic enterprise on the farm are highlighted by the emergence of a new type of capitalist enterprise on some of these larger holdings. These are essentially commercial enterprises, often financed as joint-stock companies, with capital provided by local businessmen as well as by the farmers involved in the enterprise. Corporative farming of this type reflects a growing tendency to subject agriculture to pecuniary values; in the *Economic Survey*'s words, "a clear distinction is now being made between profitable and unprofitable farmers." (ESJ, 1960-61, p. 295.) Such values have not formerly been so clearly visible in farming. That is, while agriculture in Japan has been subjected to a degree of rationalization for a very long time and has certainly been treated by the government as a part of the national economy, the values of business efficiency and profit have not played a large or consistent role in the definition of farm, farmer status, and rural cultural values. Farming has been moving away from its traditional feudal definition as a unique, class-bound occupation, culturally rewarding in its own right. Related devaluations of the virtues of rural life have been taking place in the U.S. and European countries. Agricultural policy in Japan for the past century has been based on the need to improve land holdings and tenure so as to permit the farmer to work out his own adequate, and culturally satisfying, subsistence production. Trends in the 1960's shift the emphasis. As the Government's *Survey* puts it, "Agricultural policies must undergo changes from the . . . policies based mainly on the improvement of the land conditions of the farming families . . . to those that will result in the increase in efficiency of agricultural management and the establishment of a good sales system." (ESJ, 1960-61, p. 42.)

The appearance of cooperative or corporative farms established by the pooling of resources of several small farmers was an important development, undoubtedly utilizing patterns of social relations traditional to the Japanese rural community. However, the strong business emphasis and rationality of many of these new organizations was not a traditional element, and it is probably safer to interpret the overall trend as a phase of the general commercial outlook which has been invading Japanese agriculture rather than as a simple persistence of old forms of cooperative association. In any case, there is a vast difference between commercialized cooperation and cooperation in the context of traditional subsistence socioeconomy. The economic pressures felt by Japanese agriculture—labor costs, rise in land prices, packaging and shipping costs, machinery costs—are so strong that the response has been forced along commercial, business lines. If the traditional social organization was in the picture, it was so, we believe, instrumentally and not ideologically.

Still, many Japanese farmers retain their old ways. Despite the fact that among all the ECAFE Asian countries, Japan had the greatest advance in agricultural production during the 1950's (Taiwan was next; see UNEA 1961), agricultural growth in Japan during the decade was slow in comparison to growth in all other aspects of the economy.

A Ministry of Agriculture and Forestry report[14] places the blame on attitudes traditionally associated with "peasant proprietorship," and the sense of a need for change has given rise to campaigns to promote a more innovative spirit among Japanese farmers. The ministry has stepped up its extension services, and voluntary farm organizations, like the 4-H clubs, are working intensively on local educational programs. These efforts have apparently had their effects on the attitudes of the younger generation, but it should be remembered that the basic problems of Japanese agriculture are traceable to inadequate capital and excessively small units, and

[14] 1960 World Agricultural Census (Tokyo, 1960).

that these features must be changed before massive alterations in the economic and technical status of farming can be expected.

The Cultural Scene

As Japan's consumer-oriented economy continued to expand, the traditional culture retracted in many spheres and achieved new popularity in others. Japan has experienced a phenomenon described for the United States in John K. Galbraith's book *The Affluent Society*: the expansion of the private sector of the economy at the expense of the public. In 1962 Japanese newspapers published articles and editorials on the decline of Japan's many monuments, parks, old temples and shrines, forests, and other areas of scenic beauty and historical reference owned by religious organizations. Labor costs were rising to the point where maintenance became difficult, and municipalities and the national government showed as little interest in making cultural appropriations as their American analogs—even less interest, perhaps, since capital was still in relatively short supply, and public spending tended to flow toward critical material needs like roads, buildings, unemployment relief, and the like.

Equally important has been a change of mood. The Japanese have enjoyed their beautiful country and its colorful customs, but like Americans they have shown no strong interest in preserving them at the cost of higher taxes or deprivations in the consumer sphere. Internal tourism is booming —this is an old Japanese custom—and the greatest increases in expenditures for recreation in 1960 were for food purchased outside the home, i.e. the restaurant business in the cities was doing extremely well, and better than the old-fashioned resorts in the ancient villages and historic sites. A few of these older resorts, like Atami, have been taken over by private capital and turned into something approximating Atlantic City, and the new middle class has appeared to enjoy concrete and aluminum hotels with modern facilities more than the traditional wooden inns.

Behind these changes, which may be disappointing to the Western analyst of prewar Japanese culture and damaging to his confidence in the aesthetic sensibilities of the Japanese, may lie a reinterpretation of the role of tradition in Japanese life. The relatively extensive preservation of cultural monuments and traditional arts and pastimes in prewar Japan may have been sanctioned principally by nationalistic interests, that is, they may have been mainly a reflection of official policy which, since the Meiji era, had utilized Japan's cultural past as a device to promote various national goals and to ensure the support of a dedicated and docile population. The rapid dissolution of this policy after the war removed official sanctions for preservation of the past; and with the expansion of a consumer economy, the personal interests of the Japanese people immediately began taking the route familiar in all industrializing countries—toward personal comfort and enjoyment, with little regard for tradition. Since much of the traditional culture was, in the contemporary view, an apologia for poverty, its recent decline suggests that the much-advertised investment in the past of the average Japanese was a facet of official compulsion and was not necessarily deeply felt.

A Japanese newspaper editorial remarked in 1962 that "we have lost our position in the stream of history," and went on to complain that Japanese show much more interest in Western or modern art, drama, music, architecture, and sports than in traditional Japanese pursuits. The modern things were being cultivated for their own sake, with no reference to the past or to their historical meaning. This same issue of the newspaper (*Japan Times Weekly*, March 17, 1962) also contained a panegyric for the expanding consumer industries and the favorable balance of payments, that is, the very forces which underlie the destruction of the sense of history. Moreover, when public effort has succeeded in preserving a monument or a traditional art form through subsidy, the meaning of these will be changed: they become "historical" in the self-conscious sense, and Nara merges with Williamsburg. Sooner or later American philanthropic foundations will play their role in helping to preserve the Japanese past, since the Japanese, like Americans, are preoccupied with other matters.

On the other hand, certain popular pastimes with traditional roots have shown no signs of decline. The annual visits to the Yasukuni Jinja have been more popular than ever; visits to certain traditional temples and their shops and tourist facilities are extremely popular, even though the pilgrims may arrive on motorcycles instead of on foot. Wherever the new prosperity has sought out a traditional pastime, that pastime will be reinforced (e.g. geisha houses and business expense accounts); thus the cultural past is not all dead. However, its survival will be often part of the general hedonism and movement of modern life, and thus its meaning changes.

This has been evident in religious trends. The most important religious development in Japan since the end of the war has been the appearance of several new cults or sects which now number several million adherents. These "religions" resemble the Father Divine movement far more than any traditional Buddhist, Shinto, or Christian sect. Hedonism, guarantees of wish fulfillment, and in one case militant nationalism have been the dominant themes. Such organizations may represent the seamy side of social change in Japan: people in large numbers are failing to achieve emotional satisfaction from traditional Oriental faiths or from Christianity. The conclusion is somewhat tempered by the fact that Christian sects have registered considerable gains in the 1960's, and private financial support for Buddhist and Shinto sects has been substantial, and their festivals and benefits well attended. Religion thus has benefited from prosperity, although the insecurities attendant upon rapid social change have also been visible in religious behavior.

We have spoken elsewhere of the decline in traditional crafts. Much of this has been due to their uneconomic nature in a high-wage, highly productive economy. An equally important explanation is found in the necessity to change old techniques because new equipment demands it. Japanese domestic architecture has been undergoing a radical change from the thin-walled wooden and wattled structure with extensive window area to an adapted Western-style construction. The basic causes are to be found in the need to build heavier walls and floors to accommodate the conduits for modern conveniences, and also to secure better insulation and protection against fire. Japan's forests also have reached a critical stage of depletion; hence new building materials must be sought. Public and private housing developments in an era of inflated land prices must make the most efficient use of that land; hence the single family dwelling has been giving way to the concrete and steel apartment building. The typical and traditional Japanese domestic house may eventually survive mainly in the lowest income districts, which is one more symptom of the situational reversal of cultural values.

Following the encouragement given Japanese craftsmen by Americans in the Occupation, and by the growth of the international snob market in the past decade, Japanese crafts in the 1960's have entered a "new age," as a trade publication put it. In every field—architecture, furniture, ceramics, textiles, wooden ware, lacquer—Japanese craftsmen have been merging their designs with those produced in Denmark, Sweden, France, the U.S., and Italy. American interior decorator and specialty firms sent their own designers to Japan to work with the local craftsmen, and the Fulbright Commission sent Japanese craftsmen to the U.S. to learn and to teach. Traditional items like Mashiko pottery were no longer the autonomous local products they were earlier, but have become international in their market and styling. In the process they have changed their form: a note of standardization has crept in, a glossy perfection and sameness which characterizes handicrafts that have attained a semivolume market.

While the survival of crafts may depend upon international trade and invisible exports, the domestic market has shifted to plastics and synthetics. In the 1960's Japan was the fourth-ranking plastics producer in the world, after the U.S., England, and Germany. Plastics has been one of the industries in which smaller firms have thrived, since plastic-molding equipment is relatively simple and cheap. Japan had 2,316 plastic-molding enterprises in 1960, as against 1,800 for the U.S. Only 10 percent of the output of these many companies was exported; the remainder poured into the Japanese market, where it has been replacing practically everything made earlier from wood, ceramics, bamboo, and leather.

MASS MEDIA

Along with the focusing of attention on consumption, with its fads and fashions and pastimes, there goes a general re-definition of the Japanese national entity, away from the historic macro-paternalistic conception of a nation of loyal children of the emperor animated by a mystical "Spirit of Yamato," and toward the secular commercial state, with its representative government, opposed interest groups, and "public opinion." That is, Japan has been becoming what anyone chooses to define it, and in the contemporary period this has tended to be equivalent to the national economy and its vicissitudes. The eagerness with which the Japanese have sought a definition of their national identity was indicated by the popularity of public opinion polls and the rapid expansion of newspaper and magazine readership and radio-television. In 1961 the *Asahi* had a circulation of 7.6 million copies, and the total circulation of the daily press was 26,104,926—equal to the combined circulation of the entire U.S. daily press. Since in 1961 Japan had a population of about 96 million, one daily paper was read by about 1 in every 3.5 persons, or the average family of 4.8 persons took more than one newspaper. These figures placed Japan around fourth in readership among the nations of the world. In 1961 there were 59 private television stations and 109 radio stations; and NHK operated 54 stations, each with 2 radio and 2 television channels—all these for 96 million people in a country the size of the state of Montana. These various outlets provide news broadcasts hourly, and a wide range of entertainment and public service programs. Radio and TV sets in use in January 1961 were estimated at 12,500,000 and 7,820,000, respectively, and these increased by one or more million sets each in 1962.

Japan was in the early 1960's the world's largest producer of motion pictures (India produces the next largest number). While the U.S. produced 270 feature films in 1961, Japan made 493. Japanese film exports doubled between 1955 and 1960 and had a value of 3 million dollars, putting Japan as second or third, after the U.S. and Italy. Change in content of these films over the prewar period was striking: the export business encouraged Japanese producers to make films with an eye to the international market as well as the domestic, hence the modern Japanese movies have been cast in terms of internationally comprehensive themes and logic, from the art film to the domestic drama. Even the *chambara* film on samurai deeds of valor became Westernized in the special sense of using themes and patterns derived from the U.S. Western movie. (However, in 1960 an *American* Western was modeled on a Japanese samurai film, *Seven Samurai*!). Japanese films have contained many indigenous cultural elements, but there has been a growing trend toward treating these elements objectively in ways understandable to audiences anywhere.

Advertising has shown comparable development. The consumer economy produced a doubling of advertising output and revenue in the 1960's. Dentsu, the third largest ad agency in the world, had in 1962 a total annual revenue of 190 million dollars; its nearest competitor less than a third of this amount. It may be a sign of the times that the corporation which most nearly resembles the absolute monopolies typical of prewar Japan should be in the field of advertising. Advertising content and style has been heavily influenced by American models, and the slogans and logic of appeal which bombard the Japanese consumer have helped to create in his mind's eye a picture of the world very similar to that held by the average American when he is attentive to the mass media.

Conclusions

In the introduction we described a number of social changes that seem to accompany the development of industry and a nationally integrated rationalized economy in any nation-society. In the preceding sections of this paper enough data has been presented to suggest that most of these changes are under way, though their degree and rate are undetermined. In any case, it is our belief that Japan's current industrial growth and urbanization is producing or reinforcing institutional patterns of a general type familiar to all the highly industrialized societies of the West, and that for most macroscopic purposes it is necessary to consider Japan in the context of Western, rather than Asian or perhaps "feudal," society. This point of view seems also to be popular among some Japanese intellectuals, who, when they return from their Asian research or travels, experience a "shock of recognition" in the perception of the growing non-Asian or non-Oriental character of their homeland. They, like many Western visitors, tend to see the traditional arts and crafts and surviving social customs as survivals of a charming past or as cultivated enterprises catering to the tourist trade. Other intellectuals regret the decline and endeavor to cultivate the traditions. For both the Japanese and the foreigner, Japanese traditional culture can be seen as interesting or as old-fashioned, depending upon current fashion and ideologies (especially pro- and anti-Americanism), and this means that there will be revivals, as well as disappearances, of the old ways. But these revivals or reinforcements will be set in the matrix of a modern industrial society and will take much of their meaning, and their economic base, from this society.

Sociologically, these changes have heralded the appearance of an important middle category in the socioeconomic structure. Before World War II the middle class in Japanese society was hard to discern. Scholarly discussions of the Japanese class system emphasized the inconclusive nature of this system, pointing out that feudal and localized social relationships, as well as an unequal distribution of wealth, tended to blur the lines of division. In contemporary Japan, however, the consumer revolution has resembled its middle-class-dominated analog in the U.S., and its chief spokesmen have been in large part self-made men aspiring to security, respectability, and prestige. Progress, prosperity, and happy conformity are their slogans, just as they are in the U.S. The new middle class throngs the new resort hotels, often with wives and children in tow, and these scenes provide a picture of social stratification resembling the West in considerable detail.[15]

[15] It is precisely this type of conclusion that appears to be negated by contemporary viewpoints on Japanese social change among sociologists and anthropologists. Or at least, whether or not the hypothesis or conclusion about a Western-style social class system can be defended, many of these observers would uphold the position that there has been little change in traditional forms of status and social relations. Since writing this, we have read Ezra Vogel's *Japan's New Middle Class* (Berkeley: University of California Press, 1963), which exemplifies this point of view. This informative account of life among salary men in a Tokyo suburb acknowledges many macroscopic changes and the rise in the level of living, but presents a picture of conservatism in the family and home. Basically "social change" from this point of view contrasts evident or acknowledged change in macroscopic levels with persistence of traditional features at the microscopic. However, the perception of microscopic stability might obscure evidence of change on a broad and general scale. To cite an example: Vogel states that despite changes in social outlook, husbands do not go out in public with their wives any more frequently than before the war. Possibly

From a political standpoint, economic change in Japan has signified the beginning of a shift in power from an aristocratic-military oligarchy to an economic elite, with labor union leadership in its typical Western position of public challenge to this new elite. Along with this shift in power has gone a change in the national mood: Japanese concern for the traditional culture, the "Japanese spirit," or national prestige in the imperialistic sense has given way to an emphasis on progress and the health of the national economy. Daily newspapers headline economic events; the barometers of national well-being, the balance of payments and rate of economic growth, are given daily treatment, like a weather report. Housewives buy stocks in the department stores, and cash savings are being used in many other ways to increase income rather than to prepare for the rainy day. A strong note of national pride, again reminiscent of the U.S. in the 1920's, runs through all this: a pride in general accomplishment, in the fact that Japan now exports expensive electronics instead of cheap fountain pens.

Psychologically, then, these social and economic developments seem to have been accompanied by a considerable increase in Japanese self-esteem. The "Japanese character" of prewar and early postwar times, with its reticence and embarrassment, has become a rare commodity, at least in the middle and upper socioeconomic groups. Much of this "cultural character" originally must have been a situational re-

---

this is true for certain types of social visiting and business affairs. On the other hand, observers of contemporary Japanese life (including the writer) have been struck with the fact that middle-class husbands, wives, and children are a frequent and common sight in resorts, which is a change from the prewar situation. Economic data on expenditures for internal tourism and recreation are high in categories which may reflect family outgoings. Perhaps the fundamental question is whether any tendency to conserve the "traditional" pattern of family relations is a lag phenomenon, or whether it represents a stable adaptation to the new macroscopic Japan. In the position taken in this paper, we would have to adopt the former of these two alternatives.

action to a pervading sense of inferiority brought about by the national effort to equal or outdo the West at its own game. That the behavior had roots in the Japanese social structure is of course true, but in light of current trends one is inclined to feel that the cultural determinants were exaggerated by the Western analysts.

The approach taken in this paper also contains some implications for a theory of Japanese society which has up to now formed the basis of Western scholarship on Japan. This theory held that while Japan in her Meiji and Taisho eras took over much of the technical apparatus of Western institutions, she preserved much or most of her preindustrial social structure, and even utilized this structure to the hilt to provide the social discipline needed for modernization. While features of this generalization may continue to apply to certain social sectors and geographical regions, it is inadequate as an explanation of events in contemporary Japan as a national society. From an historical standpoint it is our view that the "modernization without Westernization" theory of change really applied to a particular period or to a transitional phase in the change process. Whether or not one wishes to explore the meaning of the term "Westernization," it would seem on the basis of various indices of change in contemporary Japan that feudal-familial forms of social structure *are* changing, and the macroscopic social patterns are rapidly shifting toward those associated with high industrialization and urbanization elsewhere in the world.

The extreme rapidity of the changes associated with the modern economy are of course intimately connected with World War II and the political situation which led up to it. The authoritarian interlude of the 1930's and 1940's, while it served to step up certain aspects of technical modernization, also reimposed certain traditional social controls, the existence of which in turn tended to reinforce scholarly interpretation based on the approach outlined previously. The avidity with which the Japanese people and many of their leaders accepted the reforms of the Occupation period was an indication of the extent to which social changes associated with industrialization had been prepared under cover, so to speak, during the authoritarian epoch. Consequently the rapidity of current change in Japanese economy and society is due, in addition to many other causes, to a "catching-up" process. That is, it is in part at least a social readjustment, and not merely something new.

In the past decade we have witnessed a remarkable shift in the character of the Japanese elite: the businessman, oriented to efficiency, change, and prosperity and with diverse social origins, has come to the fore in a manner resembling his analog in the United States during the 1920's. Japan's culture is coming more and more to reflect the motives and interests of this group, and these cannot be described as conservative in the same sense as the gentry and samurai elites. They may be dedicated to free enterprise, but they are *not* noticeably concerned with the conservation of Japan's traditional society and culture. The flowering of private capital has removed much necessity for reliance upon oligarchic or rural sources. Hence the interpreters of Japanese society in the contemporary period will have to shift their sights from the oligarchy to the business class, and perhaps to the middle class in general.

The outlook of this powerful business class is well summarized in the words of the writers of the *Economic Survey of Japan, 1960–1961*, p. 53 (my italics):

> In order to improve the quality of the Japanese economy by changing the production and regional structures and reorganize the financial structure, the Government [should] reinforce its measures to increase public investments, develop technology, fostering human resources and others which are the bases of economic growth, as well as expand measures for the smaller enterprises, farming, labor migration and social security in order to achieve a smooth adaptation to the structural changes. . . . [Also] necessary

in the adaptation to structural changes is a change in outlook by *management,* . . . [which] should become more conscious of its social obligations as well as take a wider international view, while the *operators of small and medium-sized enterprises* must change their method of management which had hitherto been based on low wages. The *farmers* . . . must carry out their structural improvement through selective expansion, while the *housewife* today is required to engage in more modern and rationalized consumer activity.

In other words, everyone is now required to change one's previous way of thinking in the respective roles one is playing in the national economy.

Whether or not this program will be carried out, the attitudes reflected in this quotation—a self-conscious awareness of economic patterns and processes and a search for planned readjustments in social and political institutions—will continue to be shared by the dominant elite, whatever the political complexion of future governments. A strong note of pragmatic rationality has always characterized Japanese society, and thus the current trends are built upon an ancient foundation. Actually, economic planning in contemporary Japan is more extensive than in any democratic capitalist country of the West. As we have noted, the ministries responsible for the health of the economy can exercise prompt and effective control over the balance of payments, credit, and the export-import ratio. While this effective control may require modifications in the picture of Japan as a modern nation on the Western laissez-faire model, it serves to strengthen the picture of Japan as a nation developing a highly rationalized modern economy. These controls, moreover, are exercised not for nationalistic and imperialistic objectives, as they used to be, but in the general interest of public and business well-being. The Japanese businessman to an extent far greater than his Western counterpart has learned to rely on government as a means for effective stabilization and protection. If a socialist government ever comes to power in contemporary Japan, much of this partnership between business and government will be exposed as corruption and favoritism;[16] but however it is viewed, its operation has given Japan a remarkably steady and expanding, if somewhat inflated, economy. It has also given Japanese society the motive power for extensive continued change toward what, despite some reversals and paradoxes, is in broad and relevant outline the society of the West.

[16] Added in 1967: the Diet election campaign of 1966, and the political commentary surrounding it, laid considerable emphasis on this issue. A series of "scandals" involving relations between business and the Sato government became the major domestic issue in the campaign, and was exploited by the socialists. On the other hand, in 1965 and 1966 a rising chorus of criticism from Japan's new breed of "objective" political analysts deplored the "corruption" in the ranks of the socialists themselves—their willingness to accept cash donations from big business, and their unwillingness to attack business domination of the government and the nation. We have in this situation an example of the duality of the change process in Japan: on one hand, the emergence of objective political analysis, along with a sense of "corruption," is evidence of change toward a more open society. On the other, the failure of a political party to adhere to ideological definitions of social issues, and instead, to blur its program in favor of maintaining power at any price, can be taken as an example of the survival of the old Japanese power-consensus system. The existence of these apparently contradictory indices of change is responsible for the contradictions in the social-scientific analysis of change made by Western observers, noted in an earlier footnote. Another interesting trend is that in the 1964-66 period the two modes of interpretation—material change but not social change, and material change *and* social change (granting some lag)—began emerging in Japanese social science and educated commentary. This too is a sign of change toward the more open frame of intellectual reference.

LIST OF CONTRIBUTORS

REINHARD BENDIX, Professor of Sociology, University of California, Berkeley, taught at the Universities of Chicago and Colorado before moving to Berkeley in 1947 and has since been a visiting professor at the Free University of Berlin and at Oxford. He received the MacIver Award of the American Sociological Association in 1958 and is author of *Work and Authority in Industry*, 1956; *Social Mobility in Industrial Society*, with S. M. Lipset, 1959; *Max Weber: An Intellectual Portrait*, 1960; *Nation-Building and Citizenship*, 1964; and numerous articles in professional journals. He edited, with S. M. Lipset, *Class, Status, and Power*, 2nd edn., 1966.

JOHN W. BENNETT has been Professor of Anthropology and Sociology at Washington University, St. Louis, since 1959. After receiving a University of Chicago Ph.D. in anthropology he was Chief of the Public Opinion and Sociological Research Division of the Japan Occupation Army Headquarters from 1949 to 1951. He has done field research in rural North America, Mexico, Japan, and Israel and is the author of *In Search of Identity: The Japanese Scholar in America and Japan*, 1958; *Paternalism in the Japanese Economy*, 1963; and *Hutterian Brethren: A Study of Settlement, Economy, and Social Organization* to be published by Stanford University Press in 1967. He is currently engaged in comparative studies of the social aspects of agricultural cooperation in several countries.

JOHN B. CORNELL is Professor of Anthropology, University of Texas. He was trained in anthropology (doctorate) and Far Eastern Languages and Literatures (masters) at the University of Michigan and has taught at Wayne State University, Kyoto University, Michigan, and the Escola de Sociologia e Politica de São Paulo. He is presently in charge of the Asian studies program and acting chairman of the Department of Anthropology at the University of Texas. He did field work in Japan in 1950-51 and 1957-59, and is co-author of *Two*

Japanese Villages (1956) and author of articles on various aspects of Japanese social structure, especially on outcastes and on the Ainu of Hokkaido. Professor Cornell has recently worked on Japanese acculturation in Brazil where he directed the Texas-Cornell project.

GEORGE A. DE VOS, Professor of Anthropology and Chairman, Center for Japanese and Korean Studies at the University of California, Berkeley, was trained as a psychologist and has conducted research on, among other topics, comparative patterns of delinquency in Japan and the United States, the acculturation of Japanese-Americans in the United States, normative personality characteristics of urban and rural Japanese, Japanese outcastes (he has recently edited, with Hiroshi Wagatsuma, *Japan's Invisible Race*), the scoring of Rorschach responses, and the acculturation and personality of Algerian Arabs, on which he has written a book jointly with Horace Minor. He contributed the chapter on culture and personality to the *Handbook of Social Psychology*.

TAKEO DOI, Psychiatrist-in-Chief, St. Luke's International Hospital, Tokyo, is a lecturer at Tokyo University, where he gives a seminar in psychotherapy, and at Waseda University, where he uses the novels of Natsume Sōseki to teach depth psychology. He is the author of numerous articles on psychiatry and psychoanalysis.

R. P. DORE is a Fellow of the Institute of Development Studies at the University of Sussex. He previously taught at the University of British Columbia, Vancouver, and at the London School of Economics and Political Science and School of Oriental and African Studies, University of London. Professor Dore has made several research visits to Japan and is the author of *City Life in Japan* (1958), *Land Reform in Japan* (1959), and *Education in Tokugawa Japan* (1964). He is presently at work on a comparative study of factory organization in Japan and England.

456

ERWIN H. JOHNSON, Associate Professor of Anthropology, The State University of New York at Buffalo, was a Robert Gilder Fellow at Columbia University where he took a Ph.D. in anthropology. He did field work in a Japanese mountain village in 1956-58 as a Research Associate with Nagoya National University. He has published several articles on Japan.

SOLOMON B. LEVINE, Professor of Economics and Business, and Chairman, East Asian Studies Program, University of Wisconsin, was educated at Harvard and the Massachusetts Institute of Technology. He has taught at MIT, Pennsylvania State University, University of Illinois, and Keio University. He has made several trips to Japan as research scholar, visiting professor and consultant to foundations, and is the author of *Industrial Relations in Postwar Japan* and a number of articles dealing with Japanese labor affairs.

KEIICHI MIZUSHIMA is Professor, Risshō Women's University, Saitama-ken and Lecturer at the Counselling Center, Taishō University, Tokyo. He holds a Ph.D. from Waseda University and has served as a clinical psychologist in a juvenile detention home and a child guidance center, in addition to being Chief Psychologist at the Serigayaen Mental Hospital in Yokohama. He has written two books and several articles on the clinical psychology of delinquency and on counselling.

EDWARD NORBECK is Dean of Humanities and Professor of Anthropology at Rice University. He was born in Canada and received a doctorate in anthropology from the University of Michigan. He has conducted field research in Japan intermittently since 1950 and has published several books on Japanese culture and other anthropological subjects.

THOMAS C. SMITH, Professor of History at the University of California, Berkeley, and formerly of Stanford University, is the author of several articles and two books on Japan—*Political Change and Industrialization in Japan, 1868-1880* (1955) and *The Agrarian Origins of Modern Japan* (1959).

GEORGE OAKLEY TOTTEN, III, Professor of Political Science, University of Southern California, learned Japanese during the war and took higher degrees at Columbia and Yale, where he wrote theses on Japanese politics and history. He has taught at Columbia, M.I.T., Boston, and the University of Rhode Island, and is the author of *The Social Democratic Movement in Prewar Japan* and co-author of *Socialist Parties in Postwar Japan*.

HIROSHI WAGATSUMA is Professor of Social Psychology, University of Pittsburgh. He was born and educated in Tokyo and received higher degrees from the University of Michigan and the University of Tokyo. He has published articles and books mainly in the field of culture and personality, both in Japanese and English. He was co-editor with George De Vos of *Japan's Invisible Race* and is currently working with him on a study of lower class families in Tokyo.

EZRA F. VOGEL, Professor of Sociology and Associate Director, East Asian Research Center, Harvard University, has training in psychology as well as sociology and anthropology and has done field work in Japan and Hong Kong. He is the author of *Japan's New Middle Class* (1963) and co-editor of *A Modern Introduction to the Family* (1960); his current research is on Communist Chinese society, though he keeps up an interest in Japan.

INDEX

459